Passing Interest

SUNY series in Multiethnic Literature

Mary Jo Bona, editor

Passing Interest

Racial Passing in US Novels, Memoirs, Television, and Film, 1990–2010

Edited by

Julie Cary Nerad

SUNY
PRESS

Published by State University of New York Press, Albany

Printed in the United States of America

For information, contact State University of New York Press, Albany, NY
www.sunypress.edu

Production by Ryan Morris
Marketing by Kate Seburyamo

Library of Congress Cataloging-in-Publication Data

Passing interest : racial passing in US novels, memoirs, television, and film, 1990–2010 / edited by Julie Cary Nerad.
pages cm. — (SUNY series in multiethnic literature)
Includes bibliographical references and index.
ISBN 978-1-4384-5227-2 (hc : alk. paper) 978-1-4384-5228-9 (pb : alk. paper)
1. American literature—20th century—History and criticism. 2. American literature—21st century—History and criticism. 3. Passing (Identity)—United States—History—20th century. 4. Passing (Identity)—United States—History—21st century. 5. Passing (Identity) in literature. 6. Passing (Identity) in motion pictures 7. Race in literature. 8. Race in motion pictures. I. Nerad, Julie, 1969–

PS228.P35P37 2014
813'.5093520396073—dc23 2013029955

10 9 8 7 6 5 4 3 2 1

Contents

Preface: The "Posts" of Passing — vii
Gayle Wald

Acknowledgments — xi

1. Introduction: The (Not So) New Face of America — 1
Julie Cary Nerad

2. On the Margins of a Movement: Passing in Three Contemporary Memoirs — 39
Irina Negrea

3. "A Cousin to Blackness": Race and Identity in Bliss Broyard's *One Drop: My Father's Hidden Life* — 69
Lynn Washington and Julie Cary Nerad

4. Can One Really Choose? Passing and Self-Identification at the Turn of the Twenty-First Century — 95
Jené Schoenfeld

5. Passing in Blackface: The Intimate Drama of Post-Racialism on *Black.White.* — 123
Eden Osucha

6. Broke Right in Half: Passing of/in Alice Randall's *The Wind Done Gone* — 149
Julie Cary Nerad

7. Passing for Chicano, Passing for White: Negotiating Filipino American Identity in Brian Ascalon Roley's *American Son* 179
Amanda Page

8. Race in the Marketplace: Postmodern Passing and Ali G 203
Ana Cristina Mendes

9. Passing for Black, White, and Jewish: Mixed-Race Identity in Rebecca Walker and Danzy Senna 229
Lori Harrison-Kahan

10. Smiling Faces: *Chameleon Street*, Racial Passing/Performativity, and Film Blackness 255
Michael B. Gillespie

11. Consuming Performances: Race, Media, and the Failure of the Cultural Mulatto in *Bamboozled* and *Erasure* 283
Meredith McCarroll

Bibliography 307

Contributor Biographies 329

Index 333

Preface

The "Posts" of Passing

Passing Interest: Racial Passing in U.S. Novels, Memoirs, Television, & Film, 1990–2010 is a most welcome addition to the scholarship on racial passing in the United States, a country uniquely defined by its historical obsession with a binaristic (black/white) racial discourse. In particular, this book expands upon a rich body of scholarship on passing by exploring recent literary and visual texts produced in an era often referred to as "post-racial," and by bringing a host of new voices to the scholarly conversation. As these essays collectively attest, the *post* of post-racial, insofar as it is meant to signify the obsolescence or superseding of our national obsession, fails to capture both the ongoing, if changing, significance of race and the ongoing relevance of passing as a narrative theme or a strategy of racial critique. As the assembled essays show, the fluidity of racial-ethnic categorization and of visualized markers of race (such as skin color, hair texture, and the like) make passing a still-potent site of exploration into issues of identity, national belonging, post–civil rights political discourse, gender and sexuality, and ideologies of the visible. Passing also serves to illuminate complex questions of performance (how we "do" who we "are") knowledge (how we "know" who we "are"), and authenticity (how we validate ourselves or receive validation for who we "are").

The historical framing of this volume, from 1990 to 2010, is additionally interesting since it brackets a two-decades-long period that saw heightened interest in passing as a subject of research among humanities scholars, myself included. In this preface, then, I want to briefly historicize the scholarly discourse of passing, using my own experience as a point of entrance, before returning to the theme of the "post-racial," which these essays eloquently engage.

It is beyond me to produce empirical data to back up this assertion, but from my perspective as someone who began graduate studies in

English in 1988 at Princeton University, then and now a hub of African Americanist scholarship, it was late-1980s theorizing about race, ideology, and textuality/performance that created the conditions for "passing" to be seen, by many of us, as a productive site of theoretical and historical exploration. This is not to dismiss important scholarship on passing that predated the 1990s, but rather to locate the proliferation of "passing studies" in that decade as one legacy of the enabling and groundbreaking work done by such scholars-artists as Houston Baker, Kimberly Bentson, Barbara Christian, Henry Louis Gates Jr., Cheryl I. Harris, Adrian Piper, Werner Sollors, Valerie Smith, and others too numerous to mention here. That is to say, it was pioneering work by a generation of African Americanists—many of whom emerged from the flowering of Black Studies in the 1960s and '70s, and who had taken up positions of visibility and increasing authority in formerly white institutions—who provided the tools with which someone like me could begin to entertain certain questions, and even to think of those questions as the basis of future scholarly projects.

To cite one concrete example: It is difficult to overstate the importance, especially to my cohort of future African Americanists, of the publication of *"Race," Writing and Difference,* edited by Henry Louis Gates Jr. in 1986 (republished in 1992). In my memory, we all had the paperback edition with its stark black and red cover artwork, and we all read it with pens in hand. My "we" here is obviously a construct produced through the haze of memory and nostalgia, but that book, which originally appeared in two issues of the journal *Critical Inquiry* (Autumn 1995, vol. 12, no. 1 and Autumn 1986, vol. 13, no. 1) was the equivalent of a scholarly blockbuster in its day. To be sure, we all had our critiques of various positions staked out in that volume, which was itself far from univocal, but many of us used it as a starting point for discussion and debate. The phrase "social construct" or variations thereof (e.g., "Race is a social construct, but it is also real") were enormously enabling. Those quotation marks around "race" in the title of the book meant that we could begin to imagine a strategy of negotiating an important conundrum, which was how to write critically about race and its histories and legacies without reifying race in language, if not in practice. *"Race," Writing, and Difference* had the imprint of Derrida and other poststructuralist philosophers in its very title—"Difference" registering as both racial-ethnic difference and an Anglicization of Derridean *différence*—so the notion of a "way out" of such problems of language, which were also problems of the social, was always already an object of scrutiny and careful appraisal. And yet, antiessentialist critiques of race that emerged from U.S. scholars' engagement with the poststructuralist turn of the late 1960s and 1970s (including critical engagements with the philosophical foundations of poststructuralism), and the intensified intellectual atmosphere of post-1968 Black Studies, Ethnic Studies, and Feminist Studies, constitute the groundwork upon which my and others' engagements with racial passing were based.

In retrospect, and as this volume bears out, some of the intellectual giddiness associated with that moment was unwarranted. Indeed, by early 1995, when I defended my dissertation on twentieth-century cultural representations of racial passing, I had already begun to contemplate the political limitations of the quotation marks that many people habitually placed around *race*. That is, I had begun to wonder whether those quotation marks might be merely gestural. This was borne out by my teaching, in the mid-1990s and now. Today, the by and large economically privileged students I teach enter the classroom having internalized what scholars might call a language of social constructionism. They "know" that race is a social product, or at least they have absorbed that lesson even if they haven't learned it through their lived experiences. When I assign them Danzy Senna's *Caucasia,* in a class about "post-soul" aesthetics, politics, and culture, they talk easily and readily about the struggles of its biracial protagonist; can grasp the complex mediation through Jewishness of the black-white binary in that novel; and offer wise insights into the narrative's explicit critique of a post-racial discourse, as it is given voice by the protagonist's father, Deck. Many of my students use the novel as a jumping-off point to talk about their own experiences of hybridity and the complexity of their social and racial formations.

And yet. I am hardly the first to assert that such a shared understanding of the discursive limitations of so-called post-racialism in the Age of Obama does not mitigate the persistence of racism, or of the various crises—of incarceration, of HIV, of failed educational institutions, of heart disease and diabetes, of police profiling—that disproportionately affect people of color, especially African Americans. Indeed, that contradiction is in part what the essays in this book are about. How is it that in a supposedly post-racial age we continue to live our lives through "race," and how do cultural productions use passing as a productive *way in* to thinking about—examining, critiquing, exploring—this contradiction? In some ways, the essays in *Passing Interest* are about the conditions of possibility of *post-ness* itself. How are we "post"? Post what? Why has post-ness become a dominant paradigm for conceptualizing race (and perhaps ethnicity)? *Passing Interest* cannot definitively answer these questions, but the many fine essays collected here go a long way toward investigating them by putting "passing"—a supposedly passé concept—at the center.

Gayle Wald

Acknowledgments

An earlier version of Lori Harrison-Kahan's "Passing for Black, White, and Jewish: Mixed Race Identity in Rebecca Walker and Danzy Senna" appeared in *MELUS* 30:1 (Spring 2005): 19–48 under the title "Passing for White, Passing for Jewish: Mixed Race Identity in Danzy Senna and Rebecca Walker." It is reprinted here, in revised form, by permission of MELUS, the Society for the Study of Multi-Ethnic Literature of the United States, and Oxford University Press. MELUS, founded in 1973, "endeavors to expand the definition of American literature through the study and teaching of Latino American, Native American, African American, Asian and Pacific American, and ethnically specific Euro-American literary works, their authors, and their cultural contexts." For more information, go to www.melus.org.

Of the many people I owe my thanks, I would like to offer a special acknowledgment to each of the contributors to this volume. I am a better scholar for having had the opportunity to work with them over the past several years, and they have confirmed for me many times over the vast benefits of scholarly collaboration. I am grateful, both as a scholar and a human, to know them. I would also like to thank Dr. Beth Bouloukos, Rafael Chaiken, and all the staff of SUNY Press, who were so supportive, insightful, and knowledgeable at each step of the publication process. I appreciate their always quick and helpful responses to my many queries. The anonymous readers throughout this process also have my deep gratitude. They provided invaluable advice on the manuscript, and I thank them sincerely for their thoughtful reading, their incisive comments, and their expert guidance on each essay.

I offer my thanks, also, to the Office of Faculty Professional Development at Morgan State University for a Summer Research Grant that helped fund research for this project in its early stages, as well as to the

Northeast Modern Language Association for approving a Special Session at which I first met several of the contributors. I thank my chairperson—Dr. Dolan Hubbard—and the three deans of the College of Liberal Arts under which I have had the pleasure to serve—former longtime dean Dr. Burney J. Hollis, interim dean Dr. M'Bare N'gom, and interim dean Pamela Scott-Johnson. My colleagues in the department of English at Morgan State deserve special acknowledgment for their encouragement and support over the years. An individual thanks to Karl Henzy, who read an early draft of my essay on Alice Randall's *The Wind Done Gone* included in this collection. To my mentor/friends—Monifa Love Asante, Dana D. Nelson, and Steven Weisenburger—I owe a debt of gratitude that I cannot adequately express here. I will simply say that they are everything a mentor should be—wise, generous, supportive, compassionate, dependable, and appropriately demanding. They set the bar high and they continue to inspire me every day.

Personal and deep thanks go to my family, especially Charlie and Olivia, as well as Jane, Buck, Kathy, Sandy, Don, Mitchell, and Kendell, who support and strengthen me in ways too numerous to list. I also thank Jack, Bob, Priscilla, Guy, Becca, Isabel, and Clay. And, finally, I want to thank my friends, who enrich my life and see me through: Aimee, Amy, Anika, Dan, Doug, Heidi, Isaac, Jennifer, Joy, Karl, Kat, Kimberly, Lori, Lulan, Patrick, Peet, Rebecca, Tracy. I dedicate this book to all of them, and to Princess, because black and white still make Gray.

1

Introduction

The (Not So) New Face of America

Julie Cary Nerad

In a *Politico* story that reads somewhat like a postmodern, absurdist version of a news report, Stella O'Leary, the president of the Irish American Democrats, is quoted as saying that United States President Barack Obama is "as much Irish as he is Kenyan," although, she adds, "he's been very wrapped up in his African-American heritage" (Lovely par. 5). In this same spirit of recognizing Obama's interracial—or, more precisely, international—heritage, the Irish band The Corrigan Brothers (nee "Hardy Drew and the Nancy Boys") recorded a hit song entitled "There's No One as Irish as Barack O'Bama" that went viral on the Internet in 2009.[1] Notwithstanding that according to the song his "granddaddy's granddaddy came from Moneygall," President Obama identifies as an African American. Of this fact, he has been consistent despite the media's debate over just "how black" he is. Beginning with the run-up to his declaration of candidacy for the presidency through the actual presidential election of 2008, various "political pundits" and scholars cast and recast his racial identity as Black (he is phenotypically "black"); as African American (his father was from Kenya); as not "really" Black (his ancestors were not held in the American slave system); as bi- or multiracial (his mother was white); back to Black (he can't hail a cab in Chicago); or as African American (as a respectful term of identity). His election in 2008 at least temporarily stemmed the tide of debate: Barack Hussein Obama is now almost universally hailed as the "first African American President," even if the "birthers" still insist on questioning his American birth.

Regardless of the "degree" or quality of his "blackness"—after all, historically in America, *any* black makes you *all* black, despite the disagreements noted above—his election and inauguration are certainly significant moments in U.S. history. Indeed, many Americans framed Obama's presidency as heralding the end of racism, as signaling the ascendency of a "post-racial" society, or, at the very least, as evincing to the world an America that has finally overcome its legacy of slavery and Jim Crow segregation. President Obama is, as the white, British commentator Andrew Sullivan writes in *The Atlantic,* the "new face of America":

> [W]hat does he offer? First and foremost: his face. . . . Consider this hypothetical. It's November 2008. A young Pakistani Muslim is watching television and sees that this man—Barack Hussein Obama—is the new face of America. In one simple image, America's soft power has been ratcheted up not a notch, but a logarithm. A brown-skinned man whose father was an African, who grew up in Indonesia and Hawaii, who attended a majority-Muslim school as a boy, is now the alleged enemy. If you wanted the crudest but most effective weapon against the demonization of America that fuels Islamist ideology, Obama's face gets close. It proves them wrong about what America is in ways no words can. (par. 1, 2)

This passage implicitly heralds the "brown-skinned" Obama as America's savior against extremist Islamists. But it is explicitly Obama's *face* and not his political position that enables him to change how the world "sees" America. In this hypothetical situation, Obama's face undercuts any religious and cultural differences between America and a "young Pakistani Muslim," who is (we are to assume) a possible future terrorist, because what he sees in the televised image is presumably his own blackness reflected in Obama's. In other words, Obama's skin trumps every other marker of his identity, including nationality, religion, class, age, etc. that might otherwise mark him as "the alleged enemy." Of course, what the young Pakistani cannot possibly "see" in Obama's face is that childhood spent in Indonesia and Hawaii, his (brief) Muslim schooling, or his current religious affiliation. More important here, however, is what Sullivan cannot imagine him seeing: despite Obama's lighter skin tone, what is *not* "apparent" to the young Pakistani (through Sullivan's lens) is Obama's white mother or the white grandparents who raised him. In short, Sullivan's young Pakistani Muslim does not see Obama's *Irish* heritage; he sees only his *African* (or, more precisely, nonwhite) heritage. He sees, in Sullivan's imagination, the image of a man *like him*. This passage tells us as much or more about what Sullivan "sees" than what a young Pakistani Muslim might see. In short, the (il)logics of this passage highlight both the continued importance of race in the Western imagination and the ocularity of the racial system in the United States. It also illustrates the unidirectional nature of racialization via the lingering power of hypodescent—better known as the "one-drop rule"—the Irish American Democrats' "open arms" notwithstanding.

The continuous importance placed on Obama's racial and national heritages demonstrates a paradox of twenty-first-century racial discourse: part of America wants to claim that we have moved "beyond race" and that the election of President Obama demonstrates that racism is a thing of the past. However, ironically, we can only make that claim by *emphasizing* his race.[2] That is, we must point out the significance of his racial identity, only then to dismiss it as irrelevant or secondary. These countervailing trends were evident in one of Obama's own press conferences in March 2009. Referencing his "historic presidency," ABC reporter Ann Compton asked President Obama if, over the first sixty-four days of his presidency, he felt that race had shaped his image or whether it had been "a relatively color-blind time." In response, President Obama recognized the social significance of his personal racial identity, but then quickly moved to depersonalize his presidency by shifting the focus to economic issues. He explained:

> [A]t the inauguration, I think that there was justifiable pride on the part of the country that we had taken a step to move us beyond some of the searing legacies of racial discrimination in this country, but that lasted about a day. . . . [R]ight now, the American people are judging me exactly the way I should be judged. And that is: Are we taking the steps to improve liquidity in the financial markets, create jobs, get businesses to reopen, keep America safe? (Obama)

As opposed to Sullivan's image of the young Pakistani whose religio-political beliefs are effectively scrambled by President Obama's face, Obama's response does imagine a "color-blind" citizenry who will judge him on his ability to grapple with economic affairs. His answer, that is, posits a public able to see him as just "the president," a body politic who can effectively sever our cultural racial epistemology from a particular embodied man. His dismissal of racial identity as irrelevant to his ability to perform his job is not a new strategy. In the earlier twentieth century, for instance, Harlem Renaissance authors such as Claude McKay and Jean Toomer wanted to be known as talented poets, not as talented (for) "Negro" poets. While the implicit suggestion that Obama's skin color has no bearing on his capacity to manage national and international affairs is certainly true, a sidelining of racial issues is perhaps both overly optimistic and slightly disingenuous—and even potentially dangerous—because his response problematically conceptualizes race as a distraction: the celebration of our historic (if partial) triumph over the "searing legacies of racial discrimination" lasted "about a day" before we had to get down to the *real* business at hand. Certainly, President Obama understands that race largely played a role in the housing and credit crises, the rising unemployment rate, and the breakdown of the healthcare and education systems that occurred in the first decade of the twenty-first century. Thus, continued socioeconomic disparities among racial groups—"the searing legacies of racial discrimination"—can only be addressed, once again, by *highlighting* race, not by *sidelining* it.

As Gayle Wald explains, however, many see color blindness as the means to a democratic society:

> [I]t is now commonly held, by liberals and conservatives alike, that a purposeful indifference to race and a corresponding elevation of the "individual" as a social agent is an effective strategy of achieving the end of a just, democratic society. According to such color-blind arguments, a concerted "blindness" to race presents that most promising alternative to a society in which racialization—however unstable, shifting, or unenforceable—historically has played a role in governing social opportunity and status. (183)

Those critical of color-blind policies, however, might note the alternative way of reading the phrase "the *end* of a just, democratic society."[3] Indeed, in twenty-first-century America, being "color blind"—refusing to recognize race as a significant component of identity—is coming to mean being blind to continued systemic racial disparity, the kinds of disparity that were dramatically and publicly exposed after Hurricanes Katrina and Rita during the George W. Bush administration.[4] Thus, what some Americans want to do in this "post-Bush" world is simply to pat ourselves on the back for electing an African American president, offer that achievement as evidence that race no longer matters, and then maintain policies that continue to increase socioeconomic and educational gaps among racial groups. Jodi Melamed names this type of willed blindness and the political and economic policies that grow from it "neoliberal multiculturalism" in which "esteeming some people of color of the same race, according to conventional categories, makes it easier to accept that others of the same race may be systematically treated unequally" (153).[5]

In the United States, race *does* still matter. Indeed, the concept of race continues to be a fundamental element of identity in America. The tenacity (and centrality) of race is due in part to the fact that, notwithstanding scientific evidence that debunks the claim of significant genetic difference among races, America as a culture—and Americans as individuals—continues to believe in the *biological* reality of race.[6] In a kind of circular logic, we still believe in the "reality" of race because lived experience continues to validate race as a significant marker of identity and kinship, and because race continues to have real social and economic consequences. Telling people that race isn't biologically "real" doesn't erase history or trump personal experience, both which continue to reinforce the reality of race. As Baz Dreisinger puts it: "Theoretical jive about race as a 'disproved' concept is, well, jive; good old Race, rigid and old hat, lives on in our hearts and minds. Slay something—blackness, whiteness, Latino-ness—in concept and you still haven't slain it in the flesh" (125). Dreisinger here articulates the significant gap between theory and praxis. And nothing continues to highlight this gap like racial passing, the lens through which the contributors to *Passing Interest* each explore contemporary understandings of race and racial identity in the United States, particularly as represented in texts produced between 1990 and 2010.

While any limitation of time frame is to some extent arbitrary, I selected 1990 as the beginning point for this collection for several reasons. The first few years of the 1990s were a watershed of national and international events that marked a new phase in history—a breaking down of barriers—that may, arguably, have set the stage for the 2008 election of an interracial president, one who so motivated the young voters of Generation Mix.[7] Nineteen ninety was the last year of the Cold War. It was also the year of German reunification (the Berlin Wall fell in November 1989). In South Africa, in February 1990, Nelson Mandela was freed after twenty-seven years of imprisonment. While the changes were not all peaceful—1990 also saw the start of the Persian Gulf War—American culture was flooded with images of walls literally and figuratively crumbling. On the home front, George H. W. Bush vetoed the Civil Rights Bill of 1990, before signing the Civil Rights Bill of 1991 into law in November 1991.[8] William Jefferson Clinton, later affectionately and sometimes derisively known as our "first black president," was elected in November 1992.[9] The Rodney King beating by Los Angeles police officers in March 1991, and the resulting "not guilty" verdict announced in April 1992, sparked both a violent six-day race riot and a national conversation on race in the United States.[10]

All this happened in the very years that the Multiracial Movement—a movement founded on the idea of barrier breaking—was coming into its own. In 1993, the U.S. House Subcommittee on Census, Statistics, and Postal Personnel held hearings to discuss the racial and ethnic classifications that would be available on the 2000 U.S. Census. Representatives of the Association of Multiethnic Americans argued for "either a simple 'multiracial' check box or the possibility of checking all applicable racial categories" (DaCosta 1). By the time of the hearings, of the roughly sixty social support organizations for mixed race people that existed, most had been formed in the preceding five years (DaCosta 3).[11]

While certainly this movement toward recognizing multi*racial* identity grew in part from the multi*cultural* movements of the late 1960s, 1970s, and 1980s, and is sometimes still collapsed into that term, it is unique from that earlier effort in that rather than highlighting and demanding equality for distinct identities—the thrust of identity politics—multiracials highlight points of intersection in a way more akin to a feminist theoretics that attempts to balance a collective identity with innumerable articulations of difference/subject positions.[12] In other words, multiracials specifically insist on their multiplicity and diversity, and use this "as a basis of collective identification" (DaCosta 17). No one individual represents the multiracial.

Although the Census debate may not have concerned the "average American"—whoever that might be—most Americans witnessed this emergent multiplicity/identity in multiple forms of media that, not coincidentally, highlight the visual component of racial and ethnic identification: Michael Jackson's single "Black or White"—from the *Dangerous* album—was released in November 1991. The video begins with a catalog of nationalities in traditional cultural dress dancing with Jackson, and ends with a computer generated morphing of faces, sexes, (presumably) nationalities, and races. The video was an almost immediate national and international success. This facial morphing/melding surfaced again in 1993 when *Time* magazine published a Special Issue entitled "The New

Face of America" precisely the label Sullivan passed on to Obama. On the cover was a woman's face: this new "Eve" is a composite image of various races: "15% Anglo-Saxon, 17.5% Middle Eastern, 17.5% African, 7.5% Asian, 35% Southern European and 7.5% Hispanic" ("New Face of America" 2).[13] A few years later, in 2000, *Newsweek* offered its own Special Report entitled "Redefining Race in America." Its article, "The New Face of Race," features the face of a child whose "ethnicity" is listed as "Nigerian, Irish, African-American, Native American, Russian Jewish, Polish Jewish" (38), with little awareness of the slippage from the classifiers of "race" to "ethnicity."

While Jackson's video and song are clearly antiracist statements that suggest that cultural and racial melding are good things (the original video also featured Jackson destroying objects with racist graffiti, scenes purportedly cut for their violence), the magazine articles evidence an undercurrent of resistance. In addition to propagating the long-standing tendency to consider distinctions of nationality, race, ethnicity, and even religion as synonymous types of identity markers, these articles reported (or warned?) of the shrinking "white" population in the United States, emphasizing the rapidly coming minority status of whites and the ever-increasing waves of "brown" immigrants.[14] For instance, the subtitle of *Time's* "New Face of America" issue reads "How Immigrants Are Shaping the World's First Multicultural Society." While generally optimistic and celebratory in tone, such articles also have the potential to create a defensive animosity on the part of whites. In this sense, they are reminiscent of eugenicist works such as Madison Grant's *The Passing* [meaning "death of"] *of the Great Race* (1916) or Lothrop Stoddard's *The Rising Tide of Color Against White World Supremacy* (1920), texts that were key in the anti-immigration legislation act of 1924.[15] The articles, meant to document current trends in immigration and intermarriage, implicitly (and even explicitly) suggest that whiteness will be subsumed by a new "multicultural" (nee "mulatto") face.[16] As Shawn Michelle Smith argues, such articles also paradoxically reaffirm the assumptions that there are discernible, distinct racial "types" and that blood or race can be quantified and classified. She notes: "[C]ontemporary attempts to envision, to define, and to codify racial and national identities, as well as to determine where and when those constructs intersect, diverge, and can be challenged, are haunted by their explicitly racist nineteenth-century origins" (Smith 225). This is so even if the articles are not themselves "racist" in message or tone.

Similarly, even the change instituted for the 2000 U.S. Census—the opportunity to check multiple racial labels—can also be seen as just another way of compartmentalizing one's self into racial "parts." Although the opportunity to recognize multiple aspects of one's racial identity was liberating for many, it certainly did not eliminate the de facto one-drop rule, under which *any* amount of African heritage makes one black. For instance, Obama may have checked boxes to recognize both his mother's and his father's racial identity. But he is still our first African American president. Or we might think of Tiger Woods, whose self-labeling in 1997 as "Cablinasian" was intended to be liberatory and reflective of the multiplicity of his racial heritage. Instead, it garnered him considerable (and still ongoing) criticism from those who read the term as evidence of internalized racism against his blackness. Furthermore, the term "Cablinasian" ultimately fails to destabilize the racial *system*. That is, because "Cablinasian" has no unique referent in U.S. racial discourse; the term simply loads Woods with multiple racial signifiers—Caucasian, Black, Indian, and Asian—with the "black" understood (by most Americans if not Woods himself) as his primary racial identity because of both the residue of the one-drop rule and Woods's physical appearance. Finally, Woods's neologism highlights the cultural pressure to have *some* kind of racial label, albeit one that strives to blur the lines.

Part of the problem is that, while we as a culture now (theoretically at least) recognize the absurdity of a racial system based on "divisions" and "drops" of blood, we continue to use racial rhetoric and terminology that relies on such proportioning because that remains the primary language we have to discuss race. In turn, that language in many cases continues to limit our conceptual ability to understand ourselves in race-neutral terms even as more Americans find themselves uncomfortable wearing one particular racial label. As Jennifer Ho argues, "(Generally speaking) there is not a space or a language for mixed race people to claim a multiple, hybrid, or heterogeneous subjectivity" (143). What Woods and the "new face" articles attest to is our continuing belief in the embodiment and the quantifiability of race—and the visibility of racial faces—even into the twenty-first century.

This desire to compartmentalize, to label, to know *who* someone is by *what* that person is—black, white, brown; gay, straight, bisexual; male, female, transgender; American, immigrant, illegal; Christian, Muslim, Jew—and to be able to confirm that information visually perhaps unsurprisingly reflects our desire for control in a postmodern (or perhaps *post*-postmodern) world where rapid cultural, social, and technological changes seem to blur even further the line that has historically separated fact from fiction—to meld, for instance, six different faces into one. While the epistemology of racial visibility has never been reliable, the advances in technology that let us "see" the new Eve assure us only that we cannot be assured that what we "see" is "real."[17] Ironically, in one sense such technologies seem fabulously anachronistic, as the "new" face of Eve (or Woods or Obama) isn't really "new" at all. As Kimberly McClain DaCosta—among many others—succinctly notes: "People of mixed descent have existed in American society since its inception" (7).[18] It is those bodies of "mixed descent"—and the texts that treat such bodies through the trope of racial passing—that are the focus of the essays collected in *Passing Interest*.

Specifically, the essays included in this collection explore contemporary engagements with racial passers in four genres: novels, memoirs, television, and film. Multiracialism put in conversation with the trope of racial passing provides a particularly fruitful intersection for the study of race in the United States. On the one hand, as Michelle Elam persuasively argues, "because mixed race has been often represented since the 1990s as hip testimony to American democracy, the corporeal resolution of racial diversity and national unity, it is also represented as a painless antidote to the centuries-old practice of racial passing. Passing, then, seems a particularly antique phenomenon in this 'mulatto millennium'" (*The Souls* 96). On the other hand, the merging of racial identities into a single body outside the strictures of a one-drop rule—a process that generates a state of unified multiplicity—further muddies the water by creating *more* rather than *fewer* opportunities/possibilities for passing by multiplying racial indeterminacy and the options for identification, by both the self and others. The opportunities for *mis*recognition—the primary strategy through which passing functions—multiply as quickly.

Passing, in the broadest sense, is now understood by many scholars as synonymous with *performance*: it is the iteration of a set of behaviors, cultural codes, language, etc. ascribed to a specific identity category such as race, gender, sexuality, class, religion, and so on. This understanding of all identity as performance/passing challenges at a fundamental level the idea of biological essentialism, that we are *who* we are because of *what* we are. As Samira Kawash puts it: "[M]y identity is not what I am but what I am passing for" (73). This position—that we're all passing all the time; that passing is constituent of identity—suggests that there can actually be no such thing as passing in the more traditional sense. Werner Sollors offers a general definition of passing in this traditional sense: "Passing, an Americanism not listed in the first edition of the *Oxford English Dictionary*, may refer to the crossing of any line that divides social groups" (*Neither* 247).[19] Passing, then, as a social practice of transgression, is usually understood as a particular performance of an identity that is not "one's own." As many scholars have noted, this conception of passing paradoxically undercuts *and* reinscribes an antiessentialist position.

On the one hand, passing recognizes that identities are performed rather than innate by the very act of the successful pass. Passers perform quite convincingly and with apparent authenticity in ways that do not fit their legal or cultural classification, classifications which have historically been assigned based on biological heritage and the body—and read on faces. Passing thus also highlights and problematizes the importance of specularity in identity construction (internal and external—identity and corporeality—are supposed to match). As Linda Schlossberg explains, "we are subjects constituted by our visions of ourselves and others, and we trust that what we see and read carries with it a certain degree of epistemological certainty" (1). Because passing disrupts visual expectations, because the passer doesn't "look like" how one of a category "should" look, passing "becomes a highly charged site for anxieties regarding visibility, invisibility, classification, and social demarcation" (Schlossberg 1). In sum, passing highlights our cultural tendency to assign individuals into mutually exclusive, singular boxes (gay or straight; white or black) *and* exposes as unreliable a visually based system of identification and classification by troubling the illusion that you *are* what you *look like* you are.[20]

On the other hand, passers are often understood as performing an identity that they do not "own" legally, psychologically, or culturally. The trope of passing can also simultaneously reinscribe the very categories that the pass destabilizes (and thus underwrite an essentialist position) because it is often conceptualized as a betrayal of one's "real" identity or as an "inauthentic" performance. Such passing is usually assumed to be intentional. As Elaine K. Ginsberg argues: "[A]lthough the cultural logic of passing suggests that passing is usually motivated by a desire to shed the identity of an oppressed group to gain access to social and economic opportunities, the rationale for passing may be more or less complex or ambiguous and motivated by other kinds of perceived rewards" (3). The rationale might also stem from the avoidance of persecution (rather than to garner a reward): for instance, in a homophobic culture, a gay man might pass as straight to have access to socioeconomic opportunities he would otherwise be excluded from, but he also might pass to avoid violence he would be subjected to as an openly gay man. Despite the motivation of the pass, the logics behind it often turn on the idea that the passer is concealing or repressing a "true" identity and is performing an assumed or "false" one.

This is the framework within which *racial* passing has generally been understood: the performance of a racial identity other than what one "is" biologically, a classification that is assumed to be visually verifiable.[21] Although racial passing challenges the idea of fixed, immutable, mutually exclusive racial categories, because it is also often understood as an act of betrayal (of one's true self, as well as of family and community), it can simultaneously undergird essentialist beliefs about race. Representations and discussions of passing thus often reproduce the antithetical tendencies in our understandings of race itself: the movement toward understanding identity as performance rather than essence, *and* the movement to fit individuals into neat, containable, policeable categories.

Although there are incidences of white-to-black passing,[22] because of the history of slavery, Jim Crow segregation, and racism in the United States, the most common iteration of racial passing has been black-to-white (a "light-skinned" black person living as white). Racial passing in this more specific sense goes back as far as—at least—the 1740s, as evidenced by advertisements for runaway slaves who might use their light skin to help them escape.[23] Because the act of passing depends upon the ability to blend into the targeted group—to go undetected—there is no way of knowing how many people actually "crossed the color line" over the last few hundred years. Estimates vary widely. As Daniel J. Sharfstein writes, "For nearly a century, sociologists and others have attempted to estimate the percentage of whites in the United States who have some African ancestry; speculation ranges from 1 to 20 percent" (338).[24] Elam suggests, however, that ultimately racial passing's "relative statistical irrelevance bears little on its cultural and literary relevance to the national drama over it" (*The Souls* 99). Indeed, what we can easily document is that the trope of racial passing has been a significant part of American *literature* since—at least—the middle of the nineteenth century.

Some of the earliest published texts written by African American authors are racial passing texts, including William Wells Brown's *Clotel or, The President's Daughter* (1853) and Frank J. Webb's *The Garies and Their Friends* (1857). Harriet Jacobs's autobiographical novel, *Incidents in the Life of a Slave Girl* (1861), also includes race (and gender) passing scenes. The trope appealed early to white writers as well. Cora in James Fenimore Cooper's *Last of the Mohicans* (1826) is passing for white, and Harriet Beecher Stowe's *Uncle Tom's Cabin* (1851–52) includes the well-known "Spanish masquerade" scene, in which George Harris darkens his skin and passes as a Spanish gentleman to escape enslavement.[25] As readers even of these few early texts will recognize, there is a wide range of variation in the trope of racial passing. Some of these variations include those who pass situationally for momentary convenience or access; those who pass primarily for economic reasons (white at work; black at home); those who pass as tricksters or as undercover agents; those who pass unintentionally (they do not realize their "true" racial classification); those who pass to marry a person of another race; those who pass deliberately to escape the systemic inequities of racism; those who pass as a result of internalized racism; and so on, and in various combinations. In short, racial passing has both served as a tool to subvert the American system of racial classification throughout U.S. history and captured the imagination of American writers. It has been documented or represented in novels, plays, poems, memoirs, essays, songs, comic strips, family lore, journalistic exposés, biography, autobiography, and more recently, films and television; and has been the object of study for, at least, ethnologists, historians, law theorists, psychologists, sociologists, and literary and cultural scholars.

Indeed, since the 1990s, a vast body of scholarship has been produced on racial passing. Three key works are Elaine K. Ginsberg's edited collection *Passing and the Fictions of Identity* (1996); Gayle Wald's *Crossing the Line: Racial Passing in Twentieth-Century U.S. Literature and Culture* (2000); and Maria Carla Sánchez and Linda Schlossberg's edited collection *Passing: Identity and Interpretation in Sexuality, Race, and Religion* (2001).[26] Since the publication of these foundational works, many other insightful studies—from journal articles, to special focus journal issues, to monographs—have been published. These works generally read passing texts from early American literature up to the Civil Rights Era.[27] An important recent collection that focuses on passing specifically in the work of Charles W. Chesnutt, perhaps the single author who dealt the most with passing, is *Passing in the Works of Charles W. Chesnutt* (2010), edited by Susan Prothro Wright and Ernestine Pickens Glass.

Contemporaneous to this growing list of scholarly studies on passing, however, we have also seen repeated declarations over the last two decades that "passing is passé."[28] Maria P. P. Root argues that "[t]he dialogues about mixed race identity reflecting pathology, self-hate, or 'passing' are relics of an era of history that is gone" (4). Similarly, in "Toni Morrison and the Burden of the Passing Narrative," Juda Bennett assumes that "passing for white . . . no longer seems to engage contemporary novelists" and assumes as a starting point the "relative disappearance of the passing figure from contemporary literature" (205). He characterizes Charles Johnson's *The Oxherding Tale* (1982), Danzy Senna's *Caucasia* (1998), Ralph Ellison's *Juneteenth* (1999), and Philip Roth's *The Human Stain* (2000) as "anomalies" in a body of literature no longer interested in passing as a trope (note 1). In contrast to those who suggest that passing is a trope that has come and gone, however, I side with those who recognize that the production of passing texts (new, newly published, or republished) over the last two decades is significant, sustained, and substantial. Among others, Elam notes that "the theme of passing lives on—is, in fact, resurrected to assume a spectacular new life" (*The Souls* 97), and Dreisinger acknowledges that "[r]ecent years have witnessed an upsurge in racial passing narratives" (121). Similarly, Sollors suggests that "contemporary writers and artists may be returning to representations of racial passing" (*Neither* 284). Indeed they are, if, that is, they ever left.

In addition to the novels Bennett listed (noted above), we could add Walter Mosley's *Devil in a Blue Dress* (1990), J. California Cooper's *Family* (1991), John Gregory Brown's *Decorations in a Ruined Cemetery* (1994), Colson Whitehead's *The Intuitionist* (1999), Wesley Brown's *Darktown Strutters* (1994), Elizabeth Atkins Bowman's *Dark Secret* (2001), Alice Randall's *The Wind Done Gone* (2001), and Karen E. Quinones Miller's *Passin': a novel* (2008), among others. The last two decades have also seen the publication of several previously unpublished novels (Ellison's *Juneteenth* could actually fall into this category), including *Paul Marchand, F. M. C.* (1998), *Mandy Oxendine* (1997), and *The Quarry* (1999), all by Chesnutt, as well as Hannah Craft's *The Bondswoman's Narrative* (2002), a novel discovered by Henry Louis Gates Jr. New editions of several other passing novels have been printed. Complementing this list of fiction is the remarkable surge in the production of memoirs that explore race and passing in familial and historical contexts, including the 2007 memoir of Bliss Broyard (daughter of the famed *New York Times* literary critic Anatole Broyard) and those by Elaine Galindo, Shirlee Taylor Haizlip, Neil Henry, Clarence Major, David Matthews, Rebecca Walker, and Gregory Howard Williams, to name a few. Perhaps the most highly *visible* evidence of the continued relevance of racial passing in American culture are Ice Cube's recent FX network series *Black.White.*, as well as episodes of the popular television dramas *Angel, Cold Case, Law & Order,* and *Without a Trace,* and recent films such as *The Human Stain,* based on the Roth's 2000 novel of the same name, a film version of Mosley's *Devil in a Blue Dress* (1995), or Wayne Booth's *Slow Burn* (2005).[29]

Thus, the title of this collection—*Passing Interest*—recalls both what I see as the unwavering interest in passing *and* the notion or suggestion that passing is no longer relevant/necessary or no longer appeals to writers—that it is a "relic of the past." Perhaps the numbers of actual people who pass into whiteness in a traditional sense are on the decline. But the textual explorations and representations of passing are certainly still multiplying. In fact, the trope of racial passing remains an ideal means for exploring and for representing the shifting multiplicity and performativity of racial and national identities, as well as the boundaries that police those categories, in this increasingly multiracial, interethnic culture. The fluid, multicultural citizen has become an almost ideal body upon/through which to write the twenty-first century passing narrative.[30] Indeed, Dreisinger argues that "[a]s Americans become reacquainted with their racial mixed heritages, and as we slowly begin to recognize how much cultural borrowing has shaped our intellectual landscape, we consume narratives about passing and multiracialism with avidity" (123). Furthermore, as Elam puts it, authors find passing "a particularly timely medium to explore the ongoing relevance of race amidst the recent rise in anti-identitarianism and post-racialism" (*The Souls* 122). Racial passing continues to serve as a touchstone for gauging public beliefs and anxieties about race, for pressing the paradoxes inherent in the discourse of "color blindness," and for evidencing the reactionary backlash and fundamentalist tendencies that significant cultural changes such as increased immigration, economic instability, and rapid globalization provoke. Finally, in an age and culture increasingly inundated with visual media in both communal and private spaces—from police cameras watching citizens, to individuals capturing images of others with cell phones—and the almost limitless ability to manipulate the visual image—to create the "new face" of Eve—television and film (as well as other visual technologies) have become as fundamental to the construction and maintenance of race and identity categories as the novel was to nineteenth- and early-twentieth-century audiences. Racial passing—a trope dependent in large part upon the embodied, visual cues that construct and police racial identity—is perhaps, then, particularly suited for televisual and filmic exploration.[31]

In their analyses of recent passing narratives, the contributors to *Passing Interest* attempt to address a set of questions that helped me shape this project as a whole. At the most basic level were questions about the use, relevancy, and popularity of racial passing as a narrative trope: In this multiracial, post–civil rights era, how has the trope of racial passing—as a structural element of texts—changed? Or how has it remained the same? How have authors of the last two decades used passing to explore the construction of a bi- or multiracial individual's sense of racial identity? Does "one drop" of blood still reign supreme in the American court of popular culture? To what extent does contemporary American culture allow for the racially indeterminate individual? Or does it? Do we continue to exoticize such individuals? Another set of questions focused on passing at a thematic level, as a means to examine cultural constructs about race and national identity. To that end, I asked: In what ways does passing challenge or fortify social, economic, and political hierarchies structured through a rhetoric of racial difference? Are we moving toward a truly color-blind society or one in which racial intermixture is increasing the reactionary impulse to ossify racial categories? Where is the intersection between cultural borrowing and passing? And, finally, I asked: How is the trope of passing—which is mired in issues of visibility—used in a technological age so fundamentally mediated by the visual image and saturated by media?

The essays in *Passing Interest* answer such questions in multiple—and sometimes contradictory—ways. The conclusions the essays reach are not monolithic, nor are they definitive. Because the concept of race itself has shifted and adapted to different historical moments, passing—both the actual, historical practice of passing and our textual representations of it—has adjusted correspondingly. There is no one way to describe all contemporary racial passing texts, and consequently, the working definition of "passing" in this collection has a bit of deliberate elasticity to it without, I hope, emptying the term of useful meaning. Under this approach, certain general trends surfaced that help us see both continuities and differences from earlier, traditional treatments of racial passing. In some texts, the traditional passing trope survives unchanged. Like their predecessors, these texts explore (either explicitly or implicitly) how racial identity is constructed, how those processes are policed and/or can be subverted, and the identity crisis that can occur in the bi- or multiracial individual. Others look at passing texts whose underlying racial conservatism subverts their purported racial and social liberalism. Another group focuses on the "ethnic" passer in texts that complicate the black-white binary of the traditional racial passer. And the remainder explores the slippage between traditional racial passing and related forms of racial performance (such as blackface minstrelsy, racial masquerade, or the more contemporary concept of cultural borrowing). Thus, while the essays in the collection are loosely organized around the texts' treatment and choice of passing subjects and passing as a trope (as listed above), the essays could have been grouped in various ways. They might instead have been grouped by genre. Or by theme: some link issues of racial performance to the matrix of self-community-nation in unique ways that highlight political, capitalist, and social investment in a racial hierarchy, while others focus specifically on the role of the consumerist-driven media in the maintenance of racial categories and stereotypes within the capitalist marketplace. Alternatively, they might have been organized through the various cultural discourses and phenomenon they engage, such as immigration law/nationality, the Post-Soul Aesthetic, contemporary political satire, affirmative action, or the rhetoric of "post-racialism." In any arrangement, these essays show that, as the culture becomes more (openly) multiracial/multicultural and as visual technologies proliferate, passing as a trope becomes more rather than less fluid and malleable, and it is this very elasticity that enables it to serve as a tool to explore the increasing complexities of racio-national identity within the United States.

The opening pair of essays explores relatively traditional uses of the passing trope within contemporary memoirs and records how interracial families, usually over multiple generations, have been and continue to be affected by racial passing.[32] The memoirists in many cases continue to reproduce language that conceptualizes race as a biological element of identity: they evidence the tenacity of the one-drop rule and even a belief in racial atavism (the reappearance in children of the racial traits of grandparents or more remote ancestors). However, some of the memoirs also implicitly illustrate how this reactionary, or at least traditional, understanding of race survives not *just* because those in control would like to stay in control or because it is so deeply engrained in the language we have to talk about race. Biology has been used to make race, to fuel racism, to fracture families, but it has also made families, communities, and a sense of collective identity used to *resist* racism. Resistance movements (such as the civil rights movement) were built largely by a sense of group identity based on authenticity—an authenticity primarily based on that same biological system of racial classification.[33] That power lingers and supports, rather than destabilizes, a system of rigid and singular racial classification. Thus, the memoirists often vacillate between traditional conceptualizations of race and the language of hybridity or racial-multiplicity, specifically within a framework of multiracialism. Put differently, they maintain racial difference while foregrounding the shift from "mulatto" to "multiracial" that began in the 1990s.

In "On the Margins of a Movement: Passing in Three Contemporary Memoirs," Irina Negrea offers a close reading of three early memoirs: Shirlee Taylor Haizlip's *The Sweeter the Juice* (1994), Gregory Howard Williams's *Life on the Color Line* (1995), and Judy Scales-Trent's *Notes of a White Black Woman* (1995). Negrea examines the traditional use of passing in the memoirs, focusing part of her argument on the psychological consequences of those family members left behind. According to Negrea, Haizlip, Williams, and Scales-Trent—in contrast to their ancestors—ultimately try to situate themselves in a place of *in-betweeness,* a space *on* the color line, in an attempt simultaneously to elude an exclusive racial classification and to claim multiple familial histories. These memoirists' somewhat tenuous conclusion that identity is ultimately based not on an assigned racial category, but on an individual's choice, mark them as forerunners of the multiracial movement. That claim also highlights a contemporary trend in racial classification *not* to choose a single racial identity. Their own difficulty with *not* choosing—with not having a clear racial label to affix to themselves—however, surfaces in their language, which paradoxically continues to describe them as black and evidences the lingering power of the color line at the end of the twentieth century.

In "'A Cousin to Blackness': Race and Identity in Bliss Broyard's *One Drop: My Father's Hidden Life,*" Lynn Washington and I argue that Broyard—like the earlier memoirists—claims all the racial branches on her family tree. However, rather than situating herself on the color line while also being black, Broyard ultimately exits the novel as biracial, but still white. The discovery of her father's "one drop" does not essentially change her primary racial identification. Broyard admits that she initially believes it *should* alter her sense of identity, but through her quest she discovers that having black ancestors does not translate into a sense of blackness. Nor, the memoir suggests, should it. As importantly, Broyard ultimately invests blackness with a specific cultural value: blackness becomes property that one must earn and that is not inherited automatically through blood. This positive valuation of blackness allows her to maintain a primary white identification without being subject to the accusation of self-hate that racial passers, such as her father, bore. Finally, the memoir highlights the dramatic sociocultural changes that happened between her father's generation and hers—and even in the decade between the early memoirs and her own—changes that allow her to be a "cousin" to blackness rather than a "tragic mulatto."

The next set of essays read texts that counter the movement toward multiplicity and racial liberalism suggested (if not always reached) by the memoirs. The first two examine television episodes/shows that, on the surface, expose the horrors of segregation and racism. However, the contributors demonstrate through their analyses that these texts conceptualize passers primarily as transgressors, cultural thieves, self-haters, or imitators. Like passers from earlier generations, these passers demonstrate the tragic consequences of not staying in one's culturally sanctioned racial box and thus suggest that life-in-the-box is actually the better option.[34] Such texts ultimately suggest that rather than moving toward a multiracial, color-blind, or post-racial society, we continue to operate within a system in which racial ambiguity serves primarily to fuel a reactionary, exclusionist impulse to ossify racial categories. The third essay in this section looks at a text whose reception—rather than the text itself—evidences such a reactionary impulse to maintain racial categories and white hegemonies.

In "Can One Really Choose?: Passing and Self-Identification at the Turn of the 21st Century," Jené Schoenfeld argues that despite their pretenses to being narratives of racial progress, passing episodes of two popular drama series—*Law & Order* and *Angel*—are clearly invested in maintaining a present-day racial order in which identity is fixed, such that one may (temporarily) assume an identity through passing, but one cannot define a new identity simply by choosing. Indeed, these episodes often trade on the lingering residue of the one-drop rule and regressively frame the new "multiracial" through the older stereotype of the "mulatto." Through their resuscitation of the tropes of passing, the tragic mulatto, and the "black baby," Schoenfeld argues, the episodes illustrate the tension between an apparently progressive racial attitude and a deeper cultural conservatism about race and identity.

In "Passing in Blackface: The Intimate Drama of Post-Racialism on *Black. White.*," Eden Osucha examines competing discourses of cultural authenticity and critical spectatorship involved in the production of "blackness" in the 2006 race-changing "reality" miniseries *Black. White.* Osucha contextualizes her discussion within the contemporary discourse of post-racialism and American culture's ever-growing obsession with "reality" television, linking these seemingly disparate issues through their shared impetus toward the construction of racial epistemology in the United States. According to Osucha, the point of the show was not to highlight the constructedness of race itself, but to make into profitable spectacle the overt performance of racial stereotypes that blends into caricature and does little to destabilize fixed racial identity categories.

In the final essay in this group, it is not the text, but the text's reception that evidences a reactionary backlash. In "Broke Right in Half: Passing of/in Alice Randall's *The Wind Done Gone*," I argue that Randall's 2001 novel, a parallel novel to Margaret Mitchell's 1936 now-mythic novel *Gone With the Wind*, attempts to (re)write history on a larger scale and suggest that the legal battle surrounding the publication of Randall's novel illustrates how deeply America is still invested in its own denial of racism: in order to see print this postmodern novel itself had to pass as a parody rather than be recognized as a serious indictment of historical and contemporary racism. Thus, the essay discusses the novel in the context of the rise of contemporary political satire. But I argue that the novel's most transgressive element is that Other—Randall's version of Scarlett O'Hara—is a light-skinned black woman. This revelation is the fulcrum of the novel's politics and what makes the novel so threatening.

The next three essays take a step away from the traditional black-white passer to focus on multiethnic passers, those who live not on or across "the color line" but in the neo-borderlands, where multiplicities seem to proliferate exponentially. The multiethnic passer can arguably highlight a much more complex socio-racial-national nexus, one that understands the production of individual identity not within the either-or dichotomy of a Jim Crow society, but through the diversity of globalization, immigration, and cultural fusion. The language that dominates the texts themselves and the critical explorations of those texts is thus filled with words of motion: "flux," "fluidity," "indeterminacy," "hybridity," "ambiguity," "ambivalence." That some of these passers retreat to the safety of monocultural subjectivity that offers a sense of racial closure because it corresponds to a traditional definition of race (they select one box) perhaps speaks to the lingering cultural power of whiteness within the United States. That others don't—that they insist on multiplicity not as a transgressive challenge but as a normative state of being—is indicative of the larger social, economic, political, and demographic shifts in the United States in the twenty-first century.

In "Passing for Chicano, Passing for White: Negotiating Filipino American Identity in Brian Ascalon Roley's *American Son*," Amanda Page reads Roley's 2001 novel, which focuses on two brothers of Filipino and German heritage who pass for Chicano or white. The liminal position of these brothers as "invisible" Filipino Americans allows Roley to extend the boundaries of traditional passing narratives to groups who remain outside of the dominant racial discourse, moving the ethnic Other from margin to center. Page situates her reading within a discussion of anti-immigration nativist rhetoric in the United States and examines how the passing narrative is transformed when applied to "ethnic" subjects. Page argues that despite the potential for interethnic affiliation, however, white hegemonic power continues to divide ethnic minorities and to work against a mestizo sense of collective identification.

Ana Mendes's "Race in the Marketplace: Postmodern Passing and Ali G" also explores indeterminacy and ambiguity in a cultural borderland where the performance of race, ethnicity, religion, and nationality collide.

Framing her argument within a discussion of the (globalizing) consumerist impulse that drives the production of a Western conception of race, Mendes argues that Ali G—a character developed and acted by the British Jewish comedian Sacha Baron Cohen—is the postmodern passer.[35] The light-skinned Ali G claims a black identity by overtly relying on racial stereotypes that render visible the discursive nature of race. However, Ali G complicates the black-white binary by employing a Middle Eastern name and Asian cultural references. Commentators label him concurrently as a black man, a white man pretending to be black, an Asian being black, or a Jew being an Asian being black. Mendes argues that the kind of "racial morphing" documented in Ali G's passing, or in a technologically blacked-up image of Kate Moss, or in the conscious racialization of the body in Japanese *ganguro,* suggests a readiness to recognize openly—and indeed to manipulate—the performative nature of identity categories such as race, ethnicity, and nationality but that such a recognition does not necessarily destabilize the stereotypes upon which it functions. Instead, the very indeterminancy of identity, highlighted through the reproduction of fixed stereotypes, generates a new market for capitalist consumption.

In the next essay, Lori Harrison-Kahan examines one novel—Danzy Senna's *Caucasia* (1998)—and one memoir—Rebecca Walker's *Black, White and Jewish* (2001)—to explore the increasing tendency of passing narratives to feature mixed-race protagonists who pass for Jewish.[36] These texts reflect the current trend to convey the social construction of race through what she calls "the metaphorics of performance." Furthermore, she argues that texts in which African American protagonists pass as Jewish shift the paradigm of the passing narrative to rewrite the biracial binary of black and white in terms of more complex categories of identity: black, white, *and* Jewish. Jewishness, Harrison-Kahan argues, "functions as a representation of multiplicity and ambivalence in contemporary multiracial literature" and is particularly suited to the passing narrative because Jewishness itself is a multiple signifier as, variably, a religion, a race, an ethnicity, and/or a culture.

The final pair of essays takes what was most transgressive about earlier passing narratives—the idea that race is a performance—as their starting point. These essays (and the texts they study) work to show how alternate operative strategies of racial performance, such as racial masquerade, cultural borrowing, satire/parody, blackface, etc., have moved closer to the trope of passing as our understandings of racial production have shifted. These works engage the concepts of (racial) fluidity and hybridity at a textual or generic level through a playful postmodern genre shifting and blending. In them, racial identity and the trope of passing are much more likely to be treated comically or satirically than tragically.[37] The explorations pry loose even further the connection between race and biology/embodiment, suggesting that racial identity is more about a cultural position, authorized not by ancestors but by experience. Race becomes a property not primarily passed down through biological inheritance, but one that is acquired through a matrix of location, language, associations, and psychological ownership. In these texts, the "objective" system of racial classification through "divisions" or "drops" of blood gives way to a subjective system of identification. In other words, while traditional racial passers embrace one part of the self (determined biologically) over another part, these postmodern passers claim ownership in a racial identity without that biological grounding or even without the phenotype that might support a specific racial claim. For instance, a dark-skinned person might occupy whiteness (understood in cultural terms), a move that truly divests racial identity from a biological basis and moves it firmly into the realm of cultural production; here, the property of whiteness is located much more overtly in material property. These texts, like some of the earlier memoirs, albeit in a very different way, generally present race as ultimately resistant to demarcation: race, as one articulation of identity, is always in motion, in process, and indeterminate. They push toward a concept of racial identity that is pure, disembodied performance dependent as much upon the (often manipulable and credulous) audience as upon the embodied individual. However, the visual ontology of skin, backed by centuries of practice and continued through systemic inequities, continues to push hard against this understanding of race(s) as truly cultural properties open for acquisition and exchange in a free market, as the privative fates of the passer-protagonists suggest.

In "Smiling Faces: *Chameleon Street,* Racial Passing/Performativity, and Film Blackness," Michael B. Gillespie looks at *Chameleon Street,* Wendell B. Harris's 1989 film about Detroit confidence man Douglas Street, and suggests that the film employs the trope of passing in four distinct ways that revolve not on phenotype (Harris, who plays Street, is not light-skinned enough to pass as white) but on performance.[38] According to Gillespie, Harris's film suggests that identity, in any register, is unfinalizable. Gillespie argues that the film offers a unique conceptual sense of passing as a critical trope, thus shifting the ideal from the existential to the epistemological. The film takes for granted, openly manipulates, and even dismisses visual racial cues in its exploration of *how* race is enacted and how various audiences respond to racial performance and, in a larger sense, identity.

In the final essay in the collection, "Consuming Performances: Race, Media, and the Failure of the Cultural Mulatto in *Bamboozled* and *Erasure,*" Meredith McCarroll examines Spike Lee's *Bamboozled* (2000) and Percival Everett's *Erasure* (2001). McCarroll frames her argument with Trey Ellis's concept of the "cultural mulatto." McCarroll argues that the texts' protagonists are not the "thriving hybrids" Ellis projected, but instead are "cultural mulattos," individuals who are not freed of racial constraints, but rather pass as white *and* as black, threatening both individual identity and cultural authenticity. In these texts, McCarroll suggests, Lee and Everett reveal the absurdity of racial constructs that determine the legitimacy of art and individuals through framed parodies that are grounded in the rich and often problematic artistic history of black America—namely, minstrel shows and protest novels. The texts, according to McCarroll, thus foreground the hypocrisy of a culture that is fundamentally structured by race yet unable to acknowledge its own racism. Instead, the public is complicit in the capitalist enterprise that profits from the continued promulgation of racist stereotypes, even in a post–civil rights era.

A Final Reflection

For some, challenges to distinct, "pure" racial groups and the prediction that whites will be a minority in the United States by the year 2042 is simply bad news.[39] Indeed, the "browning" of the traditional black/white racial dichotomy represented by popular, high-profile figures/celebrities and the revised Census categories, coupled with the "changing face" of the nation due to increasing immigration and a mixed-race, African American president, is understood by some as a threat to the cultural currency of whiteness.[40] The resultant white anxiety is spawning white supremacist groups that are proliferating at unprecedented rates through the Internet, and fostering a "Juan Crow" system of restrictive and punitive legislation to keep nonwhite immigrants outside U.S. borders. For many, the ever-expanding neo-borderlands are dangerous ground, and the individuals who locate themselves there—now more than ever—need to be policed. These reactionary impulses—and desires—to reinscribe racial boundaries push against the liberatory impulses that would see those boundaries dissolved and generate a string of paradoxical tendencies: in a time when the "color line" has purportedly been dismantled, the United States has built a literal wall between itself and Mexico to fortify national borders.[41] Anti-immigrant sentiment and white supremacist and other hate groups (that often hide behind a nationalist rhetoric of antiterrorism and neo-liberalism) are on the rise; however, so is interracial marriage.[42] The same year that a man of multiple racial, ethnic, and national heritages was first inaugurated as the President of the United States, African American men were in prison or unemployed in record numbers. It was the same year a white actor performing a role in modern blackface was nominated for an Academy Award.[43] And all of this is in a culture trumpeting its color blindness, post-racialism, and multiculturalism.

These contradictory movements likely do not surprise given the historical, psychological, ideological, economic, and sociostructural history of race in America. Whether understood as biological or sociological, essential or performative, "race" has been and continues to be fundamental to our identity at individual, familial, communal, and national levels. But it has never been—and still is not—easy or simple to define, identify, or police. The process arguably becomes even more complicated as the number of boxes we can check proliferates and as immigration by Latinos (Mexicans, Puerto Ricans, Dominicans, etc), Asians, and other racial and ethnic minorities continues to increase. Racial passing, which disrupts the idea of fixed identity categories that can be described and proscribed, and troubles our visual epistemology of race, thus continues to be an apt trope for examining how we rewrite ourselves and our history, for the process of writing itself, like the process of *being,* is an act of negotiation between author/self and audience/nation. And America is still in many ways trying to figure out just what/who we are (becoming).

Notes

1. There is, of course, an unintended irony in this association with Obama's Irish heritage, given the historical elision between the Irish and African Americans in the United States, especially in the late nineteenth century. See Noel Ignatiev's *How the Irish Became White* on the history of the Irish in America. See Matthew Frye Jacobson's *Whiteness of a Different Color* for a broader study of whiteness and European immigrants.

2. Jodi Melamed highlights a similar paradox in her discussion of what she calls neoliberal multiculturalism: "[T]he new world-historical formation that emerged out of [the collapse of white supremacy as a structuring logic] was also unified by race. Indeed, it could not have been otherwise; the fact that race was identified as the central problem—the crux of everything wrong and unequal in governance, economy, and society—itself called for resolutions in the register of race" (x).

3. For an extended discussion of color-blind political policies and the concept of "color consciousness," see Appiah and Gutman.

4. Hurricanes Katrina and Rita hit the U.S. Gulf Coast in, respectively, August and September 2005. The storms and their consequences, including the failure of the New Orleans levees, devastated much of lower Louisiana and parts of the Texas and Mississippi Gulf Coast. The combined death toll of the two storms was almost two thousand, and as of 2009 hundreds remained listed as missing. The George W. Bush administration was heavily criticized for its failure to respond adequately to the storms, which overwhelmingly affected people of color.

5. In *Represent and Destroy: Rationalizing Violence in the New Racial Capitalism,* Melamed defines neoliberal multiculturalism, in part, as "a market ideology turned social philosophy. It portrays an ethnic of multiculturalism to be the spirit of neoliberalism and, conversely, posits neoliberal restructuring across the globe to be the key to a postracist world of freedom and opportunity" (xxi).

6. As Elise Lemire puts it: "In short, we hold on to biology when faced with the issue of race and sex even in the face of our many claims that race is purely a social fiction" (145). For a concise summary of current scientific understandings that debunk the idea of significant distinctions between "races" and the paradoxical tenacity of "race" as a concept, see Goldstein and Thacker. I understand "race" as a socially constructed category of identity, the conceptualization of which was linked to biological "difference" in the United States in the seventeenth and eighteenth centuries in conjunction with the rise of the U.S. as a nation-state and with the proliferation of the slave system. For more on the construction of race and racism in the United States, see Theodore W. Allen's *The Invention of the White Race: The Origins of Racial Oppression in Anglo-America* (1997); David Theo Goldberg's *The Racial State* (2002); Thomas F. Gossett's *Race: The History of an Idea in America* (1963; 1997) and Werner Sollors's *Neither Black Nor White Yet Both: Thematic Explorations of Interracial Literature* (1997).

7. This is Rainier Spencer's term for this younger generation in *Reproducing Race: The Paradox of Generation Mix* (2010).

8. The Acts, shaped in response to Supreme Court decisions in the late 1980s that weakened aspects of the Civil Rights Act of 1964, were designed to increase protections for individuals against discrimination in the workplace (specifically in hiring/firing practices) and to ensure petitioners' rights to rewards after specific judgments. For more, see "Civil Rights Act of 1990" and "Civil Rights Act of 1991." The Americans with Disabilities Act also became law in 1990.

9. In a *The New Yorker* "Talk of the Town" editorial, Toni Morrison famously referred to Clinton's metaphoric blackness, writing: "Years ago, in the middle of the Whitewater investigation, one heard the first murmurs: white skin notwithstanding, this is our first black President. Blacker than any actual black person who could ever be elected in our children's lifetime. After all, Clinton displays almost every trope of blackness: single-parent household, born poor, working-class, saxophone-playing, McDonald's-and-junk-food-loving boy from Arkansas" (2). By

analogy, *Newsweek* ran a cover (May 21, 2012) with a head shot of Obama and the line "The First Gay President," likening Obama's support of gays to Clinton's relationship with African Americans.

10. Timothy J. Meagher summarizes the casualties: "On April 29, 1992, shortly after the verdict became known publicly, minority neighborhoods in Los Angeles exploded in angry violence over the verdict. When the violence subsided, fifty-eight people were dead, more than thirteen thousand were arrested, and more than one thousand buildings were destroyed" (221–22).

11. The AMEA itself was officially founded in 1988; however, it grew in part from a few smaller interracial and biracial family support groups. The Organizing Committee for a national group was formed in 1986. According to the AMEA Web site, the oldest existing multiracial group is Interracial Intercultural Pride (I-Pride), founded in San Francisco in 1978–79 ("AMEA's").

12. Drawing on the work of black feminists in the 1970s and 1980s, Kimberlé Crenshaw coined the term *intersectionality* in 1989 to note the ways in which aspects of identity (such as race, class, gender, sexual orientation, etc.) intersect and inform each other to produce specific types of marginalization and systemic inequalities. For a succinct and informative overview of race and ethnicity, particularly relevant to multiculturalism in the United States from 1965–2000, see Meagher.

13. While the name "Eve" is used to symbolize the creation of the new multiracial/cultural individual, within the Judeo-Christian tradition, it also continues to carry the connotations of sin, transgression, and downfall as well.

14. As Melamed explains: "In the 1970s, *brown* emerged as an antiracist coalition-building term among people of color, a shorthand for racial pride and solidarity that short-circuited restrictive black-or-white notions of race relations" (145). "Browning," however, has become shorthand for the population challenge to the white majority in the United States.

15. The Immigration Act of 1924, also known as the Johnson-Reid Act, greatly limited immigration quotas from many countries outside of Western Europe. See Jacobson.

16. Approximately nine million people (or about 3 percent of the U.S. population) reported being of more than one race on the 2010 U.S. Census, with black/white being the largest combination ("2010 Census"). This is up roughly 30 percent from the 2000 U.S. Census. There is a quickly growing body of scholarship on the multiracial millennial. See, for instance, G. Reginald Daniel's *More Than Black: Multiracial Identity and New Racial Order* (2001), Loretta I. Winters and Herman L. DeBose's *New Faces in a Changing America: Multiracial Identity in the 21st Century* (2002); Kimberly McClain DaCosta's *Making Multiracials: State, Family, Market, and the Redrawing of the Color Line* (2007); Heather Dalmage's *The Politics of Multiracialism: Challenging Racial Thinking* (2004); and Kim M. Williams's *Mark One or More: Civil Rights in Multiracial America* (2008), just to name a few.

17. See Smith for an in-depth study of the use of technologies such as photography to police identity.

18. For a wide-ranging study of "interracialism" particularly focused on black/white mixture in the United States, see Sollors's edited collection, *Interracialism: Black-White Intermarriage in American History, Literature, and Law*. In his essay in that collection, Joel Perlmann argues that "American history would be unrecognizable without ethnic intermarriage" (509). Perlmann conscientiously distinguishes "ethnicity" from "race" but suggests that the "ethnic model" could be used as a guide for handling "racial intermarriage sensibly in courts and in law" (508).

19. Sollors continues: "Everett Stonequist cites a great variety of cases, including Jews passing for Gentiles, Polish immigrants preferring to be German, Italians pretending to be Jewish, the Japanese Eta concealing their group identity to avoid discrimination, the Anglo-Indians passing as British, and the Cape Coloured as well as mixed bloods in the Caribbean and in Latin America moving into the white groups; one could add many other instances, such as Chinese Americans passing as Japanese Americans—and vice versa" (*Neither* 247).

20. In *Looking Like What You Are: Sexual Style, Race, and Lesbian Identity* (2001), Lisa Walker examines these issues specifically within the context of a lesbian identity, arguing that "the visibility of any identity group is necessarily linked to the paradigm of racial visibility . . . [and] the feminine lesbian cannot be studied in isolation from the idiom of race passing" (10, 11).

21. Sollors reminds us, however, that racism adjusted to the "unmarked" black body: "[C]ertain descent characteristics, even invisible ones, were viewed as essential and more deeply defining than physical appearance, individual volition, and self-description" (*Neither* 248).

22. The two best-known instances of white-to-black passing are likely John Howard Griffin's *Black Like Me* (1961) and Grace Halsell's *Soul Sister* (1969), both journalistic accounts of whites who darkened their skin to experience life as a black in the United States. Dreisinger's *Near Black: White to Black Passing in American Culture* is the first book-length study of white-to-black passing; however, Sollors lists in an extended endnote cases of and sources on white-to-black passing (*Neither* note 7). Martha A. Sandweiss also offers a recent account of historical white-to-black passing in *Passing Strange: A Gilded Age Tale of Love and Deception across the Color Line* (2009).

23. See Sollors, "Passing; or, Sacrificing a *Parvenu*," in *Neither Black Nor White* for a thorough, meticulously researched historical discussion of passing (246–84). In this chapter, Sollors surveys passing in literature and history and provides a wealth of resources for any scholar of passing. A general discussion of the history of passing in American culture, especially as it relates to the concept of "selling out," can be found in Randall Kennedy's *Selling Out* (144–85).

24. Sharfstein includes two endnotes (notes 3 and 6) with extensive lists of scholars who have discussed the issue of numbers (338–39). In *Neither Black nor White,* Sollors also offers a survey of sources and notes that most scholars "have offered estimates that are . . . dramatically heterogeneous and range from hundreds to millions" (281). Daniel, writing within the field of sociology, also

summarizes the scholarship on the estimates of passers. He notes: "The most recent, most careful calculations, made in 1946, estimated that between 2,500 and 2,700 individuals crossed over yearly" (53).

25. For a reading of George Harris's "Spanish masquerade," see Stern.

26. Ginsberg's book, the first critical collection to explore texts of racial and gender passing, covers works from the eighteenth-century autobiography of Olaudah Equiano to Griffin's 1961 exposé, *Black Like Me*. Wald's monograph offers a tighter focus on passing in the first half of the twentieth century, including narratives of the Harlem Renaissance, to the 1949 passing films *Pinky* and *Lost Boundaries,* to the denunciations of passing in black magazines of the 1950s, to Griffin's *Black Like Me*. Sánchez and Schlossberg's collection takes, in the editors' terms, a more "playful" look at passing and understands identity as primarily a means of storytelling. One significant contribution of this collection is its inclusive discussion of forms of passing, from homosexual to straight, female to male, Mexican and Jewish to white, even Catholic to Protestant.

27. The scholarship on passing is too plentiful to list in entirety. However, I will note several that are, among others, deserving of mention: In addition to critical works such as Sollors's *Neither Black Nor White* (1997) that considers passing in its discussions of related topics, several monograph studies of racial passing have been published in the last decade, including Juda Bennett's *The Passing Figure: Racial Confusion in Modern American Literature* (1996), Pamela L. Caughie's *Passing and Pedagogy: The Dynamics of Responsibility* (1999), M. Giulia Fabi's *Passing and the Rise of the African American Novel* (2001), Kathleen Pfeiffer's *Race Passing and American Individualism* (2003), Mar Gallego's *Passing Novels in the Harlem Renaissance: Identity Politics, and Textual Strategies* (2003), and Steven J. Belluscio's *To Be Suddenly White: Literary Realism and Racial Passing* (2006). These monographs all focus generally on racial passing during or before the Harlem Renaissance/Modernism, and they are complemented by a vast number of journal articles that read nineteenth- and twentieth-century passing novels. A handful of journal articles or chapters, and a single monograph—Sinéad Moynihan's *Passing Into the Present: Contemporary American Fiction of Racial and Gender Passing* (2011)—have been published on contemporary passing narratives. Moynihan reads works of both racial and gender passing, focusing more on the relationship between passing and issues of authorship, and expanding the threads of her discussion to include religion and death. Michelle Elam devotes chapter 3 of *The Souls of Mixed Folk: Race, Politics, and Aesthetics in the New Millennium* to passing in three contemporary passing novels: Danzy Senna's *Caucasia,* Philip Roth's *The Human Stain,* and Colson Whitehead's *The Intuitionist* (the chapter is a version of an earlier *African American Review* article). Dreisinger also mentions some recent passing texts in *Near Black: White-to-Black Passing in American Culture* (2008). Most recently, Marcia Alesan Dawkins's *Clearly Visible: Racial Passing and the Color of Cultural Identity* (2012) reads selected passing texts (from Plato to *The Human Stain*) through a framework of rhetorical terms and concepts. A recent Special Issue of *LIT:*

Literature, Interpretation, Theory (Summer 2007)—"Minstrelsy, Passing, and the Location of an American Racial Identity"—focuses on passing and blackface, and one issue of *Women & Performance: a journal of feminist theory* (2005) entitled "pass•ing" approaches passing as a means of negotiating various facets of identity. Although some of the essays in these journal issues focus on passing narratives published since 1989, the issues do not focus solely on recent passing texts. A 1992 issue of *Transition: An International Review* published by Oxford UP is also entitled "Passing." The issue includes Adrian Piper's essay "Passing for White, Passing for Black" (also published in Ginsberg's collection), but does not otherwise focus on the issue of passing as we understand it herein. Other studies that are written more for a lay audience include Brooke Kroeger's *Passing: When People Can't Be Who They Are* (2004)—a collection of case studies; and A. D. Powell's *"Passing" for Who You Really Are: Essays in Support of Multiracial Whiteness* (2005).

28. Nathan Huggins's brief essay "Passing is Passe" is included in *Revelations*. He opens the essay by stating that "Black people, it seems, don't 'pass' anymore" (245). Wald dedicates a chapter of *Crossing the Line* to articles from the 1950s that suggest passing is no longer necessary, including titles such as "I Refuse to Pass," "Why Passing is Passing Out," or "Is Passing for White a Dying Fad?" (116–51).

29. The television episodes are "Are You Now or Have You Ever Been?" (*Angel,* 2000); "Libertyville" (*Cold Case,* 2009); "Blood" (*Law & Order,* 1997); and "Absalom" (*Without a Trace,* 2007). Other films that overtly use the trope of passing but whose passers need to alter their appearance to pass (usually through cosmetics) include Charles Lane's *True Identity* (1991), a comedy in which a black man passes as white to escape a mobster; the Wayans brothers' *White Chicks* (2004), a comedy in which two black police officers pose as rich white debutantes; and Ben Stiller's *Tropic Thunder* (2008), a satiric film in which one of the actors (played by Robert Downey Jr.) is a white Australian who has undergone a medical procedure to make him look like a black man to enable him to play the role of an African American soldier. A slightly earlier film comedy is *Soul Man* (1986), starring C. Thomas Howell, which plays on whites' complaints over minority scholarships in colleges. Some of these films blend into whiteface, blackface, or racial masquerade, but they also function on the passing premise that their disguise is not recognized by their intended audience.

30. Arguing in a different register, Melamed suggests that this "multicultural citizen"—defined against a newly re-racialized monocultural subject and whose race corresponds as much (or more) to economic status than skin color—may be the new privileged subject in the neoliberal multicultural global society promoted by the United States (153).

31. For more on passing and images of the racialized body in film and other visual media, see Wald's *Crossing the Line*; Richard Dyer's *White*; Susan Gubar's *White Skin, Black Face in American Cinema*; Shawn Michelle Smith's *American Archives: Gender, Race, and Class in Visual Culture*; Caroline Streeter's "The Hazards of Visibility: 'Biracial' Women, Media Images, and Narratives of Identity"; Linda

Williams's *Playing the Race Card: Melodramas of Black and White from Uncle Tom to O. J. Simpson*; and various essays in the "pass·ing" issue of *Women & Performance*.

32. Although not a focus of this collection, biographies that turn on racial passing have also been published over the last two decades, including three recent ones: Sandweiss's *Passing Strange* (2009); Elizabeth M. Smith-Pryor's *Property Rites: The Rhinelander Trial, Passing, and the Protection of Whiteness* (2009); and Sharfstein's *The Invisible Line: Three American Families and the Secret Journey from Black to White* (2011).

33. G. Reginald Daniel explains: "Many African Americans have argued that the one-drop rule, although originally oppressive, has been a means of mobilizing African Americans in the struggle against white racial privilege. These people also view the rule as a means of preventing erosion in the number of individuals who under the current system are counted as black. These numbers, they argue, are needed to enforce and support civil rights legislation and claims aimed at tracking historical and contemporary patterns of discrimination, and in arriving at goals of achieving social and economic equity" (7).

34. One such text(s) not studied in detail in this collection is Philip Roth's novel and Robert Benton's film, *The Human Stain*. The film, like the novel, directly employs the traditional structure of passing novels: Coleman Silk (a light-skinned black man) passes for white (although Jewish, which is a deviation from the traditional black-white structure) so that he will not forever be known as "the black classics professor" and so that he can marry a white woman. His end is a typically tragic one. Thus, it is quite similar structurally and thematically to films of the 1940s and 1950s, such as *Pinky* (1949), *Imitation of Life* (1934, 1959), *Lost Boundaries* (1949), or *Band of Angels* (1957). For more on *The Human Stain,* see Elam and Ibrahim.

35. Although Sacha Baron Cohen's character Ali G is British (rather than American), the character has significant appeal in the United States. *Da Ali G Show* began airing in the United States on HBO in 2003. Cohen has since made several films directed by American directors and produced in the United States.

36. For more on a comparison of African American and Jewish American literary texts in the early twentieth century, and the relationship between race and ethnicity, especially in the context of passing, see Rottenberg.

37. Perhaps the best known early satire of racial passing is George Schuyler's *Black No More* (1931). A less-known parody is Langston Hughes's play *Limitations of Life* (1938), which lampoons the 1934 film *Imitation of Life.*

38. Although the film's premiere at the Venice Film Festival slightly precedes this collection's date range; the film was not released in the United States until 1990.

39. According to a 2008 U.S. Census Bureau press release, "Minorities, now roughly one-third of the U.S. population, are expected to become the majority in 2042, with the nation projected to be 54 percent minority in 2050" ("An Older"). On May 12, 2012, the U.S. Census Bureau reported that "50.4 percent

of our nation's population younger than age 1 were minorities as of July 1, 2011." It also reported that by 2011 there were five majority-minority states or equivalents (Hawaii, Washington D.C., California, New Mexico, and Texas). Hispanics, numbering 52 million in 2011, outnumbered African Americans (at just under 44 million) and were also the fastest growing minority population. However, the Census Bureau treats "Hispanic origin" and "race" as separate indicators, and notes that "Hispanics may be of any race" ("Most Children"). Such reports neatly highlight the long-standing slippage between race, ethnicity, and nationality.

40. Melamed explains the current value of whiteness in relation to the United States' co-opting of an originally antiracist multiculturalism and a concurrent remobilizing of older racial categories:

> As economic citizenship becomes more central to racial procedures and while *whiteness* as property is still operational, globalization also creates *multicultural* as a new form of *whiteness,* or rather the category of *whiteness* and its privileges are sublated into the category of *multiculturalism*. Traditional white privilege still comes into play in the United States, even as some white folks are left behind or left unprotected as the government shifts from service to its (historically favored white) citizens to capital maximization within globalization, which requires and produces a multiracial, multilingual, multicultural elite. At the same time, neoliberal racialization can intensify technologies for disqualifying, civilizing, and disciplining people of color without class privilege, renewing older racial schemas. (152–53)

41. According to a U.S. Army Corps of Engineers/U.S. Customs Border Protection Web site:

> In Section 102(b) of the Illegal Immigration Reform and Immigrant Responsibility Act (IIRIRA), Congress mandated the U.S. Department of Homeland Security (DHS) to install fencing, barriers, roads, lighting, cameras, and sensors on not less than 700 miles of the southwestern border. This total includes 370 miles of primary pedestrian fencing to be completed in 2008, in areas most practical and effective in deterring smugglers and aliens attempting to gain illegal entry into the United States. In addition, DHS has committed to completing a total of 300 miles of vehicle fence along the southwestern border by the end of 2008. . . . Primary pedestrian and vehicle fence are needed because of high levels of illegal entry along the U.S./Mexico international border. The mission of the U.S. Customs and Border Protection (CBP) is to prevent terrorists and terrorist weapons from entering the United States, while also facilitating the flow of legitimate trade and travel. (*Border Fence* par. 1–2)

The Office of Border Patrol Program Management Office has announced that as of January 8, 2010, the Vehicle Fence 300 project was complete ("TI Timeline").

42. According to the Southern Poverty Law Center (a group that tracks hate groups and hate crimes), the number of hate groups has also risen in the United States "by more than 50% since 2000. [The SPLC's *Intelligence Report*] attributed that growth mainly to fears about nonwhite immigration, but pointed out that the rise of a black man to the White House also appears to have contributed. And it said the ongoing economic meltdown, which some have already blamed on racial minorities and undocumented Latino immigrants, could well add to a worsening situation" (Potok par. 2). However, a study published in 2011 in *Journal of Marriage and Family* finds that, 10.7 percent of blacks who married in 2008 married whites, up from 3 percent in 1980; and overall black/white marriage increased threefold between 1980 and 2008. Almost 34 percent of Asians in 2008 married whites; more than 28 percent of Hispanics married non-Hispanic whites (Qian and Lichter).

43. Downey was nominated for Actor in a Supporting Role for Stiller's *Tropic Thunder*. He did not win.

Works Cited

"2010 Census Shows America's Diversity." *U.S. Census 2010 News Releases*. U.S. Census Bureau. Web. 24 Mar. 2011. 12 June 2012.

"Absalom." *Without a Trace*. CBS. WJZ. Baltimore, MD. 15 Nov. 2007.

Ali G Indahouse. Dir. Mark Mylod. Universal Pictures, 2002.

Allen, Theodore W. *The Invention of the White Race: The Origin of Racial Oppression in Anglo-America*. New York: Verso, 1997. Print.

"AMEA's History." *AMEA: Association of Multiethnic Americans*. Web. 18 June 2012.

Appiah, K. Anthony, and Amy Gutman. *Color Conscious: The Political Morality of Race*. Princeton: Princeton UP, 1996. Print.

"Are You Now or Have You Ever Been?" *Angel*. Warner Brothers Network. 3 Oct. 2000.

Bamboozled. Dir. Spike Lee. Forty Acres and a Mule Filmworks, 2000.

Band of Angels. Dir. Raoul Walsh. 1957. DVD. Warner Home Studios, 2007.

Belluscio, Steven J. *To Be Suddenly White: Literary Realism and Racial Passing*. St. Louis: U of Missouri P, 2006. Print.

Bennett, Juda. *The Passing Figure: Racial Confusion in Modern American Literature*. New York: Peter Lang, 1996. Print.

———. "Toni Morrison and the Burden of the Passing Narrative." *African American Review* 35 (2001): 205–17. Print.

Black. White. Dir. R.J. Cutler. fX Networks, 2006.

"Blood." *Law & Order*. NBC. LEX18. Lexington, KY. 19 Nov. 1997.

Border Fence Environmental Planning. U.S. Army Corps of Engineers/U.S. Customs and Border Protection. Web. 28 June 2009.

Bowman, Elizabeth Atkins. *Dark Secret*. New York: Forge, 2000. Print.

Brown, John Gregory. *Decorations in a Ruined Cemetery*. 1994. New York: Mariner Books, 2001. Print.

Brown, Wesley. *Darktown Strutters*. Amherst: U of Massachusetts P, 1994. Print.

Brown, William Wells. *Clotel; or, the President's Daughter*. 1853. *Three Classic African American Novels*. Ed. Henry Louis Gates Jr. Vintage Classics. New York: Random House, 1990. 3–224. Print.

Broyard, Bliss. *One Drop: My Father's Hidden Life—A Story of Race and Family Secrets*. New York: Little Brown, 2007. Print.

Caughie, Pamela L. *Passing and Pedagogy: The Dynamics of Responsibility*. Urbana: U of Illinois P, 1999. Print.

Chameleon Street. Dir. Wendell B. Harris. Gethsemane 84, Inc./ Prismatic Images, Inc., 1989.

Chesnutt, Charles W. *Mandy Oxendine*. Foreword Williams L. Andrews. Intro. Charles Hackenberry. Urbana and Chicago: U of Illinois P, 1997. Print.

———. *Paul Marchand, F.M.C.* Intro. Matthew Wilson. Jackson: UP of Mississippi, 1998. Print.

———. *The Quarry*. Intro. Dean McWilliams. Princeton: Princeton UP, 1999. Print.

"Civil Rights Act of 1990." *Govtrack.us*. Web. 22 June 2012.

"Civil Rights Act of 1991." *EEOC 35th Anniversary*. Web. 22 June 2012.

Cooper, J. California. *Family*. New York: Anchor Books, 1991. Print.

Cooper, James Fenimore. *The Last of the Mohicans*. 1826. Ed. and Intro. Paul C. Gutjahr. Ontario: Broadview P, 2009. Print.

Crafts, Hannah. *The Bondswoman's Narrative*. ca. 1857. Ed. Henry Louis Gates Jr. New York: Warner Books, 2002. Print.

Crenshaw, Kimberlé. "Demarginalizing the Intersection of Race and Sex: A Black Feminist Critique of Antidiscrimination Doctrine, Feminist Theory, and Antiracist Politics." *University of Chicago Legal Forum* 139 (1989): 139–67. Print.

DaCosta, Kimberly McClain. *Making Multiracials: State, Family, Market, and the Redrawing of the Color Line*. Stanford: Stanford UP, 2007. Print.

Dalmage, Heather. *The Politics of Multiracialism: Challenging Racial Thinking*. Albany: State U of New York P, 2004. Print.

Daniel, G. Reginald. *More Than Black? Multiracial Identity and New Racial Order*. Philadelphia: Temple UP, 2001. Print.

Devil in a Blue Dress. Dir. Carl Franklin. TriStar Pictures, 1995.

Dreisinger, Baz. *Near Black: White to Black Passing in American Culture*. Amherst: U of Massachusetts P, 2008. Print.

Dyer, Richard. *White*. London: Routledge, 1997. Print.

Elam, Michele. "Passing in the Post-Soul Race Era: Danzy Senna, Philip Roth, and Colson Whitehead." *African American Review* 41 (2007): 749–68. Print.

———. *The Souls of Mixed Folk: Race, Politics, and Aesthetics in the New Millennium.* Stanford: Stanford UP, 2011. Print.

Ellis, Trey. "The New Black Aesthetic." *Callaloo* 12.1 (1989): 185–203. Print.

Ellison, Ralph. *Juneteenth.* Ed. John F. Callahan. New York: Random House, 1999. Print.

Erasure. Dir. Percival Everett. Hyperion, 2001.

Fabi, M. Giulia. *Passing and the Rise of the African American Novel.* Urbana: U of Illinois P, 2001. Print.

Galindo, Elaine. *Beyond Passing.* Bloomington, IN: Xlibris, 2011.

Gallego, Mar. *Passing Novels in the Harlem Renaissance: Identity Politics and Textual Strategies.* Hamburg: Lit Verlag, 2003. Print.

Ginsberg, Elaine K. "Introduction: The Politics of Passing." In Ginsberg 1–18. Print.

———, ed. *Passing and the Fictions of Identity.* Durham, NC: Duke UP, 1996. Print.

Goldberg, David Theo. *The Racial State.* Malden, MA: Blackwell, 2002. Print

Goldstein, David S. and Audrey B. Thacker, eds. *Complicating Constructions: Race, Ethnicity, and Hybridity in American Texts.* Seattle: U of Washington P, 2007. Print.

Gossett, Thomas F. *Race: The History of an Idea in America.* New Ed. New York: Oxford UP, 1997. Print.

Grant, Madison. *The Passing of the Great Race.* 1916. New York: Scribner's, 1921. Print.

Griffin, John Howard. *Black Like Me.* 1961. Boston: Houghton Mifflin, 1971. Print.

Gubar, Susan. *Racechanges: White Skin, Black Face in American Culture.* New York: Oxford UP, 1997. Print.

Haizlip, Shirlee Taylor. *The Sweeter the Juice: A Family Memoir in Black and White.* New York: Simon and Schuster, 1994. Print.

Halsell, Grace. *Soul Sister.* 30th Anniversary Ed. Washington, DC: Crossroads International, 1999. Print.

Henry, Neil. *Pearl's Secret: A Black Man's Search for his White Family.* Berkeley: U of California P, 2001. Print.

Ho, Jennifer. "Ambiguous Movements: Paisley Rekdal's Passing Identity in The Night My Mother Met Bruce Lee: Observations on Not Fitting In." *Women & Performance: A Journal of Feminist Theory* 15.1 (2005): 141–65. Print.

Huggins, Nathan. "Passing is Passe." *Revelations: American History, American Myths.* Ed. Brenda Smith Huggins. New York: Oxford UP, 1995. 245–47. Print.

Hughes, Langston. "Limitations of Life." *Black Theatre U.S.A.* Ed. James Hatch and Ted Shine. New York: Free Press, 1974. 655–57. Print.

The Human Stain. Dir. Robert Benton. Miramax Films, 2003.

"I Refuse to Pass." Janice Kingslow. *Negro Digest* (May 1950): 22–31. Print.

Ibrahim, Habiba. *Troubling the Family: The Promise of Personhood and the Rise of Multiracialism.* Minneapolis: U of Minnesota P, 2012. Print.

Ignatiev, Noel. *How the Irish Became White.* New York: Routledge, 1995. Print.

Imitation of Life. Dir. Douglas Sirk. Universal International Pictures, 1959.

———. Dir. John M. Stahl. Universal Pictures, 1934.

"Is Passing for White a Dying Fad?" L. Masco Young. *Color* (April 1957): 46–49. Print.

Jacobs, Harriet. *Incidents in the Life of a Slave Girl.* 1861. Ed. Jean Fagin Yellin. Cambridge: Harvard UP, 1987. Print.

Jacobson, Matthew Frye. *Whiteness of a Different Color.* Cambridge: Harvard UP, 1998. Print.

Johnson, Charles. *The Oxherding Tale.* 1982. New York: Plume, 1995. Print.

Johnson, James Weldon. *The Autobiography of an Ex-Colored Man.* 1927. *Three Negro Classics.* Intro. John Hope Franklin. New York: Avon Books, 1965. 393–511. Print.

Kawash, Samira. "*The Autobiography of an Ex-Coloured Man*: (Passing for) Black Passing for White." In Ginsberg 59–74. Print.

Kennedy, Randall. *Selling Out: The Politics of Racial Betrayal.* New York: Random House, 2008. Print.

Kroeger, Brooke. *Passing: When People Can't Be Who They Are.* New York: Public Affairs, 2004. Print.

Lemire, Elise. *"Miscegenation": Making Race in America.* Philadelphia: U of Pennsylvania P, 2002. Print.

"Libertyville." *Cold Case.* CBS. WJZ. Baltimore. 29 March 2009.

Lost Boundaries. Dir. Alfred L. Werker. Film Classics, 1949.

Lovely, Erica. "Obama's Roots Have Irish Smiling Eyes." *Politico.* Web. 11 March 2009.

Major, Clarence. *Come By Here: My Mother's Life.* New York: John Wiley and Sons, 2002. Print.

Matthews, David. *Ace of Spades: A Memoir.* New York: Henry Holt, 2007. Print.

Meagher, Timothy J. "Racial and Ethnic Relations in America, 1965–2000." *Race and Ethnicity in America: A Concise History.* Ed. Ronald H. Bayor. New York: Columbia UP, 2003. 193–240. Print.

Melamed, Jodi. *Represent and Destroy: Rationalizing Violence in the New Racial Capitalism.* Minneapolis: U of Minnesota P, 2011. Print.

Miller, Karen E. Quinones. *Passin': a novel.* New York: Grand Central Publishing, 2008. Print.

"Minstrelsy, Passing, and the Location of an American Racial Identity." Special Issue. Guest Ed. Joshua J. Masters. *LIT: Literature, Interpretation, Theory* 18.2 (2007). Print.

Mitchell, Margaret. *Gone With the Wind.* 1936. New York: Scribner's, 2007. Print.

Morrison, Toni. "Comment." *The New Yorker.* Web. 5 Oct. 1998: 1–2.

Mosley, Walter. *Devil in a Blue Dress.* New York: Washington Square P, 1990. Print.

"Most Children Younger Than Age 1 Are Minorities, Census Bureau Reports." *United States Census Bureau.* Department of Commerce. May 17, 2012. Web. 12 June 2012.

Moynihan, Sinéad. *Passing Into the Present: Contemporary American Fiction of Racial and Gender Passing.* Manchester: Manchester UP, 2011. Print.

"The New Face of America: How Immigrants Are Shaping the World's First Multicultural Society." *Time* Special Issue. 18 Nov. 1993. 2. Print.

"The New Face of Race." *Newsweek* Special Report. Web. 18 Sept. 2000. 38–41.

Obama, Barack. "Press Conference of the President." The White House, Washington, DC. Web. 24 Mar. 2009.

"Older and More Diverse Nation by Midcentury." *United States Census Bureau.* Department of Commerce. Web. 14 Aug. 2008.

"pass·ing." *Women & Performance: a journal of feminist theory* 15.29 (2005). Print.

"Passing." *Transition: An International Review* 58 (1992). Print.

Perlmann, Joel. "Reflecting the Changing Face of America: Multiracials, Racial Classification, and American Intermarriage." *Interracialism: Black-White Intermarriage in American History, Literature, and Law.* Ed. Werner Sollors. New York: Oxford UP, 2000. 506–33. Print.

Pfeiffer, Kathleen. *Race Passing and American Individualism.* Amherst: U of Massachusetts P, 2003. Print.

Pinky. Dir. Elia Kazan. Twentieth Century Fox, 1949.

Potok, Mark, ed. "Resurgence on the Right." *Intelligence Report.* Southern Poverty Law Center. Summer 2009. Web. 28 June 2009.

Powell, A. D. *"Passing" for Who You Really Are: Essays in Support of Multiracial Whiteness.* Palm Coast, FL: Backintyme, 2005. Print.

Qian, Zhenchao, and Daniel T. Lichter. "Changing Patterns of Interracial Marriage in a Multiracial Society." *The Journal of Marriage and Family* 73.5 (Oct. 2011): 1065–84. Print.

Randall, Alice. *The Wind Done Gone.* New York: Houghton Mifflin, 2001. Print.

Roley, Brian Ascalon. *American Son.* New York: W.W. Norton, 2001. Print.

Root, Maria P. P. "Five Mixed Race Identities: From Relic to Revolution." In Winters and DeBose. 3–20. Print.

Roth, Philip. *The Human Stain.* Boston and New York: Houghton Mifflin, 2000. Print.

Rottenberg, Catherine. *Performing Americanness: Race, Class, and Gender in Modern African-American and Jewish-American Literature.* Hanover, NH: UP of New England, 2008. Print.

Sánchez, Maria Carla, and Linda Schlossberg, eds. *Passing: Identity and Interpretation in Sexuality, Race, and Religion.* New York: New York UP, 2001. Print.

Sandweiss, Martha A. *Passing Strange: A Gilded Age Tale of Love and Deception Across the Color Line.* New York: Penguin, 2009. Print.

Scales-Trent, Judy. *Notes of a White Black Woman.* 1995. University Park: Pennsylvania State UP, 2001. Print.

Schlossberg, Linda. "Introduction: Rites of Passing." *Passing: Identity and Interpretation in Sexuality, Race, and Religion.* Ed. Maria Carla Sánchez and Linda Schlossberg. New York: New York UP, 2001. 1–12. Print.

Schuyler, George. *Black No More.* New York: Macaulay, 1931. Print.

Senna, Danzy. *Caucasia.* New York: Riverhead Books, 1998. Print.

Sharfstein, Daniel J. *The Invisible Line: Three American Families and the Secret Journey from Black to White.* New York: Penguin, 2011. Print.

Slow Burn. Dir. Wayne Beach. Lionsgate Productions, 1995.

Smith, Shawn Michelle. *American Archives: Gender, Race, and Class in Visual Culture.* Princeton: Princeton UP, 1999. Print.

Smith-Pryor, Elizabeth M. *Property Rites: The Rhinelander Trial, Passing, and the Protection of Whiteness.* Chapel Hill: U of North Carolina P, 2009. Print.

Sollors, Werner. *Neither Black Nor White Yet Both: Thematic Explorations of Interracial Literature.* New York: Oxford UP, 1997. Print.

———, ed. *Interracialism: Black-White Intermarriage in American History, Literature, and Law.* New York: Oxford UP, 2000. Print.

Soul Man. Dir. Steve Miner. New World Pictures, 1986.

Spencer, Rainier. *Reproducing Race: The Paradox of Generation Mix.* Boulder, CO: Lynne Rienner, 2010.

Stern, Julia. "Spanish Masquerade and the Drama of Racial Identity in *Uncle Tom's Cabin.*" In Ginsberg. 103–30.

Stoddard, Lothrop. *The Rising Tide of Color Against White World Supremacy.* Intro. Madison Grant. New York: Scribner's, 1920. Print.

Stowe, Harriet Beecher. *Uncle Tom's Cabin.* 1851–52. Ed. and Intro. Christopher G. Diller. Ontario: Broadview P, 2009. Print.

Streeter, Caroline. "The Hazards of Visibility: 'Biracial' Women, Media Images, and Narratives of Identity." In Winters and DeBose. 301–22. Print.

Sullivan, Andrew. "Good Bye to All That: Why Obama Matters." *The Atlantic Online.* Web. Dec. 2007.

"TI Timeline." *CBP.gov.* Web. 10 Nov. 2011.

Time (Fall 1993) 142:21. Special Issue. Web.

Tropic Thunder. Dir. Ben Stiller. Dreamworks, 2008.

True Identity. Dir. Charles Lane. Sandollar Productions, 1991.

Wald, Gayle. *Crossing the Line: Racial Passing in Twentieth-Century U.S. Literature and Culture.* Durham: Duke UP, 2000. Print.

Walker, Lisa. *Looking Like What You Are: Sexual Style, Race, and Lesbian Identity.* New York: New York UP, 2001. Print.

Walker, Rebecca. *Black, White, and Jewish: Autobiography of a Shifting Self.* New York: Riverhead, 2001. Print.

Webb, Frank J. *The Garies and Their Friends.* 1857. Intro. Robert Reid-Pharr. Baltimore: Johns Hopkins UP, 1997. Print.

White Chicks. Dir. Keenen Ivory Wayans. Columbia Pictures, 2004.

Whitehead, Colson. *The Intuitionist.* New York: Anchor, 1999. Print.

"Why 'Passing' Is Passing Out." *Jet* (July 17, 1952): 12–16. Print.

Williams, Gregory Howard. *Life on the Color Line: The True Story of a White Boy Who Discovered He Was Black.* New York: Penguin, 1995. Print.

Williams, Kim M. *Mark One or More: Civil Rights in Multiracial America.* Ann Arbor:

U of Michigan P, 2008. Print.

Williams, Linda. *Playing the Race Card: Melodramas of Black and White from Uncle Tom to O.J. Simpson.* Princeton: Princeton UP, 2001. Print.

Winters, Loretta I., and Herman L. DeBose, eds. *New Faces in a Changing America: Multiracial Identity in the 21st Century.* New York: Sage, 2002. Print.

Wright, Susan Protho, and Ernestine Pickens Glass, eds. *Passing in the Works of Charles W. Chesnutt.* Jackson: U of Mississippi P, 2010. Print.

2

On the Margins of a Movement

Passing in Three Contemporary Memoirs

Irina Negrea

> I am a black American with white skin, an African American with both African and European ancestors. Thus, I live a life that is often disjointed, troubling. I also see the world in a different way. There is something about living on the margins of the race that gives me a unique view of the categories "black" and white, that presents a different picture of white Americans and black Americans. For my position does not allow me the luxury of thinking that the notion of race makes any sense . . . my existence unsettles expectations of "race."
>
> —Judy Scales-Trent, *Notes of a White Black Woman*

Like the history of race in the United States, racial passing is usually messy, much messier than the growing body of scholarship on the phenomenon has yet addressed. Scholars such as Elaine K. Ginsberg, Werner Sollors, and Gayle Wald, among others, have laid a sound foundation and acknowledged how passing is, in fact, a double-edged sword: the act undermines racial categories so that white supremacists cannot claim whiteness as an exclusive property, but passing also undergirds those same racial categories by documenting how light-skinned "blacks" who choose to live as white reify the racial boundaries that their passing exposes as socially constructed.[1] In other words, passers stress the faults in the system precisely by relying on and perpetuating the hegemonic power of whiteness: their existence as "both" gives lie to the mutual exclusivity of racial identity categories, and the fact that they *choose* to live as white undermines the idea of *biologically* determined race, but their choice to live exclusively as white still tacitly empowers (them and) the very system that would otherwise oppress them and that continues to oppress darker-skinned family members. Furthermore, since the act of passing requires secrecy, its power to subvert racial categories is visible only when the passer is made visible, either to a community or to a reader.

Because the strategy of passing itself depends upon *not* being visible, then, we can never know the actual number of people involved in passing.[2] However, the plethora of accounts of passing—in fiction, journalism, memoir, and film—over the last 160 years underscores its significance as a means of coping with and negotiating racial inequities and racism in the United States. Despite both its historical longevity and its continuing tenacity, the act of passing lacks clear-cut edges or definitions. However, it is perhaps because of its malleability that the trope has survived. Indeed, underscoring the complexity and adaptability of the phenomenon is the variability we find in accounts of passing: some passers choose to pass, either for a lifetime or situationally; others find themselves passing without their own volition and as a result of circumstances beyond their control (people assume them to be white). Still others live much of their lives unaware that they are "passing." Only after their history is revealed to them—if it is—do they have a "choice." And, having been raised with a specific racial identity (usually white), their racial "choice" is experienced differently than someone raised with a black racial identity.

Often, passers who choose to pass capitalize on their phenotypic whiteness to escape the socioeconomic discrimination and even cultural and physical violence they would potentially be subjected to as members of an oppressed group. But factors that help individuals decide to live as/become white can be material, economic, social, emotional, and/or psychological in nature. Passing also carries a different weight for different individuals, depending on the individual's own unique familial situation, the historical specificity and the assumptions about race that are functioning in society and culture at that given time, as well as on the political possibilities available at that particular moment and place. As Daniel J. Sharfstein notes in his biography of three families who crossed the color line, "The conventional understanding of passing as masquerade does not begin to approach the broad range of individuals' experiences as they migrated from black to white" (8). Across this range, though, emotional "costs" usually run high. Because U.S. racial categories have historically been exclusive (one race per person; "biracial" or "multiracial" has defaulted to "black" under the law of hypodescent—the "one-drop" rule), becoming white has often necessitated cutting ties with black family and friends. Those who do this, no matter the reason, are often constructed as "race traitors."[3] The idea that people who pass are betraying their race can be found in the earliest passing stories through contemporary ones. To leave behind one's oppressed identity—to reject the project of racial uplift and, later, race solidarity—is regularly characterized as crass materialism, moral corruption, self-hatred, or even (in the case of male passers) a lack of manhood.[4] Accounts of passing thus often suggest that passing takes a tremendous emotional toll both on the passer and on those members of the family with whom the passer has severed contact. As a result, some passers "return" to "their race," but others continue to live (sometimes even happily) as white. Some stay in the United States; others leave these shores for (they hope) more equitable treatment in Europe. On an extratextual level, some authors use passing to substantiate claims of an innate racial hierarchy, while others use passing to suggest an inherent equality across races. As a consequence of all of the factors highlighted above, stories of passing are often saturated with ambiguity and contradictions.

Passing is thus messy not only for the individuals and the families involved, but also for those of us who try to parse the mechanics of passing as a trope with the goal of understanding something about race, identity, and culture in the United States. This essay works toward that goal by probing some of the structural differences in passing situations—and the experiential consequences of those variations—as recorded in memoirs of interracial families living in the latter half of the twentieth century, a yet largely un-mined body of texts. The memoirs—Shirlee Taylor Haizlip's *The Sweeter the Juice: A Family Memoir in Black and White* (1994), Judy Scales-Trent's *Notes of a White Black Woman* (1995), and Gregory Howard Williams's *Life on the Color Line: The True Story of a White Boy Who Discovered He Was Black* (1995)—record the stories of real families made and split across the racial divide. The discussion also acknowledges how each of these family stories is grounded in particular historical moments that come with specific assumptions about race and the color line in the United States. Because that ground shifts from one generation to the next, this essay tries to resist too many generalizations about passing as a monolithic trope, while still attempting to draw some conclusions about what these three memoirs suggest about race and identity in their own historical moment.[5]

The three memoirs under study here—all published in the mid-1990s—have several key points of intersection relevant to a discussion of passing. All three memoirs discuss at length the racism that African Americans face in their daily lives and its varying intensity and virulence, according to historic specificity. They also show how the U.S. racial system at the close of the twentieth century—despite post–civil rights progress toward racial equity and the demise of Jim Crow segregation—still could not easily accommodate individuals whose phenotype failed to match their racial identity. Haizlip, Scales-Trent, and Williams—all light-skinned individuals—attest to how they unsettle both whites and blacks by virtue of their physical appearance in a racial system grounded in the illusion of fixed, exclusive categories. For some, the disjunction between their appearance and their racial heritage threatens white identity itself. The memoirs also all narrate what passing meant/means for the family members left behind by passers, particularly exploring the emotional and psychological impact on those unable or unwilling to pass, and revealing conflicting feelings of anger, betrayal, inadequacy, and helplessness. Finally, all come to some resolution that involves recognition of both "sides" of the family and of the self.

Important in this study is the fact that, first, these contemporary texts are not *fiction,* but *memoirs*[6] and thus detail the lives of actual (if narrativized) families and individuals, many still living when the texts were published. Second is that, as a group, they seem to mark the beginning of a stream of racially focused memoirs that has continued unabated through the first decade of the twenty-first century. Two questions here, then, are: Why the 1990s? And, how do these texts differ from earlier accounts? The autobiographical or biographical texts that dealt with passing published before the 1990s are most notably the spate of texts published in the 1940s and 1950s—at the nascence of the civil rights movement.[7] These texts include (but aren't limited to) Walter White's autobiography, *A Man Called White* (1948); W. L. White's "true story" account of the Johnson family, *Lost Boundaries* (1947); Reba Lee's fictionalized (auto)biography, *I Passed For White* (1955); an explosion of magazine articles published in the 1950s decrying passing; and, a bit later, John Howard Griffin's journalistic narrative, *Black Like Me* (1961). However, while all of these texts acknowledge passing as an actual phenomenon and despite the ways they trouble the color line, none of the texts are developed memoirs that situate passing in the kind of historical exploration of family in the ways the memoirs under study here do.[8] Furthermore, the contemporary memoirs (to varying degrees) "out" their family members—some long dead, some still living—as passers. Perhaps most importantly, these more recent memoirists conceptualize themselves not primarily in a black/white dichotomy, as do the vast majority of earlier writers/subjects, but as light-skinned multiracial individuals who to some extent have the liberty of "choice" in their racial identity.

These significant differences document a level of change in the racial landscape—a fissure in the bulwarks of whiteness—in the early 1990s. Just as the earlier burst of confessional/exposé passing narratives erupted at the onset of the civil rights movement, these later memoirs appeared at the genesis of the multiracial movement.[9] Kimberly McClain DaCosta argues that from the mid-1990s "multiracialism has emerged as a topic of public discussion, and 'multiracial' has become a recognizable social category and mode of identification" (2–3). She suggests further that as a consequence, "the multiracial family is no longer a contradiction in terms" (174). The proliferation of racially focused memoirs—Paul Spickard has called it the "boom in biracial biography"—is part of this groundswell that opened up possibilities for multiracial identification.[10] The authors consider themselves, in various situations and at various (or even simultaneous) moments as black, white, mulatto, biracial, multiracial, neither, both, or all of the above. Thus, even as they maintain the language of racial categories, they also each conceptualize their racial identity as a form of hybridity—as an *in-betweenness*—that creates enormous potential for freedom from a binaric racial system.[11] The moments at which their own language resists their attempts to break down racial categories do not necessarily reflect a failure of their vision, but instead evidence the historical complexity of race in the United States and its reliance on a paradoxical "logic" of visibility and invisibility.

At the end of their physical and spiritual journeys, Haizlip, Scales-Trent, and Williams situate themselves *on* the color line, in a move that is ultimately meant to elude any attempt at racial classification and to empower the individual to claim a complex family history. They challenge the racial system, then, not by *choosing* to pass as white but by *resisting* the cultural pressure to choose (or be forced into) one identity or another, an option that does not involve the trauma of leaving family and community behind and that functions as a more dynamic metaphor for a multiracial twenty-first century America. They attempt to tie together, to bridge, and to heal their families that have been divided by the color line, and suggest that those who have passed should not be judged too harshly for their choices, no matter how traumatic their actions prove to be for those they leave behind. They claim a new kind of visibility, one that acknowledges the multiplicity inscribed upon their bodies and that demands cultural recognition as well. Their representations of the struggles of (in today's parlance) multiracial members of their families and of themselves, as well as their complicated family trees, serve as poignant reminders that the problem of the twenty-first century remains the color line at both macrocosmic and microcosmic levels.[12]

Left Behind, Moving Ahead

Shirlee Taylor Haizlip's *The Sweeter the Juice* is, as she subtitles it, "A Family Memoir in Black and White." Haizlip herself, along with her mother and her siblings, is phenotypically white, but her immediate family identifies as black. Published in 1994, the memoir is the fruit of a long search—undertaken on behalf of Haizlip's mother—for a branch of the family that crossed the color line to "become white" (13). Haizlip begins her story with Margaret Maher, the white, abandoned daughter of an Irish immigrant who, around 1875, married Edward Everett Morris, a light-skinned ex-slave. The couple had four children, including William C. Morris, the author's maternal grandfather. Dire circumstances cause the dissolution of William Morris's family: his wife dies; William (who is an alcoholic) abandons the family; the older siblings go out on their own. The younger daughter Margaret (the author's mother) is left behind in the care of her black godmother. Later, when Margaret tries to reunite with her brothers and sister, she discovers that they are passing as white and that they do not want to acknowledge her because she is "black." Her father ends up passing as well, and while he keeps in contact with Margaret's "white" sister, Grace, he never acknowledges or tries to contact Margaret. In short, Margaret's siblings and father reject her to protect themselves from exposure. From there, the narrative weaves its way through the vicissitudes of racial passing, racism, family history, and personal struggle, and thus provides ample material for analysis. For the purposes of this essay, I will focus on the moment of racial fracture in the family, looking specifically at what it tells us about how race—and particularly whiteness—functions in the United States.

A key question in the narrative is why they didn't take Margaret with them, especially given that Margaret herself was light enough to pass. All of the children (including Margaret) had attended a whites-only school in Washington, where admission was based on visual inspection. Given her mother's light skin, Haizlip recalls that she was "confused when my mother told me that she was not with her father, or her brothers and sister, because she was too brown" (32). The explanation Haizlip ultimately posits for Margaret's abandonment revolves around how whiteness functions in the United States: "My mother was the scapegoat for her entire family. As the youngest survivor, she was the logical choice. The family divested all its blackness into her. She was their Other" (267). Haizlip is suggesting here that it is the *process* of renunciation—the distance they place between her and themselves—that actually bolsters their own claim to whiteness. In other words, once the color line is crossed, the passer has to ensure that it is firmly drawn between him and the family left behind. In doing so, the passer (dis)places his blackness onto other family members. However, although they reject her, they also cannot exist without her because she represents the "other" against which their whiteness is constructed. Valerie Babb explains the process thus: "Once conceived, whiteness maintained itself hegemonically," mainly through the exclusion of those who are not white, a fact that reveals, paradoxically, that whiteness needs nonwhiteness "to give it form and expression" (41–43). In order for them to become white, Margaret's family needs someone to be left behind, to "stay" black, so that they can be defined and define themselves as white. Margaret indeed becomes the Other against whom her siblings can compare and find themselves superior. They project their blackness—physical and cultural—onto her, as she is tacitly chosen to bear the "stigma" of blackness for the rest of the siblings and her father, none of whom realizes (or cares) how traumatic it is for her to be left behind and abandoned, the modern emotional equivalent of being "sold down the river."

Margaret is thus simultaneously marked as "other" (made visible) by a stigma of race and erased by both the act of familial disavowal and the social invisibility of being nonwhite, highlighting the paradox of visibility/invisibility central to race in the United States. In other words, Margaret—despite her "white" skin—becomes hyper-visible as black, a visibility that paradoxically makes her socially and politically *invisible*.[13] Like Ralph Ellison's Invisible Man, Margaret is not seen because of the "psychological 'construction of [whites'] *inner* eyes,' which conceptually erases [their] existence" (Mills 8–9). For the other family members, the situation is reversed: as passers, they need to be "invisible" as whites—that is, they need not to stand out among whites—but they also become invisible in that whiteness is conceptualized as the absence of race. As Sterling L. Bland explains, whiteness "brought with it the privilege of not being classified at all, since whiteness is considered a point of reference or of origin, used to define and classify 'the others'" (141).[14] Individuals passing for white, then, enter a state of invisibility. However—here once again is a paradox—that state is also a site of privilege and (potential) socioeconomic and political empowerment/visibility. Margaret's family bolsters their own whiteness by their repeated refusals to acknowledge her relationship to them—by their repeated erasure/marking of her as black. When Margaret tries to contact her siblings by mail in 1936, her letters are returned marked "unknown addressee," even though she has the correct addresses. Three years later, her husband, Julian, uses his influence as a minister and writes to the chief of police in Cleveland, asking him for help in reuniting his wife with her family. Contacted, the two brothers and one sister reply that they did not know a Margaret Morris. Thus, Margaret becomes the family's best kept secret, "her family's heart of darkness," as Haizlip puts it (267).

Margaret's desire to find and be acknowledged by her siblings certainly grows from her deep psychological disappointment at being rejected,[15] but it also reverberates within the legacy of familial reconstruction within the African American community. The importance of reclaiming relatives for African Americans dates from slavery, when families were broken up at the whim of or economic pressures upon the slave master, and their members sold away to different states or regions. In such a hostile climate, one important part of African American culture is to claim, to know, and to acknowledge members of one's family. When it necessitated disavowal of family members, as it did in Margaret Morris's case, passing fractured the African American family just as surely as did the slave system and is one reason why passing has generally been condemned within the African American community. However, Haizlip comes to understand that, more often than not, passing historically happened out of economic necessity, a desire for physical safety, or the unwillingness to accept second-class citizenship—and that passing itself represents a means to cope with all the adversities that a person faces as black. She thus suggests that those who crossed over should not be judged for their choices: "I have more sympathy for those who made the choice to leave the black part of their lives behind. In my eagerness to condemn, I had never looked too closely at the circumstances that provoked such decisions" (267). Haizlip concludes that one should judge *the system* that makes passing possible and enticing in the first place. Or, even better, we should change the system to afford all individuals, regardless of race, access to economic opportunity, civil and human rights, and self-respect. Thus, by exposing the pass, Haizlip's memoir is not an act of racial retribution against race traitors, but an attempt at public reclamation, reconstruction, and reconciliation of the (interracial) family, processes dependent upon identification and revelation. That is, the memoir must make *visible* all members of the family, regardless of race, just as it makes visible the *process* of racialization itself.

When Haizlip finds Grace, her mother's "white" sister, Grace at first denies ever having a sister, then recants and allows Haizlip and Margaret to pay her a visit. Grace recounts the story of her life after the separation, not mentioning anything about the separation itself or about her race. Family pictures are exchanged and stories told, but even then race does not enter the conversation: "Despite all the years of longing and conjecture, despite the fact that race was the central issue, I could not bring myself to broach it yet," the author comments (247). Haizlip senses that to approach the issue of race means to break the tenuous connection she has finally established, and further realizes that Grace "had no conscious memories of her colored years. In fact, she had no colored memories at all" (250). What is more, when Margaret visits her, Grace criticizes her own granddaughter for dating a Hispanic man who is dark "like a black man," asserting her preference that she date a white man, asking: "What's wrong with a good white man?" (257). Associating "goodness" with whiteness, and secure in her own whiteness, Grace—deliberately or not—insults both her sister and niece. Since neither is yet willing to discuss race, they let the offending remark go unaddressed; however, the comment serves to highlight the divisiveness of race and the ways in which it shapes identity. Discussing individuals whose families had, at some point, crossed the color line, Sharfstein notes that "on a daily basis, in ways large and small, they asserted their new racial status" and their descendants "[l]ike most Americans . . . were taught to believe that the line between white and black is and always has been a natural barrier supported by science and religion and fortified by politics and law" (3). Grace's remarks evidence a white identity shaped by twentieth-century racism.

In the end, the one who integrates the family—and begins to repair the fracture opened when Margaret's father and siblings became white—is Jeff, Grace's grandson. After finding out that he is "part" black, Jeff organizes a family reunion, attended by Grace, his father (Grace's son-in-law), Margaret, and her daughters—Shirlee and Jewelle. Once again, Haizlip notes, everyone avoids the topic of race. However, the presence of dark-skinned African American men (Shirlee's and Jewelle's husbands); the discussion of African tribal music and dance; and Jewelle's demonstration of a Liberian dance, all indicate that race is the undercurrent flowing in the room and that the color line, drawn in the middle of this family and separating its members for so many years, is breaking down. Grace's reaction is telling. Haizlip recounts: "Grace sat quietly, hugging herself with both arms as if holding herself together. . . . [She] smiled and gripped my mother's hand tightly as she watched her past become her present" (264). If in the beginning Grace had the reaction of someone whose world is slowly crumbling and is trying to hold herself (and that world) together, in the end, she hangs on to the person she actually left behind, to the person she once rejected and did not want to acknowledge, but to whom now she feels connected by virtue of a potential future and, briefly, a shared past.

Reclaiming that shared past, however, has limited power to reshape Grace's own sense of racial identity. In the end, after detailing what she calls "the geography of despair and flight and fear" (265), Haizlip herself realizes that her relatives who have crossed the color line have, in fact, *become* white:

> I began the search for my mother's family believing that I was looking for black people "passing for white." And they did indeed pass. But what I ultimately found, I realized, were black people who had become white. After all, if you look white, act white, live white, vacation white, go to school white, marry white and die white, are you not "white"? Can race be simply a matter of context? (266)

Haizlip's last question is one of the overarching questions in any exploration of race, and the memoir suggests that the answer is "yes." The uncle who moves to Buffalo becomes white, while Margaret, taken into the house of a black relative, becomes black.[16] Such cases illustrate the contextual nature of both blackness and whiteness.

Haizlip also records the transformation of her own racial consciousness over the course of the memoir. She is specific in delineating the components of her racial heritage and in articulating the anxiety that heritage often creates:

> Genes and chromosomes from Africa, Europe and a pristine America commingled and created me. I have been called Egyptian, Italian, Jewish, French, Iranian, Armenian, Syrian, Spanish, Portuguese and Greek. I have also been called black and Peola and nigger and high yellow and bright. I am an American anomaly. I am an American ideal. I am the American nightmare. I am the Martin Luther King dream. I am the new America. (15)

Unlike with the passer, there is no attempt to conceal, nor a wish to use ambiguity in her favor. There is also, as Paul Spickard notes, "no torment here" (83). Instead, there is only an acknowledgment that the names she is called—whether they represent different ethnicities, nationalities, or derogatory racial terms—all represent attempts to classify her. For race purists, she is an "anomaly" and a "nightmare." But for those who see the solution to the "race problem" in (continued) race mixing and erasing a color line that has never truly been impermeable, she is an "ideal" or "Martin Luther King dream," or the "new America."

Thus, at the end of her journey, Haizlip tries to avoid an oppositional or binaric construct of race by describing herself as a "person of mixed race": "If asked, I would probably now describe myself as a person of mixed race rather than as black, although I know I will never lose my black feelings" (267). Her position on the color line is one that gives her the advantage of perspective: "My color, I said, had allowed me to sit on top of and look over both sides of the high wall that separates the black and white experiences. And yes, that has been an advantage in the revelation of the dark secrets people have in their white souls" (238). Haizlip realizes that being *on* the color line gives her a unique perspective on racial categories. That liminality puts her directly in the politically charged space between races, a space that Renato Rosaldo considers important because it is inhabited by hybrid figures who challenge the status quo by resisting the dominant culture through their positioning on the border: "Claiming the border amounts to a declaration of interdisciplinary—and narrative—freedom: the border, porous and open, emerges as a zone capable of nourishing a rich grid of 'crisscrossed,' multiple identities, a celebration of ambiguity" (qtd. in Weber 532). The possibility to celebrate one's ambiguity without the need to capitulate to a system that demands racial exclusivity—with the often attendant destruction of the family—is one alternative to passing that Haizlip suggests for biracial or multiracial individuals.

The Measure of Difference

In *Notes of a White Black Woman*, Judy Scales-Trent also embraces racial (and textual) multiplicity and ambiguity. Published in 1995, her book is what the title suggests—a collection of notes, diary entries, short pieces, and anecdotes, all written from the particular perspective of one standing on the color line. Like Haizlip, Trent realizes that a liminal position between classifications is what frees her from the system and gives her the advantage of a clear view, as her self-definition attests:

> I am a black American with white skin, an African American with both African and European ancestors. Thus, I live a life that is often disjointed, troubling. I also see the world in a different way. There is something about living on the margins of the race that gives me a unique view of the categories "black" and "white," that presents a different picture of white Americans and black Americans. For my position does not allow me the luxury of thinking that the notion of race makes any sense . . . my existence unsettles expectations of "race." (7)

Like Haizlip, Scales-Trent acknowledges her mixed racial heritage, emphasizing that her racial identity gives her a different perspective on life and on racial categories. Her biraciality undermines the myth of white purity and her physical appearance leaves people at a loss as to where she fits within the racial system. Living on what she considers the margins of race(s), she is what Rosaldo calls "a borderland dweller"—one whose existence defies immutable blackness and whiteness, and one who is most feared by white purists, living in the politically charged space between the races.[17] Like Haizlip, even without passing, Scales-Trent causes anxiety and doubt in the whites she encounters because she does not "look" black, nor does she conform to many whites' expectations of blackness.

In "Shock and Fear in America," Scales-Trent writes that she considers herself an ordinary person, with the same hopes and fears as anyone else. However, she is made to feel different and she is given the measure of that difference in the fact that people (usually whites) perceive her as an "object of shock and fear" (57). At first impression, people assume she is white, and then something happens that destroys that perception, even though she still "looks" white. Scales-Trent describes how an East Indian checkout clerk who sees her hair (what she calls "true African hair") is shocked because the hair does not "match" her white complexion, so he advises her to straighten it in order to look white (57). He takes it for granted that she wants to be white, according to Scales-Trent, because of the advantages whiteness offers (58). In another instance, an old white woman in a restaurant asks her where she is from and then hits her when Trent explains that she is of African and European heritage, but does not know what specific European nationality, since slave owners did not disclose their heritage to their slaves (58). "And that's when she hit me," the author relates. "It was just a slap on the arm, delivered with a tight smile . . . [but] she was definitely angry" (58–59). Scales-Trent's comments on these incidents reveal that she realizes how destabilizing her presence is:

> While I was just going along leading my quiet, humdrum life, I apparently inspired shock, fear, anger. These people got upset because there was not a good fit between what they saw and heard, and what they expected to see and hear. This disjuncture upset them and they wanted me to do something to make them feel better. (59)

Instead of apologizing for the destabilizing effect of her physical presence, or absolving them from their guilt, assumptions, or anger, the author encourages their discomfort and highlights the historical racism that both created and desires to deny her presence. The author disrupts these people's vision of a world ordered into mutually exclusive categories of black and white. Their reaction is Procrustean: unwilling to accept the truth that *their* perspective is skewed, they want *her* to conform and make changes in order to fit *their* vision of the world. The same reaction is often provoked in white people when a passer is outed: anxiety, anger, and shock. In fact, Scales-Trent is placed into the position of the passer by her interlocutor's assumptions about how race is embodied. When her race becomes "visible"—when she outs herself as black—her selfhood must become invisible as a black person and, perhaps even more so, as a light-skinned black person.

According to Scales-Trent, one other reaction of whites is complete denial, compounded by a limitless arrogance that the world *is* the way they see it. In "Definitions," the author tells a white man at a party that she is black. His reaction is unexpected: "He replied, with a smile: 'No, you're not.' " (72). The interesting fact, she notes, is that the words were not uttered with shock, denial, amazement, or even dismay, but "calmly, with a certainty that the speaker, not I, controlled my identity" (74). The certainty comes, of course, with whiteness and the deeply embedded belief that whites possess the power to define (which, historically, they have).[18] Behind the speaker stand centuries of deciding who was black and who joined the ranks of white privilege, and centuries of legally awarded power to do so. White conductors on Jim Crow trains, for instance, had the power to force people to move from one carriage to another based on their judgment of the passenger's race. In a clear association with the Jim Crow era, Scales-Trent tells the reader that nowadays there still are government clerks who are empowered to categorize individuals when filing forms.[19] After a cursory visual inspection of the individual in front of them, they check the box they find appropriate.

Scales-Trent thus alludes to what every student of African American history knows: that to name oneself means to own oneself, not to *be* owned. The difference between the passive voice of slavery and the active voice of agency represents the difference between a life of oppression and a life of freedom. Freedom, however, is subject to the racial system, and Scales-Trent is contemplating it historically, thinking about "the categories, the racial purity laws, the lives that are stomped, mangled, ruined because of those categories and those laws" (74). The power to identify—to name or, here, to race—one's self is a sign of owning oneself, and deciding on which side of the color line one belongs is a sign of agency. This is one of the more subtle threats of passing: the passer claims the power and authority of naming/racing herself.

Scales-Trent folds her discussion of the power of self-identification—if briefly—within a framework of the nation-state. In "Lost Great-Uncle Charles," Scales-Trent relates how Charles ran away from home when he was young, with the intention to pass, and never returned. She sees her great-uncle as an immigrant to a new country—aptly named "Whiteland"—a political refugee who could not stay in his native land because he "got tired of being persecuted for holding the very dangerous political belief that he was, indeed, a man" (97). The analogy is limited in the sense that after escaping the oppressive regime, political refugees often do not need to hide their nationality, while in the case of passing for white, it is the denial of the black identity and the family (the racial nation-state) that makes "immigration" possible. However, the analogy does highlight how for the passer, as for the immigrant, assimilation may be imperative, or even desired. But both may simultaneously feel "homesick" for friends, family, and the identity left behind. In the existing racial state, dual citizenship is not possible.

In discussing her great-uncle, Scales-Trent turns more explicitly to the context of family. Although she mentions those Charles left behind—his three siblings, one of whom was Mary Mosby, the author's grandmother—Scales-Trent focuses more on Charles himself. She is sympathetic toward her great-uncle but adds that "if I thought that he had escaped to a good life in Whiteland and, in so doing, had left his family back in the old country, destitute and ill[,] If this were the case, . . . I would consider him beneath contempt" (97). But she cannot muster any lasting anger toward her long-lost relative because when she looks at her family and at their accomplishments, she sees how much *he* lost by leaving what she calls "this wonderful family" behind (98). She recognizes not only what he may have gained in access to economic, social, or political opportunity, but also what he lost by choosing to become a citizen of Whiteland.

Like Haizlip, Scales-Trent ultimately does not see passing as a betrayal: political refugees in host countries are not (or should not be) considered traitors for escaping a regime that threatened their lives. On the contrary, the regime—or, in this case, the racial/racist system—is at fault for causing racial refugees to seek safety and cross the color line in the first place: "I think about how mean a country must be to force someone to make such a cruel choice" (Trent 98). She aligns herself with Haizlip in blaming the system for creating the necessity or desire to pass. One solution that would not "mangle" lives in this way is recognizing a state of racial in-betweenness, a location with porous borders.

Scales-Trent discusses the notion of mestiza consciousness, a term originated by Gloria Anzaldúa, to describe the necessity to develop a "tolerance for contradictions" and for ambiguity, to operate in a "pluralistic mode," to stand where "phenomena tend to collide" and where "the possibility of uniting all that is separate occurs" (155). Haizlip adopts a similar position: she wants to elude classification, especially being boxed in a single, limiting racial category that is—problematically—inscribed on the body. Although claiming oneself as "racially in-between" or "multiracial" is also an act of (self-)classification, occupying such a position is, she implies, a better alternative than either passing or occupying a single racial identity for bi- or multiracial individuals, since it causes less trauma and does not require the erasure or abandonment of family on either side of the color line. Hybridity and liminality instead open possibilities for freedom and a fuller self-definition.

The Klan's Nightmare

The third author under examination here, Gregory Howard Williams, explores the consequences of a different type of passing: Williams spent the early years of his life as white, then lived through his adolescence and early adulthood as black. Despite this difference, he ends up placing himself in, and advocating for, the same liminal position as do Haizlip and Scales-Trent. Williams records his experience in *Life on the Color Line: The True Story of a White Boy Who Discovered He Was Black,* published in 1995. "My black grandmother and my white grandmother both died in the 1970s. They lived within two miles of each other, but they never met," Williams writes, effectively describing one divisive aspect of a life generated from both sides of the color line (283). If Haizlip's narrative focuses on the maternal line, Williams's is centered primarily on the paternal. Buster Williams, a pivotal figure in the young boy's life and a larger-than-life character, dominates the memoir. Himself a light-skinned man of mixed race, James Anthony (Tony) "Buster" Williams is portrayed as a very intelligent—but easily bored—idealistic alcoholic who, in turns, makes and breaks the lives of his two sons, Greg and Mike.

After dropping out of Howard University, Buster returns to his home town of Muncie, Indiana, and has an affair with a young white woman. They marry and move away from Muncie, so that Buster can pass for white. His voluntary exile—his racial invisibility—pays off. Living in Virginia as a white man, he owns and operates a roadside café. As with his passing, his way of operating his business simultaneously reinforces and subverts racial categories: he upholds Jim Crow segregation by serving white customers in the front of his café and black customers in the back. However, in 1950s Virginia, it was against the law to serve both races under the same roof in any capacity. Despite this sanction, Tony Williams creates a space where the two races actually come together in the deeply segregated South. The café thus stands as a microcosm of the racially divided nation, with Tony literally crossing the line as he moves back and forth through the building, and as a metaphor for Tony himself, who is "neither black nor white, yet both," as Werner Sollors aptly describes interracial individuals.

Raised in the café and thus reminded daily of the U.S. system of segregation, the four Williams children have no inkling that legally they would be considered black. They are, in Julie Cary Nerad's term, "unintentional passers."[20] Greg and Mike do, however, have some suspicions that something is amiss when they visit their mother's parents in Muncie: "We were always greeted warmly in Muncie, but hardly a day passed without some abrupt silence when I entered a room filled with relatives. The silence indicated to me that aunts, uncles, and even older cousins shared a secret I must not know" (16). The secrecy that surrounds Greg's racial heritage is necessary in Virginia, but in Muncie the (shared) secret is kept by his mother's white family out of shame.

After one family visit to Indiana, Greg and Mike come home to find that their mother has taken their younger siblings and left because of the physical abuse she has suffered at her husband's hands.[21] From this point on, Tony drinks away his economic assets to the point where Greg and Mike are literally starving. When their poverty reaches this extreme, Tony decides to return to Muncie to his mother. This is the moment when he tells Mike and Greg that they are not white. The boys' reactions are unexceptional:

> I didn't understand Dad. I knew I wasn't colored, and neither was he. My skin was white. All of us are white, I said to myself. But for the first time, I had to admit that Dad didn't exactly look white. His deeply tanned skin puzzled me as I sat there trying to classify my own father. Goose bumps covered my arms as I realized that whatever he was, I was. Colored! Colored! Colored! (33)

Greg's reaction to his fall into race is reminiscent of the one James Weldon Johnson's ex-colored man has after he finds out he is black—he looks at his mother with "white" eyes and "sees" her blackness. And, as with many earlier fictional passers, the knowledge terrifies Greg so much that his initial responses are physical ("goose bumps"), followed by horror and denial. But he continues: "The veil dropped from [my father's] face and features. Before my eyes he was transformed from a swarthy Italian to his true self—a high-yellow mulatto. My father was a Negro! We were colored! After ten years in Virginia on the white side of the color line, I knew what that meant" (34). In a Du Boisian turn of phrase, Williams describes how young Greg "sees" his father's blackness where before there was none. His father's race becomes visible before his very eyes.

With the confidence that the privilege of whiteness confers, Greg thinks he knows what it means to be black because he lives within a segregated society, but nothing in his white life has prepared him for the life that is waiting for him in Muncie, Indiana, this time in the "colored" part of the town. As Tony explains: " 'This is the Projects, boys. Colored families live on this side of Madison, and crackers the other. Stay outta there. If the crackers learn you're colored, they'll beat the hell out of you. You gotta be careful here, too. Coloreds don't like half-breeds either' " (38). Tony's warning suggests that Greg and his brother have no place on either side of the literal and figurative color line: black children reject them because they "look" white and whites are suspicious of them because they thwart their expectations of how "coloreds" are "supposed" to look. The boys must simultaneously learn to negotiate their new sociocultural space as well as their new racial identities, neither of which seem to be grounded in anything fixed or stable. Indeed, Greg finds himself in the absurd situation of being white in Virginia and "colored" in Indiana, and his father tells him: "We can still be white, but not in Muncie" (34).

Not only must they enter a state of racial visibility and sociocultural invisibility, but they do so knowing that they have been abandoned by their mother and that their younger siblings continue to live, in Scales-Trent's language, in "Whiteland." Rather than being left behind or choosing to immigrate into a white state, Greg and Mike are forcibly exiled, their identity—their racial citizenship—shifted literally overnight, their whiteness revoked. However, because they are very light-skinned, their new racial state rejects them as well. Thus, they function perhaps even more so than Scales-Trent's Uncle Charles as racial refugees.

Even though they are too young to know it, Greg's and Mike's liminal position challenges dominant white hierarchies because they are not either/or, black or white, and thus they embody a certain level of power. That power, however, is ideological at best and does little to prevent the kind of violence often incited by such racial in-betweenness or hybridity. Indeed, one could not often overtly stay in such a politically charged border space through much of the twentieth century without incurring the wrath of white racists, and the Williams boys find out on their own how that wrath is manifested in daily encounters with racial hate and discrimination. When Greg's first school friends, white Molly and Sally, find out that he is related to one of the black students, they reject him. "Even from a distance," Williams writes, "I saw shock register on their faces. . . . As I walked through the door [of the classroom], their heads snapped toward the small window. . . . When the girls saw me approach, they turned their backs to me" (46). The school episode, which echoes the one related by W. E. B. Du Bois in *The Souls of Black Folk,* is the first in a series of harsh rejections that the boys have to endure from both races, while doing what their father calls "learning how to be niggers" (58). For Greg, learning to be black—to learn the laws of being a citizen of the black racial state—is sometimes even a matter of survival.[22] In one instance, as a member of the high school basketball team, Greg and a few of his black teammates are forced to face an angry white mob among whom he recognizes classmates who have rooted for him at games: "They could see we were four well-known Muncie Central athletes. These same students cheered wildly when we mastered conference rivals. From somewhere in the darkness, I heard, 'Get the black bastards' " (225).

Greg becomes a "black bastard" despite his "white" skin. In fact, as Haizlip and Scales-Trent both highlight, it is the lightness of his skin that marks him as a particular target for whites. The white reactions he records betray a deep-seated fear of blackness, of "mixed" blood, of the possible unreliability of the entire racial system. When the boys are in an accident and their dark-skinned grandmother is in the same car, a state trooper interrogates them:

> On the way to the hospital he asked us if we were runaways. We denied it.
>
> "Then what are you doing with those colored people?"
>
> "They're family," I said.
>
> "Don't lie to me. You better tell me the truth before you really get into trouble.
>
> You're lying. We can keep you in jail until you tell the truth, and not some bullshit about being kin to those niggers." (142)

The trooper works himself into an anxious/angry state of mind when he reluctantly realizes he has to let himself believe that the boys are telling the truth. He does not *want* them to be kin to the black people because their blackness is not visible. Instead, what their bodies testify to is a crossing of the color line and the instability of race itself.

Greg gets yet another taste of how these "white" unsettled expectations can turn lethal: he remembers watching a KKK rally on TV and listening to a speaker ranting against "the bestial mongrel mulatto, the dreg of human society" (91). In the beginning, Greg does not realize who the KKK leader was talking about, but then he has an epiphany: "He was talking about me. I was the Klan's worst nightmare. I was what the violence directed at the integration was all about. I was what they hated and wanted to destroy. And that was the biggest puzzle in the world to me because I had absolutely nothing" (91). Actually, Greg does not realize that he possesses a most valuable property: the "white blood" that racist whites want to keep "pure" and pass to another generation of racists who would keep the system in place.

Perhaps most telling of the negative ramifications of the American racial system are the ways that Buster himself attempts to groom his sons to take distinctly divergent paths in life. His actions amount to tracing the color line *between* the two of them. Buster takes the boys along on what Greg calls "his rounds," in the eating and drinking joints of Muncie, where he makes his sons perform in order to con drinking money out of the "audience":

> Ladies and Gentlemen, tonight I am going to present my two sons in performance. Greg, my white boy, is going to quote Lincoln's Gettysburg Address, and Mike, the nigger and small-time hustler—just like me—will exhibit the same athletic prowess I did during my Golden Gloves days. (154)

Tony himself is the one who turns his sons into stereotypes and freak shows because his own twoness is inarticulable in the existing racial system. His own struggle with race and the system of racial classification therefore must be split and displaced onto the bodies of his sons. Mike becomes the product of an inequitable system of oppression and discrimination—the stereotype of the powerless black man—while Greg is the complement—the successful white man free from the stigma of race. Tony thus tries, in God-like fashion, to dictate the future of his sons by assigning their race. He wants Greg to leave Muncie and pass so that he can become a lawyer, but he has no such expectations for Mike, on whom he displaces all the blackness of the family. Interestingly enough, Tony considers himself black, according to his own words—since he likens Mike to himself—but his act of deciding his children's racial makeup is a fundamentally "white" gesture, the stuff *Plessy v. Ferguson* is made of. Again like the government clerk, or the train conductor who decides who stays in the "white" car and who has to go to the "colored" one, Tony metaphorically sends Mike to the colored car, while ushering Greg to the whites-only one.

The reasons for this racial splitting of his children are never made explicit to readers. However, we can see how the splitting of his children enacts the racial "division" of Tony's own identity. Arguably, the acute failures and limitations of the binaric American racial system with its paradox of invisibility are what fuels Tony's own conflicted emotions about race. He is a black man by legal definition and socialization. Thus, he is marked by race and simultaneously made culturally invisible. However, his light skin allows him to disappear unnoticed into the white world whenever he chooses, granting him a sociocultural presence. For Tony, the paradox of visibility/invisibility and power/powerlessness manifest themselves in the understanding of racial performance (and particularly of passing) as a con. This construct is reminiscent of the ex-colored man's attitude, who confesses his pleasure in playing a "practical joke on society" (778). Tony confesses he sometimes has a laugh about how easy it is to fool whites.

Greg's theory is that Tony has always hated his white side, so his passing can be construed as revenge on whites: "Dad related how, when passing for white in Virginia, he became the first 'spook' president of the whites-only Forty-and-eighth American Legion Post" (63). It definitely looks like a "capital joke" that Tony plays on whites and a way of getting his revenge on his rich white father, a father who never acknowledged him and in whose house his black mother was a servant.[23] His larger revenge seems to rest in the future he imagines for—and attempts to force upon—Greg. He wants Greg to continue his education and pass into the white world to become a lawyer, thus realizing his dream through his son. What Greg wants for himself is irrelevant to Tony: "He's gonna be the man I wanted to be," Tony brags to the drinking and partying crowd that gathers almost nightly at his mother's house (64).

The expectations that Tony has for his son are a burden on Greg, especially since Greg decides he does not want to pass/be white—for multiple reasons, one of them being the categorical rejection from the white community he has experienced. He admits that "too much had happened to me in Muncie to be a part of the white world that had rejected me so completely" (157). A significant part of that "white world" is made of his family. Williams's two families (black and white) lived in the same town for years but never met, with the exception of a hurried visit from his white racist grandmother who was scared to drive in the "colored" section of the town and who has always been openly hostile to the boys because of their father's race (111).[24] Greg also learns later in life that his grandmother withheld the letters and money their mother sent them. But perhaps the most painful blow comes from his mother. When Williams finally gets to see his mother after ten long years, she does not want to talk about their lives as "colored"; instead, she presses Williams and his brother to come to live with her in Washington, and of course, be white. Williams explains:

> We could reenter her world if we rejected the one in which we had lived for the past ten years. She knew little about our life in Muncie, nor did she want to know. She expected us to move back into her life without a past, without roots, without feelings for the people who had sheltered and cared for us when our need was greatest. (281)

When asked why she did not visit them in so many years, their mother answers that—as a white woman—she was afraid of the neighborhood and of her ex-husband. Since her primary aim was to hide from Tony, her fear is stronger than the desire to communicate with the children she has left behind. Greg refuses to accompany his mother and decides to stay in Muncie: "I knew that [passing as white] was something we could never do" (281). Greg is convinced that passing was one of the causes of his father's downfall, and, furthermore, Williams claims: "No matter what Dad or anyone else said or thought, I knew who I was and who I wanted to be" (157).

Ultimately, however, rather than claiming a space in either racial state, Williams argues that his place is *on* the color line, as the title of his book shows, although he admits that it is not an option that many whites—and many blacks, for other reasons—are prepared to accept because it would expose the faults of the binaric racial system. He realizes that the color line—the borderland—is a politically charged place and a place not very many have been able to occupy: those like him either "pass" or spend the rest of their lives trying to explain that they are, in fact, "colored." Neither option seems the right one for Williams, who, like Haizlip and Scales-Trent, thinks that hybridity and liminality, when practiced overtly, are the better alternatives, the ones that hold the key to freedom from classification.[25] At the end of his book, with an optimism that is not necessarily justified by the way he has been treated by whites most of his life, Williams expresses hope that perhaps his position will help bridge the gap between races, bringing them closer.

Life on the Line

Gregory Howard Williams, Judy Scales-Trent, and Shirlee Taylor Haizlip all suggest that the traditional racial system in America is ultimately untenable and is, if slowly, crumbling. It fails to accommodate adequately or even at times to acknowledge the existence of millions of biracial or multiracial individuals who do not fit neatly on one side of the color line or the other. For those with "white" skin and "black" families, those who insist on claiming rather than denying their complex racial and familial history, the stakes are even higher. The color line marks its course through the middle of their families, their histories, their identities. Disclaiming one part of that heritage is to engage in the very act of erasure that allows those in power to oppress the powerless. But they also recognize that the blame should lie on the system as much as—or more than—on the individual who decides to slip from racial visibility and social invisibility into racial invisibility and the social agency that accompanies it. The very issue of racial mobility, which is at the heart of the concept of passing, illuminates possibilities for freedom from limiting racial classifications. By being racially mobile and taking advantage of that mobility, by being invisible when the system wants them visible and contained, by causing white anxiety, and, finally, by inhabiting spaces to which they are not "entitled," passers (intentional or unintentional) expose the tenuousness of the entire racial system on which American society is based. But that end carries a high price, one that these authors are unwilling to pay. Instead, as part of the multiracial movement that picked up steam in the late 1990s and flowered in the first decade of the twenty-first century, they insist on situating themselves in the borderland where black and white merge. Although their sometimes troubled and contradictory conceptualizations of their own racial identity highlight that thinking outside a binaric system remains difficult for Americans raised on and in Jim Crow, their memoirs document in a very personal and specific way the fictionality of the color line. On a larger level, their personal histories enact American history. As they suggest, America as a culture—even in this post–civil rights era—still has a long way to go to reach true racial equity and to admit the complicated interconnections that bind us together as a society. Until we are able truly to dismantle remaining vestiges of the color line, however, they remain hopeful in their refusal to choose.

Notes

My acknowledgment to Julie Cary Nerad for editing this essay, particularly to meet length and style requirements, and for bringing forward arguments that were implicit in earlier versions.

1. For more on the concept of whiteness as a form of property, see Harris; and Lipsitz. For more on racial passing see Ginsberg; Wald; and Sánchez and Schlossberg.

2. In 1991, F. James Davis (drawing from sources cited) estimated the numbers of passers in the United States as follows: "The peak years for passing as white were probably from 1880 to 1925, with perhaps from 10,000 to 25,000 crossing the color line each year, although such estimates are likely inflated. By 1940, the annual number had apparently declined to no more than 2,500 to 2,750 a year (Burma, 1946:1822; Williamson, 1980:103)" (22). In addition to citing Burma (as does Davis), Randall Kennedy summarizes: "Estimates regarding the incidence of passing have varied greatly. Walter White claimed that annually 'approximately 12,000 white-skinned Negroes disappear' into white society. Roi

Ottley asserted that there were 5 million 'white Negroes' in the United States and that forty to fifty thousand passed annually" (28).

3. "Race Traitor" in a more contemporary context is also the title of a journal and book (edited by Noel Ignatiev and John Garvey). Ignatiev calls for the abolition of whiteness (not the abolition of all people who are light-skinned) because whiteness carries with it cultural privilege that maintains an oppressive racial system. For an extended discussion of the political and social reasons why black Americans generally condemn passing, see Davis.

4. Pauline E. Hopkins (writing under the name of Sarah A. Allen), for instance, entitles one of her passing stories "The Test of Manhood; A Christmas Story" (1902). In this story, Mark Myers can only ascend to true manhood by revealing himself as a passer and acknowledging his dark-skinned mother. Rebecca Harding Davis's passing protagonist, John Broderip, in *Waiting for the Verdict* (1867) faces a similar test of his manhood.

5. I want to recognize that while I attempt to draw some general conclusions, the essay does not—and cannot—reflect the experience of all biracial or multiracial individuals or families. Furthermore, other contemporary memoirs that include passing, such as David Matthews's *Ace of Spades: A Memoir* (2007), Bliss Broyard's *One Drop: My Father's Hidden Life* (2007), or Elaine Galindo's *Beyond Passing* (2011), certainly offer additional possibilities for analysis.

6. For my purposes here, "memoir" refers to a type of autobiographical writing that recalls a certain period in or aspect of the author's life, rather than narrating his or her whole life. It is based on accurate, factual details and/or events from the author's life but also includes the author's subjective interpretation of those facts and events. Granted, although we tend to conceive of memoir as "true," it is arguably similar to "fiction" in that the memoir, too, is crafted and shaped by an author. According to William Zinsser, "Memoir writers must manufacture a text, imposing narrative order on a jumble of half remembered events. With that feat of manipulation they arrive at a truth that is theirs alone, not quite like that of anybody else who was present at the same event" (6). For more on memoir and life writing as a form, also see Barrington; and Smith and Watson.

7. As Gayle Wald notes, black presses in the 1930s and 1940s also published stories of racial passing. Most notable was the sensational story of Elsie Roxborough, a wealthy black socialite who passed for white and was found dead in her apartment in 1949, a possible suicide (82–84).

8. Walter White's autobiography primarily focuses on his decades at the N.A.A.C.P. and documents his passing in relation to his political work. W. L. White's *Lost Boundaries,* which was dramatized for film in 1949, is not actually memoir. It is instead White's documentary account of the Johnsons, a family who passed in a small New Hampshire town. Reba Lee's text is problematic as memoir, also, as it is reportedly Lee's account of her life "written down by" author Mary Hastings Bradley. The text might more accurately be described as semi-fictionalized (auto)biography, dictated and edited. Furthermore, "Lee" is a

pseudonym and the text does not expose her family. The 1960 film based on Lee's story was further dramatized. For an in-depth look at the 1950s magazine articles, see "'I'm Through with Passing': Postpassing Narratives in Black Popular Literary Culture" in Wald (117–51). Finally, Griffin's text is primarily sociopolitical exposé, and his passing was enabled by medical intervention (again, see Wald, 152–81).

9. For a discussion on the relationship between the civil rights movement and the multiracial movement, see Kim M. Williams. Williams argues that, despite what were understood as antithetical impulses revolving largely around potentially negative consequences of a new system of racial classification, the multiracial movement could not have happened if not for the earlier [civil rights] movement (85).

10. In "The Subject is Mixed Race: The Boom in Biracial Biography," Spickard notes the "dozens" of "autobiographical and biographical treatments of the lives of people with multiple ancestries" that have been published since the early 1990s (77). Similarly, Laura Browder argues that "a striking trend emerged in the 1990s: autobiographies that describe not temporary racial passage but racial redefinition" (274). Referring to the same decade, David A. Hollinger adds that "[a] society that often has policed the black-white color line with terror now registers a more relaxed fascination with the crossing of that line, even widespread acceptance of such crossings. Hollywood movies explore the theme with increasing frequency, and family memoirs of black-white fusion fill the display tables at bookstores" (1370).

11. In the history of race in the United Sates, the term *hybrid* has more often had negative connotations. Nineteenth-century pseudo-scientists referred to biracial and multiracial individuals as "hybrids" to suggest that people of different races were of different species. One particularly tenacious consequence of such arguments is the term *mulatto,* which suggested an analogy between a biracial person and a mule—a "hybrid" of two species (donkey and horse), which is incapable of breeding. For a discussion of the etymology of the term *mulatto* as well as more on hybridity, see Sollors (125–35). For a summary of the concept of the "hybrid degenerate," see Squires. Late-twentieth-century multiracials such as the authors under consideration here attempt to (re)claim the word, re-conceptualizing it in a way more akin to Anzaldúa's use of the term *mestiza.*

12. W. E. B. Du Bois famously declared in *The Souls of Black Folk* (1903) that the problem of the twentieth century is the problem of the color line.

13. Linda Schlossberg puts it this way: "Historically in the United States, racial readability has been translated into social immobility and, ironically, social invisibility. 'Visibility' in this context, functions as metaphor rather than objective phenomenon: to be marked is to be marked out" (5).

14. Indeed, whiteness is both *absence* of categorization *and* a *category* that is chosen. Gayle Wald argues that it is in the interest of white ideology to represent whiteness as "the absence of the racial sign" because it can maintain the myth of white purity (13–14). The same myth is perpetuated by establish-

ing whiteness as a point of origin, or of reference, against which all other races are defined as deviant. Nineteenth-century scholar Harlow S. Orton, in "The History and Development of Races: Annual Address Before the State Historical Society of Wisconsin, Feb 23, 1869," put it thus: "What we call the Caucasian race, is no type; it is the original, the primeval race, the most perfect form of physical beauty, symmetry and proportion—the crowning work of the creation, and the worthy cabinet of the Divinity that stirs within it" (qtd. in John David Smith 342). As Werner Sollors records the self-flattering Western racial "logic": "[M]ankind's initial color must have been white," as white was considered to be the initial purity from which all the other races deviated (76).

15. Margaret's need to be recognized as a member of the family may also stem from a lack of self-esteem generated by an internalized "white" system of values. Again discussing the Invisible Man, Mills argues: "Moreover, because of the intellectual domination [whites] have over [the Invisible Man's] world, he may also be frequently assailed by self-doubts, doubts about whether he *is* a real person who deserves their respect or perhaps an inferior being who deserves the treatment he has received" (8–9). Even though the reader is not offered a clear explanation, it seems that Margaret at some point finally gives up trying to contact her siblings and devotes herself to her own family. Haizlip takes over her disillusioned mother's quest in 1992.

16. Haizlip's memoir also relates the story of Margaret's uncle Edward, who moved to Buffalo, where he and his wife were unknown, in order to start a life as white. Illustrating an instance when family ties *weren't* completely severed, in Buffalo, they are visited by family, but only by those in the family who are also light-skinned enough to pass. Even so, during visits, Edward and his wife keep their shades drawn and do not invite any of their neighbors or friends to meet their family members (68–69).

17. Discussing social spaces and border theory in American Studies, anthropologist Renato Rosaldo identifies the social border as a very important and politically charged space. The border is inhabited by "hybrid figures"—figures that already challenge the status quo by resisting the dominant culture through their positioning *on* the border and by being hybrid. These figures claim the border.

18. Scales-Trent also tells of the time in the 1960s when she taught at a high school in New Jersey. After the principal found out that she was in fact black, he told her: "I have just found out that you are a Negro. I am worried that something might happen in the school, some kind of disruption or violence. So I thought I would make an announcement over the PA system and let everyone know you are a Negro. Just to avoid trouble. *You* understand" (43–44). The principal's announcement is another instance of a white assuming the authority to name/race another person, this time quite publicly.

19. Davis cites as an example of this phenomenon the "race clerks" that functioned through the middle of the twentieth century in Louisiana, noting one example in particular: "[T]he deputy registrar in the Office of Vital Records

for the City of New Orleans, was fired in 1965 for insubordination. For fifteen years she had been the city's self-appointed arbiter of who could have a 'white' birth certificate and who could not, and thus of who could marry whom" (157).

20. In an essay on racial passing in late-nineteenth-century texts, Nerad argues that such unintentional passers *are* actually *white* if we recognize race as a sociological construct and reject the one-drop rule as invalid. This way of categorizing unintentional passers such as Frances E. W. Harper's Iola Leroy actually works to destabilize the color line more so than does an approach (such as Harper herself takes in the novel) that realigns such passers with a black identity.

21. Mary Williams had made several previous attempts to leave Tony, and all the children were included in those attempts. The final opportunity arose when Tony was away in Indiana to bring Greg and Mike home. Mary takes that opportunity and runs away with the children she has with her at the time.

22. To exacerbate his situation, Greg also has to learn to deal with the daily embarrassment of picking his father up from the bars where he passes out in an alcohol-induced haze and of carrying him home in plain sight through the neighborhood. He also has to deal with the insults and demeaning abuse that Tony piles on him every time he is drunk—which is most of the time. And, he has to cope with the abject poverty in which they have to live when every penny goes to feed his father's, and his grandmother's, addiction to alcohol.

23. As a passer, Tony also is subject to nightmarish moments. For instance, while passing, he infiltrates the festive white crowd gathered to witness the last recorded public lynching in Indiana in 1930. Williams writes: "Four thousand white citizens had stormed the jail and applauded as the youths were killed. Dad shared the horror of Indiana's lynching with Muncie's black community. It was as if he had walked into hell and come out with a report on it" (64). On August 7, 1930, a large crowd stormed the city jail in Marion, Indiana, where three African American young men were held. Thomas Shipp, Abram Smith, and James Cameron were charged with murdering a white factory worker and raping his white girlfriend. The crowd lynched Shipp and Smith, but Cameron escaped lynching when a participant claimed he was innocent. James Cameron died in January 2009 at ninety-two, after devoting his life to fighting against racial injustice. For many, the scene will recall Walter White's famous accounts of being present in lynch crowds in the Atlanta 1906 race riot and later being threatened while passing as white in order to gather information on white violence against blacks in Phillips County, Arkansas.

24. Greg's white relatives avoid him at school as well. He recalls: "At lunch I entered the cafeteria and saw Ben Cook, a white cousin. In the joy of a new beginning, I gave him a friendly smile. His eyes widened in panic, and he quickly avoided my gaze" (190). The reaction of Greg's cousin makes it clear that his white family did not care to be associated with him in any way.

25. Spickard disagrees, arguing that Williams never questions the racial categories of "black" and "white," and that the memoir does not engage the issue

of racial mixing. In comparison, Browder argues that Williams's book (along with Haizlip's) describes "race as a choice that can be made by some people of ambiguously light-skinned appearance [and shows] racial classification as arbitrary, albeit with very real consequences. These autobiographies refuse to posit racial identity as essential" (274).

Works Cited

Allen, Sarah A. "The Test of Manhood, A Christmas Story." *Colored American Magazine.* Dec. 1906. Print.

Anzaldúa, Gloria. *Borderlands/La Frontera: The New Mestiza.*1987. San Francisco: Aunt Lute Books, 1999. Print.

Babb, Valerie. *Whiteness Visible: The Meaning of Whiteness in American Literature and Culture.* New York: New York UP, 1998. Print.

Barrington, Judith. *Writing the Memoir: From Truth to Art.* Portland, OR: The Eight Mountain Press, 2002. Print.

Bland, Sterling Lecater Jr. *Voices of the Fugitives: Runaway Slave Stories and their Fictions of Self-Creation.* Westport: Greenwood, 2000. Print.

Browder, Laura. *Slippery Characters: Ethnic Impersonators and American Identities.* Chapel Hill: U of North Carolina P, 2000. Print.

Broyard, Bliss. *One Drop: My Father's Hidden Life—A Story of Race and Family Secrets.* New York: Little Brown, 2007. Print.

DaCosta, Kimberly McClain. *Making Multiracials: State, Family, and Market in the Redrawing of the Color Line.* Stanford: Stanford UP, 2007. Print.

Davis, F. James. *Who Is Black? One Nation's Definition.* Tenth Anniversary Ed. University Park, PA: Pennsylvania State UP, 2001. Print.

Davis, Rebecca Harding. *Waiting for the Verdict.* 1867. Ed. Donald Dingledine. Albany: NCUP, 1995. Print.

Du Bois, W. E. B. *The Souls of Black Folk.* New York: Dover, 1994. Print.

Galindo, Elaine. *Beyond Passing.* Bloomington, IN: Xlibris, 2011. Print.

Ginsberg, Elaine K. "Introduction: The Politics of Passing." *Passing and the Fictions of Identity.* Ed. Elaine K. Ginsberg. Durham: Duke UP, 1996. 1–18. Print.

Griffin, John Howard. *Black Like Me.* 1961. Boston: Houghton Mifflin, 1971. Print.

Haizlip, Shirlee Taylor. *The Sweeter the Juice: A Family Memoir in Black and White.* New York: Simon and Schuster, 1994. Print.

Harper, Frances E. W. *Iola Leroy.* 1892. Boston: Beacon, 1999. Print.

Harris, Cheryl I. "Whiteness as Property." *Harvard Law Review* 106.8 (June 1993): 1710–91. Print.

Hollinger, David A. "Amalgamation and Hypodescent: The Question of Ethnoracial Mixture in the History of the United States." *American Historical Review* 108.5 (Dec. 2003): 1363–90. Print.

Ignatiev, Noel, and John Garvey, eds. *Race Traitor.* New York: Routledge, 1996. Print.

Johnson, James Weldon. "The Autobiography of an Ex-Colored Man." *The Norton Anthology of African American Literature*. Ed. Henry Louis Gates Jr. and Nellie Y. McKay. New York: W. W. Norton, 1977. 777–861. Print.

Kennedy, Randall. "Racial Passing." *Mixed Race America and the Law: A Reader*. Ed. Kevin Johnson. New York: New York UP, 2003. 157–68. Print.

Lipsitz, George. *The Possessive Investment in Whiteness: How White People Profit from Identity Politics*. Rev. ed. Philadelphia: Temple UP, 2006. Print.

Matthews, David. *Ace of Spades: A Memoir*. New York: Henry Holt, 2007. Print.

Nerad, Julie Cary. "Slippery Language and False Dilemmas in Passing Novels by Child, Howells, and Harper." *American Literature* 75.4 (2003): 813–41. Print.

Rosaldo, Renato. *Culture and the Remaking of Social Analysis*. Boston: Beacon, 1989. Print.

Sánchez, Maria Carla, and Linda Schlossberg, eds. *Passing: Identity and Interpretation in Sexuality, Race, and Religion*. New York: New York UP, 2001. Print.

Scales-Trent, Judy. *Notes of a White Black Woman: Race Color Community*. 1995. University Park: Pennsylvania State UP, 2001. Print.

Smith, John David. *Anti-Black Thought: 1863–1925*. New York: Garland, 1993. Print.

Smith, Sidonie, and Julia Watson. *Reading Autobiography: A Guide for Interpreting Life Narratives*. 2nd ed. Minneapolis: U of Minnesota P, 2010. Print.

Sollors, Werner. *Neither Black Nor White Yet Both: Thematic Explorations of Interracial Literature*. New York: Oxford UP, 1997. Print.

Spickard, Paul. "The Subject is Mixed Race: The Boom in Biracial Biography." *Rethinking "Mixed Race."* Ed. David Parker and Miri Song. London, VA: Pluto Press, 2001. 76–98. Print.

Squires, Catherine R. *Dispatches from the Color Line: The Press and Multiracial America*. Albany: State U of New York P, 2007. Print.

Wald, Gayle. *Crossing the Line: Racial Passing in Twentieth-Century U.S. Literature and Culture*. Durham: Duke UP, 2000. Print.

Weber, Donald. "From Limen to Border: A Meditation on the Legacy of Victor Turner for American Cultural Studies." *American Quarterly* 47.3 (Sept. 1995): 525–36. Print.

White, W. L. *Lost Boundaries*. New York: Harcourt, Brace, & Co., 1947. Print.

White, Walter. *A Man Called White: The Autobiography of Walter White*. 1948. Foreword Andrew Young. Athens: U of Georgia P, 1995. Print.

Williams, Gregory Howard. *Life on the Color Line: The True Story of a White Boy Who Discovered He Was Black*. New York: Penguin, 1995. Print.

Williams, Kim M. "From Civil Rights to the Multiracial Movement." *New Faces in a Changing America: Multiracial Identity in the 21st Century*. Ed. Loretta I. Winters and Herman L. DeBose. Thousand Oaks, CA: Sage, 2002. 85–98. Print.

Zinsser, William, ed. *Inventing the Truth: The Art and Craft of Memoir.* New York: Mariner Books, 1998. Print.

3

"A Cousin to Blackness"

Race and Identity in Bliss Broyard's *One Drop: My Father's Hidden Life*

Lynn Washington and Julie Cary Nerad

> The vagaries of racial identity were increased by what anthropolcgists call the rule of "hypodescent"—the one drop rule. When those of mixed ancestry—and the majority of blacks are of mixed ancestry—disappear into the white majority, they are traditionally accused of running from their "blackness."
>
> —Henry Louis Gates Jr., "The Passing of Anatole Broyard"

In a video clip of the February 6, 2008, episode of "African American Lives 2" with Dr. Henry Louis Gates Jr., Bliss Broyard offers a detailed description of her racial background:

> I sort of think of myself as an ex-patriot to the black community. Being black is not a result of my DNA tests, it's not finding out that I have this ancestry, it's experience, the way that you've lived. I think of myself as someone who has mixed-race ancestry. . . . I feel like a cousin to blackness, but I don't feel like I've earned the right to call myself black. (2)

Broyard's relationship to blackness is explicated more fully in her memoir, *One Drop: My Father's Hidden Life—A Story of Race and Family Secrets*

(2007), which details an extensive, well-researched foray into the Broyard family history. The narrative pivots on the fact that her father, famed *New York Times* literary critic Anatole Broyard, spent the majority of his life passing for white. Despite years of speculation among those close to the family, it was only upon Anatole's death—when Bliss was in her early twenties—that his racial identity was publicly confirmed. Bliss and her brother Todd were, by her account, the last to know. In *One Drop,* Bliss Broyard traces her father's transition across the color line, hoping to learn more about him, his "other" family, and, finally, herself. Like the traditional "tragic mulatto" of much racial passing fiction, Bliss, although she must negotiate feelings of displacement when confronted with the social implications (as she perceives them) of her black racial ancestry, acknowledges her link with the black community.[1] In this sense, she ostensibly represents her father's polar opposite by deciding not to hide her blackness. Indeed, Bliss's decision not to conceal her black familial heritage challenges her father's beliefs about the link between race and identity, as well as his own decision to keep his blackness hidden. He is the passer unredeemed; she is the passer reclaimed.

In divergence from the traditional fictional female passer who somehow discovers her black heritage—such as Frances E. W. Harper's *Iola Leroy*—however, Bliss ultimately concludes that race is a social construction. The culture has changed, the text suggests, since her father's youth, when the "one-drop rule" of hypodescent linked individuals of mixed race with blackness by mandate rather than by choice. Blackness now is not necessarily or automatically the default for anyone with black family forebears. Seeing herself as *akin* to blackness—a cousin to blackness, as she puts it—is an option that would not have been available in the more binaric racial system of her father's youth. Furthermore, she recognizes many—although not all—of her own previously unexamined attitudes about race and the stereotypes she has about African Americans. She suggests finally that one must "earn the right" to call oneself black, a notion that evidences a significant shift both in racial ideology and in the cultural politics of race from her father's generation.

Bliss Broyard's approach to race and her (ultimately) positive valuation of blackness places her memoir well within contemporary critical understandings of racial identity. Certainly the post–civil rights generation of which she is a part often continues to understand race as written upon the body, as visible, and even as biological—a reality that easily exposes the lie of "post-racialism." But there has been a significant shift, birthed as and nurtured in the multiracial movement of the 1990s, that has recalibrated the lens through which many Americans now view race. Images of interracial couples, interracial adoptions, and multiraced celebrities that now populate media—from print advertisements to television to film—would have been near unimaginable only a few decades earlier. The proliferation of such images (and realities) at least reflects and perhaps contributes to an increasing acceptance of bi- or multiracial identities that resist easy classification or categorization (other than as "multi"). Indeed, many are now seeking out information about their (genetic/familial) past. Daniel J. Sharfstein explains:

> Thanks to technological advances of the past decade, extraordinary amounts to genealogical material have been digitized, and companies have marketed DNA tests to determine a person's racial background. Millions of Americans are swabbing their cheeks, watching television shows about celebrity genealogies, posting family trees on popular ancestry Web sites—and stumbling across family secrets. (5)

This impetus to know, to discover one's racial heritage, is antithetical to the long tradition of hiding any "black blood" that motivates much racial passing and suggests, then, that the consequences of finding one of those "family secrets" is something, potentially, to be welcomed. Canvassing the expanding field of recent memoirs that incorporate the trope of passing, one frequently finds evidence of this shift in perception.

Furthermore, recognizing race primarily as a social construct rather than a biological essence, these authors regularly emphasize that (light-skinned) biracial or multiracial individuals now often have a choice whether to identify or dissociate with a particular racial group. Race, according to Alaina Lemon, functions as

> an organic metaphor . . . not only about bodies (nationalism and gender rely on bodily imagery too) but about a particular connection among bodies, bodies whose substance is bound over time, unmixed with other bodies' substance. It is the means by which people index connections among bodies that is key: individual bodies may be visibly represented as raced, but connections among them cannot always be, not in the same way. They can only be mapped out or pointed to. That's why race is not always about skin color. (58)

Skin color may still be the result of biology, but the familial body exceeds biology. If race cannot be always and easily mapped onto the individual, it is even less so for the family or the nation. Similarly, blackness itself is now more than ever also about connections between bodies moreso than it is about skin color or "drops" of blood.

Although the shift is neither monolithic nor immediate, for a growing segment of the population, blackness is something that must be *earned* rather than something that cannot be denied. There is a sea change between conceiving of the "right" to call oneself black and the idea of blackness being automatic (and sometimes unwanted) if one had even a remote black ancestor. Raised after the heyday of the social and economic discrimination of Jim Crow, and in the era of Affirmative Action, many in this younger generation understand the politics of race in these new terms: while still being grounded in family, race is also discursive, performative, and relational (even if they don't use those terms). It is this performativity that makes the act of racial passing—upon which Broyard's memoir turns—possible in one sense and impossible in another: if race is performed, one can pass; but if race is just performance, there's really no such thing as passing (as something you are not). This paradox is one of the points contemporary memoirists such as Broyard or David Matthews press.[2] Both Broyard and Matthews, through their exploration of racial difference and passing within a single family, precisely reflect the complex interactions between bodies, race, reproduction, and relationships, just as they explore the dynamics of racial performance, identity, and interaction. These contemporary texts, then, reflect a shift from traditional passing texts, which often assumed a biological basis for race (even those that made some attempt to debunk mutually exclusive racial categories) and which concerned themselves primarily with issues of legality, responsibility, and purity.

They also (re)invest blackness with a value divested from the discourse of racial uplift that resonates throughout much earlier passing fiction and (autobiographical) confessional essays.[3] Indeed, earlier depictions of passing regularly reflect a different set of cultural, economic, and social limitations for African Americans and often argue that (perhaps especially) white-skinned blacks had a responsibility to help other blacks rise above the effects of discrimination. There is also in these earlier texts a corresponding rhetoric of belonging and betrayal, homecoming and desertion. Thus, much traditional passing fiction explores the passer's psychosocial condition preceding her crossing the color line. The psychosocial approach tends to evaluate the intraracial factors that foster and/or complicate the passer's worldview. In the article "It Takes One to Know One: Passing and Communities of Common Interest," Amy Robinson refers to the "group from which one has passed" as an "in-group" (715). Blacks with visible "black" phenotypic features had no choice but to identify with the African American community, while biracial or fair-skinned blacks were not physically restricted to that community. They could leave the "in-group" and pass as white. Their departure, however, was often understood as a desertion, a denial of the common interests with and responsibility to other oppressed Africans Americans. Whiteness was not understood as an actual, available, acceptable choice for an authentic alternative identity; it was a deception and a desertion. Even the social marginalization and economic discrimination blacks faced usually did not justify, within the morality of the text/community, passing on a permanent basis. It made the desire to pass understandable, but it did not make the choice to pass permanently as white excusable.

In fiction, such judgment usually worked on the passer in ways that either brought him home to the black community—as in Harper's *Iola Leroy*—or brought him misery or even death—as in Frank J. Webb's *The Garies and their Friends* (1853).[4] In the latter case, the passer becomes the "tragic mulatto." This archetype survived throughout twentieth-century American popular culture, most visibly in the medium of film. Films such as *Imitation of Life* (1934, 1959), based on the novel by Fannie Hurst, depict the "tragic mulatto" passer and her struggles with self-identity that result from a phenotype that does not match her racial category, and from the desire to escape discrimination and have access to social and economic equality, and, ultimately she believes, happiness. The price the passer pays for this access, however, is too high. For example, Peola/Sarah Jane, the passer respectively in the film versions of *Imitation of Life,* is often characterized by the final moments of the films, in which she throws herself on her black mother's casket in a fit of grief—not only at the loss of her mother but also because of the realization that she has paid the ultimate price for whiteness: in rejecting her blackness, she also rejected her mother, who died in essence of a broken heart.[5] In the films, Peola/Sarah Jane has betrayed herself, her family, and her race. Her transgression is condemned implicitly (or explicitly, as when in the 1959 version her white boyfriend beats her after discovering her secret) by both white and black communities, but her real punishment seems inflicted by her own guilt.[6]

In explaining the condition of the "tragic mulatto/a" myth as represented in early-twentieth-century texts, David Pilgrim notes that "the literary and cinematic portrayals of the tragic mulatto emphasized . . . personal pathologies: self hatred, depression, alcoholism, sexual perversion, and suicide attempts being the most common. If light enough to 'pass' as white, she did, but passing led to a deeper self-loathing" (n.p.). Indeed, each of these personal pathologies, resulting from the historical marginalization of "mixed-race" people, is frequently cited in the archetypal makeup of the "tragic mulatto" (and the passer). Despite the growing tendency to think of race as a sociological construct and to reject rigid and exclusionary definitions of race, the tendency to condemn passing survives, although the reasons why have shifted, as we will discuss below. For example, in "Passing For What? Racial Masquerade and the Demands of Upward Mobility" (1998), Phillip Brian Harper writes that his African American literature students—his "students of the practice" of passing in literary works—"tend to see it [passing] in psychic-orientational terms, as signifying only the protagonist's disavowal of an identity that proper race pride and healthy self-regard would lead him or her to enthusiastically embrace" (381). This assessment of passing again highlights self-hatred as one of the major personal pathologies of the "tragic mulatto" while also raising an interesting question: Does having a demonstrated sense of race pride and a healthy self-regard prevent one from crossing the color line for purely socioeconomic reasons? The answer to this question is textured and often dependent upon the historical period to which it is applied.

Specifically, from about 1870 to the early 1960s, many passers chose to live as white strictly as a means of finding better employment and greater potential for social mobility.[7] In short, some passed occasionally and only for social convenience, others for access to jobs. In these cases, the passers often maintained connections to the black community and understood passing as a strategy to beat the system. Even Harper's students had to admit there were definite financial benefits in passing and could "acknowledge the material gain potentially enjoyed by anyone who, while legally designated as black, lives successfully as white for a significant time" (381). Passers motivated by such impulses did not necessarily experience feelings of self-loathing. Rather, the pass could be experienced as liberatory, the passer as an updated trickster. Although passing for economic gains did not *always* demand a complete break from the black community, it did demand some degree of disavowal of that community and of the black family. Economic passers walked a thin line: as long as they passed to better the condition of the black family, the (temporary, even if repeated) pass was acceptable. If they forgot which side of the line "home" actually was, their act transformed from one that supported the black family to one that denied it. No one, after all, wants to *be* the family secret.[8]

Furthermore, when educational and employment opportunities for blacks and other nonwhites increased following the civil rights movement, the need to pass for socioeconomic reasons was reduced. This shift in American racial socioeconomic dynamics during the latter twentieth century thus corresponds to a shift in the reasons why passing is generally condemned and why contemporary audiences tend to view passing as largely a *symptom* rather than a result of the passer's inner conflict. That is, the traditional perspective often weighs the passer's need for social equality and upward mobility against the psychosocial "pathologies" in the passer's ideological framework, while the contemporary perspective suggests that a lack of "race pride" and "self-regard" are at the root of one's decision to cross the color line. In the first, the passer is motivated by self-interest and is primarily punished by self-hate/guilt; in the latter, she is motivated by self-hate and is primarily punished by the black community who judges her actions.[9] In attempting to deconstruct her father's decision to cross the color line, Broyard unwittingly represents this shift in consciousness: if her father didn't need to pass for socioeconomic necessity, then he must have done so for psychological reasons.

Bliss's curiosity about her father's blackness—articulated primarily through a general obsession with discovering just "how black" he was and why he began to pass as white—takes her first to Anatole's black family.[10] In an early conversation with her darker-skinned Aunt Shirley, Bliss gains some insight into the family's approach to race that specifically links the family with the historical practice of passing as socioeconomically motivated. The Broyards moved from New Orleans to Brooklyn when Anatole was six years old. The move forced a dynamic shift in the family's racial identity because, unlike in New Orleans—where the Broyards were recognized to be among a "better class" of blacks because of their pale skin and illustrious family connections—in Brooklyn, his father Nat was "just another light-skinned black guy who could only make it in the larger world by presenting himself as something he wasn't" (337). Nat felt somewhat "trapped" by his new home, but because the opportunities for work were greater in New York than in New Orleans, he knew he would never be going back. He also knew that to gain access to those opportunities, he and his wife Edna would need to pass for white—but only at work. At home in Bedford-Stuyvesant, an area of Brooklyn once considered the cultural center for its African American residents, the family lived as black and, accordingly, bonded with other light-skinned black families in the neighborhood. The family's racial politics were, at this point, not much different than their associates' in that they all wanted to be recognized as "better" than other neighborhood blacks by virtue of either phenotypic or (perceived) intellectual differences. Since neither Nat nor Edna was very educated, they had to rely on their light skin to be accepted. Their light skin also helped them maintain a decent lifestyle, and their passing for economic reasons seemed a matter of course to the Broyard children. Shirley says: "My parents passed sometimes for work. A lot of black people did if it could bring some advantage" (82). Shirley's matter-of-factness illustrates how passing for economic reasons—and in a temporary situation—was, as we have suggested above, at least understandable as long as the pass was not permanent. Shirley's comment also suggests a certain long-standing awareness on the part of blacks about the artificiality of racial categories and how those categories fit into sociocultural and economic hierarchies. African Americans have clearly always understood how skin color could either provide or prevent access to social and economic power.

Young Anatole learned early about this relationship between skin color and empowerment. As a child, he was socialized with other children whose families "were mixed-race and tended more toward a middle class lifestyle than 'blacks' " (322). During his teen years, Anatole and his friends circulated among the social elite of black Brooklyn, attending invitation-only dances hosted by private clubs that excluded the larger (and poorer) segment of the black community. Consequently, as recalled by Robbie King, one of Anatole's childhood friends, "other blacks were jealous of us. We got into lots of fights" (335).[11] Despite spending many afternoons shuffling past his father with various cuts, bruises, and torn clothing from these fights, Anatole was likely already impressed with the idea that being light-skinned in the black community could be advantageous. In this, Anatole would not be unusual. Melvin Seeman finds in observing the social practices of young children that "friendship choices, personality, reputations, and self-images were color-related. Light Negroes were more acceptable as friends, dark children were nominated as possessors of negative personality traits (bully or hot-tempered, for example) and there was a clear tendency for children to distort in the light direction when asked to describe their own color (assigning themselves a lighter rating than independent adult observers)" (69). Seeman's research, and common sense, suggests that Anatole would likely have understood even as a child—and even without his parents' passing—how his phenotypic whiteness could benefit him both within and outside of the black community.

As he grew, Anatole, who would be privy to greater educational opportunities than his parents, also passed for work; however, unlike his parents, his professional and personal identities would become inextricably linked. In creating his professional identity, Anatole escaped the socioeconomic restrictions placed upon African Americans by omitting—although not explicitly denying—his blackness. That is, when asked about his racial background, he often responded, "Creole." When asked to elaborate by those unfamiliar with the term, he emphasized the French and Spanish cultural elements without mentioning the equally important African component.[12] Near the end of the memoir, Bliss suggests that "by describing himself that way, my father could avoid the black/white question and let people draw their own conclusion" (338).[13] But in her conversation with her aunt Shirley earlier in the narrative, Bliss suggests a different possibility. She asks: If young Anatole grew up watching his parents use race interchangeably for socioeconomic reasons, might he feasibly be confused about his racial identity and the significance of race? Given that his parents looked white and passed for white, and were rewarded with job security, it also makes sense that Anatole would be conditioned to associate whiteness with success and learn to rely on the ambiguity of his physical appearance as a rejection of social restrictions based largely on racial identity.

Shirley, however, clearly rejects any suggestion that Anatole was confused about his racial identity. She says that, despite their parents' situational passing, "there was no question when we were growing up that we were black" (82). For Shirley, the recognition that racial codes can be manipulated (by her parents, her brother, or anyone) does not destabilize a primary racial identity or a racial responsibility: "we were black." Shirley also accepts her parents' reasons for passing. They passed for economic gain. What mattered was that they came home at the end of the day to pick up their black lives and love their black children. She reads her brother's decision to pass permanently as white, however, as an act of desertion, an act of voluntary estrangement that, especially in a post–civil rights era, was difficult to understand, and even harder to forgive. Especially given his education, Anatole could have met with personal and professional success as a black man—as, indeed, did Shirley's and Lorraine's husbands.[14] His reasons to hide his blackness, then, had to extend (in his sisters' reasoning) beyond the economic. If Anatole hated his own blackness enough to deny it, then did he not by extension hate (or at best was ashamed of) his black family? Although unwilling to go so far as to suggest her father hated himself for being black, Bliss would later recall several instances of hearing her father speak negatively about blacks—in fact, she remembers once telling him that he sounded racist. In these moments, his sisters' unwillingness to forgive their brother seems justified.

In short, the Broyard children (Anatole, Shirley, and Lorraine) grew up with the understanding that passing was acceptable as a tool, but not as a way of life.[15] When Anatole decided to pass permanently, he effectively severed his relationship with his black family, even with those who—like Lorraine—were light enough to pass but who chose to be black. Tellingly, it is Lorraine (who only passed occasionally) who is ultimately less able to forgive her brother than Shirley. Lorraine cuts her brother from her will just as he cut his black family from his life. Arguably, Lorraine's choice to remain loyal to her black family—and thus reject the path that Anatole took—is precisely what fuels her more vehement feelings toward her brother. She did not need to reject her blackness to live a happy life.

Both Shirley's and Lorraine's reactions are common historically among the relatives of passers and the African American community at large. And, as we have seen through Philip Brian Harper's research, such judgment survived to a certain extent at least into the 1990s. Blacks who pass permanently into whiteness and deny any connection to the black community and family engender anger and resentment. And indeed, Bliss would encounter these feelings throughout the process of researching her father's life. Later in the text, for instance, when discussing her findings with a black woman named Beverly, she is reminded that

> [m]ost African Americans didn't have the same option as your father did. My grandmother, for example, had to endure prejudice. She never had the choice where she could sit on the bus. . . . But your dad just glided on through without having to deal with Jim Crow or desegregating the schools or any of that. And he didn't do anything to help the people who were stuck on the other side. That's why your father makes black people so angry. (181)

Here, again, we hear the language of betrayal, which grew from a system of inequity and disenfranchisement based on the vagaries of skin pigmentation. Anger at the system is redirected to those who manipulated the system for personal gain and left behind those who couldn't do so to suffer. Shirley herself admits that her occasional thoughts about her brother's family were not always the most benevolent. Sometimes, Shirley tells Bliss, her husband Franklin "would threaten to put the kids in the car and show up in Connecticut and present ourselves on your doorstep" (82). However, Shirley (and her husband) ultimately honored her brother's choice by staying away, at least until he died. It is Shirley who ultimately gives Bliss direction in her search for identity via her father's life by suggesting that she first "find out what it [identity] meant to your father" (84).

To do that, Bliss travels to New Orleans—Anatole's hometown. Armed with only his birth certificate,[16] Bliss is propelled into researching his family history which, at times, reads like a journey through the racial complexities of historical Louisiana. The Louisiana Broyards, of whom Anatole was a direct descendant, were Creole. In the eyes of American society, which was long anchored by the one-drop rule, the Louisiana Broyards (and so many others like them) were officially black, although many of them were not much different in physical appearance from people with the legal status of white.[17] However, the mélange of social traditions associated with Creole culture distinguished them from both white and black cultures. Indeed, in Louisiana, most light-skinned Creoles enjoyed a relatively decent potential for social and economic mobility, and "one drop" of black blood was historically less of a cause for social and economic ostracism than it would be in New York City, where the approach to racial identity and/or classification was more definitive. In the midst of these complicated and rather paradoxical movements toward both separation and intermixture within Creole history, Bliss's desire to quantify her father's blackness (how black is he?) seems even more futile. Her persistence in this conceptual approach to her father's identity, however, is consistent with her admission that she had not thought much about race before beginning her quest. Initially for her, her father's race should be quantifiable and definable through mapping his family tree. What she fails to see at this point, is how such a belief in the quantifiability of race fails to correspond with her own racial experience. The implication of her initial belief in quantifiable race is that she will know "how black" to feel herself, if she knows "how black" her father was biologically (and, thus, how black she is biologically). Any reader who rejects the idea that race is quantifiable through biological inheritance, however, will recognize what Bliss herself initially does not: finding out the number of white and black and mixed ancestors she has will not help Bliss feel any more or less black or white than she already feels. That is, a "percentage" of black heritage will not translate into a particular level of "feeling black."

Bliss's approach to her research also suggests that she is hoping to find information in his family history that will explain away his deception and, accordingly, allow him to remain heroic in her memory. Perhaps she will find that they aren't really black, or perhaps, as noted earlier, that her father was confused about his race. To her credit, Broyard does not hide from her own confusion and her occasional reluctance about confronting the complexities of race in America. For example, immediately following the publication of a Henry Louis Gates Jr. article that outed Anatole Broyard as black, Bliss receives a call from a cousin, Vivian. Vivian had read the article and in response, calls to reassure Bliss that it "was full of lies. Your father was white" (119). Vivian also tells Bliss about the population of "white" Broyards living, like her, on the West Coast and encourages her to come see for herself. This new information momentarily ignites Bliss's desire to exonerate her father's perceived cowardice in passing for white, and, when reflecting on Gates's article, she acknowledges "fantasizing about proving Gates wrong, forcing *The New Yorker* to print a retraction explaining that all of this had turned out to be a colossal mistake" (119). Bliss finds momentary comfort in the hope that all this racial mess might go away. To her credit, her fleeting desire is presented in the text not only as idealistic, but also as rather reactionary. Bliss recognizes her resistance as the lingering remnants of a passive racism that is expressed more desperately and defensively by Vivian.

Bliss continues to see parallels between herself and Vivian again later in the text when the two meet in person. While discussing the family's racial history, Vivian adamantly insists that many folks were incorrectly identified as black by the flawed New Orleans records department. Having left Louisiana during the mid-twentieth century, Vivian refuses to allow "some outdated one-drop rule held over from slavery times tell her who she could be" (124). Besides, she says, she "doesn't feel black." Vivian's decision to create an identity based on how she felt rather than "some outdated one-drop rule" suggests a contemporary approach to identity, although there is clearly a racist undertone to Vivian's comments. She makes the claim she does to reject the offensive suggestion that "one drop" makes her black. As much as Bliss resists her cousin's implicit racism, Bliss recognizes in Vivian's reasoning some of her own thoughts and ideas. In attempting to find the "right" way to identify herself while telling the truth about her ancestry, Bliss unwittingly uses the same process of quantification to determine racial identity as does Vivian. Furthermore, Vivian's unapologetic connection between African American identity and an "inferior" attitude mirrors some of Bliss's own unexamined assumptions about race and behavior.[18] Indeed, Bliss admits to having very little exposure to nonwhite culture during her formative years. This, coupled with the absence of an ongoing dialogue about race with her parents, fueled a "void" in Bliss's racial consciousness that complicated her ability to see blacks and whites as equal—despite her willingness to accept her black heritage.

Discussing her previously unexamined beliefs about race and racial identity, Broyard notes early in the text that "whatever I came to believe about the difference between blacks and whites grew up in that void, fed by the racism in the world at-large" (49). Given her upbringing in the predominantly white city of Fairfield, Connecticut, as well as with her father's conflicted approach to race and race issues, her rather abstract conceptualizations about being nonwhite are not surprising. She recalls a classmate named Dawn, who was one of the few black students at Green Farms Academy, once saying that there were "only a few chips in this cookie." In retrospect, she admits, this was "the closest I ever came to having a conversation about race" (47). Race was not a popular topic of conversation in her small, relatively rural hometown, as is often the norm for areas of minimal diversity that tend toward perpetuating the racial order. In the memoir, Bliss makes a somewhat ironic reference to this limited potential for expanded discussions on race in her community: "Being black or mixed race when my brother and I were growing up wouldn't have marked us with the social inferiority the way that it did in the 1930s. But out in Connecticut, snug in our antique farmhouse, the clocks might as well have turned back a generation or two . . . it was almost possible to put African Americans out of one's mind if it weren't for the nightly news" (47). The inference here is that, although race relations had improved since her father's childhood, her (and her community's) exposure to the lives of black Americans was limited to sound bites that, most probably, perpetuated primarily negative stereotypes.[19]

As her comment suggests, then, the absence of a larger, reflective, and critical discussion about race neither makes race invisible, nor does it preclude one from developing racial stereotypes or beliefs about the connection between race and identity. Unguarded and frank moments and comparisons such as these help give the memoir its depth and help the reader tolerate Broyard's occasional (and seemingly unexamined) slips into racial stereotyping. After all, Bliss was raised in American culture as white, with all the insidious and subtle (and sometimes not so subtle) beliefs about race. Her childhood doesn't excuse the presence of stereotypes in the memoir, but it does, at least, help explain how they come to be there. What is more redemptive is that, throughout the memoir, Broyard is feeling her way through to a new understanding about race, if not necessarily to the new identity she initially believes her father's secret should engender. It is this attempt to recognize and analyze her own racial beliefs that marks her as different from Vivian. This self-reflection also allows her to understand that she lacks the knowledge and personal history necessary to deconstruct—or even construct—her father's story.

Thus, Bliss revises the focus of her research. She begins to move from historical records to living people, from facts and percentages to emotion and experience. Specifically, Bliss widens the lens of her research to include the experiences of some extended family members who have faced difficulties when negotiating the complexities of the color line. She makes contact with a cousin, Mark, who identifies himself and all the other Broyards he knows as "black." Their conversation extinguishes any fantasy for a return to a less complicated racial identity and instead heightens Bliss's desire to find her place in the new interracial family. Consequently, she prepares to visit the West Coast branch of the family—including Mark and his family, *and* Vivian and the "white Broyards." After meeting the extended Broyard clans (white and black), Bliss is amazed at the similarities between herself and the group—particularly with respect to skin complexion: "If I hadn't been told exactly who was living as white and who was living as black, I would have never known . . . we all appear to be roughly the same shade of golden brown" (120). Recognizing these phenotypic similarities debunks her expectation of finding family members who fall into distinct categories of black and white as well as the hope of finding a simple explanation of her family history. Instead, she becomes fascinated with the stories of her relatives who experienced racial discrimination firsthand, from both whites *and* blacks, in addition to the experiences of those who decided, like her father, to pass for white. Bliss finds the childhood experiences of her cousins Mark, Erin, Robert, and Marchele interesting because they represent critical aspects of the black experience such as intraracial discrimination and its subsequent social marginalization. Although Bliss knew of such things, she had never heard firsthand accounts of the effects of such discrimination. Her cousins' stories help Bliss understand race not as some legal or biological category, but as an element of self shaped through experience. As importantly, Bliss begins to realize that blackness is not something that she can decide to claim or to reject on her own (white) authority. Blackness has a value, and she has not earned the right to that property.[20]

Even after first learning that her father was black, Bliss suggests that blackness somehow enriches her identity: "I had always bought into the idea of the American melting pot, and now I was an example of it. The idea thrilled me, as though I had been reading a history book and then discovered my name in the index. I felt like I mattered in a way that I hadn't before" (17). Although her celebratory tone smacks a bit of the historic and problematic fascination with the exotic, her positive valuation of newly discovered blackness is far different than that of earlier (and fictional) passers under similar circumstances, perhaps a paradigmatic example being found in Harper's *Iola Leroy*. Upon learning the news of her legal racial designation, Iola's first (and fictionally common) reaction is disbelief, followed quickly by dismay, and finally replaced by a determination to accept her blackness. Her decision is not based on a sense of freedom to choose a racial identity, but on a feeling of moral rectitude and a feeling of responsibility to her mother and other oppressed blacks. If she chose to live as white, she would be "running away" from that duty. She would also be living a fraudulent life and thus would be subject to constant fear of exposure. And, she adds, the possibility of having dark-skinned children, even if she marries the white suitor who wishes her to pass as white, makes a future life as white impossible.[21] Like Iola, Bliss decides not to hide her black heritage after being told the truth about her father's racial heritage. However, Bliss does not do so under pressure to uplift the black race or the threat of otherwise being forever separated from her black family. She also does not face the social ostracism that historically accompanied the recognition of biracial ancestry. Instead, in the current and aesthetically multicultural American society, being multiracial, as she says, makes her more a part of the "American melting pot."

While both Iola and Bliss struggle throughout their texts to inhabit a black identity, the necessity to do so is, for Iola, a foregone conclusion unless she is willing to pass. She is black according to both the one-drop rule and the custom of the day, and she must adjust her consciousness to that fact. For Bliss, the struggle is significantly different. Broyard is willing—and even happy—to acknowledge her black heritage, but it does not necessarily and automatically redefine her primary racial category. Even her Aunt Shirley seems to have different criteria for blackness in relation to her brother than to her niece. She does not lecture Bliss about the young woman's responsibility to proclaim herself black, nor does she necessarily encourage Bliss to think of herself as black. Bliss's potential to continue being white, then, does not call up for Shirley the same racial discourse or philosophical factors that Anatole's whiteness conjured. Bliss can be white in a way that Anatole could never be. The shift is partially a result of the fact that Bliss did not willingly deny the black family—she did not choose to pass—but it also reflects a shift in racial ideology. Bliss's one drop connects her to the black community, but it does not necessarily define her as black. She is, for Shirley also, only a "cousin to blackness." Within their cultural contexts, for Iola, claiming whiteness is fraudulent;

for Bliss, claiming blackness is. Indeed, *claiming* blackness might easily be considered a transgression. In this sense, Broyard's developing approach to racial identity inverts the trope of passing and also distinguishes her not only from Harper's fictional heroine, but also from her father who fits the more traditional passing story of the tragic mulatto. While Anatole is constructed by Bliss, by himself, by his family, and by the community as black, Bliss cannot confidently self-identify as "black." Because Bliss has been raised as white—because she *is* white if we throw out the one-drop rule—there are elements of blackness that she can never "own."

Questions of value and ownership of a racial identity thus lead Bliss into questions of racial authenticity (360). The information she uncovers in a second trip to New Orleans—and her reactions to that information—speak tellingly of Bliss's unexamined assumptions about what it means to be black in America. First, the discovery that some of her ancestors were free people of color, *gens de couleur,* comes as a surprise. But the results of further research are even more startling for Bliss: some of the Creole and black Broyards owned slaves. Her ancestors' complicity in the racialized cultural hierarchy unmoors her idea that blacks were simply victims. She writes: "That my white Louisiana ancestors had owned slaves wasn't surprising, but the fact that my black ancestors had also partaken in the 'peculiar institution' astounded me. These weren't the notable tragic figures I'd been expecting to encounter" (268). In other words, finding out that some of her black ancestors were slaves fit into her romanticized notions of blackness; finding out that some of them *owned* slaves did not. She has unwittingly associated blackness with unrelieved oppression. We see this equation repeated when she discovers that her great-great-great-grandmother was not a slave raped by her master. Instead, the interracial "mixing" of the Broyard family was the result of a voluntary, presumably loving relationship. Rather than feeling relieved that her ancestor was not subjected to physical violation, she is problematically disappointed. It's not tragic enough; it's not romantic enough. She continues: "My claim to an authentic black identity felt more distant than ever" (268). So steeped in stereotypes about whiteness and blackness, Bliss has difficulty reconciling history with her romanticized expectations of black suffering. Perhaps more importantly, she also fails to recognize the implications of those expectations. We don't mean to suggest here that blacks—and Creoles—did not suffer from oppression and discrimination, even those who were themselves slaveowners. What we are highlighting, instead, is that throughout the majority of the narrative Bliss has a relatively simple and limited idea of blackness that she must replace with a more complicated understanding of racial identity if she is to find a resolution to her own racial identity crisis. Initially for Bliss, blackness is about dancing and swaggering, speaking slang and liking jazz, but it is also evidently about unrelieved victimization. She learns through her research and through meeting her cousins that there is much more to being "authentically" black in America.

Her interest in questions of racial authenticity is deepened when she realizes that her father, too, was interested in the subject. Reading his essays that focused on social and racial identity reveals his own ambivalence about his racial performance. For example, "Portrait of the Inauthentic Negro," one of Anatole Broyard's most popular essays, was written from a theoretical position similar to Jean Paul Sartre's "Portrait of the Inauthentic Jew" and likens the struggle of the Negro to present himself "authentically," without either succumbing to the "cool Negro" escape or practicing "minstrelization" as a means of conforming to the generally accepted Negro stereotype (Seeman 68). He writes that

> [a]uthenticity, as I take it, would mean stubborn adherence to one's essential self, in spite of the distorting pressures of one's situation. By the Negro's essential self, I mean his innate qualities and developed characteristics as an individual, as distinguished from his preponderantly defensive reactions as a member of an embattled minority. . . . Minstrelization results from the inauthentic Negro's acceptance of his situation as defined by the anti-Negro, and his attempt to make himself comfortable in it. (57)

Here Anatole is suggesting an essential racial identity separate from the stereotypes of blackness forced upon him by a racist culture. While retaining the biological rhetoric of "essential" and "innate," he nevertheless finds room for the language of performance. He can be black, without being "black" (as a racist American culture defines it). Being "black"—that is, acting the "cool Negro"—is about performance: "Thoughtlessly accepting the white's attribution of greater rhythmicality to them, many inauthentic Negroes have made themselves arbiters of jazz music, popular dancing, and, by extension, all matters of extreme sensation and stimulation, including sexual behavior. Dramatizing this role, they have developed special rhythms in walking, speech intonation, etc." (58). Ironically, in her memoir, Bliss initially not only reproduces the language and stereotypes her father is critiquing in "Portrait," but she also applies them to his own behavior.

When describing an evening on the town with her family, she writes that "the Broyards were graceful, cool, and confident on the dance floor; sensual, witty, soulful, earthy, and fun; a center of attention, while at the same time remaining one step removed. Mostly it was my father who was these things" (59). Paradoxically, his "coolness" is what (retrospectively) marks him as black to Bliss, while Anatole himself argues that such behavior would mark him as "inauthentic" because such behavior would be a performative concession to white stereotypes of blackness. That is, Bliss reads his blackness precisely through the performative stereotypes that he would recognize as evidence of minstrelization (rather than true blackness) and which he seemed to disdain. Given Anatole Broyard's writings on the subject of authenticity, the text leads the reader (but, interestingly, not Bliss herself) to ask whether his "coolness" and his use of slang are deliberate attempts to expose himself. For instance, before dying, Anatole cryptically suggests to Bliss that if she wants to learn more about him to read his writing: he wanted his writing to be a key to his identity, a way to read his performance, a way to tell the secret that he resisted telling, even on his deathbed (although for many, especially blacks who knew him well, his racial background was not really a secret). Bliss never seems to recognize fully this paradox; instead, she offers a simpler, postmodern alternative. Perhaps, she writes, he "truly believed that there wasn't any essential difference between blacks and whites and that the only person responsible for determining who he was supposed to be was himself" (395).

Bliss begins her research for her book with the aim of finding out "how black" her father really was—as if she can quantify blackness in a contemporary revision of the one-drop rule—and quickly realizes that the answer to that question lies within a long cultural history of African Americans in the United States that she had never truly imagined because, as an upper-middle-class white girl living in a white rural community, she had never needed to imagine it. The search that is initiated by her father's "family secret" thus morphs into a burgeoning interest in her own identity and a corresponding exploration of her own racial attitudes. In discovering more about Anatole Broyard's family history, Bliss also learns about the history of race in America as it intersects with social progress, identity, and her sense of self. According to Bliss, the internal changes occurring "over the course of learning about the history of my father's family" engendered a "shift in my world view, away from the 'white' one I'd grown up with" (Broyard 228). Although Bliss Broyard's worldview has perhaps shifted—or, at least, grown more complex and less naïve—as a result of her research, her approach to race and questions of racial identity remains somewhat problematic, even at the text's end. Erin Kaplan puts it this way in her review of *One Drop* for the *LA Times*:

> Broyard ultimately cops out on the racial question by declining to state. In the end, she retreats into the neo-liberal view that color doesn't matter, that it's a social and scientific fiction. But that is, of course, the ultimate white privilege—the freedom to decide, after careful consideration, that color doesn't matter to you. Blacks have no such freedom to choose. Even Creoles like Anatole knew they had to purge themselves of their blackness to some degree to even aspire to such consideration. (R10)

Kaplan rightly points out that the freedom to choose a racial identity is largely limited for African Americans in this sense to those who are phenotypically "white." Darker-skinned blacks such as Bliss's aunt Shirley do not have access to such culturally authorized power. However, Kaplan is also arguably missing what part of Broyard's memoir does. Bliss does not, for instance, suggest that race or color doesn't "matter" culturally or psychologically. And it is historically not only whites who have suggested that race is—and thus dismissed it as—a "social and scientific fiction." Broyard, in short, isn't arguing that race is not a significant factor of individual and cultural identity. Instead, she learns that the opposite is true in ways that she had never considered: her cousins' stories about the discrimination they have encountered, the historical complexity of race and identity in the Creole community, and the reactions she received from her black family (which covered the spectrum from wariness to welcome), all deepen her understanding about the cost and value of racial identity in America. These experiences help her understand why her father passed and why he was haunted by his act of denial. They help her reflect on why he could attack in his essays what he saw as black behavior that played into negative stereotypes held by whites, while still potentially embodying and performing those behaviors. Anatole, it seems, devalued his blackness and thus his moments of performing blackness slide in the direction of the minstrel. Bliss, in comparison, invests blackness with a value that she feels she has not yet earned and is thus uncomfortable whenever she consciously attempts to embody what she thinks of as a black self.

Thus, *One Drop* does not suggest that because race is a "fiction" it is unimportant. Rather, the memoir suggests that although race is a fiction, it is still a fundamental element of American identity with real consequences. Broyard also recognizes what Maria Balshaw suggests in her discussion on passing: "Identity is not a matter of ontological distinction, what you can see, but is a much more muddy epistemological question of what one knows, or thinks one knows" (320). What Anatole Broyard knew about life—what he had lived as a boy—made him a black man passing as white, and it was his struggle with his racial identity that made him a tragic mulatto. Bliss, on the other hand, is neither tragic nor black. Unlike Iola Leroy, and unlike her father, she suggests that she "may never be able to answer the question *What am I?* yet the fault lies not with me but with the question itself" (463). Instead of perfunctorily proffering an identity based upon fractions of blood (the definition of race she begins with), she ultimately suggests that the history of racial classification in this country is flawed. And by meeting her family members and seeing herself from the outside—for the first time in her life—Bliss is forced to call into question her inherent beliefs about racial identity. That she sometimes fails to recognize objectively (and thus fails to unpack) the racial stereotypes that remain with her does not negate the significance of the revelations about race, family, identity, and self that she does come to. Furthermore, by acknowledging that she hasn't "earned the right" to call herself black, she invests blackness with a cultural and historical value—something it lacks in the traditional approach to passing and passing narratives and that it lacked for her father. Bliss Broyard, unlike many fictional and real forebears, can be white without rejecting her black racial ancestry. She can, indeed, be a cousin to blackness.

Notes

1. We want to acknowledge that comparing Broyard herself to the fictional "tragic mulatto" is, of course, engaging in some genre boundary crossing. Certainly, Broyard's articulation of her own lived experience is not reducible to one narrative trope, and memoir itself differs from the novel as a form. (For more on various kinds of life writing, see Sidonie Smith and Julia Watson's *Reading Autobiography: A Guide for Interpreting Life Narratives*). However, as is made clear throughout the memoir, Broyard's understanding of her racial identity and of her father's racial history is certainly shaped by her rather stereotypical notions of what it means to "be black" and of the act of passing that have proliferated in U.S. culture primarily through fiction and, later, film. In short, she articulates her "racial quest" as a young white woman whose knowledge about passing has been limited to the realm of fiction, not as a young black woman with the kind of cultural knowledge of passing that is often passed down within the family or

community. This perceptual difference is, in fact, one primary distinction between her and her "black" family.

2. Matthews, born in 1967, is the son of a white, Jewish mother and an African American father. His memoir *Ace of Spades: A Memoir* was published in 2007.

3. Some of these confessional magazine articles, many of which are essentially very brief memoirs or personal exposés, are Langston Hughes's "Fooling Our White Folks," *Negro Digest* (Apr. 1950): 38–41; Janice Kingslow's "I Refuse to Pass," *Negro Digest* (May 1950): 22–31; "I'm Through with Passing," *Ebony* (Mar. 1951): 22–27; "White by Day, Negro by Night," *Ebony* (Apr. 1952): 31–36; "Why 'Passing' is Passing Out," *Jet* (July 17, 1952): 12–16; "I Passed for Love," *Tan* (Mar. 1953): 33; "The Curse of Passing," *Ebony* (Dec. 1955): 50–56; "Have Negroes Stopped Passing?" *Jet* (Sept. 13, 1956): 10–12; L. Masco Young's "Is Passing for White a Dying Fad?" *Color* (Apr. 1957): 46–49; "I Lived Two Lives for 30 Years," *Ebony* (Dec. 1958): 156–58, 160–62; "Why I Never Want to Pass," *Ebony* (June 1959): 49–54. Gayle Wald devotes an entire chapter of *Crossing the Line* to what she calls "postpassing narratives," explaining that "the prefix 'post' referenc[es] their collective interpretation of changes in the material and social well-being of black people as grounds for the obsolescence of racial passing as a social practice" (119). They do, however, advocate acknowledging one's (inherent) blackness as a responsibility. Social and political improvements serve as enticements for doing the right thing ethically and racially.

4. In Webb's novel, Clarence and Emily Garies are interracial (he is white, she was his slave). They move from the South to Philadelphia and marry. After the Garies die in a race riot, their son Clarence is advised to let himself be raised as white and pass. Emily, his younger sister, remains living in the black community even though she is also white-skinned. Clarence falls in love with a white woman whose father forbids the relationship after his passing is exposed. Clarence dies a heartbroken man, while Emily exits the novel happily married and with a loving extended black family.

5. It is interesting to note that in Hurst's 1933 novel, readers do not leave Peola sobbing on her mother's casket. Although Delilah does also die in the novel, Peola never knows about her death because she has married a white man and moved to Bolivia. She is, however, torn over the choice she must make either to accept her mother (and hence her own blackness) or to be happy (and live as white). She has also sterilized herself to avoid the possibility of having darker-skinned children that would betray her racial heritage to her husband.

6. Black and white *audiences* also generally—and sometimes emphatically—condemned Peola/Sarah Jane for deserting her mother and her race.

7. This kind of temporary passing is much less represented in fiction than the kind of passing that required complete (and often dramatic) severing of familial ties and removal from the black community. In life, as Broyard's memoir documents, passing was often both a public secret—at least within the immediate black community—and carried out in varying degrees.

8. Indeed, the feeling of being abandoned or rejected is one of the main reasons for anger following familial estrangement. The required level of deception involved in permanent or long-term passing precludes family ties, and it has often been a theme in traditional passing narratives. To cite just one example, in Jessie Redmon Fauset's *Plum Bun,* Angela Murray, the light-skinned protagonist, decides to pass for white after the death of her parents and it nearly costs her a relationship with her darker-skinned sister Jinny. The sisters' relationship is only restored after Angela reclaims her black identity (and family). Many of the confessional essays noted above also highlight the reclamation of family as a key motivation for their condemnation of passing. In Broyard's memoir, such a restorative moment is left to Bliss.

9. Granted, even in earlier texts, internalized racism sometimes played a part in the passer's decision to pass and in her self-punishment, as is the case for Peola/Sarah Jane. However, often this self-hate is understood as *stemming from* the socioeconomic disadvantages and is thus, to some degree, understandable. In a more equitable (although far from perfect) racial climate, that self-hate has fewer external justifications. Also important to note is that these claims primarily hold for texts in which the character has always known she is black. The dynamics shift when the individual has been raised as white and only discovers later that she "is" black. Thus, Anatole's intentional passing is structurally and psychologically different than Bliss's unintentional passing.

10. Bliss first meets her aunts, Lorraine and Shirley, at her father's memorial service. In a moment that rings with an objectifying white voice, she reminds herself: "*This is my father's family and they are black. . . . It's really true!*" (36; italics in original). She had known of the existence of her aunts and grandmother, Edna. In fact, she later recalls meeting (the light-skinned) Lorraine on the single occasion that she met her paternal grandmother, who was also light-skinned. But Bliss had not understood at that meeting that the women were black. After all, if her father was white, then his mother and sister were white, too. The single visit was never repeated, and Edna dies while Bliss is still relatively young. Although Lorraine would phone periodically over the years, she did not call often enough to allow them to establish a relationship. Nor is Bliss able to reconnect with Lorraine after Anatole's death because Lorraine dies shortly thereafter. Lorraine's will—which explicitly disinherits Anatole—provides the catalyst for a conversation with her darker-skinned aunt Shirley, whom Bliss meets for the first time at the memorial service.

11. The jealousy experienced by "other blacks" at their school was not simply a result of the differences in skin color; intraracial class issues (which, granted, are related to skin color in many cases) also played a significant role. In this same segment of the memoir, Marjorie Costa, one of Anatole's sisters' friends, notes that "most of our groups were snobs and didn't want to talk with [other kids] if they weren't the right color and didn't dress the right way" (335).

12. "Creole" is generally defined as the mixture of French and Spanish cultures; Louisiana Creoles tend to be a mixture of French, Spanish, Caribbean, and African cultures. An in-depth discussion on the unique racial history of Creoles in Louisiana is beyond the scope of this essay. For more information, see *Creole: The History and Legacy of Louisiana's Free People of Color* (2000) by Sybil Klein; *Africans in Colonial Louisiana: The Development of Afro-Creole Culture in the 18th Century* (1995) by Gwendolyn Midlo Hall; or *White By Definition: Social Classification in Creole Louisiana* (1994) by Virginia Dominguez.

13. His response here recalls James Weldon Johnson's famous passer in *Autobiography of An Ex-Colored Man*. The narrator proclaims: "I finally made up my mind that I would neither disclaim the black race nor claim the white race; but that I would change my name, raise a moustache, and let the world take me for what it would; that it was not necessary for me to go about with a label of inferiority pasted across my forehead" (499).

14. Shirley's husband was Franklin Williams, a leading activist for the N.A.A.C.P.

15. Shirley is well aware that her sister Lorraine, like their parents, passed for white in order to find better employment opportunities. However, as is implied by her earlier statement, passing was only for work. Outside of that, her sister lived as black.

16. In its original form, Anatole's birth certificate has a "C' in the category for race—he would often say that the "C" stood for Creole.

17. Etienne Broyard was the first member of the family to settle in America, arriving in New Orleans in 1753 from a town called Port Rochelle (on the Atlantic coast of France) as a part of the French Royal Army (Broyard 148). He married a local white woman named Marie, as did his son, Henry, and for at least two generations following Etienne's arrival in Louisiana, the Broyards did not practice the local tradition of racial intermarriage. The first generation of "black Broyards" are the children of Gilbert, Etienne's grandson, and yet another Marie. This Marie, however, was a free black woman. From this point forward, the family's racial identity is described as Creole and, as such, rests at the juncture of three major cultural groups: European, Caribbean, and African.

18. See page 124 of *One Drop* for further elaboration on Vivian's and Anthony's perception of the "black" attitude. Broyard had earlier acknowledged harboring some previously unexamined negative associations between blacks and expected modes of social behavior. For instance, after moving to Charlottesville, Bliss notes, "In the drugstore I watched as my annoyance with a slow cashier, who was black, widened into a general condemnation of certain types of young African American women as lazy. In the past these thoughts had passed stealthily through my brain . . . now I began to try to intercept them" (99).

19. Indeed, the quote suggests that the media encouraged a link for its viewers between African Americans and criminal behavior.

20. Broyard does not necessarily use the term *value,* but the reasoning she follows suggests that she is attaching a sense of value to blackness much as whiteness has historically carried a value. See Lipsitz for more on the "possessive investment in whiteness."

21. She says: "Doctor, . . . suppose we should marry, and little children in after years should nestle in our arms, and one of them show the unmistakable signs of color, would you be satisfied?" (117). Iola's belief here reminds readers that race was understood as a biological—and thus transmittable—essence. Despite her general conclusion that race is socially constructed, Bliss also seems to believe in the possibility of atavism. For example, when explaining her reason for wanting to tell the truth about her racial ancestry, she says, "I said that I didn't want to hide anything. That I was afraid of being caught in a lie. 'What if I have a child and it comes out dark?' "(125).

Works Cited

"African American Lives 2: Bliss Broyard." *African American Lives 2 With Dr. Henry Louis Gates, Jr.* PBS. New York. 6 Feb. 2008.

Balshaw, Maria. " 'Black Was White': Urbanity, Passing, and the Spectacle of Harlem." *Journal of American Studies* 33 (1999): 307–22. Print.

Broyard, Anatole. "Portrait of the Inauthentic Negro." *Commentary* (July 1950): 56–64. Print.

Broyard, Bliss. *One Drop: My Father's Hidden Life—A Story of Race and Family Secrets.* New York: Little Brown, 2007. Print.

Dominguez, Virginia. *White By Definition: Social Classification in Creole Louisiana.* Piscataway: Rutgers UP, 1994. Print.

Fauset, Jessie R. *Plum Bun: A Novel Without a Moral.* 1928. 2nd ed. Boston: Beacon, 1990. Print.

Gates Jr., Henry Louis. "The Passing of Anatole Broyard." *Thirteen Ways of Looking at a Black Man.* New York: Random House, 1997. 180–214. Print.

Hall, Gwendolyn Midlo. *Africans in Colonial Louisiana: The Development of Afro-Creole Culture in the 18th Century.* Baton Rouge: Louisiana State UP, 1995. Print.

Harper, Frances E. W. *Iola Leroy.* 1892. Boston: Beacon, 1999. Print.

Harper, Phillip Brian. "Passing for What? Racial Masquerade and the Demands of Upward Mobility." *Callaloo* 21.2 (1998): 381–97. Print.

Hurst, Fannie. *Imitation of Life.* Ed. Daniel Itzkovitz. Durham: Duke UP, 2004. Print.

Imitation of Life. Dir. Douglas Sirk. Universal International Pictures, 1959.

———. Dir. John M. Stahl. Universal Pictures, 1934.

Johnson, James W. *The Autobiography of an Ex-Colored Man.* 1927. *Three Negro Classics.* Intro. John Hope Franklin. New York: Avon Books. 1965. 391–511. Print.

Kaplan, Erin Aubry. "Sort of Black Like Me." Review of *One Drop: My Father's Hidden Life—A Story of Race and Family Secrets* by Bliss Broyard. *Los Angeles Times.* 30 Sept. 2007: R10. Print.

Klein, Sybil. *Creole: The History and Legacy of Louisiana's Free People of Color.* Baton Rouge: Louisiana State UP, 2000. Print.

Lemon, Alaina. "Without a 'Concept'? Race as Discursive Practice." *Slavic Review* 61.1 (2002): 54–61. Print.

Lipsitz, George. *The Possessive Investment in Whiteness: How White People Profit from Identity Politics.* Rev. ed. Philadelphia: Temple UP, 2006. Print.

Matthews, David. *Ace of Spades: A Memoir.* New York: Henry Holt, 2007. Print.

Pilgrim, David. "The Tragic Mulatto Myth." *Jim Crow Museum of Racist Memorabilia at Ferris State University.* Web. Nov. 2000.

Robinson, Amy. "It Takes One to Know One: 'Passing' and Communities of Common Interest." *Critical Inquiry* 20.4 (1994): 715–36. Print.

Sartre, Jean Paul. "Portrait of the Inauthentic Jew." *Commentary* 5.5 (May 1948): 389–97. Print.

Seeman, Melvin. "Status and Identity: The Problem of Inauthenticity." *The Pacific Sociological Review* 9.2 (1966): 67–73. Print.

Smith, Sidonie, and Julia Watson. *Reading Autobiography: A Guide for Interpreting Life Narratives.* 2nd ed. Minneapolis: U of Minnesota P, 2010. Print.

Webb, Frank J. *The Garies and Their Friends.* 1857. Intro. Robert Reid-Pharr. Baltimore: The Johns Hopkins UP, 1997. Print.

4

Can One Really Choose?

Passing and Self-Identification at the Turn of the Twenty-First Century

Jené Schoenfeld

If racial passing was relevant enough in the year 2000 to devote an episode of a popular television show to the theme, why did that same show pretend that passing had not actually been relevant for almost fifty years? The WB's show *Angel* evoked just such a conundrum when, in the fall of 2000, it set its passing episode—called "Are You Now or Have You Ever Been?"—in 1952.[1] *Angel*, however, is not the only popular television show to have addressed the theme of passing at the turn of the twenty-first century; NBC's original *Law & Order* featured a passing episode titled "Blood" in November 1997.[2] It, too, framed passing as a concern of primarily historical relevance. Both episodes represent racism as a thing of the past, whose only vestiges are manifested in the personal feelings and expressions of a few isolated individuals. In their denial of the contemporary relevance of racial passing and, with it, the contemporary impact of racism, both of these television episodes broadcast a sense of racial "progress," but beneath this shiny, happy surface, their representations of the passer are fundamentally conservative. Indeed, the representations of racial passing in these episodes share many elements with representations of passing from the Jim Crow era and, like them, tend to reinscribe the binary structure of race upon which racism in the United States has historically depended.

The air dates of these particular episodes are not coincidental; on the cusp of the new millennium, there were notable indications—or at least promises—of racial progress having been achieved in the United States. One of those markers was a change in the racial classification system on the 2000 U.S. Census. Interest in classifying people's race, and particularly in drawing the color line between black and white, predates the founding of the United States as an independent nation.[3] Since then, the definition of who is black has varied over time and from region to region, typically being defined based on some proportion of "black blood." The most extreme definition, the one-drop rule, which classifies anyone with any black ancestry as black, was used as a social definition of blackness in the Upper South as early as the early eighteenth century (Davis 33–34; Williamson 14). However, it was not until the 1920s that the rule became "uniformly accepted" across the nation (Davis 31).[4] The one-drop rule gained strength in connection with the consolidation of Jim Crow segregation because it eliminates—in custom and sometimes in law—the possibility of a multiracial identification, thereby dividing all neatly (and primarily) into the categories of "black" or "white."

Laws regulating distinct racial categories necessarily had to be bolstered by "miscegenation laws," which prohibited interracial intercourse and marriage. Peggy Pascoe notes that "by the end of the nineteenth century, the [miscegenation] laws had spread to cover nearly all the states of the U.S." (6). When the United States Supreme Court finally ruled in 1967 that laws against interracial marriage were unconstitutional, in a case fittingly called *Loving v. Virginia,* sixteen states still had active miscegenation laws (Zack 77).[5] In the wake of the *Loving* decision, interracial marriages increased dramatically, and, by the 1990s, a new cohort of first generation bi- or multiracials was coming of age.[6] For them, the one-drop rule was neither abstract nor automatic. Though mixed-race people who wanted to acknowledge their racial multiplicity would be accused of trying to deny their blackness, some felt that the alternative was to deny part of their family and other important aspects of their heritage and of their identity. Instead, many of them sought forms of identification that would acknowledge all of the aspects of their heritage.[7] In addition to these personal forms of identification, a critical mass of multiracial people fought to have their presence counted publicly. In July 1997, a federal task force announced its recommendation about how that would be done. On Census 2000, for the first time in American history, individuals would be able to choose to be identified by as many racial boxes as they deemed applicable. Not simply a victory for the multiracial community, this change in the Census promised to represent a major step forward in race relations, because it suggested a waning of the importance of racial difference.[8]

Yet in April 1997, only three months before the task force disclosed the new Census policy, when Tiger Woods announced on *Oprah* that he had devised his own racial signifier—Cablinasian—that took into account all four aspects of his ancestry, it produced a widespread backlash—one that might not have been expected in what appeared to be an atmosphere of increasing racial liberalism. Many resented Tiger's self-definition, labeling it self-delusion or self-hate instead. A flurry of newspaper articles responded to Woods's neologism, most of them ridiculing and/or condemning Woods's multiple self-identification. Several emphasized the importance of external signifiers over self-identification, using the example of a cab driver. For instance, Denene Millner begins her article: "Just what the hell is a Cablinasian anyway? If Tiger Woods were standing on the corner of 63rd and Park facing North, say, at about midnight, would most cabbies take him for a Cablinasian or would they raise their eyebrows and pass him up as they do so many other black men they assume are headed for Harlem?" (2). In an article that appeared in various forms in Buffalo, New York, Tampa, Florida, and New Orleans, Louisiana, Leonard Pitts voiced his more general suspicion that those claiming multiracial identity are suffering from a version of self-hate: "In some instances, the desire to be biracial seems more than anything the desire to escape being black. To escape the onus attached to that word. Given black people's long and tortuous history of self-loathing, I'm always suspicious of anyone with brown skin who says he is something else" (3B). Such responses, I would suggest, demonstrate the continuing force of the one-drop rule as the guiding principle of racial identification and labeling for people of African descent in America.[9] Though legal segregation and one-drop laws are many decades defunct, the one-drop rule has survived. Because the desire for more flexible forms of racial identification—which ultimately culminated in the new method of Census 2000—was a direct challenge to the one-drop rule, it met with resistance as surely as did Woods's attempt at self-(re)definition.[10] Thus, despite rhetoric touting the diminishing relevance of race, it seems that, as a society and often as individuals, we still cling to our traditionally defined racial identities.

Far from settling the question, then, the change in the Census reopened the conversation about the status of mixed-race people relative to a larger discourse of race, racial classification, and identity in the United States at the end of the twentieth century. This renewed discussion gave the "mulatto" figure—temporarily subsumed within discourses of class, color, and political mobilization—renewed relevance. In turn, the theme of passing provided, once again, a useful platform for meditations on the importance (or lack thereof) of racial identity and classification. Like many passers, the new multiracial was seen as resisting being labeled as "black." By implicitly aligning the two (passer/multiracial), contemporary narratives could explore potential motives for this resistance. However, by focusing on the *historical* narrative of the passer in particular, they could deny the *contemporary* relevance of one such motive—avoiding racism—and ignore new reasons, such as embracing the whole of one's interracial family. Thus, without directly addressing the new multiracial phenomenon—except for a brief allusion to Tiger Woods in the *Law & Order* episode—these contemporary representations of passing dismiss multiracial identification with a resounding affirmation of the one-drop rule.

Though the mulatto trope has developed over time and in connection with the racial politics of the historical moment in which it appears, the common purpose of the "new" mulatto trope and the Jim Crow–era mulatto trope—to impose the one-drop rule—results in certain shared features.[11] In antebellum fiction, the mulatto was used chiefly in the service of antislavery appeals. Often female, she was usually represented as physically and culturally indistinguishable from white ladies, but tragically barred from the privileges and protections that were seen as the white lady's birthright (Zanger). During the Jim Crow era, the mulatto's hidden blackness and potential pretenses to whiteness produced not sympathy, but growing anxiety, because the mulatto's ambiguity was an implicit threat to the system of segregation. The mulatto trope changes accordingly, actually splitting into two complementary variants: the tragically marginal/degenerate mulatto and the "light-skinned" elite "black." A mixed-race character who identifies according to the one-drop rule, thereby "accepting" his or her place among blacks, is represented as noble or even heroic (Zack 129). However, the marginal mulatto, who attempts to claim the privileges of whiteness through passing or who simply resists categorization entirely, would likely be represented as "depressive, moody, discontent, irrational, impulsive, fickle, criminal, chronically confused, emotionally unstable, constantly nervous, and ruled by [his or her] passions" (Nakashima 167). The common thread among the various aspects of the degenerate mulatto stereotype is the idea that mixing races is unnatural and the product of race mixing—the mulatto—will necessarily be aberrant. Pascoe provides this representative example of the widely held view: "[B]y 1869 . . . the Georgia Supreme Court proclaimed: 'The amalgamation of the races is not only unnatural, but is always productive of deplorable results. Our daily observation shows us, that the offspring of these unnatural connections are generally sickly and effeminate, and that they are inferior in physical development and strength, to the full-blood of either race' " (7). This kind of imagery contributed significantly to the pressure on the mulatto to identify according to the one-drop rule, within a binary system of race. As Naomi Zack explains: "It is difficult to imagine how any American of mixed race could feel assured of an ordinary existence *as a person of mixed race* after having been exposed to the prevailing scientific and popular images of mulattoness in the late nineteenth century" (122; my emphasis). In Zack's rather dramatic terms, this imagery could be seen as "genocidal to the category of mixed race" (113). By the middle of the twentieth century, any liminal space for mixed-race people was effectively eliminated: the mulatto had become black.

Significant vestiges of the degenerate mulatto figure reemerge, however, in contemporary representations under the renewed anxiety about racial classification in the late twentieth century. First, many contemporary representations seem to share their predecessors' belief in the essential blackness of the mulatto, as well as their commitment to exposing that blackness as the mulatto's "true" identity. "Blackness," imagined to comprise a set of physical and character traits, was believed to be carried in and transmitted by the blood. Thus, it should be no surprise that blood remains such a powerful and persistent motif in narratives involving mixed race. Another key continuity is the representation of the mulatto as criminal. As I will discuss further below, whatever the ostensible crime of a given passer, the underlying and often more significant crime of the passer is racial fraud or the theft of whiteness. Finally, the denouement in mulatto fiction is always significant because it comments on the possibility (or lack thereof) of a place or of a future for the mulatto. From the antebellum on, perhaps the most common denouement is death, which communicates the fundamental lack of either place or future for the mulatto (Berzon 102; Sollors *Neither* 337).[12] Alternatively, the mulatto may be "reclaimed" by the black community, which still maintains the one-drop rule, but which, in the terms of the narrative, generally constitutes a happy ending (Zack 129).[13] These two options still resonate in the narratives under study here.

The *Angel* episode, "Are You Now or Have You Ever Been?," practices fairly consistent splitting between past and present, racist and progressive. As a narrative technique, the flashback promotes such duality, and the premise of *Angel* makes it particularly well suited to flashbacks. It is a science fiction-action drama about a vampire with a soul, who spends his afterlife trying to make amends for his past evils. He runs a supernatural detective agency, helping people who have out of the ordinary problems. In this episode's present, Angel has directed his two assistants, Wesley and Cordelia, to dig up whatever they can on an abandoned hotel called the Hyperion. We later learn that Angel lived there in 1952, and most of the episode takes place through a series of flashbacks to that time.[14] To establish the repressive context of the era, in the second flashback, residents and guests of the Hyperion Hotel are assembled around a television playing the McCarthy trials, with the infamous question, "Are you now or have you ever been . . . ?" Segregation is briefly referenced when the hotel manager turns away a black family, saying that the vacancy sign was wrong. The main drama in the flashbacks, however, is the story of Judy, a damsel in distress who also happens to be a "black" woman passing for white as well as a thief hiding out from a private investigator.

When Angel first meets Judy, she is actually engaged in two forms of passing, one of which Angel detects and exposes as fraudulent immediately, the other of which is invisible to him. Judy, caught hiding in Angel's room, initially pretends to be the maid. Ironically, among a list of several reasons why she cannot be the maid, Angel tells Judy, "you're the wrong color." It is not quite clear what color the maids at the hotel are because we never actually see one. The bellhop mentions a maid called "Consuela," but the Latina-sounding name offers little clarification as to color. Yet, though he evidently notices Judy's color, it does not translate for Angel to a "correct" understanding of Judy's race. Angel and, I would suggest, the audience "misrecognize" Judy as white, until she racially recodes herself by telling her story. Visual cues clearly are not sufficient to indicate racial identity, yet it is difficult to discard one's trust in them. Indeed, after the reveal, Judy's skin appears a bit darker, and her dark, wavy hair, and dark brown eyes take on new meaning. It is unclear whether the producers of Angel had the actress's makeup changed during the course of this scene.[15] However, the post-reveal darkening of Judy's skin reminds us that the visual nature of television as a medium only heightens the issues of visibility/invisibility that are so primary to the trope of passing (and to race itself). Certainly, novels and stories sometimes include(d) illustrations of passing characters, but the television audience can literally see a body (ironically, "in color") and still not recognize her as a black woman/mulatto. In other words, television (and film) allows audiences to *see* what they earlier had to *imagine,* thus potentially increasing its impact.[16] Post-reveal, the audience must re-view Judy and reinscribe her "white" body as "black."

This kind of visual racial play would seem to challenge the idea of fixed racial categories. However, in the conversation in which Judy reveals her racial passing to Angel, we also see the tension between the episode's overt disavowal of race and racism, and a lingering subtext that affirms racial essentialism. Somewhat anachronistically, Angel insists on the fallacy of racial difference, but Judy evokes several classic motifs typically associated with the mulatto, specifically, tainted blood, belonging nowhere, illegitimacy, and criminality. In this scene, Judy implores Angel for help, sharing her secret and throwing herself at his mercy. She explains that she robbed the bank where she worked, but she has not spent any of the money. She claims that she did it because she was angry and desperate after she got fired at the bank because they "found out about her" and her fiancé left her:

> JUDY: Aren't you going to ask me why they fired me?
>
> ANGEL: Why'd they fire you?
>
> JUDY: Because I'm not what I say I am. I've been passing since I was fifteen years old.
>
> ANGEL: Passing?
>
> JUDY: For white. My mother was colored, my father—I didn't even know him! My blood isn't pure. It's tainted.
>
> ANGEL: It's just blood Judy. It—it's all just blood.
>
> JUDY: Nobody believes that! Not even my mother's family. I'm not one thing or the other. I'm nothing.
>
> ANGEL: I know what that's like.
>
> JUDY: Yes. Yes, I am. I am something. I'm a thief! I've never stolen anything before in my life. I swear it. It's just, the things that they called me.
>
> ANGEL: Fear makes people do stupid things.
>
> JUDY: It was stupid. And I wish I'd never done it.
>
> ANGEL: I didn't mean you. I meant your former employers. They were afraid. That's why they fired you. ("Are You Now")

Angel's assertion that "it's all just blood" reflects our contemporary understanding that biological differences between races are scientifically insignificant (it also reminds viewers of his experience as a vampire who sustains his afterlife by consuming blood). But Judy's rhetoric of purity and taint is older and, I would argue, more powerful. The nineteenth-century belief that racial essences were carried in and transmitted by the blood, combined with archetypal associations of white with good and black with evil, all in the service of a racial hierarchy in which whiteness dominated, led to an intense rhetoric of white purity and black pollution.[17] Indeed, those beliefs structure the one-drop rule itself, which implies that black blood is so potently corrupting that even an infinitesimal amount is significant enough to justify excluding a person from whiteness. Judy, by this logic, is effectively barred from a "legitimate" claim to whiteness: she can only "pass" for white.[18] Yet she does not see—or, we presume, want to see—herself as black.

This leaves her in a racial limbo that is untenable in segregated America. Within a binary system of racial definition, if she cannot be "one thing or the other," she must be nothing. In this context, a multiracial identity (an alternative to the strict binary of either/or) is simply unthinkable. Moreover, Judy's conclusion that the true definition of her identity is as "thief" is also consistent with what we might call a mulatto mythology. Judy's claiming of this identity stands out in this episode because she claims she has never stolen anything before she took the money. If that were true, it would be odd for her to define her identity based on a single act. The label "thief" is fitting, however, because the passer is understood as committing a sort of racial fraud that allows her to steal white privilege.[19] By that logic, Judy has been a thief for years. Given these mutually reinforcing expressions of mulatto mythology in the representation of Judy, the attempted revision of this ideology expressed by Angel—"it's all just blood"—is not very convincing. Not only are Judy's claims expressed more passionately and at greater length, but Angel is not very credible. He is completely outside of society—he is not even human; himself a hybrid—so his beliefs cannot be taken as representative of any significant competing cultural norm.

Angel's passing episode almost succeeds in its attempt to split past from present, locating racism squarely in the past. One might argue that it is no surprise that the stereotype of the degenerate mulatto is in play in the context of a flashback to 1952, that the episode is simply striving for historical realism. In the present, one might argue, racism has abated so the representation of race in the present would be quite different. Such an assertion seems logical and would be true, but for a key element of continuity between past and present in the episode: racism, among other things, is personified in the figure of a "paranoia demon." The trope of the paranoia demon locates racism in the realm of personal feelings—not even legitimate ones at that—essentially denying its systemic impact and historical reality. That trope is carried into the present where such denial reaches its peak, despite a final, very important, continuity in the representation of the mulatto figure.

Banishing the demon—represented as tantamount to banishing racism itself—is the central drama of the episode. Though the demon wreaks all kinds of havoc, such as prompting a suicide, then convincing the hotel residents that it was really a murder, the demon ultimately focuses on Judy, playing on her fear of discovery as both passer and thief. Despite his initial reluctance to become involved in anyone else's business at this point in his afterlife, Angel decides to try to help Judy. Though Angel is already helping her by hiding the bank's money in the basement when he discovers the demon, the episode implies that by banishing the demon, Angel will eliminate the source of Judy's fear and self-hatred and thereby solve her problems. If we accept the demon as the source of those feelings, however, we must totally discount the material realities of her life: when her black ancestry is discovered, she is fired from her job and dumped by her fiancé. Moreover, the episode does not address how banishing the demon would solve Judy's criminal troubles. Yet, despite its allusions to racism, the episode seems designed to produce and endorse such logical lapses.

As history ultimately has borne out, racism was too tenacious to be banished in 1952. The possible practical advantages of banishing the demon become a moot point, in the flashback at least, because Angel does not, in fact, banish the demon at that time. Instead, we see paranoia growing exponentially, as an easily suggestible crowd follows the most tenuous threads of suspicion. While Angel is out buying supplies, the demon turns the suspicious tenants into a lynch mob, seeking retribution for the "murder." As their anxiety approaches fever pitch, the private investigator seeking Judy shows up and reveals her as a thief. Quickly leaping from "thief" to "murderess," the mob grabs Judy, but she deflects their attention to Angel, outing him as a "monster" who keeps blood in his room.[20] Letting one passer go in favor of another, they lynch Angel. Of course, he is a vampire, so hanging does not actually kill him, but it does sour him on humanity in general and Judy in particular, so as soon as he is alone he leaves the hotel, abandoning Judy to her fate. Fifty years later, Angel decides it is time to deal with the demon once and for all.

The resolution of Judy's story, however, is not as simple and positive as it appears. In the episode's present, Angel and his team successfully eradicate the demon, who, it turns out, had been feeding on Judy all this time, having convinced her never to leave her room, claiming that it could "protect" her there. After banishing the demon, Angel pays a last visit to Judy, who, finally "free," peacefully dies. To those unfamiliar with the tragic mulatto trope, the banishing of the paranoia demon and Judy's subsequent death may seem to be a sort of happy ending; Judy is quite old, after all. But, as I discussed above, even in antebellum versions of the tragic mulatto trope, death—often a tragically early one—is an extremely common ending for the mulatto. Because they have no social place, mulattoes seldom get a future, *as* mulattoes. If they are not incorporated into black communities or moved out of the American context altogether, they typically die. Furthermore, it is significant that Judy has lived and died alone. Because she is revealed as a passer before her marriage, further miscegenation and, thus, the proliferation of racial ambiguity, is prevented. Living in her room, she has quite literally been contained. Thus, *Angel,* like so many passing narratives before it, effectively punishes the passer and restores the (binary) racial order.

The episode's conclusion, however, maintains the pretense that the racial climate of its present is fundamentally different, denying any continuity with the racist past. When Angel returns to the group, Cordelia expresses her desire to leave the hotel, saying, "This place gives me the heebeegeebees." She continues:

> CORDELIA: Seventy years of violence, mayhem, and paranoia . . . bad vibes.
>
> ANGEL: We're moving in.
>
> CORDELIA: I mean, a few throw pillows, what's not to love?
>
> WESLEY: Angel, surely you more than anyone must appreciate how for the better part of the last century this place has been host, not only to a malevolent demonic presence, but the very worst face of humanity! This is a house of evil.
>
> ANGEL: Not anymore. ("Are You Now")

Angel's statement, "Not anymore," signifies his belief in the possibility that racism can be fairly easily and quite completely eradicated in a single stroke, simply by destroying the paranoia demon. It is possible that the episode's writers are satirizing the simplistic approach to race through Cordelia's turn-on-a-dime response, but nothing else in the episode seems to support such a conclusion. The episode's overt message is that race is not significant in the present; it never was "real"—only a product of paranoia.

Produced and aired on the cusp of a new millennium, "Are You Now or Have You Ever Been?" is suffused with the hope of vanquishing racism once and for all. The show seems quite sincere, even a bit earnest, in that hope. We, the viewing audience, some of whom may well be part of the rising generation of "new" multiracials, are invited to embrace the hero's color-blind perspective. Yet the undercurrent of American culture's older racial narratives (and enduring racial hierarchy) seems to undermine this message of hope. Beneath its glib surface, the episode's subtext reinscribes the one-drop rule. The representation of Judy as tragic mulatto is far more compelling than Angel's proclamations of the sameness of all humanity. As a passer, Judy is exposed by the private investigator, provisionally contained by the paranoia demon, and finally contained by her death. Furthermore, the episode's commitment to the idea that racism is nothing more than misguided personal feelings may seem liberal, but in allowing the characters (and the audience) to ignore racism's deeper structures, it allows them to live on. If Angel has already destroyed the demon of racism, all we have to do is bring the throw pillows . . . and close our eyes and ears to any lingering "vibes" of inequality.

Law & Order's passing episode, "Blood," shares with the *Angel* episode its representation of racism as a problem of the past and of race as a matter of personal feeling, as well as its underlying investment in a binary racial system and in the significance of black blood, yet the *Law & Order* episode takes things further in every way. It acknowledges, to some extent, the problem of contemporary racism; it raises the stakes by introducing children into the story; and, I would argue, it ultimately reveals itself to be more committed to maintaining the racial binary. This is particularly concerning because the *Law & Order* episode also has the potential for much greater ideological impact than the *Angel* episode. Not only did *Law & Order,* as a hugely successful series on a major network, reach a wider audience than did *Angel,* the former's pretense of presenting stories "ripped from the headlines" gave it an aura of realism not to be found in (or even expected of) the WB's little science fiction show.[21] As *Law & Order*'s title suggests, the series delivers "law" and "order," neatly packaged into manageable half-hour chunks: the first half hour of each episode typically features the police investigation of a crime, while the second half hour involves its prosecution. While the restoration of law and order ostensibly means the detection and prosecution of the murderer, I would argue that in this episode, it also means the exposure of the passer and the reification of the color line.

In "Blood," the black baby is the vehicle through which the passer is exposed. Briefly, the plot of the episode is as follows: A woman named Karen Burdett is found dead in the courtyard of her apartment building. We learn that she is the mother of a three-week-old daughter, whom she has reluctantly given up for adoption, because her husband, who already has a teenage son, told her before their marriage that he did not want any more children. Suspicious circumstances surrounding the pregnancy and birth emerge. She delivers the baby at City Hospital (a public facility, despite their wealth). Her husband is detached from the whole pregnancy and birth process. Detectives Briscoe and Curtis initially suspect an affair. This suspicion is deepened when the white adoptive mother proudly displays baby Maggie, a very dark-skinned baby with a broad nose and ample lips. Further investigation reveals, however, that the baby shares an inherited medical condition with their suspect, Josh Burdett. They therefore conclude that he is the baby's father and that this means that he is black. (Karen is Danish; thus, we are to conclude, securely white.)

The detectives' deduction of Josh Burdett's race from the more visibly evident race of his child evokes the "black baby" trope. Often in both fictional and legal discourses of the nineteenth and early twentieth centuries, the racially ambiguous body of the mulatto was tied to blackness through the more clearly racially marked body of a parent.[22] However, anxieties about atavism—the possibility that racial traits long invisible might manifest in future generations—make the "black baby" fable an important variant in literary representations of the mulatto. In the late nineteenth and early twentieth century, " 'black baby' fables" were usually written by white racists and were, as Laura Dawkins observes, "chiefly designed to warn injudicious white women against the dangers of mates without pedigrees" (168).[23] In the context of racist ideology, the fantasy of atavism expresses both the fear of the total dissolution of racial boundaries and the desperately clung-to belief that racial difference is real and could reappear in the clear and concrete form of a body whose outside matches its perceived inside. Dawkins notes, however, that variations of these tales were produced by black-identified writers of the Harlem Renaissance as well. In these tales, as in the case of Josh Burdett, the black baby is feared as a potential source of exposure for the passer. Dawkins suggests that "black-authored dark child tales reflect a continuing sense of racial crisis among Harlem Renaissance writers," who may have found it safer to explore racism when presenting it as the internalized self-hatred of light-skinned blacks rather than attributing it directly to whites (170). I do not disagree, but I would add that the "black baby" trope also played a disciplinary role for the mulatto by holding out the possibility of the atavistic child to reinforce the inescapable "reality" of a blood-borne set of race traits that could betray the would-be passer at any time.[24]

The interrogation of Josh Burdett that follows the detectives' discovery of his black ancestry (and progeny) exemplifies both verbally and visually the complicated relationship between visibility and lineage that informs both the phenomenon of passing and the black baby trope. As Eva Saks has noted, the problem with blood as the chief signifier of race is that it does not make very good evidence. For example, in the antimiscegenation case of *Jones v. Commonwealth* (Va. 1885), the "prosecution could prove the color of the [defendant's] mother's skin—'yellow'—but could not prove the color of her blood" (Saks 72). It turns out that Angel is right, from the perspective of detectable difference, it is all "just [red] blood." Unless that blood carries genes that produce racial traits that are visible externally, as in the case of Burdett's black daughter, blood is not very useful as a determinant of race. The alternative criterion of visibility, however, is also insufficient because it cannot identify everyone who "is" black based on the one-drop rule, nor does it allow for the precision necessary to apply fractional definitions of blackness. As a result, alternative definitions come into play. The interrogation is a key scene, so I will include a fairly lengthy transcription of its dialogue. The scene begins with detectives Briscoe and Curtis in the room with Burdett. Their black female lieutenant, Van Buren, is watching through a two-way mirror and we see her reflected image superimposed on Burdett. As I will discuss below, this superimposition symbolically identifies Burdett as black through a phenomenon I call "black by association":

> BURDETT: First I killed Karen because she had a child by another man, then I killed her because she had my child?
>
> CURTIS: Because she wanted to keep your child.
>
> BRISCOE: And because everybody in your "just us white folks" executive suite was gonna find out you're black, Josh.
>
> BURDETT: That's absurd. I mean, look at me.

[Enter Van Buren]

VAN BUREN: I wanna talk to 'im.

[Briscoe and Curtis exit]

VAN BUREN [slipping into a down-home, mellifluous voice]: Hello my brotha. [pause] Damn, look at you. You did it. You passed. [pause] You know, I thought up close I'd be able to tell, but I swear I can't. So, what's it like when it's just you and them? You laugh along when they tell the jokes? Oh, you know what I'm talkin' 'bout, right? [leaning in] Or, do you tell nigger jokes, too, just to keep up appearances?

BURDETT [very formal]: If you don't mind.

VAN BUREN: Oh, am I sitting too close? What, I remind you of somebody? Your motha? Was she dark skinned? High yella? Redbone? You scared now, aren't you? You been scared for almost forty years and all that fear came gushing out Sunday morning. You panicked, idn't that right? You go 'head. Tell me what happened. Take the weight off, my brotha. You'll feel better.

[Lawyer enters]

LAWYER: I'm Mr. Burdett's attorney. Do you mind telling me what my client's doing here?

VAN BUREN [back to her official, authoritative, "proper" English]: We're arresting your client for the murder of his wife. Take him down to booking.

[Briscoe reads him his rights] ("Blood")

The episode reveals its commitment to the one-drop rule by completely ignoring Burdett's appeal to visibility as racial evidence—"That's absurd, I mean, look at me"—precisely because under the one-drop rule, visibility does not necessarily qualify as reliable racial evidence. Neither the detectives nor the viewers can recognize Josh Burdett as a black man just by looking at him.[25] As she notes above, not even Lieutenant Van Buren can detect his hidden blackness, though as a black woman and therefore a racial insider, she thinks she should be able to tell.[26] Nonetheless, the much more obvious blackness of Burdett's daughter serves as visual evidence of race which, through the one-drop rule, applies to Josh and, then, his older child as well. Furthermore, the episode summarily dismisses Josh's apparent self-identification with whiteness.[27] No one ever considers the possibility that if he looks white, he is white, except as a misconception. Instead, as far as the characters on the show are concerned, his "true identity" has been revealed.

Josh, who fails to register as black on the basis of his phenotype, becomes what I call "black by association," an expansion of the black baby trope that can connect lineage and visibility by appealing to the body of a relative. In this episode, Burdett's daughter is the most prominent relative who establishes his blackness, but we later learn that Burdett's first wife divorced him after his darker-skinned sister turned up on their doorstep looking for him, thus exposing him as black. The "black by association" phenomenon is extended symbolically to Lieutenant Van Buren who is mapped onto Burdett first through her reflected image superimposed on Burdett early in the interview, then by her own attempts to cultivate a connection by putting herself in the place of his mother: "Oh, am I sitting too close? What, I remind you of somebody? Your motha? Was she dark skinned? High yella? Redbone?" Van Buren's effort here, however, raises one more potential criterion of race, that of performance. Van Buren adopts a "down-home" manner of speech when talking to Josh that seems intended to signify authentic blackness, apparently in the hope that Josh will respond in kind. His formality—"if you don't mind"—and her return to the authoritative tones of "proper" English, however, may leave some viewers to question: Which is authentic and which is performance? Or, perhaps more troubling for those who cling to the one-drop rule, might both be forms of performance? This is not new terrain for scholars of race, but it may well be for many viewers of *Law & Order*. Moreover, it is precisely the position that makes the passer a threat to the one-drop rule and a source of anxiety for many. Accordingly, the *Law & Order* episode, having peered over this precipice, retreats from this line of questioning, lest it alienate its core audience. Instead, "Blood" functions in a world of "black" and "white," even when it is occasionally unclear which is which.

Though it clings to the racial logic of segregation, "Blood" nonetheless attempts to leave that past in the past. Yet it frequently fails to sustain a clear line of demarcation between a racist past and a more progressive present. The scene below directly follows the interview discussed above. In it, Assistant District Attorneys Jack McCoy and Jamie Ross are discussing the case with their boss, Adam Schiff (all three characters are white):

> ROSS: He's had everybody fooled. His whole life was a charade; it's pathetic.
>
> MCCOY: Maybe thirty-forty years ago it made more sense.
>
> SCHIFF: Back then they had lynch mobs and bullwhips. Now they use toilet plungers—[sarcastic] progress.
>
> SCHIFF: Have you confirmed that he's the father of this child?
>
> MCCOY: We're just waiting for a blood sample from the baby.
>
> SCHIFF: What else?
>
> ROSS: Weak alibi, forensics to establish the manner of death.
>
> SCHIFF: His motive being that he didn't want anyone to know he was black. Why?
>
> ROSS: Shame, loss of friends, his work . . . I could just imagine what he was afraid of.
>
> SCHIFF: Don't imagine it, prove it. ("Blood")

McCoy's supposition that Burdett's passing may have "made more sense" when he began it, thirty or forty years before, attempts to locate racism squarely in the past. (Indeed, Burdett later testifies that part of his motivation to pass was his desire to enjoy privileges reserved for whites under segregation, such as drinking from the cleaner and more plentiful whites-only water fountains.) Schiff's sarcastic response, however, referencing the 1997 case of Abner Louima, a black man sodomized by an officer while in the custody of the NYPD, collapses the distinction between the "lynch mobs and bullwhips" of the fifties and sixties and the racist violence taking place in the episode's present. Ross's hypothesis regarding the many motives why Burdett might still not want to be exposed as black also gestures at the contemporary significance of race. Ross's initial comment, however, is perhaps the strongest—if not most obvious—evidence of the episode's underlying commitment to a binary system of race. Jamie Ross is portrayed on the show as a modern woman and a liberal, but her comment that Burdett's "whole life was a charade" and her dismissal of that life as "pathetic" inadvertently reveal not only her belief in the one-drop rule that defines Burdett as black, but also her belief that racial identity constitutes the whole of one's identity. Admittedly, Burdett lied to his first wife about his background and cut himself off from his family of origin, but Ross's comment totally dismisses the validity of the life Burdett built for himself: his marriages, his children, and his career.

Despite these admissions, both deliberate and inadvertent, of the contemporary relevance of racism, the episode still works to suppress that idea. For example, a few scenes after the conversation above, Ross meets with Burdett's employer. She learns that when Burdett applied for his job in 1963, he checked "white" on the application. Asking about the legality of a race question on a job application, Burdett's boss replies, "That was filled out in nineteen sixty-three—the bad old days." The distinction between "the bad old days" and today is clear, at least to Burdett's boss. Asked what would have happened to the application in 1963 had Burdett identified himself as black, he explains that "the application would've ended up in the trash." Jamie asks about the possible consequence of the company discovering Burdett to be black now and the boss chuckles, "Now? Hell, we'd probably put him on the board . . . cheaper than Colin Powell!" ("Blood"). With this last comment, Burdett's boss implies that being black is actually advantageous in the job market, a not-so-subtle jab at Affirmative Action (which was coming under significant attack in the 1990s). In this way, the episode denies that racism has continuing force while simultaneously sustaining racism by fueling the fears of racist whites about "unfair" competition in the job market.

One might be able to dismiss Burdett's boss's optimism as naive, but the episode very cleverly manages both to raise and dismiss the question of contemporary structural racism on a much larger scale. It turns out that the murderer is Josh Burdett's ex-wife, who killed Karen Burdett to prevent her from reclaiming her visibly black daughter. As discussed above, Burdett's recognition of his black baby would mean exposing his own blackness, and, under the one-drop rule, that of his firstborn child, David. Frances Houston, Burdett's first wife, cannot accept this. Houston's (black female) lawyer argues that Houston, concerned for the possible disadvantages to her son that might result from his being labeled black, tried to persuade Karen Burdett to give up her own child. In the heat of this argument, Houston pushed Karen, who subsequently fell over the balcony to her death. As part of Houston's defense, her lawyer wants to call several expert witnesses to testify about the potential impact for David of losing the privileges of white identity, that is, to testify about the continuing effects of structural racism. The D.A.'s office, however, successfully blocks the defense's effort to put forward witnesses to the contemporary effects of racism. Within the storyline, their rationale is that what is relevant is Houston's state of mind, not the "state of the union." The significance of this legal decision, however, goes beyond its strategic value in court. It allows the episode itself to skirt the issue.

Instead, the episode represents contemporary racism primarily as a problem stemming from the personal feelings of a few aberrant individuals. It turns out that Burdett's first wife, for example, is not the loving mother she hopes the jury will believe her to be. Not only does she refer to Burdett's second child as "some nappy haired little monkey" who might ruin her family, she fought not to have custody of her own son because of his black ancestry ("Blood"). Having failed in her attempt to include arguments about systemic racism in her defense, Houston, in her testimony, invokes an instance of personal racism: "For every Tiger Woods, there's a thousand Fuzzy Zoellers and I did not want David to go through life facing that kind of prejudice" ("Blood"). She refers here to the incident after Woods's first Masters Tournament win, when Fuzzy Zoeller infamously said, "Pat him on the back. Say congratulations . . . and tell him not to serve fried chicken next year . . . or collard greens or whatever the hell they serve" ("Tiger Woods"). Even if we believe that Houston is concerned by Zoeller's comment, her testimony still allows us to believe that contemporary racism is a matter of rude comments and distasteful personal beliefs, that racism's structural aspects are no longer an issue. Zoeller's comment about what foods Tiger Woods might request for his celebratory dinner after winning the Masters is unpleasant, but it does not change the fact of Tiger Woods's success. If anything, it makes Zoeller look foolish. The episode does not reference, however, Woods's stories of having repeatedly been kicked off golf courses and of once having been tied to a tree and had rocks thrown at him (Couch). Except for a few disturbed individuals such as Frances Houston, the episode suggests, Americans have overcome any significant or widespread, systemic racism.[28]

The racial politics of "Blood" are more complex than those of "Are You Now," but are also ultimately more conservative, which may reflect a more intense contest around shifting racial definitions in the late 1990s, one that may have been closer to resolution by 2000. Though *Law & Order*'s passing episode seems to share, for the most part, the *Angel* episode's desire to represent racism as an issue that has little significance for the present, "Blood" does at least acknowledge, if only peripherally, that racism exists in its present. Yet while it alternately dismisses or condemns that racism, its own commitment to maintaining a racial order governed by the one-drop rule is more overt. Though the racist murderer goes to jail, in the course of her trial Josh Burdett and his son David have been exposed for what they "are," and very publicly have been moved back to the black side of the color line. For all its concern with maintaining the color line, "Blood" is strangely unconcerned with the fate of Burdett's children, who are generally of such concern to mulatto fiction because they represent potential future transgressions of the color line. Baby Maggie's race is never in question, due to her visibly "black" skin tone and features, but the episode never resolves whether she will remain with her adoptive parents or return to Burdett's custody. This is especially odd given that her birth and her mother's desire to reclaim her are the impetus for the entire plot line. Similarly, though his mother is allegedly fighting to protect him from racism (everyone's except her own) we never learn how the discovery of his black ancestry affects young David Burdett. His only expression in the courtroom is his pathetic mien. Even if it is not willing to acknowledge exactly how, the show represents blackness as something that matters, whether we can see it or not.

Races are defined by their borders. Consequently, stories of those who threaten or defy those boundaries tend to emerge in moments of heightened racial tension, particularly during major transitions in the definition of racial categories and/or the organization of racial hierarchy. Though no longer explicitly didactic or even overtly political like their nineteenth-century literary forebears, these television episodes are, like them, meant to appeal to a broad audience and, like them, are expressive of the tensions of their cultural moment. The tensions, it would seem, are new: the possibility of a truly multiracial identification, maybe even heralding the collapse of racial categories altogether, has never been so promising. Of course, the idea of an America with no racial boundaries is not new. Charles Chesnutt famously discoursed on this possibility in his series of articles, "The Future American." We are much closer to this situation now than we were in Chesnutt's time, but we are certainly not living in a color-blind society. Given the positive value that racial identity holds for many, the abandonment of racial categorization altogether might not even be desirable. What was new and, I think, positive, at the turn of the twentieth century is the degree to which the U.S. government, at least, was willing to acknowledge the permeability of racial categories and the right of individuals to craft their own racial definitions.

I would suggest that, in the 1990s, the answer to the question posed by my title was still generally "no," one cannot choose one's race—at least not if that choice diverges from the one-drop rule—*and* expect others to affirm that self-identification. Despite our pretenses to racial liberalism, indicated in part by the shifting of racial discourse signified by the popularity of terms such as *multiculturalism, ethnicity,* and *diversity,* we still seem to believe that "blood will out," at least to the extent that we still obsessively work to track and to label it. Will the new millennium be any different? Perhaps. One could argue that the greater optimism of the *Angel* episode, as compared to the *Law & Order* episode, represents a sort of progress that took place in the years between 1997 and 2000. Perhaps people needed time to adjust to the idea of multiracial identification as put forward both by the Census board and by Tiger Woods. Certainly, Vin Diesel, who likes to call himself "the first multiracial movie star," seems to be much more successful at claiming a multiracial identity than was Tiger Woods (Udovich 162).[29] Another example is the interesting case of Wentworth Miller, most recently known for his starring role on Fox's television series *Prison Break.* Miller, whose racial and ethnic heritages include African American, Jamaican, Native American (Cherokee), German, English, Jewish, Russian, French, Dutch, Lebanese, and Syrian, also played the role of the young Coleman Silk in the 2003 film version of Philip Roth's passing novel *The Human Stain,* published in 2000 ("Wentworth Miller"). During his audition for the part, Miller mentioned that he felt personally connected to the part because, as he said, "I'm a minority" (Paumgarten). His manager later called to tell him that the casting directors would like to have him back, but: "They want to make sure you are who you say you are" (Paumgarten). "So," writes Paumgarten, "Miller went to Kinko's and made color copies of family photographs." He got the part. Finally, as we contemplate America's relationship to racial liberalism—if we might allow that the ability to define oneself racially could be considered an index of this—we might remember that America's "first black president," is also a first-generation multiracial. We could certainly celebrate the fact that America also has its first multiracial president, but the general invisibility of this label suggests that the American racial system has not changed all that much.

Notes

1. The episode, "Are You Now or Have You Ever Been?" first aired on October 3, 2000, as the second episode of *Angel*'s second season. The series aired on the WB from October 5, 1999, through May 19, 2004.

2. "Blood" first aired on November 19, 1997, as episode 7 of season 8. The original *Law & Order* series aired on NBC from September 13, 1990, through May 24, 2010.

3. In 1662, Virginia passed its first law "designed to discourage miscegenation and to relegate mulattoes to an inferior position," establishing in the process the now-famous principle of the American system of chattel slavery of children following the condition of the mother, which broke with English common law tradition (Williamson 8). Maryland followed with a similar statute in 1664 (Williamson 10). Such laws quickly proliferated.

4. F. James Davis notes that, though other countries often assign mixed-race people a subordinate status, the extremity of the one-drop rule—the idea that any amount of "black blood" could make one black—is only applied to blacks and is unique to the United States (13). Despite the dominance the one-drop rule came to have in the court of public opinion, it never became a uniform *legal* standard. For example, in 1785, Virginia defined a "Negro" as a person with "a black parent or grandparent" which is a far less stringent definition than the one-drop rule (Williamson 13). Daniel J. Sharfstein recently argued that identifying a person's race was often not as easy as the one-drop rule suggests: courts and publics negotiated individual cases of racial identity based on how a person functioned already in the community—with the court sometimes implicitly deferring to the community through their interpretation of how race laws were written—partially because too strict adherence to a one-drop rule would destabilize the "white" community (8–9). Another obvious marker that the one-drop rule was not codified nationally is that from 1850 to 1920, the U.S. Census did include a "mulatto" category (Williamson xii). However, "mulattoes" were considered people of color (usually, black) and excluded from any claim to whiteness, demonstrating the de facto power of the one-drop rule, even when not codified de jure.

5. In addition to Virginia, those states were: "Alabama, Arkansas, Delaware, Florida, Georgia, Kentucky, Louisiana, Mississippi, Missouri, North Carolina, Oklahoma, South Carolina, Tennessee, Texas, and West Virginia" (Zack 77). Twenty-two other states had antimiscegenation laws that were no longer in force in 1967 (Zack 77). Louisiana finally "relaxed" its legal standards for defining blackness from one drop to one thirty-second in 1970 after a successful challenge "on behalf of a child whose ancestry was allegedly only one two-hundred-fifty-sixth black"

(Davis 9). The last two states to remove miscegenation provisions from their state constitutions were South Carolina (in 1997) and Alabama (in 2000) (Pascoe 5). For an in-depth study of the history of miscegenation law in the United States, see Pascoe's *What Comes Naturally: Miscegenation Law and the Making of Race in America* (2009).

6. Nancy Brown and Ramona Douglass claim that the birthrate of multiracial individuals has grown astronomically since the Supreme Court decision *Loving v. Virginia* (1967) declared laws against interracial marriage unconstitutional (Brown and Douglass 325). The numbers, however, are still low relative to the total U.S. population. According to data from Census 2000, the population reporting "two or more races" was still only 2.4 percent of the total population (Jones and Smith 7). The median age of this population was 22.7, compared to the median age for the population reporting only one race, which is 35.6 (Meyer 4). This suggests that expansion of the self-consciously multiracial population is, indeed, a recent phenomenon.

7. The responses of multiracial people—both on a creative individual basis and in various collectivities—to their limited identity options in America's "choose one box only" system have been addressed by several of the excellent essays in Maria P. P. Root's anthology *The Multiracial Experience.*

8. One might even say that such a shift was an important precursor of the election of America's first "black" president. President Barack Obama makes no secret of his multiracial identity, but in the discourse surrounding his race, he is primarily described as a black man. Although some have suggested that Obama is not black enough (see, for instance, Debra Dickerson's challenge that because Obama's ancestry does not involve a history of American enslavement, that he is somehow "less black" than other American blacks), under the one-drop rule having a white mother does not change the "fact" of his blackness. Either as a black man or a biracial one, his election is significant and does indicate some progress in terms of race relations. However, it by no means indicates that we live in a color-blind or post-racial world.

9. Davis discusses at length the reasons why the African American community continues to have a vested interest in the one-drop rule. See especially chapter 6: "Black Acceptance of the Rule" (123–39).

10. See, for example, Joanne Jacobs's article, "Mixing of Races Makes Categories Obsolete," published in the *Tampa Tribune* on July 16, 1997, and Gregory Kane's article, "Push for 'Multiracial' Label Gives Rise to Suspicions Among Blacks," published in the same paper two days later.

11. My discussion of the mulatto figure in American literature is necessarily brief and focuses on general trends in the literature. For a variety of readings on the mulatto figure, see Werner Sollors's edited collection *Interracialism: Black-White Intermarriage in American History, Literature, and Law* (2000); and Judith Berzon's foundational *Neither White Nor Black: The Mulatto Character in American Fiction* (1978).

12. About the denouement of these narratives, Judith Berzon, who wrote the first full-length study of mulatto fiction, writes, "Death through grief, murder, childbirth, abortion, and suicide; life with remorse, despair, bitterness, alienation, and insanity; this is the catalogue of tortures that are endured by various tragic mulatto characters" (102). More recently, Sollors also notes two main trends in the denouements of mulatto fiction: "Versions in the tragic mode tend to have endings in irresolvable conflicts and often in death—frequently violent death inflicted by others, suicide, or heartbreak—and those in the comic mode are likely to end with the reign of law, a marriage (often in 'a world elsewhere') and the realization or at least the promise of a descent line that will continue the story into the future" (*Neither* 337). In the *Angel* episode, we see the familiar ending in death. The *Law and Order* episode is more open-ended.

13. Zack writes, "After the Civil War, the tragic mulatto becomes the noble mulatto who gave up the opportunity to pass for white in order to benefit less culturally privileged, darker-skinned, designated black people. In fiction written by blacks, duty and decency required that the person of mixed race identify with blacks" (129).

14. While some episodes return to important moments in Angel's past, very few feature such extended flashbacks as this one and many episodes are set entirely in the present. This anomaly is significant, because it is one of the key ways in which the episode seeks to place racism squarely in the past.

15. Melissa Marsala, the actress who plays Judy, has golden-toned skin and dark hair; no information about her race is given on IMDb. She is simply identified as an "American actress." Her surname is Italian; a few unofficial Web sites list her as "Latino."

16. A discussion of the general impact of television as a medium on viewers is outside the scope of this argument, but I do want to highlight how visual media such as television or film "illustrates" racial difference—or the lack thereof—as written on the body quite graphically. As is the case here, these media can alter a character's skin through cosmetics, lighting, or graphics. Elspeth Kydd, for instance, notes how lighting codes are used to manipulate the audience's understanding of the mulatto character in the famous passing film, *Pinky* (1949). Or, as we will see in the *Law & Order* episode, television can use tricks of the medium to superimpose images of blackness on characters in ways that print media cannot.

17. Entrenched beliefs about the physicality of race and the power of a "racial genius" to determine both physical and character type led to bizarre hypotheses about effect of racial mixing on the mulatto's body (Zack 120–21). According to Naomi Zack, "Neurologists claimed there were electrical currents in the human body that flowed in one direction in black people and in the opposite direction in white people" (123). Other scientists hypothesized that "multiracial people might have circulatory systems too long or big for their bodies, arms and legs that are not compatible in length, and teeth too big or too small for their

mouths" (Nakashima 170). Paradoxically, mulattoes were also further represented both as hypersexual and as sterile.

18. Judy also implies that she may not be "legitimate" in another sense, given her claim that she didn't know her father. Illegitimacy is another familiar trope of the mulatto. It stems from laws (and/or taboos) against interracial marriage that keep the inheritance of white privilege in "purely" and legitimately white hands.

19. For a discussion of whiteness and white privilege as forms of property see Harris; and Lipsitz.

20. This move resembles that of Lucas Burch in William Faulkner's novel *Light in August*. Suspected of murder and of dubious origins himself, Burch deflects this suspicion on both counts by "outing" his roommate, Joe Christmas, as a passer.

21. To *Law & Order*'s popularity: the series ran for twenty years on NBC, and spawned four spin-offs, several video games, and a made-for-television movie. It had millions of viewers annually in the eighteen to forty-nine-year-old category. In comparison, *Angel*—itself a spin-off—ran for only five years and had a turbulent history with a smaller network and a smaller target demographic of twenty-five to thirty-five-year-olds (Abbott 5–8).

22. See, for example, Eva Saks, who writes, "The conception of the race-marked body as a readable text which represented race and, upon fulfillment of the relevant conditions, crime, is a recurrent motif in the case law of miscegenation. However, the problem with this new body-text was that it pointed not to blood, not to race, not to dispositive unmediated proof, but instead led the court only to other texts: to the body-texts of the defendant's family, in the title search for blood—parents, as in *Weaver v. State* (Ala. 1928), or children, as in *Agnew v. State* (Ala. 1921)" (75). In the infamous *Rhinelander* case, Leonard Rhinelander's attorney uses the same method for the opposite purpose. He points out the white features of Alice Rhinelander's father, betrayed only by the darkness of his skin, to argue that his whiter daughter, Alice, surely deceived her husband into thinking she was white (Wacks 173).

23. Though recessive genes do sometimes combine to produce traits not present in either parent, the fear of atavism in the Jim Crow era exaggerated this possibility out of all proportion. Robert Lee Durham's virulently racist 1908 novel *The Call of the South* offers a vivid example of both forms of the nightmare fantasy of atavism. In this novel, the all-but-white hero Hayward Graham is depicted in apparently sympathetic terms until the night when, almost literally possessed by "the demon of the blood of [his grandfather] Guinea Gumbo," he rapes his white wife (qtd. in Berzon 33). She subsequently bears a dark-skinned baby whose features are "a horrible travesty" of his white mother's in combination, not with the father's, but with those of Guinea Gumbo (qtd. in Berzon 34). The mother goes mad, tormented by the idea that she has been polluted by the "black blood" of her baby (Berzon 34).

24. J. Michael Duvall and Julie Cary Nerad further suggest that there is a specifically gendered dynamic to the racial and sexual discipline in play here. They argue that though the threat of atavism was fairly common in turn-of-the-twentieth-century mulatto fiction, "the punishment of bearing a grotesquely atavistic child was reserved for the more transgressive—and less fictionally frequent—black male/white female couplings: white women risk insanity and/or death if they procreate with black men because the act of bearing a black child threatens the very existence of whiteness" (Duvall and Nerad 56).

25. No information is available on IMDb about the race of Stephen Mendillo, the actor who plays Josh Burdett, but in his publicity photo, his skin is fair, his complexion is even a bit ruddy. The impulse to determine even the race of an actor playing a passer, as I will discuss further below, shows how thoroughly steeped we all are in the one-drop rule and in discourses of racial authenticity tied to blood. There is a long history of discussion around the politics of the race of actors relative to the race of characters, one that becomes particularly vexed in connection with the subject of passing, but extended engagement with that discussion is beyond the scope of this article.

26. See Robinson for more on the idea of the "in-group clairvoyant" in relation to passing (716).

27. I do not wish to overstate the possibility of Josh's self-identification as white. The episode does not explore the nuance of whether Josh truly identifies as a white man, given his phenotype and the majority of his genealogy, or whether he understands himself as a black man who chooses to take advantage of white privilege with the help of his phenotype. The latter is implied when he is on the stand, but as I note later, the life he has lived as a white man for several decades is evidently irrelevant once his black ancestry is made known.

28. Also worth noting here is the fact that both the fictional Houston and the real life Zoeller are applying the one-drop rule by reading Woods simply as black.

29. In the early years of the twenty-first century, several popular magazines published features on Vin Diesel, including *GQ* (Brodie) and *Details* (Udovich) and *Savoy* (Robertson). Unlike the scorn for Tiger Woods, which was more virulent in black communities, approval of Vin Diesel (who does not "look" as black as Tiger) seems to cross the color line. *GQ* and *Details* mainly target white readers and *Savoy* mainly targets black readers, yet all three depict Diesel positively. Robertson, the journalist at *Savoy*, calls Diesel "the chameleon," implicitly inserting him into a line of black trickster figures without ever challenging Diesel's self-labeling as multiracial (56–59). Robertson points out that both black and white moviegoers have claimed him as their own. "Who's right?" Robertson writes, "Is Vin Diesel black, Italian, Hispanic or maybe Jewish? (He has played or is slated to play, three of those ethnicities in various films.) Or is he the Tiger Woods of Hollywood—kickin' butt and taking our minds off the race labels we Americans cling to so tightly" (58).

Works Cited

Abbott, Stacey. *Angel.* Detroit: Wayne State UP, 2009. Print.

"Angel." *IMDb.* IMDb.com, Inc. n.d. Web. 10 Aug. 2011.

"Are You Now or Have You Ever Been?" *Angel.* Warner Brothers Network. 3 Oct. 2000.

Berzon, Judith R. *Neither White Nor Black: The Mulatto Character in American Fiction.* New York: New York UP, 1978. Print.

"Blood." *Law & Order.* NBC. LEX18. Lexington, KY. 19 Nov. 1997.

Bone, Robert. *The Negro Novel in America.* 1958. Rev. ed. New Haven: Yale UP, 1970. Print.

Brodie, John. "Diesel Power: Vin Diesel Muscles His Way to Stardom." *Gentlemen's Quarterly.* Aug. 2002: 109–13, 179. Print.

Brown, Nancy G., and Ramona E. Douglass. "Making the Invisible Visible: The Growth of Community Network Organizations." *The Multiracial Experience: Racial Borders as the New Frontier.* Thousand Oaks, CA: Sage, 1996. Print.

Chesnutt, Charles W. "The Future American: What the Race Is Likely to Become in the Process of Time." *MELUS* 15.3 (1988): 95–107. Web. 23 March 2011.

Couch, Greg. "Woods: I'm More than Black." *Chicago Sun Times.* 22 Apr. 1997, late sports final ed.: News 1. *Lexis-Nexis.* Web. 2 Dec. 2004.

Davis, F. James. *Who is Black? One Nation's Definition.* University Park: Pennsylvania State UP, 1991. Print.

Dawkins, Laura. "Black Babies, White Hysteria: The Dark Child in African-American Literature of the Harlem Renaissance." *The American Child: A Cultural Studies Reader.* Ed. Caroline F. Levander and Carol J. Singley. New Brunswick: Rutgers UP, 2003. Print.

Dickerson, Debra. "Colorblind." *Salon.* 22 Jan. 2007: n. p. Web. 5 Jan. 2009.

Durham, Robert Lee. *The Call of the South.* Boston: L. C. Page, 1908. Print.

Duvall, J. Michael, and Julie Cary Nerad. "'Suddenly and Shockingly Black': The Atavistic Child in Turn-into-the-Twentieth-Century American Fiction." *African American Review* 46.1 (2007): 51–66. Web.

Faulkner, William. *Light in August.* 1932. New York: Vintage International, 1990. Print.

Harris, Cheryl I. "Whiteness as Property." *Harvard Law Review* 106.8 (June 1993): 1710–91. Print.

Jacobs, Joanne. "Mixing of Races Makes Categories Obsolete." *Tampa Tribune.* 16 July 1997, final ed., Nation/World 7. *Lexis-Nexis.* Web. 2 Dec. 2004.

Jones, Nicholas A., and Amy Symens Smith. *The Two or More Races Population: 2000.* U.S. Census Bureau. Washington, DC: GPO, 2001. Web.

Kane, Gregory P. "Push for 'Multiracial' Label Gives Rise to Suspicions Among Blacks." *Tampa Tribune.* 18 July 1997, final ed., Nation/World: 13. *Lexis-Nexis.* Web. 2 Dec. 2004.

Kydd, Elspeth. "'The Ineffaceable Curse of Cain': Racial Marking and Embodiment in *Pinky.*" *Camera Obscura* 43.15 (2000): 95–121. Print.

"Law & Order." *IMDb.* IMDb.com, Inc. n.d. Web. 10 Aug. 2011.

Lipsitz, George. *The Possessive Investment in Whiteness: How White People Profit from Identity Politics.* Revised ed. Philadelphia: Temple UP, 2006. Print.

Meyer, Julie. *Age: 2000.* U.S. Census Bureau. Washington, DC: GPO, 2001. Web.

Millner, Denene. "In Creating a Word to Describe His Racial Makeup, Golfer Tiger Woods Has Also Stirred up a Round of Controversy Among Blacks." *New York Daily News.* 8 June 1997, Sunday Extra: 2. *Lexis-Nexis.* Web. 2 Dec. 2004.

Nakashima, Cynthia L. "An Invisible Monster: The Creation and Denial of Mixed-Race People in America." *Racially Mixed People in America.* Ed. Maria P. P. Root. Newbury Park: Sage, 1992. 162–80. Print.

Pascoe, Peggy. *What Comes Naturally: Miscegenation Law and the Making of Race in America.* New York: Oxford UP, 2009. Print.

Paumgarten, Nick. "Central Casting: The Race Card." *The New Yorker.* 10 Nov. 2003. CondéNet. Web. 2 Mar. 2007.

Pitts, Leonard. "It Comes Down to This: Black Matters." *Buffalo News.* 28 Apr. 1997, city ed.: Viewpoints 3B. *Lexis-Nexis.* Web. 2 Dec. 2004.

Robertson, Gil. "The Chameleon." *Savoy.* Sept. 2002. 56–59. Print.

Robinson, Amy. "It Takes One to Know One: 'Passing' and Communities of Common Interest." *Critical Inquiry* 20.4 (1994): 715–36. Print.

Root, Maria P. P. *The Multiracial Experience: Racial Borders as the New Frontier.* Newbury Park: Sage, 1996. Print.

Saks, Eva. "Representing Miscegenation Law." In Sollors, *Interracialism* 61–80. Print.

Sharfstein, Daniel J. *The Invisible Line: Three American Families and the Secret Journey from Black to White.* New York: Penguin, 2011. Print.

Sollors, Werner. *Neither Black Nor White Yet Both: Thematic Explorations of Interracial Literature.* Cambridge: Harvard UP, 1997. Print.

———, ed. *Interracialism: Black-White Intermarriage in American History, Literature, and Law.* New York: Oxford UP, 2000. Print.

"Tiger Woods Profile." *CNN.com.* 2001. Cable News Network. n.d. Web. 20 June 2008.

Udovitch, Mim. "Vin Diesel Shows His True Colors." *Details.* June/July 2004. 158–62. Print.

Wacks, Jamie L. "Reading Race, Rhetoric, and the Female Body in the *Rhinelander* Case." In Sollors, *Interracialism* 162–77. Print.

"Wentworth Miller." *Wikipedia.* Wikipedia: The Free Encyclopedia. 20 June 2008. Web. 23 June 2008.

Williamson, Joel. *New People: Miscegenation and Mulattoes in the United States.* Baton Rouge: Louisiana State UP, 1980. Print.

Zack, Naomi. *Race and Mixed Race.* Philadelphia: Temple UP, 1993. Print.

Zanger, Jules. "The 'Tragic Octoroon' in Pre–Civil War Fiction." In Sollors, *Interracialism* 284–90.

5

Passing in Blackface

The Intimate Drama of Post-Racialism on *Black. White.*

Eden Osucha

And my TV's always off, 'cause I see something truly Black then.

—from "Black Dialogue," a 2005 song by The Perceptionists

Prior to his election as the forty-fourth U.S. president, media depictions of then-candidate Barack Obama were frequently dominated by the question of what his candidacy meant for the durability of "race" in America. This question framed the historic election as a symbolic referendum on race-conscious identity politics. Even prior to the election, the idea that America is now a "post-racial" nation had taken hold in the popular imagination as a form of cultural common sense.[1] Writing at the time of the campaign, historian David Roediger summarizes this viewpoint as the conviction that "race is almost spent as a social force in the United States, eliminated by symbolic advances, demographic changes, and private choices, if not by structural transformations or political struggles," adding that "[n]owhere is that argument more forcefully, or more contradictorily, made than in analyses of Barack Obama's campaign for president" (B6).

If the 2008 presidential election seemed to ratify "post-racial" presupposition, its status as an emblem of racial transcendence reflects a general belief in the transformative effects of public institutions—the idea that even symbolic changes affecting the American presidency, such as the election of an African American to that office, not only reverberate across the broader culture but also reflect and concretize social change already underway. More specifically, it points to how "race" in the United States "is a matter of collectivity, of the formation of social structures: economic, political and cultural/ideological" (Omi and Winant 58). However, critical race theorists Michael Omi and Howard Winant, from whose influential account I am quoting, distinguish this "macro-level" of "racial formation" from the more intimate registers of a "micro-level" at which race coordinates the social order—that is, "the ways in which we understand ourselves and interact with others" (66).[2]

At this writing, the current discourse of "post-racialism" is largely keyed to a historical narrative in which the figure of Obama is dramatically, if contradictorily, central. The fact of his presidency grounds popular claims about the irrelevance of race as a political or social category. Yet the very claim itself reflects a continued investment in racial blackness as a coherent form of social interpellation, in as much as this president's African American identity is its linchpin. The contradictions that frame the post-racial construction of the Obama presidency dissolve at the "micro-level"—to borrow Omi and Winant's usage—where individual citizens connect with this broader national narrative as a reflection of their own self-understanding. In other words, although the contradictions of the post-racial ideological position, as Roediger, among many others, has suggested, become glaringly apparent in the popular responses to the figure of Obama, at the "micro-level" what seems to be an argument about history simply "makes sense" as a way of thinking about what racial identity means to people personally. ("Our Obama, Ourselves," if you will.)

Just prior to the announcement of Obama's campaign, a popular media text appeared that can be seen as rehearsing the popular response to the presidency and the tensions within by purporting to explore the American experience of "race" precisely in terms of Omi and Winant's micro-level model—that is, "race" construed as a matter of individual identity and individualized social relations. The 2006 reality-based FX network miniseries *Black.White.* was a show built around a structured experiment in cosmetically enhanced racial passing. Its basic plot premise is that for six weeks, an African American family and a white family—each consisting of a mother, father figure, and teenage child—would interact with each other as their "real" racial selves in private, while publicly "exchanging" racial identities via a sophisticated arsenal of special effects make-up artistry and prosthetics.

While at the time of its airing, its provocative conceit seemed entirely new, and even (intentionally) shocking to some viewers, *Black. White.*, as I will discuss later in detail, borrows from a number of generic conventions that have become staples of reality-based entertainment programming. Most centrally, and most significantly for my analysis, it is rooted in the popular trope of the multiracial reality television cast. Partly a legacy of recent histories in fictional programming—namely, late 1980s and 1990s multiracial workplace dramas such as *ER* and *LA Law*—the multiracial cast has become a consistent feature of reality-based television, a form that dominates today's media culture. Across its various genres, multiracial casting enables shows ranging from *The Bachelorette* to *Top Chef* simultaneously to acknowledge a socially diverse American reality and to disavow that difference as a relevant subject. Not infrequently, racial difference is used on reality-based television as a staging ground for interpersonal conflicts—a staple of such programming. The additional factor of racial difference in conflicts between cast members is used to frame these events as something more than entertainment spectacle; inviting viewers to also see these interpersonal clashes as depictions of interracial conflict, shows use such instances to index their social realism.[3] In other words, these scenes help make reality television seem more realistic. Yet, in this kind of narrative framing, produced via the laborious editing process behind these shows' story arcs, if the specter of racism emerges in an interaction between a white character and one of her nonwhite fellow cast members, it is subtly (or not so subtly) ascribed to the person of color's own skepticism, paranoia, or churlishness. This is a perfect mirror of post-racial logics. Race on reality television can be used as a measure of realism in terms that, paradoxically, cast race consciousness and racism as irrelevant or, indeed, unrealistic.

On *Black. White.*, these kinds of exchanges between characters were not incidental to its plotline but the very point and premise. In this way, the show seems to position itself outside of reality-based television's dominant discourse of post-racialism by taking up racial identity and its continued social relevance as its central themes. *Black. White.*'s very premise is built around the idea that race is a significant factor in American lives, shaping cultural experience and social and economic possibilities. In what follows, I discuss the show and its dramatization of the "micro-level" of racial production (that is to say, the production of racial meaning at the level of social interaction and self-understanding). I argue that, in spite of its stated investments, the show ultimately enacts post-racialism by positing a formal and essential equivalence between black and white racial identities while, at the same time, disproportionately burdening racial blackness as the site of its production of "race" as both televisual spectacle and discourse. This essentially asymmetrical coding of black and white racial identities on *Black.White.* in large part reflects the peculiar way in which the show's depiction of racial passing invokes a quite different historical form of "crossing the line": blackface performance. Through this uncanny convergence, the series anticipates many of the terms by which, as a public figure, Obama's blackness would come to be simultaneously hypostatized and deeply unsettled in the discourses surrounding first his campaign and, later, his presidency.

Both groups of participants on *Black.White.* describe their families as "normal" or "average" and "suburban" and "middle-class," but their shared identificatory position belies key differences that have nothing to do with their different racial identities yet which contribute to the signification of race on the show. The African American family, from Atlanta, Georgia, consists of Brian and Renée Sparks and their sixteen-year-old son Nick. In the course of *Black.White.,* it emerges that the parents' primary motivation for being a part of the show is their son, who has had serious trouble in school, twice failing grade levels and socializing with a friend group his parents describe as "thuggish." Brian's and Renée's explicit hope is that, by participating in the show's social experiment, Nick will mature into a more responsible and socially aware young person.

In contrast to the Sparkses, the show's white characters are not a traditional nuclear family unit—a discrepancy that goes unremarked on *Black. White.* This omission is curious given that the structural equivalence—each has two "parents" and a child"—between the families is central to the show's social experiment. Called "the Wurgel family" on the show, a label that masks the families' different arrangements, the white participants comprise Carmen Wurgel, her teenage daughter Rose Bloomfield, and Carmen's live-in boyfriend Bruno Marcotulli. All three "Wurgels" have professional ties to the Los Angeles–based entertainment industry, which suggests that their involvement with the series stemmed from those connections. The Sparks family, on the other hand, was cast in the series following an open audition process that included hundreds of other African American families. The Sparkses are a "real" family cast from a pool of similar families; in their casting process and their post–nuclear family arrangement, the white Wurgels present a less "authentic" picture.

After undergoing cosmetic makeovers that remade the families in the image of each other's racial identities, participants were periodically made to inhabit social spaces coded on the show as racially specific. For example, a suburban sports bar with what appears to be an all-white clientele and staff is presented as a "white" space that Brian surreptitiously inhabits, working behind the bar while wearing his white-face disguise. As his "black" self, Bruno was filmed strolling through a public park that screen captioning informs viewers is part of the historically African American Los Angeles neighborhood of "South Central L.A." For the two teenaged cast members, their racial reassignments targeted cultural spaces that were not only racially specific but delimited by adolescent membership: a slam poetry workshop in which the leader and all the other participants were African American and a social etiquette class in which wealthy white teenagers learn to acquire the manners and comportment deemed appropriate to their social class. In entering these social spaces, cast members concealed their own racial identities and their participation in the show, aiming to have their racial masquerade accepted as authentic in order to experience and gain insight into social realities that they would not have access to otherwise. In short, they hoped to "learn what it's like to be [black or white]."[4]

Part of what makes *Black.White.* so interesting as a text for exploring representational dilemmas about and cultural understandings of race in a United States on the cusp of post-racialism's rise as a central term of national self-understanding is that the show explicitly promises both edifying social documentary *and* reality-based entertainment, genres that we commonly understand as somewhat antithetical. As Susan Murray notes, "Documentary is seen as a valid and productive social as well as artistic endeavor, while reality TV is often vilified or dismissed" (68). Murray, among other scholars of documentary film and television, argues that these categorical distinctions are inherently unstable. Thus, the assignment of a program to either category is less a function of intrinsic textual markers of "social weight" or "artistic endeavor" than it is of extratextual markers related to the commercial and reception context—including, importantly, whether a show is advertised in ways that stress its value as socially redeeming documentary, or as entertaining reality TV.

In media interviews promoting the show before the premiere episode, the creators of *Black.White.* differentiated their series from other reality television programming by claiming that the pedagogical and therapeutic project at its core is directed at the audience as much as at the on-screen participants. Series creator R. J. Cutler promoted the show as a "premise documentary" intended to spark dialogue about race, which Cutler termed both "the central defining issue in American society and history . . . something that doesn't get spoken about" (Lee E1). Similarly, the hip hop artist and actor Ice Cube, who in addition to producing also gave the series its theme song, said that the show was intended to give viewers a presumably nonconfrontational reason to talk about race across racial lines—at work or school—to "learn a lot more about each other and maybe deal with some of the issues" (Lee E1). Their series, in other words, is offered as a vehicle to facilitate a productive discussion of real world "issues" stemming from racial difference.[5]

The structure of the show itself, however, works against such attempts to elevate the show to the status of a "documentary"—efforts that included an extensive media campaign in advance of its premiere and the show's evidently high production value. Murray argues that with "a generically unstable program" such as *Black. White.,* which seems to be in some ways a documentary and in some ways reality television, the "success of [the] rhetorical framing is contingent on an audience's preconceived ideas about the functions of that genre. . . . [T]extual signifiers commingle with present and past extratextual generic discourses to generate spectator positioning" (Murray 54). Regardless of the rhetorical framing of *Black. White.* as a "documentary," it is replete with "textual signifiers"—such as the passing premise or the group living arrangements—that gesture toward the "extratextual generic discourses" of reality TV.

Specifically, *Black. White.*'s unique premise shares generic conventions common to many reality television series, blending elements of the makeover show, the undercover show, and the fish-out-of-water show. All of these shows—staples of reality-based programming—are rooted in cultural narratives of passing or masquerade. As critic Gina Bellafante argues, the trope of passing, with its "hold . . . on the American psyche," has become a defining trait of reality-based television:

> If reality television can be said to be about anything at all, it seems to be about impersonation. . . . The crooked-nosed are made over and play the genetically good-looking. Heiresses get out of their $200,000 sports cars and enact the habits of the agriculturally inclined. A vegan mother from Boulder trades houses with an evangelical wife in Mobile, is encouraged to care about scripture and breakfast sausage, and essentially tries to pass. (Bellafante E8)[6]

Neither the makeover nor the "fish out of water" shows dramatizes passing in a traditional sense: there is no surreptitious attempt to infiltrate a singular in-group, to have oneself deliberately mistaken for what one "is not."

But staged in these types of shows are small dramas of identity transformation and of the negotiation of unfamiliar social contexts that illustrate principal psychological and intersubjective aspects of passing. Which is to say, they explore dimensions of passing at Omi and Winant's micro-level of racial experience—"the ways in which we understand ourselves and interact with others."[7] The experiments in identity trading or transformation undertaken on these shows, Bellafante suggests, all involve attempts to pass as "other," irrespective of whether a particular show's narrative structure foregrounds the conceit of the pass—as in a show such as *The Simple Life*—or conceals it—as in *Secret Millionaire.*

The trope of passing provides a particularly useful framework for considering how *Black.White.* operates as a form of reality entertainment that also purports to educate its audience by exploring the function and meaning of race in what the show's creators paradoxically describe as a color-blind, race-conscious culture. Put differently, the show *itself* is reality television attempting to pass as documentary—popular entertainment packaged as socially edifying educational media. This generic pass allows its audience to witness the *spectacle* of blackness as the spectacle of "race" writ broadly. The position of spectatorship generated by the show's formal alignment with reality-based television programming inclines toward a treatment of "blackness" as televisual spectacle rather than documentary viewpoint (a disposition that becomes manifest, as I later discuss, in the racial masquerade of the white Wurgels). This tendency, as Sasha Torres points out, serves to index "realness" in contemporary televisual representation. Torres argues that televisual authenticity and its mediated representation as "liveness" is historically linked to the production of TV "race" as a discourse of intrinsic reality. Within what Torres describes as the "liberal" tradition of African American representation in American popular culture, "a certain documentary or ethnographic impulse, an imperative to 'authenticity' " is integral to the representation of blackness" (13).[8]

Black.White. involves a rather sophisticated conflation of three forms of racial performance, all of which have historically been linked to the production of "blackness": the racial passing narrative, racial masquerade, and blackface minstrelsy. (Significantly, for the purposes of my argument, all three forms "belong" to a past that post-racialism purports to have transcended.) In literature, as Sonnet Retman observes, the passing narrative "subverts basic epistemological assumptions about race and identity [by] unmask[ing] the juridical, economic, and social structures of race" (1452).[9] On *Black.White.*, the subversive possibilities the literary genre ascribes to the representation of passing are precluded by how the show's televisual representations of this practice depend upon racial masquerade and derive from the tradition of blackface minstrelsy. Unlike the social, lived practice of racial passing, which is characterized by the surreptitious nature of the pass, literary representations of passing conventionally work to denaturalize racial difference, along the lines of Retman's formulation, by drawing readers' attention to the performativity of race. This gesture operates primarily through the passers' phenotypic likeness to the group they wish to pass into. This phenotypic sameness is the element of racial passing that most destabilizes the idea of innate biological race difference.

Unable to pass phenotypically, the participants on *Black.White.* must instead don racial disguises. Thus, their passing is always and already mediated by the audience's awareness that they are performing a racial identity that their physical bodies do not warrant, and as a consequence, they cannot function in the same way as the traditional passing subject. Instead, their performance crosses into the realm of blackface and racial masquerade. The various elements of the disguises that transform the white Carmen, Rose, and Bruno into apparent African Americans include afro wigs, hair extensions, facial prosthetics, and cosmetic technologies that color their skin an extremely dark shade of brown.

Although the grotesque exaggerations associated with the spectacular blackness of blackface minstrelsy in its more traditional guise are not directly in *Black.White.*, its effects are easily legible in the white Wurgel family's racial performance. The racial disguises for the black Sparkses are less dramatic, although they too include wigs and cosmetics. However, the Sparkses' appearances in what might be termed "whiteface" are readily interpretable as an image of light-skinned African Americans. In the composite portrait that FX circulated widely to promote the show, which compares the "four" families among its cast—the white Wurgels, the "black" Wurgels, the African American Sparkses, and the "white" Sparkses—it could be argued that the only unambiguously "white" family in the image is that of the Wurgels.

As the racial exchange of the literary passing plot does for the external audience, blackface, as spectacle entertainment, highlights for the audience the racial performance it enacts; however, it does so by virtue of the stark unnaturalness of the physiognomies drawn in its ultimately phantasmatic likeness. At the level of individual embodiment, it was also historically (though not always) a means of "crossing" the color line. However, literary narratives of passing and blackface entertainment spectacle comprise diametrically opposed teleologies of racial performance. The effects of blackface's transparency—that is the "fakeness" of its black looks—are linked to a very different set of ends. If the passing narrative can be said to materialize the codes of racial identity in order to denaturalize racial difference, blackface has the opposite effect—reproducing a set of transparently unnatural codes in order to naturalize that difference and inflect blackness as an object of white enjoyment.

On *Black. White.*, these two seemingly counterposed cultural scripts linked to the historical past of American apartheid converge through the Sparkses' and the Wurgels' racial masquerade: the passing narrative's articulation of ersatz "whiteness" and blackface performance of "blackness." How this convergence plays out over the series proves profoundly disruptive to the formal equivalence between black and white racial identities posited by the show's premise. The Sparkses' white racial passing performance closely resembles the Wurgels' own middle-class suburban whiteness, marking a sharp point of contrast with what emerges as a much more disjunctive relationship between how the Wurgels inhabit, embody, and perform "blackness" and the self-presentation of the African American family. These two images of blackness—the Wurgels in disguise, the Sparkses as their "natural" selves—produce a tension that is never directly addressed on the show but which is heightened by the lack of tension between the artificial and the "real" productions of white identity represented on the show. Whiteness effectively disappears behind the class codes that, on *Black. White.,* function to signify it, becoming once again, "unmarked" in contradistinction to blackness—and in spite of the series' explicit effort to dramatize the construction of racial whiteness in both a literal and a figurative sense. Framed by incongruity, racial blackness on *Black. White.* becomes—once again—hyper-visible. The paradoxical effect of all of this is that the white family's fabricated blackness seems both more artificial—that is, more like blackface than black passing—and, at the same time, more authentic—or, in the terms of the media genre that grounds it, more "real." It becomes the vehicle by which a troubling discourse of racial authenticity intersects the show's transracial drama.

While the "plot" of the series homologizes black and white identities, the strategies of racial representation deployed throughout disproportionately burden *blackness* as spectacle and signifier. In part, this reflects how, as a racial signifier, blackness continues to function in contemporary televisual culture as what television scholar Herman Gray terms the "dominant media trope for representations and debates about race" (163). In positing black and white racial identities as interchangeable signs, while relying on the singular discursivity of "blackness," *Black. White.* bears out the same contradictions at play in current post-racialist discourse.

Even at this late date in television's history, African American identity is frequently represented televisually via embodied spectacle and discourses of black authenticity. As noted above, these codes are today starkly and uncritically reproduced in the reality television genre. That *Black. White.* fails to circumvent these codes has less to do with the ostensibly "subversive" practices of passing and masquerade through which it explores racial discourse than it does with how this problematic approach to black identity is embedded in the generic conventions of reality television, the rules of genre that organize the show at a narrative level and thus ultimately frame its meanings. Within these conventions, whiteness is encoded as spectatorship, a positioning that reproduces—within the structures of looking and image consumption particular to media culture—the discursive construction of whiteness as the normative position of the subject and hence racially invisible. As film theorist Richard Dyer notes, "The invisibility of whiteness as a racial position in white (which is to say dominant) discourse"—including discourses of cinema and media—"is of a piece with its ubiquity" (3).

In contrast, the Wurgels' blackface masquerade presents a version of stereotypical "blackness" that tacitly calls into question the *cultural* "blackness" of the African American family. Whereas the Wurgels are made up through gender and class codes signifying an "authentic"—and monolithic—black culture, the Sparks family presents a more suburban, culturally mainstream image of a middle-class family, who happen to be African American. For instance, in contrast to the black woman Carmen presents (defined by a short "natural" hairdo, seventies-era hoop earrings, and an Africanist sartorial aesthetic), Renée's own personal look indicates that she regularly processes her hair and favors a fashion sense that is not appreciably different from the racially unmarked, middle-class feminine styles favored by Carmen and Rose when they are out of costume. Nor is Renée's preferred way of dressing and styling her hair appreciably different from her whiteface garb. The only member of the Sparks family who is shown to be in any way linked to the urban cultural aesthetic that *Black. White.* passes off as authentically black is Nick, whose teenage rebelliousness includes a predilection for a materialistic, nihilistic black masculinity marketed by the popular music industry (to a largely white consumer audience) as an emblematic hip-hop aesthetic. Ironically, the artificiality of the Sparkses' cosmetically altered bodies works to highlight the "realness" of their actual black bodies; their approximation of whiteness when made up in their racial masquerade is also easily readable as the appearance of a "light-skinned" African American family.

This asymmetrical coding of racial difference extends to the public spaces on which the show's narrative depends, as the settings for its ongoing field studies and object lessons in passing. These contexts are as critical to the show's conceit as the sophisticated makeup techniques deployed by the special effects artists. Yet what counts as a racialized location for situating blackness in the show's cultural geographies is qualitatively different than what is presented as a "white" space. In blackface, Bruno, Carmen, and Rose all variously inhabit an urban landscape in which the cultural locations of racial blackness seem untrammeled by cross-racial or even cross-class contact. These comprise a youth slam poetry group, an all-male domino game played under a visible haze of smoke and the influence of alcohol, predominantly African American neighborhoods in urban Los Angeles, and an AME church service. By contrast, the show's creators seem at pains to locate spaces that are intrinsically "white." Instead, the spaces of leisure consumption to which they deploy their undercover African American cast members come across less as exemplary of white culture than as simply frequented by white people. This reinforces an idea of racial "whiteness" as something that is merely coincidental with white bodies rather than a site of *difference* and *specificity*. The choices of setting for whiteface performance seem at once obvious and arbitrary: spaces of women's leisure activity such scrapbooking and knitting classes, a Bible study group, golfing, and suburban mall shopping, and a wine bar, country-western theme bar, and sports bar. As a young "white dude," Nick is placed in a photography class and a teenage etiquette class held in the elite neighborhood of Bel Air. These classes code whiteness as "wealth." In contrast to Rose's poetry group, the photography class suggests that whites are most interested in and capable in modes of creative expression that require technology and expertise. The slam poetry group confers intrinsic "expertise" to black teenagers in using the privileged knowledges of "emotion" and "realness."

The seeming inability of the show to locate an authentic or even coherent "whiteness" beyond the habits of bourgeois leisure and commodity consumption contributes to the overall construction of blackness as a stable site of racial difference, while whiteness disappears behind its signifiers of class. The show's discourse of black authenticity serves to dissimulate any friction between "real" whiteness and whiteface. Lacking a discourse of "authenticity," whiteness here never approximates the "real," while "blackness," on the other hand, frequently appears to be nothing but.

From the very first episode, Carmen and Bruno turn out to be eager consumers of the kinds of black authenticity in which their cosmetically altered appearances traffic.[10] As early as the first episode, Carmen presents an almost parodic version of white liberal stereotype, touting her "compassion for . . . suffering," which she claims is the moral inheritance of her parents' unspecified "involve[ment] with the civil rights movement," as her motivation for participating in the show's social experiment and, she implies, her prospects for successful racial passing. Carmen is so confident in the enlightened views and good intentions she claims for herself that, throughout the series, she seems constitutively unable to recognize her own propensity for naive, offensive, or simply bizarre statements about African Americans, such as her initial comments aligning blackness with suffering. This tendency comes to light early in the first episode in the staged "reveal" moments when the members of the individual families see each other in racial masquerade for the first time. Reflecting on her first impressions of Bruno in blackface, she enthusiastically proclaims to the camera, "I love 'black'! Somehow, heart-wise, there's that warmth."

In addition to her painfully awkward locution, Carmen seems entirely unaware of the fetishistic significations of her statement and what they broadcast about her unchecked beliefs about the "otherness" of African Americans. This becomes even more apparent when, in this same episode, Carmen admits to having "no idea what it's going to be like to live with a black family," implying that the experience would be somehow significantly different from living with strangers in general. The overall impression is of someone who identifies with African Americans in an abstract sense yet seems to have very little personal experience interacting with actual African Americans.

The second episode makes this point with particular force. Accompanied by Renée, Carmen shops for a set of outfits for her and Bruno to wear to the African American church they plan to attend the following morning in racial masquerade. Ignoring Renée's counsel that a modest dress and a man's suit would be more appropriate attire, she gravitates toward an African clothing store where she purchases highly flamboyant "traditional" garments. Reflecting on the experience later, Renée wonders to the camera what Carmen "really thinks about our race, whether we're just so different [from whites], like we're aliens?" Carmen's self-professed interest in "learn[ing] about their culture"—referring to the Sparkses—informs her approach to the show's social experiment. She seems to understand her participation in the show as an opportunity for a bit of cultural tourism—as an opportunity, framed in more positive terms, to acquire cultural knowledge. But incidents such as the shopping trip reveal instead the extreme extent to which she others the Sparkses. The naive misconceptions that Carmen gives voice to in the course of preparing her black persona stage an epistemological crisis unique to white experience on *Black. White.* as Carmen and Bruno regularly perform—albeit inadvertently—how little they know *about* how little they know about actual African Americans.[11] The show lets this stand as an index of white privilege, set off by Brian's and Renée's wry observations about their own prior knowledge of white culture, which is brought to the fore most effectively within the shared living space.

Having strangers live together has been a central premise of most reality shows since the series *Big Brother* and *The Real World* popularized this category of programming in the U.S. television market. On *Black. White.,* this generic convention is positioned as a way of extending the show's pedagogical and social documentary concerns. In living so intimately with the racial other, during the making of what the show's creators stressed was a "reality experiment," the individual participants were expected to confront issues of racism, identity politics, and cultural differences not simply as and in terms of their "experimental" selves but in relation to their own racial identifications. Thus, the show modifies the generic convention, in which the interactions of the participants themselves form the primary drama of the show (as in a show such as *Big Brother*). Here, the Sparkses' and Wurgels' public interactions with one another—mini experiments in which at least one party is always in racial drag—fuels the private interactions, which are then understood as not performances, but as "real." This public/private dichotomy also marks an oscillation between the show's "reality television" and "documentary modes" as the shared domestic space is privileged as space where emotionally authentic (and hence socially meaningful) exchanges take place.

Unmasked, the white participants reveal their approach to the living arrangements as a pedagogical opportunity, asking their African American counterparts for pointers about black culture, embodiment, and linguistic expression and to evaluate their preliminary attempts at passing from a presumed perspective of racial authenticity. Presuming a reciprocal, symmetrical relationship between their two families' experiences of racial passing, Carmen and Bruno approach black and white racial identities as mutually constituted via forms of "in-group" knowledge. They are therefore surprised when Brian and Renée explain that they don't need training in the linguistic and behavioral cues that signal white identity because, as African Americans, these are things that they have already had to learn in order to negotiate the societal mainstream.

This exchange invokes the phenomenon of black "double consciousness," which W. E. B. Du Bois, writing more than a century ago, famously described as "the peculiar sensation . . . of always looking at one's self through the eyes of others, of measuring one's soul by the tape of a world that looks on in amused contempt and pity" (11). Du Bois's formulation names the ways in which white hegemony produces in African Americans an awareness of one's self that incorporates an awareness of how one is perceived by others. The claim that Brian and Renée make here, that a compulsory knowledge of whiteness is intrinsic to African American subject formation, suggests that an awareness of how one is perceived by others encompasses an awareness of the racial other in a broader sense—including how whites perceive and relate to each other. Brian's and Renée's articulation of black identity as something formed in negotiation of whiteness is already attuned to the logic of "the pass," as what Amy Robinson argues is "a hostile encounter between two *ways of reading*" identity—one that depends on "the visible as an epistemological guarantee," the other "an acknowledgment of multiple codes of intelligibility" (716; emphasis original). In suggesting that African Americans are already compelled to present themselves in terms of codes of intelligibility particular to the "appearance" of whiteness, Renée and Brian indicate that African Americans are to some extent, always, already "passing" within white majority culture, a suggestion that paradoxically challenges the symmetrical framing of racial difference embedded in the show's premise. In depicting "race" as a form of (unevenly) situated knowledge, *Black.White.* privileges its African American cast members as skilled practitioners of that knowledge, a fact born out in the audience's initial introduction to Brian and Renée.

If Carmen can be said to approach racial passing as an opportunity for cultural tourism, the metaphor that organizes Brian's and Renée's approach to passing for white would more properly be espionage.[12] After all, as they repeatedly point out, the so-called white world is the one in which they in fact live, and so they approach becoming cosmetically "white" not so much as traveling to "another world"—a rhetorical figure that features prominently in the Wurgel family's descriptions of their experience of passing for black—but as a chance to "go underground and actually experience life as a white person in America," as Eddie Murphy puts it in his 1984 *Saturday Night Live* skit "White Like Me."[13]

In "White Like Me," through cosmetic artistry and by imitating "white" speech and bodily comportment, Murphy assumes a white racial identity in order to discover a "white America" that the skit presumes is hidden from African American view. The skit's title riffs on *Black Like Me*,

John Howard Griffin's 1961 memoir of his six-week experience traveling around the Jim Crow South cosmetically disguised (much like the Wurgels) as a black man.[14] As recounted in his book, Griffin surreptitiously crossed the color line in order to expose white prejudice from a perspective nominally unavailable to whites. Murphy's satirical representation of racial passing inverts the experiment, exploring white privilege from a perspective nominally unavailable to people of color. Disguised as a white man, Murphy discovers an alternate reality in which white salesclerks let their white customers take things for free, a normal city bus becomes transformed into a party bus (complete with cocktails and dancing) following the departure of its sole black passenger, and white bank employees freely dole out cash to white loan applicants with no application, contract, or even expectation of repayment. The skit concludes with a return to the dressing room where Murphy first assumed his racial disguise. Gesturing toward a row of African American men and women evidently undergoing similar cosmetic transformations, Murphy now reframes his experiment with racial passing. Addressing the camera directly and his white audience implicitly, Murphy delivers this "warning": "The next time you're hugging up with some really super groovy white guy or even a really great super keen white chick, don't be too sure . . . they might be black."[15] Racial passing, constructed through the narrative frame of Murphy's skit, is not simply a project of investigation or social documentary but a strategy for subversion, as Murphy and his protégés are positioned as covert operatives, whose common ability to assume the visible signs and performative cues that signify whiteness, in combination with their cosmetic disguises, stands to undermine the putatively stable and exclusive precincts of white racial identity and the social authority it delimits.[16]

In *Black.White.,* Brian and Renee are depicted in the first episode as sharing the underlying supposition of Murphy's satirical representation of passing, which is that there is a private domain of white discourse and behavior integral to the reproduction of white racial formation. They expect to discover forms of privilege conferred through intraracial recognition, though on a milder scale than what Murphy's skit depicts. But their broader concerns are more aligned with Griffin's project in *Black Like Me,* for they believe that contemporary American racism is much more likely to be expressed privately among whites than openly directed at people of color—or, in Brian's words, "what whites talk about when no other races are around."

Conversely, Bruno theorizes (albeit skeptically) that as a black man he might hear things that he does not hear as a white man. From the start he professes a desire to experience racism firsthand, as if to expose to the show's white viewers a political reality they might not otherwise consider or even be aware. It soon becomes clear that Bruno holds an extremely narrow definition of what counts as an experience of racism—namely, being subjected to racial epithets in public interactions with white strangers. This virtually guarantees that he will *not* experience racism in terms that he can recognize. During one of the families' nightly dinner table conversations in the first week of taping, Rose asks everyone else what he or she has learned so far. Bruno responds right away, sharing that, "as a black man, I'm getting the reaction from people that I usually get as white Bruno, and that's telling me a lot." What this is "telling" him is elaborated by what he says next: "I'm just waiting for someone to say, 'Hey, [n-word]!' " Bruno posits a fantasy scenario in which, masquerading as a black man, he will be randomly assaulted with a racial epithet by a self-consciously and aggressively racist white stranger. In the absence of such overt displays of racism, he claims, his experience of racial passing thus far proves to him that, in fact, "racism" no longer exists.

Although the Sparkses inform Bruno "that's not going to happen," he remains wedded to a definition of racism that ignores what Brian, in this and subsequent conversations, tells him are the more subtle coding of racist expression and the systematic, rather than individualized, ways in which racial hierarchies get reproduced. This exchange, which comes early in the series, begins an ongoing debate between Bruno and an increasingly frustrated Brian around Bruno's claim that his experiences in black masquerade affirm what he had suspected from the outset. In this argument, Bruno maintains that his forays into public in racial disguise lend authority to his opinion for he, like Brian, has now "experience[d] the world *as a black man*" (emphasis added). By the end of the first episode, he has concluded that racism in 2005—the year the show was taped—is less a social reality than the refuge of the embittered and angry, people who "find racism because [they] look for it," a characterization Bruno extends to Brian. Racism for Bruno is not a social reality but an alibi—an excuse for those who would rather eschew the ethics of personal responsibility that Bruno attributes to his own father's success as a European immigrant to the United States.

Although Nick's understanding of his own father as "out of touch" with post-racial (or at least post-racist) American realities echoes Bruno's claims about the obsolescence of racism, it becomes clear to viewers that Nick doesn't share Bruno's political inclinations—that is, Bruno's conviction that the show's passing experience will reveal the triumph of liberal individualism over racial prejudice. In fact, Nick doesn't seem to have any sense of or concern with how his own experience with passing might connect with a broader social message. He "just [wants] to pass," which he construes as a private recreational experience and not, as his father does, a public intervention with implicit political significance: in the first episode, Nick informs Rose, "I'm just here for the fun." Yet Nick's conflicts with his father over the purpose of participating in the show and rejection of his parents' ideas about its potential to educate and reform their troubled teen reinforce the narrative framing of the argument between Bruno and Brian as ultimately reflecting a personality conflict. In recuperating potentially political-racial conflict as mere interpersonal difference, *Black. White.* bears the ideological hallmarks of post-racialism, and in so doing, forecloses its own potential as antiracist critique.

From a critical race studies perspective, a more positive interpretation is that the real referent for the blackface performance on the show is a white cultural imaginary in which racial "blackness" is legible as a subject position to be tried on, a body posture to assume, a set of codes to master. Thus, while *Black. White.* fails as a televisual enterprise dedicated to teaching its white participants and viewers alike about "the black experience," it nonetheless brings to light some of the problematic desires and assumptions that its white participants—and perhaps, some of its viewers—bring to the show by depicting whites unself-consciously engaging their fantasies of otherness. This comes to light in moments on the show that temporarily suture the viewers to a critical black spectatorship.

Herman Gray argues that one reason why "blackness" maintains its force as a cultural trope in the eras of multiculturalism and by extension post-racialism—representational regimes that trouble the binary terms of the historic "color line"—is that blackness is constantly being "recode[d] and reposition[ed]" through depictions that spectacularize difference and then contain that difference. At the heart of this operation is what Gray terms a "discursive shift" that mediates between an ostensible racial realism that abolishes racial stereotype—such as the image of the self-described "normal," suburban Sparkses—and a hypostatized blackness that tacitly legitimates stereotype by recuperating race as a visual epistemology. Throughout its single short season, *Black. White.* periodically disrupts the work of narrative containment by materializing racial difference in terms that precisely recode and reposition *whiteness* by exposing the white fantasy and enjoyment that hide behind the traditional mask of blackface. As Eric Lott notes in his seminal study of the theatrical blackface minstrel tradition, whites historically engaged "blacking up" as "less a sign of absolute white power and control than of panic, anxiety, terror, and pleasure" (6). In such moments, whiteness on *Black. White.* is outed as an object of looking—that is, an object of a critical *black* spectatorship—rather than as the normative position of spectatorship itself. A critical, counterhegemonic gaze is thereby solicited and mobilized—if only temporarily—for the show's audience.

I want to be clear that I am not here referring to the dramatic, often highly entertaining failures of white cultural knowledge that recur throughout each episode of the series—that is, scenes of crisis in which white people are confronted with the fact that they don't know something they thought they knew but which the show's black participants (it is also revealed) already knew white people didn't know. A particularly illustrative example is a tense exchange in which a predictably tearful Carmen expresses frustration that Renée won't accept her apology for calling out to her, during a session with a dialogue coach intended to coach the women in their respective racial performances, "Yo Bitch!" Carmen insists that she really did not know that this was *not* a friendly term of endearment among black women. This incident also typifies how the program allows a stereotypical discourse of blackness to play a central role in the white participants' construction of their African American personae—in this case, Camen's uninterrogated construction of the vocabularies of gangster rap as representative of what she calls "African American vernacular." What's particularly striking about the scene between Carmen and Renée is that the latter has demonstrably moved on from this matter while Carmen is still quite upset. One might wager that nowhere in America is the sight of white people behaving foolishly about race matters news to people of color. The emphasis in this scene is ultimately on Renée's refusal to engage fully with what might be considered "a teachable moment." This raises the question: For whom within the show's viewership was this scene—out of the dozens of hours of footage shot for each episode—included during the editing process that produces the reality-based "narrative"? I would suggest that the dramatic significance assigned to such scenes of white epistemological crisis on *Black. White.* is a key indicator of how the show privileges its white viewers.

But the show has other lines of address. Periodically, it does construct an oppositional, even counterhegemonic gaze that draws attention to how narrative frames determine the production of blackness as spectacular object of white looking. It is in these moments that the show more successfully negotiates its racial logics. Here, epistemologies of whiteness take shape not in whites' dramatic interrogation of the failures of their own racial knowledge, but rather as unremarked failures to recognize racial fantasy—what Lott terms the twinned impulses of "pleasure and terror"—as forms of racial knowledge as such. As the driving forces behind modernity's racial knowledge project, pleasure and terror are at the core of the white relationship to racial otherness as "the organization of desire" (Lott 148). This is knowledge mediated outside of liberalism's rational discursive modes, appearing instead as something haptic or instinctual.

The show's premiere episode contains a particularly instructive depiction of white racial fantasy as an object (and not simply an engine) of spectatorship: the juxtaposed scenes of the two couples' "reveals" in racial makeup. First in the show's narrative is the scene in which Carmen, herself in "black" makeup, meets a figure she terms "black Bruno." In this instance, Lott's theory of blackface as a medium of desire that merges terror and pleasure becomes literalized. At first glance, Carmen's reaction to Bruno is deeply ambivalent, her face briefly registering shock and what seems displeasure, even horror. Almost immediately, however, *terror* is recuperated as *pleasure*. What is it that "corrects" her response? Is it white liberalism—that is her awareness of being "on camera" and therefore "caught" in a racist reaction of terror? Or white fetishism—that is, her *forgetting* to do so? The scene begs the difference. It also suggests that one way in which Carmen unwittingly negotiates these tensions is by differentiating "black Bruno" from her real (white) partner by addressing him as she would a stranger: "You look like a really nice man," she tells him. This line is delivered while the couple is holding each others' hands and staring raptly into each others' smiling faces.

Within this short sequence of reaction shot close-ups, Carmen's and Bruno's reactions to each other in blackface clearly display their eroticization of racial blackness and show how abjection easily slides easily into objectification, as the fetish of racial blackness seems to work almost like an aphrodisiac for them. The couple stares at each other, then kisses, and Bruno turns to the camera and says, with tears in his eyes, "I'm in love with this woman." Like Carmen's address to Bruno as a strange but "nice man," his affection for "this woman" seems directed at a discrete "black Carmen" persona. Rarely since Whoopi Goldberg's 1990 star turn as the queer black *Ghost* in the white desiring machine, has American popular culture presented such an explicit depiction of black embodiment in service to white heterosexual romance.[17] The mediating role of racial blackness for this performance of white heterosexual desire is instructively highlighted by its position—that is, the positioning of white heterosexuality—in the edited sequence of cross-racial makeover unveilings.

This scene is immediately followed by an analogous unveiling of white racial personae between Brian and Renée. When Brian and Renée first see each other in whiteface, the couple simultaneously bursts into laughter. Renée makes fun of Brian's shoebrush mustache and thinning blond hair. Brian teasingly calls Renée "white girl," and pretends to force her to kiss him. Their reactions are diametrically opposed to Carmen's and Bruno's. Instead of race changing being an erotic experience for Brian and Renée, finding themselves in the guise of a white heterosexual couple feels plainly ridiculous. Their laughter cues the audience to this reading but also frames the entire scene as a mirror for the behavior of the actual white couple whose encounter with blackface immediately preceded it. What is ridiculous about whiteness, by this light, is the ways in which it cathects blackness as both excluded abject and desired object.

The scene between Brian and Renée activates for the audience a counterhegemonic spectatorship that sees whiteness critically, rather than making whiteness synonymous with the position of the spectator. Throughout the series, this critical gaze is periodically rearticulated in Renée's and Brian's direct commentary on the ways in which Bruno and Carmen inhabit blackness. This occurs in private conversations between the two of them either alone or with Nick, or in the "confessional" space of the camera-directed interview, such as the scene in which Renée asks the audience, via the camera, whether Carmen's desire to purchase "African" clothing as churchgoing attire reflects her view of African Americans as so *other* as to be "alien." This interview with the camera is intercut with a depiction of Bruno and Carmen discussing their plan to wear clothing blankly described by Carmen as "traditional African dress" to an AME church service in what they assume will be a culturally sensitive, universally resonant statement of black pride. Later in this same episode, we are shown the conversation in which Renée describes for her husband and son the experience of shopping for church clothes with Carmen at the African-themed store and the outfits that Carmen eventually purchased. In response, Brian jokingly remarks, "Why don't they just dress like Aunt Jemima on the syrup bottle and get it over with? . . . or Uncle Ben?" (*BW*). His reference to infamous stereotyped commodity trademarks re-describes what Carmen and Bruno present as a display of cross-racial identification and respect as masking a desire to consume blackness as archaic stereotype. It also suggests how in the Wurgel family's racial masquerade, the ostensibly divergent scripts of blackface and passing performance are reconciled: while Rose, Carmen, and Bruno all appear successfully to "pass" under the radar of the in-group they are infiltrating, to those group members (by virtue of racial affiliation) already in the know about the nature of the pass—namely castmates Nick, Renée, and

Brian—their passing instead registers as a form of what might be called neo-blackface. This minstrelsy is much more naturalistic in appearance than the stereotyped images of an Aunt Jemima or Uncle Ben but is rooted in the same significations, the same dialectic of pleasure and danger, and the same abjecting projections of white fantasy that ground these icons of the Jim Crow past.

This footage capturing critical black commentary is edited into the extended narratives concerning Carmen shopping for the clothes and, later, Carmen and Bruno modeling and discussing their outfits. The critical meaning of this storyline showing white cast members engaged in the fetishization of blackness is inflected by intercut scenes depicting the show's African American cast members as critics of that desire. The conventions of documentary editing here position the Sparkses as spectators looking (critically) at the Wurgels by locating them outside of the scenes under discussion. In this way, *Black.White.* momentarily disrupts and reverses what is otherwise a quite conventional positioning of "black" and "white" as spectacle and spectator throughout the show's economies of the gaze.

But it is a critical potential that the show otherwise contains, both by privileging the viewing position of white spectators, in the ways I've outlined above, and by refusing to acknowledge those elements that undercut the formal symmetries upon which the show's address to racial difference depend: the fact that the Wurgels are not a nuclear family (nor even, technically, the "Wurgels"); the qualitative differences between the various spaces in which the show locates blackness and whiteness as cultural formations; and the central role that signifiers of class difference play in the construction of black and white racial identities. Although the show generally regards "race" as a political and lived reality, particularly in conversations among cast members on such subjects as racism, white privilege, and Du Boisian double consciousness, and purports to interrogate and unsettle post-racialism's assumptions about the historical obsolescence of "race," *Black.White.*'s central conceit of "race trading" is consistent with the depoliticized, culturalist understanding of "race" ascendant in "the Obama era." This is especially illustrated by the discourse of black authenticity produced within the dialectical relation of blackface to passing. But *Black. White.* does not simply recapitulate what would become post-racialism's structuring contradiction—that is, the recourse to blackness as a stable signifier in order to proclaim the instability and incoherence of race as a system of meaning. In staging whiteness in terms of epistemological failures and in soliciting and then containing a critical black perspective, the show reveals that the deeper stake of post-racial paradox such as that which frames the Obama presidency is not simply the maintenance and preservation of an old racial order but something much more subtle and entrenched.

The micro-level of post-racialism turns out to be a dramatic interplay between intimate knowledges and their refusal. At stake, then, in a discourse that incoherently posits Barack Obama as emblematic of the end of "race" by virtue of his racialization is a deep anxiety about the crisis of cultural knowledge that confronts whites in this increasingly multiracial society. Post-racialism promises the end of "having to know" (as liberalism superficially demands) about other racial experiences and about the past and present of American racisms by reassuring whites about the sufficiency of what they already think they know about race—that is, how to recognize, as Carmen does in the instance of her first glimpse of the cosmetically enhanced Bruno, a "black" face.

Notes

1. Like "color blindness," a term with its own distinct genealogies, the "post-racial" ideal remands the claims of racial injustice and exclusion to the historical past, to argue that "race" itself is the root cause of all racisms. The two terms differ functionally, however. The ideal of a color-blind nation does not claim any direct relationship to historical processes. Color blindness promises racial transcendence through the sort of individual disinvestment in racial thinking satirized by the comedian Stephen Colbert, who frequently tells African American guests on his show that he is in fact surprised to learn that they are black, explaining that, because he is *politically* "color-blind," he *literally* "cannot see race." Post-racialism, in contrast, frames the political ideal of racial transcendence as a historical formation, within which the election of the nation's first African American president marks an epochal shift. Michael Omi and Howard Winant attribute the ideology they term "post-racialism" to a particular phase in American capitalism, linking the its emergence in the 1990s to the rise of Clinton era neoliberalism. Post-racialism, they argue, provided politically centrist "New Democrats" with an ideological justification for dismantling the welfare state and race-based social justice programs in the name of racial progress (Omi and Winant 147–49). Post-racialism has also emerged as a scientific truth, especially in the wake of recent advances in the science of genomics and the now widely accepted idea that "race" has no genetic basis. See Weinbaum 227–29.

2. What Omi and Winant term "[t]he racial order" is comprised in "the continuity and reciprocity between these two 'levels' of social relations. The micro- and macro-levels, however, are only analytically distinct. In our lived experience, in politics, in culture, in economic life, they are continuous and reciprocal" (67).

3. Jon Kraszewski suggests that the MTV show *The Real World* pioneered this narrative conceit as a convention of the genre. See Kraszewski.

4. Brandi Wilkins Catonese, one of the few scholars to offer an extended reading of *Black.White.*, approaches the show through the lens of theater/performance studies. She frames it this way: "*Black.White.* does not offer us black performance as transgressive potentiality because it refuses its place in a complex, intersectional world, and traps its actors within a depthless environment" (172).

5. Just what "the issues" are, however, is never directly addressed on *Black.White.* beyond the general implication that many of the interpersonal conflicts on the show—especially around Brian's claims that Bruno refuses to acknowledge the reality of racism and Bruno's insistence that that racism is merely what Brian projects onto whites, as I discuss below—have something to do with how "American society and history" are, as Cutler states, "defined" by race.

6. The popular series behind this catalog of reality show formulas are easily recognizable. *Extreme Makeover* and *The Swan* are paradigmatic examples of the makeover show in which personal transformation is linked to extensive plastic surgery. The "heiresses" living among "the agriculturally inclined" refers to the experience of celebrity heiresses Paris Hilton and Nicole Ritchie on *The Simple Life*. Other shows that riff on this basic "fish out of water" premise include *Amish in the City*, in which Amish teenagers share a house with "modern" young people, *Secret Millionaire*, which has individuals assume false identities in impoverished communities, the British *Faking It*, a show that gives individuals a month of training in a specific profession and then films them as they try to "fake it" on the job, or Cutler's more recent series *30 Days*, in which an individual spends a month in an unfamiliar social environment (the episode "Straight Man in a Gay World" placed a self-proclaimed homophobe in the legendarily queer Castro Street neighborhood of San Francisco). Bellafante also describes as passing texts the recent spate of "spouse-trading" shows, such as *Wife Swap* and *Trading Spouses*, in which dramatic tension and hence narrative momentum derive not simply from the fact that the individual spouses are traded into strange families but that the swap occurs across distinct lines of social difference: class, regional culture, religion, politics, and—yes—race.

7. These various formulas are also linked by a common therapeutic imperative. White argues that this imperative extends throughout the genres of reality television (181–82). See also Dovey.

8. Thus, for example, race-conscious plots on fictional TV series are presumed to refer to social truth. In reality television programming, racial blackness is conventionally signified by an individual figure who is intended to embody racial difference among the otherwise white, middle-class participants. This subject is conventionally expected to create conflict; that is often the central logic behind their casting. In this way, most reality shows locate racial otherness broadly and "blackness" specifically in interpersonal conflicts framed as interracial conflict. The prevalence of such plot devices across shows as diverse as *Survivor*, the MTV *Real*

World franchise, and *Black. White.* suggest that, as a discourse, race has become integral to reality TV's ontology of the real.

9. For a rich analysis of the tradition of literary narratives of racial passing as it is consolidated and reconfigured throughout the twentieth century, in relation to depictions of passing in literature, film and television, news media, and political rhetoric, see Wald.

10. In contrast to her "parents," Rose comes across as manifestly more humble, self-reflexive, and intelligent—and ultimately more likable. At home after her first day with the group, Rose confesses her fears that her passing will be exposed and her concerns that this would seem, in the context of a group dynamic that for her is defined by honesty and trust, quite "disrespectful."

11. Whereas Carmen's naiveté is implicated in her ignorance of African American cultural and political perspectives, Bruno's ignorance is linked to (white) arrogance.

12. In contrast to his parents, Nick Sparks is represented as apathetic, self-involved, and sure that his parents' belief that "race" still matters is totally out of touch with present-day (post-racial) social realities. For some, Nick's characterization might merely register as a stereotype of the typical teen who defines himself partially in opposition to his parents, but on *Black. White.,* the marked differences between selfish Nick and the earnest, sensitive, and self-aware Rose direct viewers' attention to how his behavior and attitude register within the opposing ideological commitments on display here, as epitomized in Brian's and Bruno's arguments.

13. The skit is available for viewing online at http://www.hulu.com/saturday-night-live.

14. The skit also recalls George Schuyler's satiric novel *Black No More* (1931), in which blacks can undergo a whitening process so that they become indistinguishable from whites and enter all aspects of American society and a reality otherwise closed to blacks.

15. As Gayle Wald notes in her reading of the skit, "White Like Me" goes farther than merely "satir[izing] racial hierarchy and hidden racial entitlement." It also constitutes an explicitly critical "inquiry into the visual protocols of racial classification" as a set of embodied codes that stabilizes racial difference and yet, in their easy appropriation by Murphy and his partners in passing, also prefigure "the fluidity of racial appearances as a threat to the stability of 'white' racial authority itself" (3). In Wald's analysis, the skit's narrative framework is indispensable to its critical meanings. While *Black. White.* shares the documentary impulse humorously staged in "White Like Me"—an impulse both of these contemporary texts derive from Griffin's *Black Like Me*—and pointedly aspires to the kind of critical intervention Murphy narrates, my larger argument positions the FX series as the less critical text.

16. Murphy's parting line directly targets that authority by suggesting that white racial authority may have already have been breached. Whether or not it

has—as Murphy states, "they *might* be black"—marks the disruption of whiteness both rehearsed and promised by the skit as fundamentally indeterminate. This indeterminacy is itself a crisis for whiteness, the production of which habitually and historically relies on clear, (putatively) impassable borders.

17. Referring to Goldberg's role in *Ghost,* in which she channels a dead man so he can kiss his widow, Chris Holmlund observes that "Whoopi is the first, and so far the only, black woman who 'becomes' a straight white man in mainstream movies" (133). Herman Gray, in his reading of the film, points out that Goldberg's transformation is the result of how her "special spiritual powers . . . are put in the service of white heterosexual love" (162).

Works Cited

Abrams, Joseph. "Black Like Whom? Obama vs. the Leaders." 16 Jan. 2008. *National Review Online.* Web. 12 Oct. 2008.

Bellafante, Gina. "*Black.White.*: Reality TV for Those Infatuated with Passing." *New York Times.* 8 Mar. 2006: E8. Print.

Black.White. Dir. R. J. Cutler. fX Networks, 2006.

Catonese, Brandi Wilkins. *The Problem of the Color[blind]: Racial Transgression and the Politics of Black Performance.* Ann Arbor: U of Michigan P, 2011. Print.

Crews, Chip. "More Than Skin Deep: FX's *Black.White.*" *The Washington Post.* 8 Mar. 2006: C08. Print.

Dovey, Jon. *Freakshow: First Person Media and Factual Television.* Berkeley: U California P, 2000. Print.

Du Bois, W. E. B. *The Souls of Black Folk.* 1903. New York: Penguin, 1996. Print

Gray, Herman. *Watching Race: Television and the Struggle for "Blackness."* Minneapolis: U of Minnesota P, 1995. Print.

Griffin, John Howard. *Black Like Me.* 1961. New York: Signet, 1996. Print.

Hollinger, David A. "Obama, the Instability of Color Lines, and the Promise of a Postethnic Future." *Callaloo* 31.4 (2008): 1033–37. Print.

Holmlund, Chris. *Impossible Bodies: Femininity and Masculinity at the Movies.* New York: Routledge, 2002. Print.

Kraszewski, Jon. "Country Hicks and Urban Cliques: Mediating Race, Reality, and Liberalism on MTV's *The Real World.*" *Reality TV: Remaking Television Culture.* Ed. Susan Murray and Laurie Ouellette. New York: New York UP, 2004. 179–96. Print.

Lee, Felicia R. "Confronting America's Racial Divide, in Blackface and White." *The New York Times.* 16 Feb. 2006: E1, E7. Print.

Murray, Susan. "'I Think We Need a New Name for It': The Meeting of Documentary and Reality Television." *Reality TV: Remaking Television Culture.* Ed. Susan Murray and Laurie Ouellette. New York: New York UP, 2004. 40–56. Print.

Omi, Michael, and Howard Winant. *Racial Formation in the United States: From the 1960s to the 1990s*. 2nd ed. New York: Routledge, 1994. Print.

Retman, Sonnet. "*Black No More*: George Schuyler and Racial Capitalism." *PMLA* 123 (2008): 1448–64. Print.

Rich, Frank. "Guess Who's Coming to Dinner." *The New York Times*. 2 Nov. 2008. Late ed sec. WK: 10. Print.

Robinson, Amy. "It Takes One to Know One: 'Passing' and Communities of Common Interest." *Critical Inquiry* 20.4 (1994): 715–36. Print.

Roediger, David. "Race Will Survive the Obama Election." *The Chronicle of Higher Education: Chronicle Review* (2008): B6. Print.

Schuyler, George. *Black No More*. New York: Macaulay, 1931. Print.

Steele, Shelby. "Obama Seduced Whites with a Vision of Their Racial Innocence Precisely to Coerce Them into Acting out of a Racial Motivation." *Los Angeles Times*. 5 Nov. 2008: A31. Print.

Torres, Sasha. *Black, White and In Color: Television and Black Civil Rights*. Princeton: Princeton UP, 2003. Print.

Wald, Gayle. *Crossing the Line: Racial Passing in Twentieth-Century U.S. Literature and Culture*. Durham: Duke UP, 2000. Print.

Weinbaum, Alys Eve. *Wayward Reproductions: Genealogies of Race and Nation in Trans-Atlantic Modern Thought*. Durham: Duke UP, 2004. Print.

White, Mimi. *Tele-Advising: Therapeutic Discourse in American Television*. Chapel Hill: U of North Carolina P, 1992. Print.

6

Broke Right in Half

Passing of/in Alice Randall's *The Wind Done Gone*

Julie Cary Nerad

> "I have accepted the injustice of all of them loving her different because she was white. If she was just a nigger like me but got the chance to live as white, it's too much too bear. But maybe that's just the way it is, so I'm broke. Right in half."
>
> —Cynara (Alice Randall, *The Wind Done Gone*)

In "Telling Forgotten Stories of Slavery in the Postmodern South," Susan V. Donaldson suggests that the cultural shift(s) generated from/in a postmodern, postcolonial, postsegregation world "requires a new kind of historical novel, one that underscores its own provisional status by calling attention to its literary operations—that is, how it goes about representing the past—and that also problematizes history by unearthing discontinuities, anomalies, and multiple possibilities and by posing alternative content and alternative forms" (270).[1] Alice Randall's *The Wind Done Gone* (2001) is just such a novel. In her postmodern re-vision of Margaret Mitchell's *Gone With the Wind* (1936), Randall tells the story of Cynara Brown, a mixed-race woman who must reconcile different versions of reality in what she calls this "territory of truth and illusion" (167). Cynara's journey, recorded as a diary, is not primarily one of physical movement, although she does move from Atlanta, to Washington, D.C., to the eastern shore of Maryland. Her story is instead more a record of the development of relationships and the constant reimagining of knowledge—both self-knowledge and historical knowledge. The story specifically highlights how the construction of history and of reality affects how we construct our own identities. Change history, and we change ourselves. Change ourselves, and we change history. Arguably, it is a lesson modeled within the book for the book's readers. There is always another truth to be uncovered, while Truth is illusive or perhaps even an illusion.

The primary means through which the novel challenges history—and especially the myth of the Old South—is passing, a common trope since the mid-nineteenth century and one well at home in a neo-slave narrative.[2] That is, Randall reframes history not only by removing Scarlett O'Hara—here named "Other"—from center stage of the American sectional drama, but also by making the white Southern belle black. Tata (Tara), and by extension the plantation South as a whole, is anything but the serene paradise of benevolent white masters and their faithful black slaves that Mitchell's novel helped write into the cultural imagination. In Randall's updated version, Scarlett has "black blood"; Mammy is rumored to be a serial murderer; and Ashley Wilkes is presumably gay. Here, people cannot be separated easily into mutually exclusive categories such as black and white, and slavery and freedom are not primarily about legal status. Because of its postmodern, transgressive reimagining of a myth that has influenced American culture so deeply that it seems to many to *be* history—to be fact rather than fiction—the novel itself has also had to depend upon the strategy of passing. In order to see print, that is, the novel has been marketed as a parody, a move that dulls the edge of Randall's textual blade and thus blunts the impact of her assault on the residue of racism in American popular culture. This essay explores how cultural resistance to the passing *within* Randall's postmodern text—which proceeds through the blackening of a white cultural icon—demands the passing *of* the text as a parody, evidencing a continuing anxiety about race and the control of America's racial history in the twenty-first-century United States.

Passing as Parody

The Wind Done Gone is regularly described as a parody of *Gone With the Wind*. Indeed, its cover boasts that it is "The Unauthorized Parody" and claims *The New York Times* best-seller to be "a provocative literary parody that explodes the mythology perpetrated by a Southern classic." Randall herself identifies her first novel as a parody that answers the question: Where are all the mulatto characters in Mitchell's novel? Houghton Mifflin defends the novel it published explicitly as a parody and not a sequel, defining for the Web site's readers the terms thus:

> The goal of parody is to comment critically and to expose and explode the flaws of the original. The goal of a sequel, by contrast, is to continue a story, generally using the principal characters, style, tone, and themes of the original; a sequel might take a slightly different point of view, but it would not overturn or ridicule the basic assumptions of the original. Think of it as the difference between revolution and evolution.

Randall's novel, according to Houghton Mifflin, is a narrative *revolution*. In one of the earliest literary articles on the novel, Bettye J. Williams also defends *The Wind Done Gone* not only as "a charming parody" but also as "a classic parody in a long line of literary creations which extend back to the ancient Greeks" (310, 323).[3] Although not all authors credit Randall's book with such significant agency or literary pedigree, references to and mentions of the novel in many other scholarly articles and reviews also refer to Randall's text as a parody.[4]

The legal and literary uproar that manifested itself in a debate over the First Amendment and copyright law surrounding the novel's 2001 publication, however, is partially to blame for this characterization. Indeed, the novel was not originally marketed as a parody: on the dust jacket of the advance copy, it was hailed as "a brilliant rejoinder and an inspired act of literary creation" (cited in "*Gone With the Wind Done Gone*" 1207). However, as the *Harvard Law Review* article explains, "after the Mitchell estate filed suit . . . the jacket copy changed to read simply, 'A provocative literary parody that explodes the mythology perpetuated by a Southern classic' " (1207). Others quickly followed suit, echoing this language and further undergirding the novel's reputation as a parody. For instance, after the initial injunction that prohibited the novel's publication as a derivative work that infringed upon the rights of the Mitchell estate, authors and scholars such as Shelby Foote, Linda Hutcheon, Charles S. Johnson, Michael Kreyling, and Harper Lee signed a petition in support of Randall's novel, referring to it specifically as a parody (Bagdikian n.p.). Finally, after an extended legal battle in which writers such as Toni Morrison and Henry Louis Gates Jr. testified, the novel went to press on the authority of the Eleventh Circuit Court of Appeals. Its judgment (and the defense attorney's argument) was founded on the novel's *definition as a parody*:

> Noting that *The Wind Done Gone* appropriates a "substantial portion" of the copyrighted elements of *Gone With the Wind*, the court in *SunTrust Two* observed, "Houghton Mifflin argues that *The Wind Done Gone* takes nothing from *Gone With the Wind* that does not serve a parodic purpose, the crux of the argument being that a large number of characters had to be taken from *Gone With the Wind* because each represents a different ideal or stereotype that requires commentary, and that the work as a whole could not be adequately commented upon without revisiting substantial portions of the plot, including its most famous scenes." . . . Whether *The Wind Done Gone* took more than what was reasonable from *Gone With the Wind,* therefore, would depend on whether *The Wind Done Gone*'s overriding purpose and character was to parody *Gone With the Wind,* or in contrast to serve as a market substitute for it. (Beck 7–8)

In other words, as a sequel or a "market substitute," the novel would have been infringing upon the rights of the Mitchell estate to profit from copyrighted material from the original novel. As a parody, however, the novel was protected under the First Amendment and thus had the court's sanction to exist. The evocation of the characters from Mitchell's novel was considered fair use by the appeals court.[5]

Linking the novel to a larger question about Randall's authorial intent and her treatment of history, "*Gone With the Wind Done Gone*" reframes the Court reasoning:

> The threshold question in determining whether Randall's book constitutes protected parody is whether it had *Gone With the Wind* as a target or merely used it as a weapon with which to comment on something else. . . . Although . . . Randall may have wanted to make more general points about the treatment and perception of blacks in the antebellum South, it seems clear that the primary focus of her book was *Gone With the Wind* itself, not merely the broader historical setting. (1207)

If Randall was attacking through parody *GWTW* itself (understood as a fictional production of one woman and owned now as intellectual property by her heirs), *The Wind Done Gone* commits no legal trespass. If, however, Randall was using Mitchell's characters "merely" to critique and revise historical interpretations of the South and slavery, then she has literally broken the law. This argument, while perhaps legally sustainable, is slightly specious. For, as that same article later notes: "Randall challenged a book that defined the Civil War for many people" (1213). Precisely. Randall did use Mitchell's book as a focal point, but *Gone With the Wind* is not just any book: for many, it is *history*. As Houghton Mifflin's own Web site suggests in defense of Randall's novel: "Randall needed to take on Mitchell's work directly to undermine its myths, make readers question its world, and explode the archetypes that have leapt off its pages into America's consciousness" (n.p.). If the earlier novel did not have the iconic status and gilt of historical "accuracy" that it does, it would not have served as such a target for Randall.

Gone With the Wind was published in 1936 and won a Pulitzer Prize in 1937. Close to one and a half million copies of the first edition sold and more than thirty million copies have now been sold. The book has been issued in approximately two hundred editions in forty countries (Stewart 9). The film version, produced by David O. Selznick, debuted in 1939 to great acclaim: it won ten Academy Awards.[6] The novel, and perhaps even moreso the film, calcified a nostalgic image of the mythic South that perpetuated/s racism and Jim Crow segregation.[7] As Donaldson explains, the "master narratives that justified and acquiesced to slavery, segregation, and white supremacy and rendered African Americans virtually silent and invisible . . . had found a culmination of sorts" in Mitchell's work (268). She continues: the "*Gone with the Wind* phenomenon aided and abetted widespread historical and popular silences about slavery and its harsh realities until well into the late twentieth century" (269).[8] Similarly, in their "Letter of Support" for Randall written during the court battle, the thirty signatories argue:

> Because of the extraordinary popularity of *Gone With the Wind* and its unique mythic status, Mitchell's novel has become a prime source of knowledge about plantation life for much of mainstream America. Now is the time for the American public to hear another perspective on this legend. We feel it is urgent for the public to engage in a full discussion of the important issues raised by Ms. Randall's satiric commentary on the characters and events that have become so well known through the vehicle of *Gone With the Wind*. (Bagdikian n.p.)

Here, the letter writers acknowledge the significance of *Gone With the Wind* in the construction of "knowledge about plantation life." However, as Thomas Haddox notes, the petitioners fail to challenge an uncritical process of history making itself. They suggest that Randall's novel is just a satiric re-version of history that one might select and advocate on behalf of. He argues: "The problem of identifying and understanding a past—as opposed to constructing and advocating one—has largely vanished" (121). I would extend Haddox's complaint in that the petitioners also unintentionally reify the very version of history that, presumably, they want to see challenged by referring to "knowledge" and "the characters and *events that have become so well known* through the vehicle of *Gone With the Wind*" (my emphasis). Although certainly different in intent, their language undergirds the authenticity of Mitchell's novel and recalls, for the historically minded, the reputed words of Woodrow Wilson in response to the 1915 screening of D. W. Griffith's *The Birth of a Nation* at the White House: "It is like writing history with lightning, and my only regret is that it is all so terribly true."[9] My point here is this: yes, the novel may be parodic in tone or in the characters' names. But what Randall's novel attacks is not just one fictional exploration of the Civil War (as a parody of *Gone With the Wind*), but the *processes* of history and cultural memory that allow *Gone With the Wind* to *create* history.

As Eve Allegra Raimon notes, the court battle over Randall's novel "makes manifest the depth of the enduring contest over competing versions of America's racial past" (154–55). In short, it forces the question, "Who owns history?" Corinna Baschirotto argues, the

> action taken against Randall's exploration and explosion of *GWTW*'s story and of its racist stereotypes seems to reveal, more than the limits of her work, a desire to avoid a serious questioning of the national identity, of the past on which this identity rests and of the sources which have most powerfully articulated it. That Randall's attempt was deemed a violation implicitly suggests a kind of ownership over the contested ground of memory[.] (n.p.)

If the battle here is reduced to a question of Margaret Mitchell's individual rights as an author (and by extension her descendents' rights as legal heirs) then the answer to the question of who owns history is evidently simple: she does. For instance, no similar uproar surrounded the recent publication of Donald McCaig's *Rhett Butler's People* (2007), the *authorized* "re-imagining" of Rhett Butler's life before and during his life with Scarlett. Why not? The legal answer, of course, is that McCaig was selected by the Mitchell estate to write the sequel and therefore there was no infringement of copyright.[10] The Mitchell estate also had a significant amount of control over what could happen to the characters and over how the characters and plot were developed. As Anne Bartholomew puts it in her review of McCaig's novel:

> To pluck a character from a beloved book and recalibrate the story's point-of-view isn't an easy thing to do. Ultimately, the new must ring true with the old, and this is where *Rhett Butler's People* succeeds beyond measure. In the spirit of Mitchell's masterpiece, McCaig never questions that love—of family, lover, land, or country—is the tie that binds these characters to life, for better or worse. (n.p.)

Bartholomew hits the nail on the head—several times. McCaig's novel carries the weight of authority, the approval of the Mitchell estate. The guardians of the myth—a myth that didn't begin with Mitchell but which certainly found its cultural authority cemented in the sweeping, epic proportions of her rendition—approve precisely because McCaig's novel "rings true" to Mitchell's own "beloved" articulation of history. In the "spirit of Mitchell's masterpiece," McCaig's novel "never questions" the version of the South that America has clung to through Jim Crow segregation, the civil rights movement, and even the contemporary purportedly "color-blind" era.

The Wind Done Gone, however, challenges the verisimilitude of Mitchell's romantic, fallen South. And, if we recognize that Mitchell's creation has morphed outside the bounds of fiction and has created "knowledge" of history itself, then we must reject the reductive conclusion that the Mitchell estate should be protected against a novel that simply invokes what have come to be historical figures: no one, for instance, would sue Randall for writing a book set in the 1860s using "facts" about the Civil War and Reconstruction. Randall's use of Mitchell's characters—as types that embody a cultural history—should be understood in the same way. I do, of course, recognize an author's right to copyright protection and understand that I tread on thin ice here. But my point is not to suggest that the Mitchell estate should forfeit rights to her novel. Indeed, her heirs should benefit from all the copies of *Gone With the Wind* sold, and the film, and the sequels that extend the story as Mitchell conceived it. Instead, my point is that through the postmodern elision between fact and fiction,

Mitchell's characters have entered the public domain as articulations of the Southern Belle, the Dashing Reprobate, the Southern Gentleman, the Southern Planter, the Faithful Slave, the Steadfast Mammy, etc. These are the characters that populate Randall's novel, but we see them without the green glasses of Mitchell's southern Oz, so to speak. Furthermore, in *The Wind Done Gone* the characters born in *Gone With the Wind* seem only important as they impact the life of Randall's newly imagined protagonist, Cynara. As with the black characters in Mitchell's novel, the majority of white characters in Randall's novel function more as types rather than as developed characters. For instance, Randall's versions of Scarlett O'Hara, Ashley and Melanie Wilkes, and Gerald O'Hara barely appear in the novel. Randall also extends the story beyond Scarlett's closing dictum: "Tomorrow is another day": *The Wind Done Gone* begins after R. (Randall's reimagined Rhett) leaves Other (which is where Mitchell's novel ends), and continues through the death of Mammy, Other's drunken, fatal fall down the stairs of Tata (Scarlett's death was prohibited in the authorized sequels),[11] Cynara's marriage to and desertion of R., and finally her affair with a black congressman and the birth of their child, Cyrus—none of which is in Mitchell's novel.

These characteristics of Randall's novel, as well as the slippage between historical "fact" and "fiction" generated by *Gone With the Wind,* undercut the definition of the novel as primarily a parody (although it does have a parodic tone/elements). Rather, Randall's novel uses Mitchell's novel—as a "weapon" in process of "revolution"—to critique American culture's uncritical, widespread, and continued glorification of an understanding of history that marginalizes, stereotypes, and denigrates African Americans, while simultaneously casting white Southerners and the South in general as victims of Northern aggression, carpetbaggers, scallywags, and the "bottom rail" put on top. In Randall's novel, as in other postmodern novels such as Thomas Pynchon's *The Crying of Lot 49* or Colson Whitehead's *The Intuitionist,* reality (and history) is separated from any potential "Truth" and is revealed as a construct. Furthermore, in *The Wind Done Gone,* reality (and history) becomes the construct of the dispossessed rather than the possession of those with hegemonic control. Reframing how we see things—learning how to read, as Lila Mae Watson puts it in Whitehead's novel—is essential to the process of revisionist texts like *The Wind Done Gone*. Randall's novel, as a postmodern reflection on knowledge, oppression, and history, highlights history itself *as narrative process* rather than as an objective, unchanging Truth that can be encapsulated and owned by one (white) woman and her heirs.

Thus, despite the dust jacket's bold red sticker, the chorus of scholarly claims, and a legal judgment, I suggest here that the novel is only passing as a parody. Granted, it does reflect on another work by adapting characters and scenes to critique that work, and it does "expose and explode the flaws of the original"—thus, it comments on the original text and is transformative, two key elements in the legal parlance about the definition of "parody"—but the text itself is more accurately characterized as a historical parallel novel—a novel that uses as a framework an earlier novel but that is told from a different point of view in order to effect a critical evaluation of cultural, social, or historical events. Paul Saint-Amour calls such works "appropriative rejoinders":

> This genre of appropriative rejoinder from the margins asks to whom a text belongs, interrogating, among other things, the logic by which a work ideologically complicit in the historical subjugation of subaltern groups should remain unquestioningly celebrated or immune to powerful forms of criticism, parody, and reevaluation because of its status as private intellectual property. By repeating canonical works with critical differences, these rejoinders perform the reappropriation of a text by a character (and often by the author as well) whose dispossession and infantilization that text helped naturalize. (Saint-Amour 216)[12]

These works, in other words, might use parody as a tool, but they are more than parody. Works such as Randall's belong "to a lengthening genealogy of works, many by subaltern writers, that reproduce aspects of a canonical text's architecture but rewrite that text from its margins for political protest, rejoinder, restitution, or the working-through of historical trauma" (Saint-Amour 215). In short, the relationship between *Gone With the Wind* and *The Wind Done Gone* is similar to the relationship between Charlotte Brontë's *Jane Eyre* (1847) and Jean Rhys's *Wide Sargasso Sea* (1966) or even that between L. Frank Baum's *The Wizard of Oz* (1900) and Gregory Maguire's *Wicked* (1995).[13]

Although the point may at first glance seem relatively insignificant—what does it matter if we call the novel a parody or an "appropriative rejoinder"?—I believe it is more than just a point of definition. Calling Randall's novel a parody—for many—neutralizes its subversive potential to a large extent by equating it in the contemporary American public eye with parodies such as *Airplane* or *Scary Movie* (and all their sequels).[14] We don't have to take it seriously. It is, after all, just a parody, not serious literature or "*historical* fiction," not a serious reflection on the racism of yesterday and today or on the construction of knowledge and the control of history. "Parody" and "serious literature" are, of course, not mutually exclusive, as a long list of novels attests. Or, within the contemporary arena, we might cite Jon Stewart's and Steven Colbert's highly popular cable television shows *The Daily Show* and *The Colbert Report,* as instances in which parody can offer serious or critical social commentary. Citing Bahktin's understanding of parody, and taking Colbert specifically as an example, Jonathan Gray, Jeffrey P. Jones, and Ethan Thompson argue that such parody

> offers "new" ways to make sense of "old" texts or genres. Moreover, just as humor in general can provoke reflection on the social convention that is targeted, parody aims to provoke reflection and *re-evaluation* of how the targeted texts or genre works. . . . [W]hile parody is at root a form that is never inherently political, parody can *become* an important contributor to political discourse, encouraging critical viewing and a healthy cynicism about the mediation of politics. (18; italics in original)

Point granted. However, I would contend that, for much of the general public in the United States, the word *parody* continues to carry traditional connotations of humor, spoof, and absurdity. After all, parody *can "become"* an important contributor to social discourses and it "*aims* to provoke reflection and *re-evaluation*" of a text, but the use of parody does not guarantee such critical outcomes. Indeed, in her critical treatise *A Theory of Parody,* Linda Hutcheon notes the complicated history of "parody" in all its forms, arguing, in part, that the interpretation of parody is always culturally situated. She asks: "Is it intended as innocently reverential? ridiculing? didactic? mnemonic? ironic? Does it accept or resist the Other?" (77). Beyond this, audiences themselves are diverse and variable, and the intent of the satirist/parodist may not translate effectively onto any given audience.[15] Indeed, the willingness to accept parody as valid social or political critique depends upon the audience's willingness to question its own beliefs (if the parody threatens those beliefs) rather than dismiss it as ridiculous. There is a reason, after all, why not everyone thinks *The Colbert Report* is funny: "The presence of 'humor' in political humor can rely quite heavily on one's world view" (Gray, Jones, and Thompson 4). Thus, although parody can serve as a serious critique—even when cast in "humorous" terms—of culture, history, governments, power structures, etc., what I suggest here is that in this case branding Randall's novel as "parody" undermined rather than facilitated the text's legitimacy as cultural critique for a significant segment of the readership who is culturally invested in the myth of the Old South and the racial drama it offers. As a parody—a humorous spoof or satirical mimicry—Randall's novel can see print not only because that definition allows it to conform to copyright law, but also—and more importantly—because it de-authorizes it as a voice of history. As a potential reality or biting exposé, as a "brilliant rejoinder," as a new conceptualization of racial identity and individual agency, or of interracial relationships and the construction of history, the novel is a threat not just to the master narratives that bolster white supremacy, but to the security of history itself. To undercut *The Wind Done Gone*'s agency, the battle is articulated as revolving around legal rights, not human rights.

Certainly, historians, as well as other authors and scholars in other disciplines, have challenged the myth of the South without drawing such legal fire. And certainly one can critique the myth of the Old South without going through Tara. However—and this is a crucial point—going through Tara (as the symbolic heart of the mythic Old South) is in many ways *fundamental* to reframing U.S. history effectively. As long as U.S. culture glorifies *Gone With the Wind* not as a text or a movie, but as an embodiment and a realistic articulation of an objective *history,* the myth of the grand Old South will ride roughshod over countervailing (historical and/or academic) narratives, no matter how "post" anything the culture claims itself to be. What caused the vast public outcry against Randall's novel was that it attacked a beloved icon of (a particular version of) "history"—not Randall's alleged infringement of copyright or intellectual property law. Certainly the novel's legal battles were arguably exacerbated by the growing protectionist impulse surrounding intellectual property in the Internet age marketplace. James Boyle argues: "We have locked up most of twentieth-century culture and done it in a particularly inefficient and senseless way, creating vast costs in order to convey proportionally tiny benefits. . . . Worst of all, we have turned the system on its head. Copyright, intended to be the servant of creativity, a means of promoting access to information, is becoming an obstacle to both" (15).[16] But I would maintain that the particular public fervor over the novel arose in part from the particular subject matter that was framed as under attack. The *sanctity* of Mitchell's novel was not just about one author's legal rights. Instead, it reveals our resistance as a culture to challenge beliefs about U.S. history that continue to reinscribe racism and racial stereotypes. To see print, the novel must *pass* as a parody.

The Mirror, the Master, and M.E.

I turn now to the novel itself to examine the specific textual elements that fueled such resistance. What is most transgressive about *The Wind Done Gone* is not that Dreamy Gentleman is gay and was in love with a male slave, or that Planter (Gerald O'Hara) and most other Southern "gentlemen" are pedophiles, or that Miss Priss (Prissy) killed Mealy Mouth (Melanie Wilkes), or even that Mammy killed three newborn sons born to Lady (Ellen O'Hara), purportedly because Mammy and Garlic (Pork) didn't want sober white men around the plantation. Instead, the most threatening aspect of Randall's rewriting is that her version of Scarlett O'Hara—the center of *Gone With the Wind*'s cultural power—is, according to the "one-drop" rule, black and is thus only passing for white, even if unintentionally so.[17] Other/Scarlett, as Cynara puts it, is "just a nigger" and her daughter "just a high-yellow gal in a blue velvet riding habit" (133). The revelation that Other/Scarlett is black is the fulcrum of both the novel's racial politics and what makes the novel so threatening to the myth of the Old South: the ideal of white womanhood, the beautiful belle and her Bonnie Blue baby, the cause for which the KKK purportedly rode, is exposed as a fiction of white supremacy.[18] Given the history of race in the United States and the iconic status of *Gone With the Wind*—with its power to make history—that revision, indeed, has potentially "revolutionary" power.

Just as for Frank J. Webb in *The Garies and Their Friends* (1857), Frances E. W. Harper in *Iola Leroy* (1892), or Nella Larsen in *Passing* (1929), the trope of passing allows Randall to explore the performativity of race, while still recognizing the importance of race as an experiential identity category. In a kind of postmodernist critical pastiche, throughout the novel Randall also inflects the trope of passing through a racialized Lacanian framework of the mirrored Subject/Other, a Hegelian dialectic of Master/Slave, and the postcolonial construct of the subaltern.[19] Ultimately, however, the text rejects or undercuts all of these discourses to imagine a postmodern black female Self who, unlike the standard "depthless" white male postmodern protagonist, is a fully realized, independent Subject situated within a family, community, and nation.[20] To claim such a selfhood, Cynara must recognize that there is no fundamental, biological difference between herself and Other. Instead, their difference stems from the arbitrary distinction of race that marks/makes one biracial sister "black" and the other "white." Race thus marks not a fundamental difference (she and

Other are the same), but rather becomes a way of knowing, a process of understanding and negotiating the racist culture that surrounds us.

Cynara Brown (often called Cinnamon or Cindy) is the daughter of Planter and Pallas (Mammy). Like Lacan's infant, Cynara initially defines herself against and in relation to "Other"—in this case, her (purportedly) white half-sister. Although they are not exact physical reflections of each other (as adults, Cynara is several inches taller; Other's waist is smaller; Cynara's skin is very light brown; Other's is "white"), the half-sisters do resemble each other. The girls are also the same age, are raised in the same house, and have the same father. They share their mothers. They both love and marry the same man. They both, at different historical moments, own Tata. The primary difference between the two is their racial designations (and the sociocultural benefits or proscriptions arising from those designations). Indeed, everything Cynara knows about herself, and everything she desires, is a product of the U.S. racial system and her internalization of that system. In essence, Cynara initially experiences her own identity as a lack or absence stemming from her blackness.[21] As Baschirotto writes: "Cynara is Scarlett's double, and her life mirrors Scarlett's in many respects. The colour [*sic*] line, which divides Other's whiteness from Cynara's blackness, nicely works as a mirror through which differences are at first marked and later on, with the discovery of Other's hybridity, dissolved" (par. 23). Setting aside for later Baschirotto's final claim here that the discovery of Other's "hybridity" dissolves the differences between them, I agree that the color line functions as a mirroring surface. Other embodies the Imaginary—she is whole—primarily because she is white, while Cynara believes she lacks cohesion because she lacks whiteness.

Other's whiteness allows her to occupy the Imaginary not only because it grants her access to social and cultural privilege denied (the black) Cynara, but also because it allows her access to Mammy, Cynara's own biological mother. At the novel's opening, a dying Mammy has asked Cynara to return to Tata. As Cynara struggles with her decision whether to go, she records in her diary (which serves as the text of the novel) a tumult of emotions. She avidly desires an affirmation of her mother's affection, but she fears returning to the place from which she was sold at the age of thirteen and to a mother who, in her mind, *let* her be sold—she cannot, she writes, forgive her mother for the minutes she stood bare-breasted in the Charleston slave market (31).[22] More significantly, Cynara cannot forgive Pallas for her mothering of Other, articulated most succinctly through another memory of bare breasts. In a formative scene,

Cynara witnesses Other publicly demand—and receive—Mammy's milk. She recalls:

> [Other] was old enough to walk. She walked right past me, past Lady, she walked right past Lady and me, over to Mammy, reached up for Mammy, and my Mama reached down to pull Other up onto her hip. Other reached into the top of Mammy's dress and pulled out my Mother's breast. "I want some titty-tip," she said, and I ached in some place I didn't know I had, where my heart should have been but wasn't. . . . I flushed in a rage of possession as those little white hands drew the nipple toward the pink mouth, then clasped on. (13)

Because she is white, the three-year-old Other receives the nourishment (both physical and psychological) from Mammy that should have been Cynara's. The scene thus literally enacts Cynara's association between whiteness and fullness/wholeness, as well as that between blackness and absence/lack. Patricia Yaeger, exploring how this scene creates both a sense of desire and identification while also alienating Cynara from her mother, argues: "Seeing her mother's body whole while watching Scarlett [*sic*—Other] suck, Cynara also wants to be Scarlett, to have access to excess, to her own mother's milk that makes Scarlett run. A scene of labor and exclusion is simultaneously a scene of eros and identification, and a strange and unexpected sisterhood, a ghostly mother and daughter-hood, is born out of cross-racial envy and work" (Yaeger, "Circum-Atlantic" 791). Cynara identifies with Other as the suckling child of Mammy, but she also understands that her exclusion, her lack of access to Mammy, stems from her own blackness. Other is white, therefore Other has access to Mammy's milk. Cynara's desire to be suckled by Mammy (in Other's place) grows into her adult desire for R. to (mock) suckle at her breast rather than at Other's. She confesses: "I didn't start loving him till he preferred me to her. Oh God, I loved him then. So much was reconciled for me in his reach for my nipple before her breast, my kiss before her breath, so much reconciled and so much redeemed" (147). Cynara's relationship with R., then, serves primarily as a way to regain what she believes she lost to Other as a child: her Mother.

Lady, just the "oldest child on the porch" at seventeen (15), is another casualty of the patriarchal slave system with its common cultural practice of requiring the Mammy to nurse the white children of the plantation owner. In an essay exploring how whites represented black female bodies in the nineteenth century, Beverly Guy-Sheftall writes: "They [black women] were the South's perpetual wet nurses, providing from their breasts milk for Black and white babies alike. In other words, it was the exploitation of the Black woman's body—her vagina, her uterus, her breasts, and also her muscle—that set her apart from white women and that was the mark of her vulnerability" (30). In the porch scene, Randall shows that white women (denied the opportunity to nurse their own children) also suffered from this system of black female exploitation, even as they were complicit in its maintenance. As Other publicly nurses at Mammy's breast, Lady staggers back from the scene, clutching her "clinched waist." Her husband, Planter, at that moment walks out onto "the whitewashed porch" and declares the scene "My peculiar heaven, my peculiar, particular heaven" (14). Indeed, Planter—as Father (the Father here embodying the race system)—articulates the peculiar "heaven" of a cultural system dictated by white men for white male pleasure and profit. Although his "white" daughter also gets her fill of milk/pleasure as a child, Lady's situation suggests that the system is ultimately one that constrains white women as well. Mammy and Lady are interdependent cultural constructs, albeit with asymmetrical access to social privilege. Lorraine O'Grady articulates this interdependence this way:

> The female body in the West is not a unitary sign. Rather, like a coin, it has an obverse and a reverse: on the one side, it is white; on the other, not-white or, prototypically, black. The two bodies cannot be separated, nor can one body be understood in isolation from the other in the West's metaphoric construction of "woman." White is what woman is; not-white (and the stereotypes not-white gather in) is what she had better not be. (qtd. in Guy-Sheftall 14)[23]

As a minor character, Jeems, puts it, "If it's true you can't divide Mammy from Lady, maybe you can't divide Lady from Mammy" (84). The mammy performs the roles the lady is restricted from publicly performing *as a [white] lady* and the lady occupies the positions the mammy, *as a black woman,* is publicly prohibited from fulfilling.

However, Randall's novel highlights here—as in other places—that public matters did not always reflect private ones. After Mammy publicly nurses Other to Planter's delight and to Lady's and Cynara's abjection, Lady secretly nurses Cynara in her room. Cynara writes: "She [Lady] pulled me onto her lap and I suckled at her breast till her warm milk filled me. As always, it was a cheering surprise for both of us. We had been sharing these little spurred-by-envy suppers all my memory, but each time the milk came and how long it came without running out was a mystery to us both" (16). The public moment of Mammy nursing Other, paired with the private moments it generates between Cynara and Lady, allows the novel to make a further point about the directionality of racial relationships: what is "normal" in the antebellum South (a black Mammy nursing a white child) becomes perverse when reversed (a white Lady nursing a black child, no matter how white-skinned that black child is). Thus, although it seems there is an equal exchange (Mammy nurses Other; Lady nurses Cynara), the system legitimates the first and pathologizes the second. What can happen on the porch in the first case, must be closeted in the second.

Raimon argues that such "cross-racial mother love is a predominant theme in *The Wind Done Gone* and an integral component of life on 'Tata' " (156). Granted, placed where it is near the novel's opening, the scene does suggest for the reader two cross-racial mother/daughter pairings, just as it highlights the interracial relationships between white plantation owners and their female slaves. However, the passing plot that Randall weaves into the novel potentially undermines the subversiveness of these pairings. After all, Lady and Other are, according to the one-drop rule, black, thus making the interactions between the daughters and their surrogate mothers *intra*-racial rather than *inter*-racial.[24]

Readers discover Lady's concealed racial heritage through an exchange of letters reproduced in Cynara's diary between "E." (Lady) and her first cousin and true love "P." (Feleepe). The cousins are prohibited from marrying by their mothers who know of their "black blood" and fear that their children's coupling would produce dark-skinned babies. In one letter, P. explains his own mother's and aunt's fear and also records unflinchingly the lengths to which the women would have gone to protect their secret:

> She says her confinement and the confinement of her sister, my mother, were agony, greatly lessened but not ended by the arrival of perfect pink infants. She says they watched the tips of our fingers every night for signs of darkening. . . . Even if you had turned the color of butter, if she had turned the color of butter, I would have put the pillow over her face and I would have cried. Color comes in so slow over a period of ten days, if you do it quick even the Daddy don't see the dark in the

> baby. Of course the Mammy knows. They've seen all sorts of white-looking nigger children. (124–25)[25]

The revelation of their racial heritage and his aunt's reflections on the vagaries of skin color lead Feleepe to ruminate on racial identity and articulate some of the questions the novel itself presses: "Niggers Who Knew Not? Can you be a Negro if you don't know you're a Negro? I would have said a nigger knows he's a nigger. Always. Absolutely. But what if he doesn't?" (125). Lady's and Feleepe's—and, even more so, Other's—unintentional passing answers this final question. If she doesn't "know it," then she *isn't* black. Other (and her white sisters) are "white not black with a secret" (125). In this sense, then, Randall has it both ways.

On the one hand, and following the logic of the one-drop rule, Other is black. Randall thus "pollutes" the arguably best-known icon of white Southern womanhood, exposing the construct as a fiction: Southerners and Northerners have actually idealized a black woman, and the novel gets to claim for black womanhood all that even contemporary audiences love about Scarlett O'Hara. On the other hand, if we reject the one-drop rule as fundamentally illogical and void of any scientific basis—following the current critical consensus—Lady, Feleepe, and Other are *not* black. Despite Lady's professed *willingness* to accept a black racial identity as long as it comes with Feleepe's hand, Lady is raised as white and has always lived as white. Her racial self-consciousness is white up until Feleepe tells her that she is a "Negro" and continues as such afterward. Her only connection to a black racial identity is the racial classification of a long-dead Great-Grandmother and her own desire for the "brown" babies that she might have produced with Feleepe. Although haunted by the knowledge of her *legal* racial status long after Feleepe's death, Lady continues to live as white, marries a white man, and raises white daughters. Her society may have understood her to be black if the "truth" was known, but *we* as twenty-first-century readers are under no obligation to reinscribe that one-drop rule. Indeed, if we believe race to be a sociological construct, Lady—and thus Other, who dies before she ever even learns of her black ancestor—must be classified as white. They do not have the memories, experience, or consciousness necessary to be black. Mammy's milk did not "darker Other's berry" (162) any more than the "drop" of black blood she inherited from a great-great-grandmother. Within the text, this paradox—this absurdity of the U.S. racial system—is precisely what Cynara (and readers) must reckon with. Other is white, even though she is black.

My goal here is emphatically not to reclaim (the reimagined) Scarlett O'Hara as white or to "save" her from blackness. Rather, it is to highlight how the novel forces the reading public to choose between either keeping the historical icon of womanhood white or upholding the one-drop system that has been pivotal in maintaining white privilege: depending on whether we authorize a biological or a sociological model of race, Other's/Scarlett's racial identity changes.[26] This variability itself challenges the concept of race as an innate, biological essence. The passing plot thus allows Randall to illustrate that blackness—or racial identity in general—is a construct.[27] Cynara explains:

> It's not in the pigment of my skin that my Negressness lies. It is not the color of my skin. It is the color of my mind, and my mind is dark, dusky, like a beautiful night. And Other, my part-sister, had the dusky blood but not the mind, not the memory. There must be something you can do or not do. Maybe if the memories are not teased forth, they are lost; maybe if the dance is not danced, you forget the patterns. . . . [R.] thinks that the blackness is in the drop of blood, something of the body. I would have thought that he knew enough women's bodies to know that that could not be true. (162)

Cynara's phrasing does play with the language of essentialism by referring to "dusky blood." However, the balance of her reasoning leans heavily toward the recognition of race as a performed identity: it is something one *does* rather than something one *is*. One drop just does not matter against a lifetime of experience: being black is about *being,* not just about blood.

I return now to Baschirotto's claim that the "discovery of Other's hybridity" dissolves the differences between Cynara and Other. In one sense, I agree. Cynara has to reframe her understanding of everything in her life based on the knowledge that Other is actually the Same, that is, that there is no innate biological "difference" between them. However, in another sense, as is implicit from what I have argued above, suggesting that Other's remote black ancestry dissolves their "difference" is tantamount to upholding the color line (by slotting them both on the "black" side). One drop doesn't suddenly make them racial sisters, nor does it make it easier for Cynara to understand the oppression she has suffered as a result of the racial system that has marked her as black and Other as white. In fact, the knowledge of Other's "black blood" initially almost breaks her: "I have accepted the injustice of all of them loving her different because she was white. If she was a nigger like me but just got the chance to live as white, it's too much to bear. But maybe that's just the way it is, so I'm broke. Right in half" (133). The black-white binary has been fundamental to Cynara's construction of Self (as it has been—and arguably continues to be—essential to our construction of history), and what she had understood in her life as losses were made intelligible by the racial system (and Other's difference within that system). Whiteness embodied the Imaginary whole; blackness reflected absence/lack. Mammy nursed Other because Other was white. R. married Other because Other was white. As long as Cynara continues to understand herself, her family, her culture through a black/white binary, Other's "hybridity" is a crushing blow. Without a white Other, Cynara feels a void, as if she is looking in the mirror and sees no reflection. She can't see herself without the framework that (a white) Other had provided. Thus, Other's "hybridity" itself—understood as an articulation of some essential blackness—is not what allows Cynara to reconcile herself with Other. I would argue, instead, that Other's "black blood" allows Cynara to recognize the artificiality of the color line in a way that frees Cynara to see Other as white *regardless* of her "hybridity." Thus, Other's "hybridity" does dissolve the "difference" between them, but not in the way that Baschirotto's argument suggests.

Breaking out of a relational model of identity built on the concept of *biologically* distinct (and even opposite) racial categories is what allows Cynara to stop defining herself against a white, privileged Other—her mythic white sister. In short, she realizes that Other's racial identity does not need to dictate her own, and that she is already whole, already a Subject, not the fragmented object she understood herself to be: "To look in the mirror and know, not simply that my beauty eclipsed hers, but that it is elemental, that is does not require purchase or contrast to be, or to be valued, is a miracle" (176). This self-actualization also reveals to Cynara that the struggle between her Self/Other was always inherently futile and self-imposed. Earlier in the text and thinking about Other's drunken, fatal fall down the steps of Tata, Cynara writes: "Sometimes it feels like the game is over and I'm putting up the checkers, and instead of me winning, she just lost, or more like she never showed up. And that's something else altogether from how I want to feel, triumphant! Winner-ly. However it happened, I'm just glad not to lose. Other is dead. And I'm sorry for it" (104). After Cynara reframes her relationship with Other and frees herself from a relational model of identity formation, however, she can feel "winner-ly" without having "won." Or conversely, even though she ended up "winning" R., even though she realizes Mammy did love her, too, the prize no longer has the same savor. The game is over not because Other is dead, but because she no longer needs an (white) opponent/other. Cynara's acquisition of a unified sense of Self and the resulting psychological freedom lie, then, not in the reflection of an "Other" or the mastery of a "daylight version" of herself, but in the revelation of a Self not defined as an *absence* of whiteness.

Cynara's triumphant ascension to personhood is ultimately articulated in Other's un-othering: "It is a sister and a family I leave behind, not Other, not some thing" (196). Other is no longer the (imaginary) unattainable ideal. Instead, she is just a sister. Cynara and Other are not, however, sisters because they both have *black* blood; they are sisters because they both have *Planter's* blood and the shared experience of being Planter's children (and Mammy's and Lady's) on Tata, even though one of them is "black" and the other "white." She writes: "In the place we lived together, [we were] half-sisters separated by a river of notions: notions of Negroes and notions of chivalry, notions of race and place, notions of customs and rage" (194). These notions are what separated them from sisterhood. Having reframed her history and her own notions of race, reality, and identity, Cynara can now work in cooperation with (the memory of) a sister rather than in opposition to an Other. Her new story reads thus:

> Once in Georgia I had a sister who loved my mother dearly; she took care of Mama all her life, better care of her than I took. I hated her and buried her, and now I forgive her. Once in Georgia I had a mother I could not find my way to loving. I'm grateful that Other found a way and kept the path clean and brightly used. She made exquisite use of my mother's love. And now it's my turn to make good use of her mother's love. Lady loved her black man in the bright light of day. If he will have me, I will love Adam, I will love my Congressman that way. (196)

Cynara leaves Tata—and R. and slavery and Georgia—to embrace a blackness that she no longer sees as marking an essential absence or lack. Indeed, this new "fullness" is symbolized in her pregnancy by the black Congressman Adam Conyers (after her many infertile years with R.).

Cynara ultimately gives up her child (Cyrus) to Adam and his wife so that Cyrus might have a life of legitimacy and honor with an intact black family—and so black Americans might have a race leader. In Hester Prynne–like fashion, she lives out her years largely alone. However, despite her sacrifice, she has a "free-y" sense of freedom. She declares herself "[a] Negro woman who would not change her position" (144, 185). Cynara thus journeys not only from legal bondage to emancipation, but from psychological slavery to individual and emotional freedom, from fragmentation to wholeness. This process also frees her from the position of the subaltern.

Cynara finally tells R. her name as she leaves him. Given the history of naming practices for/of African Americans within the United States, the act is significant because it signals her rejection of the slave system. More importantly, however, this self-naming is the ultimate mark of her ascension into Self and the culmination of her desire to write herself into history. And, thus, to determine history. At the novel's beginning, she explains:

> This is my book. If I die tomorrow, nobody'll remember me except maybe somebody who find this book. I read *Uncle Tom's Cabin*. I didn't see me in it. . . . If I forget my real name, won't be anybody to tell it to me. No one here knows. I'm going to write down everything. Something like Mr. Frederick Douglass. (7)

Writing herself into history, naming herself, marks her desire for—and acquisition of—voice and agency in a world that had denied her individuality (or even humanity). And she claims that voice/agency not only for herself, but also for others marked by U.S. culture as subaltern. Or, more precisely, she reveals their hitherto concealed agency and thus destabilizes the very concept of the subaltern black American. The text in this way, too, offers a revised version of (white patriarchal) U.S. history: although the subaltern have ostensibly been denied subjectivity by the oppressing class/race, in Randall's reimagining, they have actually managed a subversive control. Manipulating Lady into marriage with Planter, nursing the girl children and killing the boy ones, sleeping with Planter in pleasure all their lives, Mammy was—as Garlic puts it—"the real mistress of the house" (52). Similarly, Garlic was the intellectual and emotional force—the architect and mastermind—behind the building of Tata and Planter's fortune. Thus, at novel's end, the African American characters—those who are conspicuous in Mitchell's novel either for their functional presence as stereotypes or for their absence—become not only the driving force of history, but the controlling force of the present.

However, despite Cynara's personal triumph, and although Garlic and Mammy are revealed as the true masters of Tata, Randall doesn't simply invert the racial politics of the day. Black agency in the novel is still constrained by the limitations of white racism. The black characters are, as Yaeger puts it, "still faced with the problem of internal colonization, of performing white culture and reinforcing white dominance better than the white landowners themselves" ("Circum-Atlantic" 780). Breaking free of such internal colonization is precisely the struggle Cynara engages in, and the one that Mammy arguably falls to when she nurses Other at the exclusion of her own black child. The book, too, falls victim to this white dominance if we force it to pass as a parody of *Gone With the Wind.*

Wind-ing Up

Despite the fact that cultural authorities, scientists, laymen, and authors have argued convincingly over the last few decades that race is a cultural and/or social construct, the illusion of an innate, biologically based racial identity still drives much of U.S. culture, history, economics, rhetoric, politics, power, and daily life. Race still matters, no matter the race of the forty-fourth president. However, Other's racial identity (the passing plot) has seemed of secondary importance for most reviewers and scholars writing about *The Wind Done Gone.* A representative comment is from Baschirotto: "Although Other does not know it, even she has black ancestors, since her mother's great-grandmother was 'a Negresse' (124). As a result, the book is a revelation and exploration of hybridity" (par. 21). After this acknowledgment, the essay then continues to focus on Cynara and black aesthetics/language in the novel. In such arguments, Other's racial reclassification is often relegated to the status of a parodic element. For many, such as Baschirotto, the omission is a result of argumentative focus: scholars productively explore the text primarily as a test case for the First Amendment, as a type of historical fiction, or as a neo-slave narrative.[28] For the mass of popular reviewers, Randall's postmodern pastiche and reclamation of the passing trope might itself seem too absurd to take seriously. But the silence surrounding Other's/Scarlett's racial identity potentially reflects a larger cultural dilemma generated by a media culture that is asking whether Barack Obama's presidency serves as the culmination of "color-blind" politics or even signals the beginning of a "post-racial" era.[29]

After all, to the postmodern, post–civil rights, twenty-first-century, "color-blind" reader, it shouldn't matter if "Scarlett" is black, should it? That is, if contemporary readers/reviewers *care* that she is black, the culture's current claims to racial "blindness" become empty rhetoric: in a "truly" color-blind or "post-racial" culture, Other's/Scarlett's racial identity would be inconsequential. Of course, we aren't really living in a "color-blind" culture any more than did the (fictional) Scarlett O'Hara. The continued importance of race is, as I have argued implicitly above, partially what fueled the lawsuit against Randall's novel in the first place: Scarlett O'Hara—*the* Scarlett O'Hara—historical icon of *white* womanhood—simply cannot be either *black* or dead.

Ironically, the relative silence on the issue of Other's/Scarlett's race in Randall's novel suggests its importance without engaging in the critical issues about race, history, knowledge, etc. that the racial switch engenders. It also signals the cultural anxiety that talking about race/racism still creates. In a speech delivered during Black History Month 2009, the first black U.S. Attorney General, Eric Holder, put it this way: "Though this nation has proudly thought of itself as an ethnic melting pot, in things racial we have always been and continue to be, in too many ways, essentially a nation of cowards. Though race related issues continue to occupy a significant portion of our political discussion, and though there remain many unresolved racial issues in this nation, we, average Americans, simply do not talk enough with each other about race" (par. 2). Holder argues here that although race is a recognized factor in politics, we still lack a wide-scale, productive, honest discussion about historical and continued race-based inequities and racism. Many Americans (especially, some would argue, many whites) are still uncomfortable talking about race. Not surprisingly, Holder was called out (mainly by conservative Republican media figures) for being a reverse racist, anti-patriotic, and out of touch. The reticence to talk honestly about race that Holder refers to, as well as the backlash his comments fostered, is yet another facet of the residue of racism that Randall's novel addresses. This reticence—and the discomfort that the topic of race can still generate—also contributed to the public uproar that the publication of Randall's novel initially caused, an uproar that attempted (but only partially succeeded) to shift the discussion of the novel away from race/history to a legal one about author's rights, intellectual property law, and copyright infringement.

If failing to discuss the cultural resistance to redefining Other/Scarlett—the Southern icon of white womanhood—as a black woman and to grapple openly with the consequences of such a redefinition (or race as a topic in general) further perpetuates systemic and latent racisms, however, insisting that Other/Scarlett is black runs the risk of reinscribing the one-drop rule that Randall's novel and other contemporary passing novels work to debunk in favor of a more fluid concept of racial multiplicity.

In this respect, Randall's postmodern novel is also a realistic one: race in the United States has never been a neat, simple, or easy topic, despite the illusion of a color line intended to maintain "racial purity" and easily recognizable and policeable racial categories/identities. It is precisely this messiness of race, history, and identity that *The Wind Done Gone* demands we discuss. If, that is, we aren't kept too busy having to fight for the novel's right to exist. While the definition and marketing of *The Wind Done Gone* as a parody served the purpose of giving Cynara Brown a public voice, those strategies also allowed U.S. culture to sidestep the larger issues at stake: Who owns history? Whose voice gets heard? According to the courts in this case, we can only counter the continued proliferation of (beloved) racist icons—and thus (hi)stories—through parody. Thus, the history of *The Wind Done Gone* demonstrates that, despite twenty-first-century political claims of color blindness, and even "post-racialism," we are still to some degree awash in the residue of a racism not yet gone with the wind.

Notes

A special thanks to Karl Henzy and the press readers for reading earlier drafts of this essay. Their comments were insightful and much appreciated.

1. Donaldson is drawing here on the work of Linda Hutcheon and Brian McHale.

2. See Haddox for a discussion of the novel as a neo-slave narrative.

3. Several sources, such as the Houghton Mifflin Web site ("Information About") and the Democracy Now Web site ("An African American History") attribute an identical sentence, verbatim, to Henry Louis Gates Jr. They do not specify a source, although Gates's support of Randall's novel was well publicized. Gates himself testified in the legal case surrounding the novel's publication: "[The novel] is a creative mechanism for the exercise of political speech . . . on the part of people who feel themselves oppressed . . . and wish to protest that condition. . . . African Americans have used parody since slavery to 'fight back' " (Beck 9, note 9). See Gates's *The Signifying Monkey* for more on his understanding of the use of parody, especially in the African American literary tradition.

4. For instance, see also Donaldson 270; Stewart 12; and Taylor, "Women and Dixie" 858.

5. The Mitchell Estate eventually settled out of court after the novel's publisher, Houghton Mifflin, agreed to pay an undisclosed amount to Morehouse College, a Historically Black College in Atlanta, Georgia. The novel's path to publication has become a case study in copyright law; much of the scholarly work published on the novel revolves around the court case and the appeal. For

a discussion of the case specifically in relation to copyright law, see Saint-Amour (207–20) and "Gone With the Wind Done Gone." For a more general review of the court battle and the book's initial reception by critics, see Williams.

6. The movie won eight traditional awards, plus a "Special Award for the Use of Color" and "The Irving Thalberg Memorial Award" for Selznick.

7. As Helen Taylor puts it in *Circling Dixie,* "*Gone With the Wind* . . . has sealed in popular imagination a fascinated nostalgia for the glamorous southern plantation house and an ordered hierarchical society in which slaves are 'family' and there is a mystical bond between landowner and the rich soil those slaves work for him" (29). Donaldson points out, however, that the image of the glorified Southern slave past did not escape criticism: "African Americans were particularly quick to criticize the novel and the film from their inception" (269). She quotes Alice Walker's description of the film from *In the Same River Twice*: "It is a film in which the suffering of millions of black people over hundreds of years of enslavement is trivialized to the point of laughter" (qtd. in Donaldson 269).

8. Or, as Warren Beck and Myles Clowers state: "More Americans have learned the story of the South during the years of the Civil War and Reconstruction from Margaret Mitchell's *Gone With the Wind* than from all the learned volumes on this period" (1:xi). Or, as Donaldson notes, Mary Condé has argued that "all African-American fiction about slavery since [*Gone With the Wind*'s] publication in 1936 has continued in some measure of response to it even if this is not made explicit" (qtd. in Donaldson 269).

9. Griffith's film is an adaptation of Thomas Dixon's *The Clansman, an Historical Romance of the Ku Klux Klan,* published to widespread acclaim in 1905. It is the second novel in Dixon's trilogy on the KKK. Linking the two to Mitchell's novel is not difficult in other ways as well. Grace Elizabeth Hale notes that "Mitchell claimed to have been 'practically raised on [Dixon's] books' " (262) and Helen Taylor also cites Dixon as a role model for Mitchell, although she also suggests that many Southern women writers had a greater influence ("Women and Dixie" 848).

10. Alexandra Ripley was selected by the Mitchell estate to write the sequel to *Gone With the Wind,* a novel entitled *Scarlett* published in 1991. Legally, because these two novels were authorized by the Mitchell estate, plagiarism or copyright infringement (the charges Randall faced) was not an issue. See Taylor's *Circling Dixie* for a discussion of the spinoffs of *Gone With the Wind* from a transatlantic perspective linking Southern culture and British culture.

11. James Boyle notes the trial judge's reaction to Other's death: " 'They killed Miss Scarlet!' the astonished trial judge said after reading Randall's book. My colleague Jennifer Jenkins, one of the lawyers in the case, recounts that the judge saw the case in relentlessly physical terms, seeing the parody as a 'bulldozer' and *Gone With the Wind* as a walled country estate into which the bulldozer had violently trespassed. He was consequently unimpressed with the claim that this 'bulldozer' was protected by the First Amendment" (27).

12. Taylor alternately calls such works a "literary echo" and distinguishes them from a sequel: "The 'echo' begins with the original and then plays games with readers' knowledge and expectations of the characters and narrative development; it invites them into a knowing literary conceit, teases and pleases them with surprise and shocks" (32–33).

13. Saint-Amour makes this point—and lists other paired texts—in the conclusion to his monograph in which he explores copyright law and the literary imagination. "*Gone With the Wind Done Gone*" also lists such paired texts, noting (as does Saint-Amour) that one significant difference is that the copyright protection had expired on the earlier texts in other cases.

14. *Airplane* had one sequel, *Scary Movie* has five.

15. When the audience misses the parodic nature of a performance, of course, the absurd can pass unexamined as authentic: in a moment approaching the surreal, Colbert was invited to testify as an expert on immigration in a congressional hearing by the House Judiciary Committee on Immigration (Sept. 24, 2010). He testified in character. Such a moment highlights the potential (and potentially dangerous) slippage between parody and reality. His invitation to the congressional hearing also makes one wonder how many viewers recognize Colbert's parody at all (a question supported by the seemingly perpetual list of interviewees who accept invitations to be on Colbert's show, apparently with no recognition that they are the object of the joke). A recent study conducted by the Ohio State University suggests that interpretation is tied to individual-belief: "Conservatives were more likely to report that Colbert only pretends to be joking and genuinely meant what he said while liberals were more likely to report that Colbert used satire and was not serious when offering political statements. Conservatism also significantly predicted perceptions that Colbert disliked liberalism" (LaMarre, Landreville, and Beam). Neither of these understandings—that Colbert is "joking" or that he is "not serious"—suggests a nuanced recognition of Colbert's political satire. In the second vein, Colbert's presence at the 2010 congressional hearing potentially allowed some viewers to dismiss the proceedings themselves as absurd, despite Congress's very real power to enact law/policy.

16. Boyle notes: "[C]urrent intellectual property policy is overwhelmingly and tragically *bad* in ways that everyone, and not just lawyers or economists, should care about" (xi; emphasis in original). Similarly, focusing on copyright law in the Internet age, Lawrence Lessig argues that "[f]ree cultures are cultures that leave a great deal open for others to build upon; unfree, or permission cultures, leave much less. Ours was a free culture. It is becoming much less so" (30).

17. Although outside the scope of this essay's focus, another line in the novel suggests that Other is also passing as straight. Cynara writes: "But Other liked girls real good. I almost think the reason she loved Dreamy Gentleman so, was that there was so much boy in his man and so much girl in his boy" (101). For more on unintentional passing, see Nerad.

18. Scarlett's identity flaws (that she is too headstrong, for instance) are largely linked in *GWTW* either to necessity brought about by the Civil War or

to her Irish heritage. For a discussion of the racial history of the Irish in America, especially in relation to blackness and African Americans, see Ignatiev.

19. In what follows, my reading of Randall's text is not in itself Lacanian, Hegelian, or postcolonial. Rather, I am suggesting that the novel itself plays with these theories/critical tropes as much as it does with its fictional influences.

20. "Depthlessness" (Fredric Jameson's term) as a symptom of the postmodern protagonist (and landscape) stems from poststructuralist arguments and a rejection of depth models such as Freud's understanding of the latent and the manifest. Jameson writes: "What replaces these various depth models is for the most part a conception of practices, discourses, and textual play. . . . [D]epth is replaced by surface, or by multiple surfaces" (12). The "depthless" model(s) of identity highlights performance and surface rather than a core, stable Self. *The Wind Done Gone*—as do other postmodern texts written by minority or feminist authors—however, emphasizes the performative aspects of identity while also recognizing the impact of "history" and culture on shaping identity. Such texts also often (perhaps paradoxically) recognize the danger of wholly rejecting more stable models of identity necessary for political mobilization (e.g., the civil rights movement or the women's movement). See Gregson for an accessible, introductory overview of postmodernism and gender, race, postcolonialism, etc.

21. See Fanon for more on the internalization of racism by the oppressed.

22. This same resentment over a slave mother "giving up" her girl child is explored in Toni Morrison's novel *a mercy* (2008). The mother in Morrison's novel begs to keep her still-nursing baby boy and urges the sale of her daughter, Florens, instead. The novel ultimately reveals that the mother's actions are an attempt to protect her daughter from even greater suffering. So, too, here. The novel suggests that Mammy sacrifices moments with Cynara for a greater goal of protecting her. The novel also suggests that Planter sells Cynara (for $1) to his friend so that his daughter is never in the position of having her sister's husband take her to bed, as would happen, he presumes, if "Cindy" were to stay on Tata (173). The irony, of course, is that Cynara and Other both do end up having sex with the same man. To Cynara's request that Planter set her free as an alternative, he replies: "It is better to be a slave to a rich man than a slave to poverty. Poverty is a cruel master, a cruel master every day. And there are kind masters in the world" (173). But he adds: "You distract your mother more than you know. And I have lost too many children for her to lose none" (173).

23. The Mammy/Lady pair and the Cynara/Other pair both engage this Janus-like construction of the female body in the United States, with Cynara ultimately rejecting this binaric approach.

24. Raimon later nods at this fact—"this sense of fluid maternal boundaries in *The Wind Done Gone* extends to the racial origins of Lady and Other, whom we learn are both of mixed descent" (157)—without thoroughly recognizing how it might change her original claim about the relationships being cross-racial.

25. The logic of this letter also implicitly suggests that Mammy potentially killed Lady's three sons not because they would be "three sober white men" on

the place, as Miss Priss puts it (63), but because they showed physical signs of blackness. Further evidence for this as a possibility is the suggestion that Other's daughter Precious showed black physical traits. Precious cried in the night not because she was afraid of the dark but because Mammy put a clothespin on her nose while she slept. She also rubbed lemon oil on her elbows to hide "signs" of blackness (127).

26. One way out of this dilemma, of course, is to sue Randall for copyright infringement and suppress the novel.

27. Haddox argues, in contrast, that *The Wind Done Gone* ultimately reinscribes a racial essentialism, noting particularly Cynara's reference to "blood memory." Suggesting that Cynara locates racial difference in the dangerous ground of historical memory, or a "common experience of oppression," that is overlaid upon an innate racial essence (131), he writes:

> [H]er consciousness of the personal history that she and Other share suggests that this shared consciousness is, at bottom, biological. . . . In other words, even if "memory"—the consciousness of a shared history of oppression—becomes the defining quality of racial identity, this memory is ultimately derived from a deeper, more essential source—"blood memory"—which must then be made conscious. (Haddox 132)

I disagree with Haddox's supposition here, although only perhaps by emphasizing certain of Cynara's claims at the expense of others (the desire for a postmodern protagonist to represent a logically cohesive, consistent position is arguably a desire bound to be thwarted). I believe that Cynara's reference to memory is to a more personal, direct *experience* of being black or being white in American culture.

28. For instance, Yaeger focuses her article on Randall and Kara Walker on lactation, excess, and exploitation of the black female body. Haddox focuses on the ludic in African American historical fiction, although he does discuss Other's racial identity in the essay's last few pages.

29. And this even as that same media touts the GOP momentary forerunner of the day, the African American Herman Cain (complete with historically racialized name), in the runup to the 2012 primaries. Like Obama, Cain's race was used to illustrate how race is no longer a significant restrictive element in U.S. culture. Redux 2012.

Works Cited

Airplane. Dir. Jim Abrahams, David Zucker, and Jerry Zucker. Paramount, 1980.

"An African American History Month Special: A Look at 'The Wind Done Gone,' a Parody of 'Gone With the Wind' Told From a Slave's Perspective. 21 Feb 2002. Web. 22 Dec. 2008.

Argall, Nicole. "A Rib from My Chest: Cynara's Journey as an Africana Womanist." *CLA Journal* 47:2 (2003): 231–43. Print.

Bagdikian, Ben. H. et al. "Letter of Support." 10 April 2001. Web. 19 Dec. 2008.

Bartholomew, Anne. Promotional comment on *Rhett Butler's People*. 9 January 2009. Web.

Baschirotto, Corinna. "'I want to be the rule itself, not the exception that proves it'" *The Wind Done Gone*: Rewriting *Gone With the Wind*." *The 49th Parallel: An Interdisciplinary Journal of North American Studies* 14 (2004): np. Print.

Beck, Joseph M. "Copyright and the First Amendment after *The Wind Done Gone*." *Vanderbilt Journal of Entertainment Law and Practice* 5.2 (2003): 1–10. Print.

Beck, Warren and Myles Clowers. *Understanding American History Through Fiction*. New York: McGraw-Hill, 1975. Print

Boyle, James. *The Public Domain: Enclosing the Commons of the Mind*. New Haven: Yale UP, 2010. Print.

Donaldson, Susan V. "Telling Forgotten Stories of Slavery in the Postmodern South." *Southern Literary Journal* 40:2 (2008): 267–83. Print.

Fanon, Frantz. *Black Skin White Masks*. 1952. Trans. Charles Lam Markmann. New York: Grove Press, 1967. Print.

"*Gone With the Wind Done Gone*: 'Re-Writing' and Fair Use." *Harvard Law Review* 115.4 (2002): 1193–1216. Print.

Gray, Jonathan, Jeffrey P. Jones, and Ethan Thompson. *Satire TV: Politics and Comedy in the Post-Network Era*. New York: New York UP, 2009. Print.

Gregson, Ian. *Postmodern Literature*. London: Arnold, 2004. Print.

Guy-Sheftall, Beverly. "The Body Politic: Black Female Sexuality and the Nineteenth-Century Euro-American Imagination." *Skin Deep, Spirit Strong: The Black Female Body in American Culture*. Ed. Kimberly Wallace-Sanders. Ann Arbor: U of Michigan P, 2002: 13–35. Print.

Haddox, Thomas. "Alice Randall's *The Wind Done Gone* and the Ludic in African American Historical Fiction." *Modern Fiction Studies* 53.1 (2007): 120–39. Print.

Hale, Grace Elizabeth. *Making Whiteness: The Culture of Segregation in the South, 1890–1940*. New York: Vintage, 1998. Print.

Holder, Eric. "Remarks as Prepared for Delivery by Attorney General Eric Holder at the Department of Justice African American History Month Program." 18 Feb. 2009. Web. 10 June 2009.

Hutcheon, Linda. *A Poetics of Postmodernism: History, Theory, Fiction*. New York: Routledge, 1988. Print.

———. *A Theory of Parody: The Teachings of Twentieth-Century Art Forms*. New York: Methuen, 1985. Print.

"Information About Suntrust Bank v. Houghton Mifflin Company." 17 April 2001. Web. 22 Dec. 2008.

Jameson, Fredric. *Postmodernism or, The Cultural Logic of Late Capitalism*. Durham: Duke UP, 1991. Print.

LaMarre, Heather L., Kristen D. Landreville, and Michael A. Beam. "The Irony of Satire: Political Ideology and the Motivation to See What You Want to See in The Colbert Report." *The International Journal of Press/Politics* 14.2 (2009): 212–32. Print.

Lessig, Lawrence. *Free Culture: The Nature and Future of Creativity*. New York: Penguin, 2005. Print.

McCaig, Donald. *Rhett Butler's People*. New York: St. Martin's, 2007. Print.

McHale, Brian. *Postmodernist Fiction*. New York: Methuen, 1987. Print.

Mitchell, Margaret. *Gone With the Wind*. 1936. New York: Scribner's, 2007. Print.

Morrison, Toni. *a mercy*. New York: Knopf, 2008. Print.

Nerad, Julie Cary. "Slippery Language and False Dilemmas in Passing Novels by Child, Howells, and Harper." *American Literature* 75.4 (2003): 813–41. Print.

Pynchon, Thomas. *The Crying of Lot 49*. 1965. New York: Harper Perennial, 2006. Print.

Raimon, Eve Allegra. *The "Tragic Mulatta" Revisited: Race and Nationalism in Nineteenth-Century Antislavery Fiction*. New Brunswick: Rutgers UP, 2004. Print.

Randall, Alice. *The Wind Done Gone*. New York: Houghton Mifflin, 2001. Print.

Saint-Amour, Paul K. *The Copywrights: Intellectual Property and the Literary Imagination*. Ithaca: Cornell UP, 2003. Print.

Scary Movie. Dir. Keenen Ivory Wayans. Miramax Films, 2000.

Stewart, Mart A. "Teaching *Gone With the Wind* in the Socialist Republic of Vietnam." *Southern Cultures* 11.3 (2005): 9–34. Print.

Taylor, Helen. *Circling Dixie: Contemporary Southern Culture Through a Transatlantic Lens*. New Brunswick: Rutgers UP, 2001. Print.

———. "Women and Dixie: The Feminization of Southern Women's History and Culture." *American Literary History* 18.4 (2006): 847–60. Print.

Whitehead, Colson. *The Intuitionist*. New York: Anchor Books, 1999. Print.

Williams, Bettye J. "Glimpsing Parody, Language, and Post-Reconstruction Themes in Alice Randall's *The Wind Done Gone*." *CLA Journal* 47.3 (2004): 310–25. Print.

Yaeger, Patricia. "Cicum-Atlantic Superabundance: Milk as World-Making in Alice Randall and Kara Walker." *American Literature: A Journal of Literary History, Criticism, and Bibliography* 78.4 (2006): 769–98. Print.

7

Passing for Chicano, Passing for White

Negotiating Filipino American Identity in Brian Ascalon Roley's *American Son*

Amanda Page

Just as the Civil Rights Act of 1964 changed the racial dynamics of the United States, so, too, did the Immigration Act of 1965, which rewrote immigration policy to allow an equal number of immigrants to enter the United States from all countries of the globe, drastically changing more than a century of exclusionary policies that had previously admitted immigrants "according to a hierarchy of racial desirability" (Ngai 227).[1] The passage of this legislation led to an influx of immigration that greatly altered the racial makeup of the nation by the end of the twentieth century. During the 1990s, Los Angeles saw more than 2.8 million new Asian and Latina/o immigrants, creating new racial tensions as low-wage jobs were being filled by immigrants (Kim 36). Critic Jinah Kim notes: "With the growth of these communities, Los Angeles became the first and largest U.S. city without a claim to a white majority population. This reality gave rise to a multiculturalist discourse of inclusion and anti-immigration nativist fervor" (36). The nativist "fervor" against largely Asian American and Latina/o immigrants that Kim cites has had lasting rhetorical and political staying power over the last two decades.[2]

Because of this dramatic shift in demographics, legal scholar Rachel F. Moran argues that the traditional approach to civil rights advocacy fails to redress adequately new forms of discrimination against groups such as Latina/os:

> In attacking the evils of discrimination against Blacks in the South, this [traditional civil rights] framework has elevated race and ethnicity to a position of central importance in defining equality of opportunity. However, race and ethnicity have proven to be somewhat artificial organizing principles for Latinos because they have different racial origins and come from a range of countries. Consequently, issues related to racial and ethnic identity frequently have been barriers to overcome, rather than sources of mutual identification and support. (10)

By focusing on remedying historic injustice and predicating activism on unified racial identification for mobilization, Moran suggests, the traditional civil rights framework does not meet the needs of Latina/os and, by extension, other groups who fall outside of the black-white binary of historic U.S. race relations. Instead, Latina/o activists prefer class-based approaches to improving lives, as "many Latinos believe that the most significant impediment to upward mobility is neither race nor ethnicity, but poverty" (10). This fundamental difference of approach, along with the ethnic and racial rivalries created by a changing economy, prevents lasting interracial and interethnic coalitions among Latina/os, African Americans, and other groups (Moran 12).

Brian Ascalon Roley's 2001 novel *American Son* examines these contemporary barriers to political alliances among racial and ethnic groups in 1990s Los Angeles. Indeed, as a seemingly pointed indication that the dominant American script of black-white racial conflict is inadequate in a more diverse contemporary U.S. racial landscape, the novel opens in April 1993—exactly one year after Los Angeles erupted in riots that pitted racial minority groups against each other in the aftermath of the Rodney King verdict.[3] King-Kok Cheung discusses the 1992 L.A. riot within the context of the shift in demographics, noting that "[d]uring the seventies and the eighties the community was transformed from a predominantly black to a mixed black and Latino area, with Latinos constituting nearly half the population" (6). According to Cheung, these newcomers had to compete for already scarce jobs and that, "[i]nto this volatile milieu entered Korean immigrants" who opened stores and were seen as additional economic competition (6). Cheung argues that racial and ethnic tensions in Los Angeles were further fueled by widespread beliefs in various minority stereotypes (which were magnified by the media during the riots) that ultimately worked to pit minority against minority. In its exploration of Asian American and Latina/o subject positions in 1990s L.A., *American Son* acknowledges perceived racial and ethnic difference as a real barrier to lasting interracial solidarity in the face of virulent anti-immigration rhetoric that recodes racism as nativism and pits marginalized immigrant groups against each other. However, by inserting into the traditional black-white paradigm racial and ethnic groups such as Asian Americans and Latino/s that are, as Gayle Wald notes, usually made culturally and politically invisible by the traditional U.S. racial binary (14), the novel highlights the importance of accommodating new subjects in the post–civil rights era.

In *American Son,* those new subjects are Roley's protagonists, Tomas and Gabe Sullivan, the sons of a German American father and a Filipino mother, and the primary narrative strategy is the trope of racial passing, a trope deeply embedded in the African American tradition of social protest. Almost two decades ago, critic Elaine K. Ginsberg noted how the trope of passing illuminates various processes intrinsic to the construction of identities:

> [Passing] is about identities: their creation or imposition, their adoption or rejection, their accompanying rewards or penalties. Passing is also about the boundaries established between identity categories and about the individual and cultural anxieties induced by boundary crossing. Finally, passing is about specularity: the visible and the invisible, the seen and the unseen. ("Intro" 2)

Fundamentally concerned with the establishment and transgression of boundaries, with the negotiation of new identities and cultural anxieties, passing is perhaps the perfect literary trope for contemporary authors, such as Roley, who are looking to expand the American literary canon to include the experience of the marginalized in a culture of rapidly shifting demographics and a splintering system of racial classification. The liminal position of these brothers as Filipino Americans allows Roley to extend the boundaries of traditional passing narratives to groups who remain outside the dominant binaric racial discourse and place Asian American experience at the center of the American story. The atypical permutations of passing also allow Roley to investigate the affinities and differences within and between Asian and Latino *collective* identities, as negotiated within an inadequate and reductive black-white dichotomy and a white hegemony. Although the protagonists' experiences as displaced, marginalized, invisible, ethnic Others have the potential to create unique possibilities for critique, as well as for bridging gaps between various "nonwhite" groups, I argue that interracial alliances ultimately fail in the face of persistent white supremacy in the novel.

By centralizing the Filipino American, *American Son* ventures down an avenue well suited for examining the ways that immigrants grapple with the multiplicity of racial and ethnic group dynamics they find in America, and particularly in 1990s L.A. Theorist Lisa Lowe notes that "the specific history of Asian immigration in relation to U.S. citizenship is different from the histories of other migrant or racialized groups, such as African Americans, Native Americans, and Chicanos/Latinos." However, she adds that "the Asian American critique of citizenship generated by its specific history opens the space for . . . cross-race and cross national possibilities" (35–36). Though the boundaries between the labels "Latino" and "Asian American" are themselves not well defined,[4] this kind of "cross national" potential is perhaps particularly apropos in the case of Filipino Americans. Filipinos share a history of Spanish colonization with Latinos, yet their homeland is in Asia rather than the Americas. Negotiating the relationship between Filipinos and the larger body of Latinidad in the Americas thus becomes a maze of identification and disidentification, dependent on individual definitions of and identification with Latino and/or Asian identity. This already multifaceted hybridity becomes especially difficult to negotiate in the United States where the complexity of Filipino American identification has been further complicated by the experience of U.S. imperialism in the Philippines.[5] The result of the meeting of Asian, Spanish, and Anglo-American cultures creates, in Chicana writer/theorist Gloria Anzaldúa's terminology, the [Filipino American] mestizo, individuals who fit neatly into no single category or label of collective identity.

In *Borderlands/La Frontera*, Anzaldúa illuminates the complications and contradictions of the mestizo identity:

> Cradled in one culture, sandwiched between two cultures, straddling all three cultures and their value systems, *la mestiza* undergoes a struggle of the flesh, a struggle of borders, an inner war. Like all people, we perceive the version of reality that our culture communicates. Like others having or living in more than one culture, we get multiple, often opposing messages. The coming together of two self-consistent but habitually incompatible frames of reference causes *un choque*, a cultural collision. (100)

Although Anzaldúa is describing a Chicana/o mestizo identity, her definition applies easily to the Filipino mestizo as well. The mestizo identity both produces Lowe's vision of interracial/national collaboration and the creation of alternative constructs that defy the dominant discourse, and causes individuals' inability to create sustainable relationships across ethnic boundaries. The liminality of the mestizo, which is potentially liberating for its resistance to a reductive racial binary, is in fact *un choque,* the cultural collision that generates anxiety for the mestizos in Roley's novel.

Like earlier "tragic mulattoes" of black and white descent, narrator Gabe Sullivan and his older brother Tomas must negotiate their identities in a culture that has no framework to accommodate the complications of being *both,* in this case, Asian (Filipino) and "white." Uncomfortable in this fragmented state, they try to position themselves within a single racial identity. Tomas first chooses to pass for Chicano to gain visibility in Los Angeles gang culture, while younger brother Gabe initially passes for white in northern California as a way of escaping the violence and poverty of Los Angeles. By passing, they attempt to substitute "the coherent image of the other for a complex, unstable self" (Kawash 65).[6] Put in practical terms, Roley presents each brother's passing as the result of a desire simultaneously to gain visibility as well as economic and cultural power in a society that continues to define people using narrow categories of identity. Both brothers pass in and out of various identities as it suits them (or as others project upon them). Thus, with each performance of a new identity, Roley's characters—as do other passers before them—underscore for readers the arbitrary (or, at least, performed) "nature" of identity. Although neither brother in Roley's novel finally subverts racial categorization (indeed, as I argue below, they succumb to the prevailing racial hierarchy), the novel's use of the trope of passing does specifically highlight the differing processes—and stakes—of racialization for ethnic others.

Within the traditional U.S. black-white racial binary, created and maintained by hypodescent (the cultural understanding of race as singular, exclusive, and biologically determined by the race of the subordinate parent), "mulatto" passers are usually blacks passing for white.[7] Where the traditional black-to-white passing narrative hinges upon the "one-drop rule," which determines the mulatto's "true" (i.e., black) identity however, critic Jennifer Ho argues that Asian American identity is often less fixed:

> While the "one-drop" rule guided definitions of African American subjectivity, this is not the litmus test to authenticate one's

> Asian identity, in so far as the evidence for "Asian-ness" is not based on a shared belief system and imaginary acceptance of "race" but is differently coded on the very body. For if one claims to have an Asian American grandparent but "looks" non-Asian (black or white or Latino), then the belief is that one is not Asian American but whatever one looks like (be it black, white, or Latino). (144)

"Asian-ness" thus fractures the reductive racial binary, just as it highlights the role of visibility in common practices of racial identification in the United States. Of course, as critic Antonia Darder explains, we must also understand "notions of 'race identity and difference' as *politically* formed rather than embedded in the color of the skin or a given nature (Hall, 1990a, 1990b). In other words, to identify as black or Chicano is not so much a question of color as it is a question of cultural, historical, and political difference" (137; emphasis added). Granted, racial classifications based on indices of "difference" or even on feelings of identification are always potentially in conflict with the visually based system of race, which is what makes passing possible. The deviation I want to stress here is that historically, under the one-drop rule, a black-white biracial person would usually be understood as black even if he didn't "look" black and even if he didn't identify as black. This is not necessarily the case for the Asian-white person, who might more easily claim whiteness if she "looks" white. The fact that Roley's protagonists do not "look" Asian—and are therefore not defined as Asian by those evaluating their physical appearance—should allow these subjects more leeway in claiming "authentic" identities than their "black" counterparts in traditional black-white passing narratives, individuals whose racial identity was determined by the generally accepted one-drop rule, regardless of physical appearances. This is arguably one distinction between the "mulatto" and the "mestizo." The shift from the mulatto to mestizo passing subject might open up the boundaries of identification for the multiracial subject, transforming the either/or choice of the tragic mulatto into a more fluid and dynamic identification that allows for more than one racial or ethnic identity. And indeed the novel dangles the prospect of such multiplicity and its potential for atypical interethnic affinity before the reader as a postmodern alternative to the rigid racial structures of the past.

However, even in the 1990s post–civil rights United States, the residue of hypodescent and the consequences of white racism linger, leaving those prospects unrealized alternatives to a reductive understanding of race and identity for the characters, if not for the readers. Throughout the novel, both brothers, who have internalized the rule of hypodescent even as they choose to pass, undercut the possibility of a multiracial subject position. Their hybrid identity is thus a source of tension rather than a source of power that critics such as Anzaldúa, Lowe, and Ho theorize as possible. Unable to extricate themselves from the intractable racial epistemology that has no space for the mestizo, Tomas and Gabe choose passing as a strategy not because it destabilizes racial categories but rather because it functions within the framework of discrete categories and thus allows them to inhabit a unified, single racial identity. Their world is still one where "there is not a space or language for mixed-race people to claim a multiple, hybrid, or heterogeneous subjectivity" (Ho 143) despite the greater potential liminality of Asian-ness. Thus, due to their location at the crossroads of "habitually incompatible frames of reference," neither brother is able to feel comfortable in any single *or* multiethnic political collective identity.

Indeed, echoing the language of the U.S. racial system, at the novel's opening Gabe stresses that Tomas is "really" half white and half Filipino (15). Through Gabe, the narrative describes the evolution of Tomas's passing:

> At my school—Saint Dominic's—everyone thought I was white for a while. Tomas had gone there first and he had passed as a white surfer. There were no other surfers there, but he was known as one—he even bought a board and had our mother take him to the beach three times a week—and he put Sun-In in his hair, though instead of turning blond it went all red. Then he began hanging out with Mexicans, who are tougher. He stopped surfing and dyed his hair black again. If anyone tried calling him Asian he beat them up, and he started taunting these Korean kids who could barely speak English. . . . Finally, Tomas got kicked out of school for smashing a Japanese boy's car window with a tire iron. (30)

Here, as throughout the novel, Tomas understands implicitly the relationship between performance/appearance and racial category, although his understanding never reaches the point of destabilizing racial identity itself. This paradox is not unusual in passing narratives with characters who are conditioned to believe in a racial essence: for Tomas to "pass" as Chicano, he must conceal his "authentic" Filipino identity. He wants to "be" (or be seen as) Chicano instead of Asian, without recognizing either of those identities as constructed, even as he deliberately constructs a (specific) racial/ethnic performance. Thus, he applies the racial "logic" that maintains the traditional racial system.

However, his deviation from the black-white dichotomy is significant, as is the fact that Tomas rejects both of his biologically determined "choices." From Gabe's perspective, his brother is "really half white, half Filipino" (15). The framework of their white father's racism and their Filipino mother's victimization—which replays the cultural experience of white imperialist domination in the Philippines—however, disqualifies both individual racial identities ("white" or "Filipino") as desirable alternatives. Tomas thus rejects both of those identities in favor of a Chicano one. Passing as Chicano—and specifically as a violent Mexican gangster—allows him both to claim another ethnic label and actively to oppose the groups he is denying. In other words, Tomas's alternative identity as a Chicano, he believes, resists a white supremacist/colonialist identity while offering an empowering alternative to a "weak" Asian identity stemming from the history of feminization of Filipino men under colonization.

Indeed, his rejection of his Filipino heritage is meant to obliterate any association with being a "submissive" Asian like his mother or brother, a stereotype specifically linked to the history of white colonization of the Philippines. Gary Y. Okihiro notes that Filipino men were historically "rendered feminine in their barbarism or condition of stunted intellectual development (as in children and women) and in the manliness of their women . . . the very visible racialization (and gendering and sexualizing) of Filipina/os underwrote the U.S. colonial project in the Philippines and its domestic agenda of white supremacy, patriarchy, and nationalism" (37). Tomas's self-hate manifests itself in his attacks on Asian American students and his violent reaction to being identified as Asian. Caught in the trap of patriarchal, imperialist racism, Tomas himself uses racism against fellow Asians in an attempt to reposition himself. As Ian F. Haney López notes, "Though the decision to pass may be made for many reasons, among these the power of prejudice and self-hate cannot be denied" (14). Tomas's use of violence against Asians not only distances himself from his own "Asian-ness," but also, in his eyes, solidifies his performance of a Chicano identity. Interethnic conflict—rather than coalition—becomes fundamental to establishing a masculine identity.

If Tomas is going to assume an identity that is not his own ("real") Filipino one, his family would prefer him to assimilate to white culture. Passing as white would make more sense to his family, who clearly values white culture above Chicano culture and who recognizes that being "white" would offer him potential entry into higher socioeconomic classes. Gabe, again, explains:

> [Tomas] is the son who causes [our mother] embarrassment by showing up at family parties with his muscles covered in tattoos and his head shaved down to stubble and his eyes bloodshot from pot. He . . . dresses like a Mexican, and it troubles our mother that he does this. She cannot understand why if he wants to be something he is not he does not at least try to look white. (15)

Here, Tomas's tattoos and shaved head signal (a stereotyped) "Mexican" identity to his family. Mrs. Sullivan's brother, Betino Laurel, writes letters from Manila to the family condemning Tomas's behavior, explaining that he finds it "puzzling that a Filipino boy such as Tomas should choose to spend his time with poor Mexican children when there certainly must be nice American and Asian children of successful people in Los Angeles" (12). Betino's letter reveals how racialized class values play a significant role in the Laurel family's preference for Asians and "Americans" (by which he tellingly means "white" Americans) who are more "successful" than their "poor" Latino counterparts in L.A.[8] Indeed, an explicit racial hierarchy—one in which Asians are "above" Chicanos and closer to "whites"—plays out in the novel, working against the formation of a sense of collective identity between the two marginalized groups and illustrating how a dominant group can maintain its power by forcing divisions between nonwhite groups through a process of race ranking and self-policing.[9] Specifically, by perpetuating the myth of the model Asian minority, the Laurels are able to distinguish themselves from the "lesser" minority groups such as Chicana/os and establish a superior position for themselves in the U.S. construction of ethnicity, regardless of the racism inherent in that construct—a construct that always values "white" Americans above Asian Americans.

The myth of the "model minority," as critic David Palumbo-Liu explains, "reifies Asian American identity [as hardworking, successful people] and deploys this reification programmatically against other groups, mapping out specific positionings of minorities within the U.S. political economy" (174).[10] The Laurels' distaste for Chicanos in L.A. also particularly gestures toward the family's internalization of nativist rhetoric in contemporary California, a rhetoric that positions the "model minority" against "undesirable" immigrants from Mexico. Kent A. Ono and John M. Sloop note:

> The history of media providing images of racial exceptionalism for Asian Pacific Americans, in contrast to images of African American and Chicana and Chicano undeservedness, dates at least to the early 1960s civil rights era. . . . The discourse pitted those nominated as exceptional Asian Pacific Americans against those constructed as troubled Mexicanas, Mexicanos, Chicanas, and Chicanos, rather than recognizing common and interrelated levels of experience and traditions of oppression. (163)

In the context of 1990s California, the model minority rhetoric often uses the figure of the idealized Asian immigrant to argue that Chicana/os are in fact receiving preferential treatment under U.S. immigration law to the detriment of law-abiding Asian immigrants, who are positioned as victims (Jacobson 62). By positioning one immigrant group against another, the nativist argument masks its own racism by arguing that immigration policy is itself racist against Asians. By presenting the Laurels' acceptance of such racist "American" rhetoric against Mexican immigrants, Roley critiques the ways in which Asian Americans are invested in their own "privileged" rhetorical status even as it prevents them from realizing potential solidarities with another community that shares migrant roots and labor concerns.

Tomas, by refusing to adhere to his family's preference for assimilating into the dominant culture and by instead identifying with another liminal ethnic group, could potentially reject the racism that the rest of the family takes as the natural order of race relations in the United States and enables the possibility, at least, of a collective identity not based on biology ("blood") or even nationality. In other words, Tomas's claim to Chicano identity can potentially be recast as a rejection of arbitrary boundaries between and as a validation of the common aspects of Chicano and Filipino experience. Disillusioned by overt racism and limited economic possibilities, Tomas's affinity with Chicanos reveals to the reader the similarity between subsequent generations of Asian American and Latina/o immigrants that the larger nativist rhetoric of the anti-immigration movement works to undermine. Laura Pulido notes that the children of first-generation immigrants "grew up in this society and have had to confront the reality of prejudice as well as interethnic contact, regardless of their class position, [and] often see things differently than their parents" (233).

Similarly, sociologists Min Zhou and Yang Sao Xiong note that second-generation Asian Americans born in the United States are more attuned to racism than their foreign-born parents, and despite their supposed "model minority" status, they are "still keenly aware of their inferior racial status, internalizing the disadvantages associated with it" (1149). As a second-generation Filipino American, Tomas's passing could reflect the larger discontent among many children of immigrants with the racialized class system within the United States.

However, as critic Martha J. Cutter notes, "only when 'passing' becomes a subversive strategy for *avoiding* the enclosures of a racist, classist, and sexist society does it become truly liberating" (75). Again, Tomas is not interested in building interethnic alliances across groups that are economically marginalized. Instead, in addition to providing psychological distance from his white imperialist father, passing as Chicano allows him to exploit an economic opportunity latent in the racism that permeates the system. Tomas's Chicano gangster identity offers him an avenue to economic empowerment that is in distinct opposition to the avenues open to the "model minority." As Chicano, Tomas starts a business selling attack dogs to wealthy white clients who assume that the attack dogs are "authentic" because he is Chicano gangster—an association an Asian identity would not establish. This dynamic plays out when Gabe accompanies Tomas on a sale. Tomas orders Gabe to "[s]it down. If the client sees you standing there like that he's gonna think you're my houseboy" (18). Tomas views Gabe's "submissive" appearance as an economic detriment when selling attack dogs. His presumption is not without some justification, as one white client's (racist) hysteria around Tomas disappears around ostensibly "Asian" Gabe, who is not perceived as threatening when alone. Indeed, Tomas specifically exploits his white clients' racism for his business's success:

> He never tells his clients he is not Mexican. Sometimes he buys pit bulls in Venice or downtown where all the black people have them chained in their alleys and when you drive through the alleyways you can hear them barking for miles. The sound echoes between the buildings. He can buy them for forty dollars there and then place an ad in a West LA newspaper like the Evening Outlook and sell them for a couple hundred dollars. (20)

By buying the dogs on the cheap in black neighborhoods where wealthy white clients would never go, Tomas acts an intermediary and makes a large profit. Having selected to perform an identity racially in between black and white, Tomas literally becomes the go-between for white people looking to buy "tough" dogs. Implicit in this arrangement is the white clients' unspoken preference for doing business with seemingly "tough" Chicanos who are not as tough as the black people who are raising the dogs. Many black to white passers (both fictional and real) passed for economic opportunity as a means of manipulating and/or critiquing inequitable labor and capital in the United States, but here, Roley uses Tomas's business to satirize the larger structures of racialized labor. He also illustrates how minority groups, too, become invested in the dominant system in ways that work against minority cooperation and the formation of a collective identity.

Ultimately, the possibilities for a multiracial/mestizo collective identity generated by Tomas's choice to identify as Chicano unravel because his performance of a Chicano identity is based almost entirely on superficial and stereotyped markers. In addition to—or to augment—his business, which is dependent upon racial stereotypes and white racism, Tomas wears gang clothes and drives "a white Oldsmobile, the type Mexican gangsters prefer because they can pile so many people into the back seat" (40). And, his tattoos are "mostly gang, Spanish, and old-lady Catholic. As he leans forward, the thin fabric of his shirt moves over his Virgin of Guadalupe tattoo that covers his back from his neck down to his pants" (17). When his family finds out about the tattoos, his uncle writes, "The Virgin Mary! I hardly think his motives were ones of reverence" (135). Though his family is Catholic, Tomas's motivations for tattooing this particular incarnation of the Virgin Mary have less to do with celebrating his own heritage (imposed by colonizers) or religion than they do appropriating a powerful symbol of Chicano identity. Anzaldúa identifies the Virgin of Guadalupe as "the single most potent religious, political and cultural image of the Chicano/*mexicano*" (52). Tomas uses this tattoo as a way literally to mark his body with signs of Chicano identity, allowing him only to masquerade as a member of an ethnic/racial group to which he understands he has no "authentic" biological claim.

Paradoxically, this most overt sign of Chicano identity causes him anxiety with "authentic" Chicanos who might see past the body to detect flaws in his performance. This is because the tattoo is meant to signify primarily to a *non*-Chicano audience. For instance, Tomas wears a thin T-shirt to show off his tattoo to a white client, but, with Chicanos, he "seems embarrassed . . . and he keeps it turned away" (45). The fear of exposure is a common element of passing narratives. However, in a marked deviation from traditional black-white passing narratives, Tomas believes he can only successfully pass *outside of* the group he is trying to appropriate as his own. His telling discomfort with Chicanos exposes that, despite his seeming subversion of racial identification, he, like so many passing subjects, is performing a racialized identity primarily for a *white* audience. That is, Tomas's racial performance is not primarily targeted toward the group into which he wishes to pass but instead toward non-Chicano whites. Even as Roley's shift from traditional mulatto to mestizo passing works to show the multiple planes of racial interaction in American race relations, his character's performance of Chicano identity, as in traditional passing, continues to be motivated by the need for white approval as a means of gaining an economic advantage. Tomas rejects both white and Filipino identities, and instead uses white racist logic to assume an identity that gives him access to economic advantages his Asian identity cannot. Passing for Chicano is an economic exchange; Chicano acceptance of his performance is unnecessary as it is a white audience that must "buy" his Chicano identity.

As the ultimate marker of culture and identity, language becomes the telling limit of Tomas's ability to "sell" his performance. Because of his inability to speak Spanish, Tomas is particularly nervous around "real" Chicanos who could expose his "inauthenticity" and undermine his performance for white clients.[11] For example, when the brothers meet the Chicana wife of a white client, she studies Tomas closely "wondering if he is a real Mexican" after he speaks choppy Spanglish (45). Gabe, who has accompanied his brother, does speak Spanish, and he is able to connect to the Chicana in a way that Tomas cannot, thus saving Tomas's deal and, more importantly, suggesting that language acquisition could serve to unite different nonwhite ethnic groups. However, angry and humiliated, Tomas physically attacks Gabe, accusing him of upstaging Tomas with his "Flip, peasant Spanish" (54). Tomas's association of Spanish with a colonized, "peasant" status makes his assumption of a Chicano identity especially ironic given his reasons for rejecting his Filipino one. Racked with his own sense of shame of Filipino colonization, Tomas resists fully identifying with another colonized culture. His resistance to the Spanish language illustrates the way nativist discourse works to keep immigrant groups self-policing the barriers among themselves. Rather than embrace the Spanish language as part of his Filipino heritage and make a seemingly "authentic" claim to an affinity with a Latino identity, he rejects the very characteristic that could form the basis of a Chicano identity, or create an interracial solidarity or collective identity: His underlying belief in white supremacy cements Tomas's privileging of English as superior (even as he passes as Chicano). Thus, his own "English-only" policy—echoing, of course, one common trope of nativist rhetoric—serves to reify racial and ethnic boundaries.

Roley deploys Tomas's unusual permutation of passing to show the complex competing interethnic/racial racisms at play under white supremacy, but even in Gabe's more traditional passing-for-white plot, Roley highlights in a new way how American racisms are interdependent. Gabe steals his brother's car and runs away from L.A., out into "Another California"—the "white" California to the north, which is filled with quiet, small towns (59). Gabe crosses a cultural border without leaving his home state, a circumstance that marks the internal geographic divisions of class, race, and ethnicity within the state. Once outside of L.A., in this new, "foreign" context, Gabe feels inadequate and ashamed of himself because he wants to blend into the town as quietly as possible, a feat he believes his poverty and ethnicity (both, he fears, indicated by Tomas's car) will deny him. He suddenly feels ashamed of Tomas's beat-up Oldsmobile and notes that "[a]t home it seems like a normal car to have, but here I feel like throwing a damned blanket over it" (72).

When the car breaks down, Gabe is befriended by a white tow truck driver. It soon becomes clear that the driver thinks Gabe is white, and he promptly begins a tirade about the "fucking Mexicans," "Cambodians, Vietnamese, Laotians," and "all those mute Asians [who] won't even learn to speak English" (84). Gabe does not react to this speech, and he certainly does not mention that his mother is Filipina and struggles with English. But Gabe does not merely "pass" as white by omission to avoid a potentially dangerous situation. Instead, Gabe actively performs whiteness through an appropriation of white racist discourse, as he begins his own tirade against Mexicans and Cambodians:

> We get all kinds [in L.A.]. The Mexicans come up and it's like they're still roaming all the barrios killing each other down in Mexico. They have their neighborhoods they mark up with graffiti. Like pissing dogs. The new ones have macho mustaches and slick their hair back like their some kind of Spanish Casanovas, but they're like these short Indian-looking guys. The Cambodians are the worst. It's like their war isn't over yet. (86)

Gabe gains approval from the driver for his racist rant and elicits "fatherly concern" that causes an "overwhelming warmth" inside him. The white racist stranger both validates Gabe's performance of whiteness and functions as a substitute for his absent (and racist) father.

The folly of Gabe's desire for the man's approval through his participation in popular nativist rhetoric becomes evident later when the driver confuses the "Mexicans" of Gabe's story with "Asians" (a slippage that begins even in Gabe's speech as he shifts his complaints from Mexicans to Cambodians). The driver's conflation of the two groups reveals the similarity of their positioning in the white, racist imaginary (92). Significantly, this slippage mimics (and mocks) the rhetorical sleight-of-hand of the anti-immigration activists in California in the 1990s, as epitomized in the struggle over Proposition 187, which sought to prevent undocumented immigrants from receiving public services. Ono and Sloop write:

> [Proposition 187] recreated demeaning depictions of undocumented workers, primarily from Mexico, and attempted to rally the general public against them. For many, the policy conjured up memories of the racialized "alien" land law restrictions against Japanese Americans; legislation severely limiting Asian immigration; the incarceration of Japanese Americans during World War II; the 1930s repatriation campaigns to force Mexicans in the United States and their children to move back to Mexico; and the 1954 "Operation Wetback," in which more than a million Mexican migrant workers were forcibly deported from the United States to Mexico. Proposition 187 was punitive, because the law already denied health and welfare benefits to undocumented workers. Proponents of Proposition 187 falsely suggested that workers were getting "benefits" they were already ineligible to receive; then, using a tortured logic, proponents called for a "new" policy to end such benefits. (3–4)

The anti-Mexican rhetoric of Proposition 187 supporters was successful with California voters.[12] Participating in this nativist discourse to solidify his performance of whiteness, Gabe ignores the obvious implications of this racially coded nativism for other immigrant communities and its echoes of past rhetoric deployed against Asian Americans. Furthermore, Gabe's racist speech here only articulates in a more overt way the implications of his own family's earlier privileging of whiteness. Again echoing the rhetoric he so frequently hears in California, Gabe asks how the town keeps "undesirables out" to which the driver excitedly exclaims: "Well there's plenty of abductions, but it isn't aliens that do it. . . . When undesirables come up, they tell them to get lost, and if they don't, that's their own peril" (88). Though Gabe feels "menace" in the air after these remarks, he still ponders the possibility of moving to this part of California with his mother, where there are "a million places you could buy a plot of land and build a small house and live for really cheap" (88). Drawn in by the opportunities he imagines possible in "white" California, Gabe willfully ignores the driver's implied threat against "undesirables" in his fantasy of a different life. Gabe's desire for a home outside of L.A., which would be the culmination of his family's "American Dream," is made untenable by white racism, but he refuses to recognize it. The disjunction between Gabe's musings and the overt racism of the conversation suggests that despite the stereotype of Asian Americans as the "model minority," they are still a minority not wholly welcome in the white nation. As importantly, Gabe's daydream, of sorts, further suggests that white supremacy sustains itself in part precisely by maintaining the illusion that the American Dream is attainable for all, regardless of what one's actual experience attests.

Gabe ultimately wakes from his daydream to a very embodied sense of the situation. He begins to feel that he "appears so obviously Asian" that others will tell the driver that Gabe is not white. Gabe's fear compounds when the driver calls his mother to have her pick him up at the diner: "I can't imagine Stone meeting her and mistaking her for being white" (113). Rather than simply admit that his mother is Filipina, he claims his white Aunt Jessica as his mother and declares his mother is the "maid" (116). Claiming a white mother helps undergird his white identity through a biological link to a white woman, but Gabe's reduction of his mother to the status of maid also reveals the economic dynamics of racial identification. The dark mother is acceptable only as "the help," recreating in microcosm the colonial relationship of Anglo-Americans and Filipinos, and thus reinscribing his mother's subjugation.

As with many racial passers, Gabe's rejection of his mother/Filipino identity leaves him with deep feelings of guilt, especially as he becomes more aware of the daily abuse his mother suffers as a Filipina immigrant once he returns to his life in L.A. Just as he was ashamed *of* his mother, he is also ashamed *for* her and, by extension, for himself. That shame—of being in an exploited and subjugated position—fuels both guilt and rage. When the mother of a white classmate extorts money from Mrs. Sullivan after she accidentally dents the woman's S.U.V., Gabe savagely beats the classmate with a tire iron, giving him a feeling of power that he mistakes for respect: "A couple times in the past I have been with a small group of people when someone said a few smart-aleck things about me and Ben laughed even though I was older. But now he is respectful, his head bowed. And though my stomach wrenches, I feel a rush not of anxiety but of confidence. In a scary way I realize I like it" (215). Gabe, like Tomas before him, gains what critic Eleanor Ty calls a "hypermasculine identity" that counteracts the stereotype of Asian American men as "feminized" and weak (125) and allows Gabe to vent his frustration with white racism and the economic exploitation of minorities that maintains it.[13] Gabe—like Tomas—turns to "hypermasculine" violence to overcome his sense of emasculation, a move that arguably positions him closer to whiteness than his earlier episode of passing for white did. His rhetorical violence becomes actual violence.

By the time the Sullivan brothers attack Gabe's classmate, Tomas has given up most of his outward affiliation to Chicano identity. He has not, however, become less violent. Tomas initially identifies as Chicano to avoid Asian stereotypes while still refusing to embrace a white identity, but that Chicano identity ultimately cannot supply full access to the cultural power Tomas desires. Tomas's Chicano identity, performed for whites, thus succumbs to the white racist pressures that motivated it in the first place. Tomas now drives a Ford Explorer, and Gabe notes that they have not been pulled over since Tomas "got his new car and started wearing straighter clothes (he says too many white kids dress like gangsters now)" (156). Ironically turned off Chicano gang-style clothing worn by the overabundance of white kids "passing" for gangsters, Tomas has "straightened" his appearance. By "straightening" his appearance (i.e., blending into dominant white culture) and passing as white, he is able to continue his criminal behavior under the radar, as whiteness comes without scrutiny. Tomas's passing as white allows the novel to press a key point about race, power, and economics. Because Tomas had first to steal in order to be able to create a white identity—to buy the visible markers of whiteness—he literalizes white economic exploitation of racial others in the United States: (his) whiteness is created and maintained by violence, theft, exploitation, and racialized economic injustice. By making Tomas engage in criminal activity, by having him literally *steal* (for) his whiteness, the novel also literalizes the understanding of whiteness as a form of property,[14] just as it highlights the process of racial construction/othering itself. In this way, Roley's critique of the intersection of racial and economic constructs in U.S. culture complicates the preoccupation with passing as simply a means of economic advancement in many earlier passing narratives.

Having dangled alternative constructions of identity before the reader, the novel concludes with that most pessimistic of the passing tropes—"selling out"—with the economic connotations of that word fully highlighted. Like Johnson's nameless narrator in *The Autobiography of an Ex-Colored Man,* Tomas sells his "birthright for a mess of pottage" (154). But what Tomas betrays is not the inherent racial essence posited by many earlier passing novels. It is, instead, a possibility for reimagining interethnic/racial affinity in the United States, one that might challenge a reactionary economic system with whites holding the purse strings. The struggle, and potential rewards, of negotiating his mestizo identity is abandoned in exchange for material gain offered by unambiguous whiteness. Tomas cannot fulfill the latent potential for connection to others outside the traditional racial binary because he has internalized American racism, so he embraces an American consumerism structured by the racial hierarchy instead.[15] Tomas's embrace of materialism via whiteness reflects his acceptance of the dominant American cultural "values"—the values his family ironically preferred he pursue when they protested his connections to "poor Mexican" teens (12).

Gabe Sullivan also does not find peace with his mestizo identity as a Filipino American.[16] Instead, by using racism and violence to gain a fleeting illusion of supremacy, he follows in his father's footsteps and becomes an "American Son," a title that signifies on Richard Wright's classic *Native Son* (1940). Gabe's acts of violence, like those of Bigger Thomas, can only doom him even as Roley seems to also suggest that Gabe's development from oppressed to oppressor is what finally makes him unequivocally American. The tortured internalization of white supremacy that manifests itself in both novels leaves little hope for Gabe's future. Roley, by alluding to Wright's work in his title, forces a reevaluation of contemporary race relations and the "progress" made in the last seventy years.

Breaking down the dominant and intertwined U.S. constructions of race and economics is ultimately too difficult for Roley's teenaged protagonists. The Sullivan brothers' internalized sense of racial inferiority leads them toward violence as a limited means of gaining a sense of masculinity and power, and neither brother is able to transcend the racial and economic inequality they have inherited while maintaining or claiming a mestizo identity. Seduced by the lure of white American materialism and economic empowerment, the brothers are unable to envision an alternative value system in their community. They have unconsciously adopted the racist, nativist worldview embodied in the tide of anti-immigration rhetoric. Thus, through the fates of his protagonists, Roley depicts the ways that racism—in nativist disguise—continues to mask economic injustice and serves to divide the similarly marginalized to prevent the formation of interracial and interethnic coalitions that could potentially resist structural economic inequalities. The novel thus serves as a reminder that, in a political atmosphere of increasing and even reactionary anti-immigration agitation, knowing how to recognize and counter the mechanisms and rhetorical strategies of racism outside of the black-white binary has become essential to forming a more comprehensive and equitable understanding of civil rights within the United States.

Notes

1. In *Impossible Subjects: Illegal Aliens and the Making of Modern America,* Mae Ngai goes on to argue that even as this radical change of immigration policy opened doors to previously excluded groups, it created new immigration problems, particularly for immigrants from Mexico who were subject to the same numerical quota cap as other nationalities despite the obvious geographical proximity (227–28).

2. Though this essay focuses on the repercussions of anti-immigration rhetoric in 1990s California, the nationwide controversy over the 2010 passage of Arizona's Senate Bill 1070 illustrates how deeply this nativist rhetoric continues to permeate the entire country. On June 25, 2012, the Supreme Court ruled in *Arizona v. United States* that while the majority of the law's provisions were the purview of federal, not state, immigration jurisdiction, it upheld a controversial provision allowing police to check the immigration status of those detained who are suspected to be undocumented. Critics of the law continue to argue that this provision encourages racial profiling.

3. Min-Hyoung Song summarizes the impact of the riot, especially on Asians and Latinos: fifty-four people were killed; 30 percent of the dead were Latinos; more than two thousand people were injured; Almost $1 billion in property damage was done, with more than eight hundred buildings burned. Latino businesses accounted for 40 percent of the damaged. Only one Korean American died, but Korean American businesses suffered the most damage, accounting for about half. Nearly half of the 12,000+ arrested were Latinos; of those, almost 80 percent were recent immigrants (Song 6).

4. Scholars Michael Omi and Howard Winant describe how Asian and Latino Americans were arbitrarily assigned racial designations by the U.S. legal system in order to fit a dominant racial construction. Because Latino and Asian Americans are not comfortably categorized as simply black, white, or "Indian," they were left to negotiate their position in the United States without allegiance to the dominant terms of the historical racial discourse; both groups were placed in similarly liminal positions that simply mapped preexisting labels onto these distinctive ethnic groups (82). The act of legal categorization continues to be prob-

lematic today, as evidenced in the confused label of "Hispanic" on the U.S. census form.

5. After defeat in the Spanish-American War, Spain signed the Treaty of Paris, which gave the United States control over the Philippines in 1898 despite the Declaration of Independence made months earlier by Filipino revolutionaries. Neither Spain nor the United States recognized the declaration, and in 1899, the Philippine-American War began. Not until 1946 did the Philippines achieve independence. The relationship between the United States and the Philippines began during the period of U.S. occupation and led to racialized colonial violence during the war and throughout the occupation. See Paul A. Kramer's *The Blood of Government: Race, Empire, the United States, and the Philippines* (2006) for a history of the complex racial dynamics of the U.S. occupation of the Philippines.

6. Samira Kawash, drawing on Lacan's concept of the mirror stage, is discussing the process of identity formation in James Weldon Johnson's *Autobiography of an Ex-Colored Man* (65). However, her description fits Tomas's and Gabe's internal processes in the novel, particularly their use of passing. Both attempt to create a stable self by substituting the (illusion) of wholeness located in some singular racial designation: Chicano or white. The underlying irony of Tomas's appropriation of a Chicano identity, of course, is that he selects a politicized ethnic identity that has made its own hybridity a source of pride and power as a way to deny his own hybrid identity.

7. Hypodescent is the cultural assumption that the racial status of a child is determined to be that of the racially subordinate parent in a racially hierarchal society. In the United States, this has often been referred to as the "one-drop" rule. See Omi and Winant for further discussion of the history of American policies of hypodescent. While most passing narratives are preoccupied with an exclusively black-white racial dichotomy (usually blacks pass for white; occasionally whites pass for black; see Dreisinger), there are several notable exceptions of narratives that try to expand the racial framework. In *The Autobiography of an Ex-Colored Man*, Johnson uses his narrator's affinity for Cuban American culture as a way to suggest alternative racial and ethnic paradigms that might allow his narrator to escape the dilemma of living as a mulatto in the Jim Crow South. Walter White's 1926 novel *Flight* more explicitly explores the potential for interethnic alliances through his Creole protagonist's relationship with a Chinese intellectual who articulates a theory of worldwide resistance to white domination. White strategically presents a Chinese character that is outside the narrow confines of an American construct of race as the catalyst for Mimi's return to her black identity. The gestures toward interracial solidarity that both Johnson and White make in their novels reflect a larger move toward global civil rights advocacy by African American intellectuals in the early twentieth century.

8. This version of "class"-based hierarchy among minority groups is a familiar phenomenon (either as a strategy for uplift or a social critique) in the passing narrative, but class is often coded as if it were an inherent character attribute rather than one based on economic position. In Howells's *An Imperative Duty*

(1892), Dr. Olney convinces his beloved Rhoda Aldgate that she is truly white because she belongs "incomparably more to the oppressors than the oppressed" (231), presumably as much for her social position as for her color. Similarly, Charles Chesnutt's Rena and John Walden in *The House Behind the Cedars* (1900) are justified in their decision to pass in part because their "superior blood and breeding" separates them from the rest of their poor, black community (21). These versions of variegated blackness based on class and caste parallel the positional hierarchies within and among minority groups in Roley's novel.

9. Furthermore, Mrs. Sullivan is color conscious, which Roley carefully frames in the context of Spanish colonization of the Philippines: "My mother's brother Betino looks white—they both have Spanish blood—but my mother appears really dark—very Filipino—even though she avoids the sun" (113). The irony of her caste consciousness lies in its similarity to themes of caste consciousness evident in many Latino texts. Piri Thomas's *Down These Mean Streets,* for example, dwells at length on color consciousness among Puerto Ricans, which is also a result of Spanish colonization and the privileged position of white "Spanish" skin.

10. Claire Jean Kim's theoretical method of "racial triangulation" identifies two codependent formations that enable the "model minority" myth to operate: "relative valorization" when the dominant (usually white) group privileges one subordinate group over another as a means of domination, and "civic ostracism" in which the dominant group carefully constructs the "privileged" subordinate group as "foreign and unassimilable" in order to disenfranchise that group as well (107). Kim's examination of the triangulation of racial dynamics requires an acknowledgment of the white supremacy that underlies all of these interactions. She writes: "White racial power may not tell the whole story, but it does generate a distinct structure of opportunities, constraints, and possibilities—parameters of resistance—with which groups of color must contend" (129).

11. Language difference is another potential complication of the shift from mulatto to mestizo passing. Certainly, African American passers would have had to "sound white," but they would not have had to speak another language in the traditional sense of the term. Passers of other national-racial groups may very well have the expectation of speaking another language in order to make their performance appear "authentic."

12. Jacobson notes, "Whites supported the measure two to one, while over 70 percent of Latinos voted against it. Blacks and Asians marginally opposed the measure, with around 52 percent voting against it" (xix). Despite voter support, the measure was struck down as unconstitutional by federal court.

13. Eleanor Ty's 2004 article, "Abjection, Masculinity, and Violence in Brian Roley's *American Son* and Han Ong's *Fixer Chao,*" illuminates the racialized interplay of violence and masculinity in the American context of globalization in novels by Roley and Han Ong.

14. See Cheryl I. Harris's "Whiteness as Property." Her argument that whiteness functions as a form of property in the United States has become a generally accepted position in whiteness studies and critical race theory.

15. As "model minority" Asian Americans, Tomas's behavior is also not surprising. Zhou and Xiong note that "despite felt or experienced discrimination, Asian Americans were also less likely than other racial minority groups to take collective action against unequal treatment and instead more likely to buy into American individualism" (1143).

16. In his preface to "*American Son* Epilogue," which appeared independently in a 2003 short story collection entitled *Growing Up Filipino,* Roley explains that the story appearing in the collection was the original conclusion to his novel. Though "*American Son* Epilogue" continues Gabe's story where the novel left off, it ends with the same bleak ambiguity about Gabe's future as the novel.

Works Cited

Anzaldúa, Gloria. *Borderlands/La Frontera: The New Mestiza.* 1987. San Francisco: Aunt Lute Books, 1999. Print.

Chesnutt, Charles W. *The House Behind the Cedars.* 1900. New York: Penguin, 1993. Print.

Cheung, King-Kok. "(Mis)Interpretations and (In)justice: The 1992 Los Angeles 'Riots' and the 'Black-Korean Conflict.'" *MELUS* 30.3 (Fall 2005): 3–40. Print.

Cutter, Martha J. "Sliding Significations: Passing as a Narrative and Textual Strategy in Nella Larsen's Fiction." In Ginsberg 75–100. Print.

Darder, Antonia. "The Politics of Biculturalism: Culture and Difference in the Formation of *Warriors for Gringostroika* and *The New Mestizas.*" *The Latino Studies Reader.* Ed. Antonia Darder and Rodolfo D. Torres. Malden, MA: Blackwell, 1998. 129–42. Print.

Dreisinger, Baz. *Near Black: White to Black Passing in American Culture.* Amherst: U of Massachusetts P, 2008. Print.

Ginsberg, Elaine K. "Introduction: The Politics of Passing." In Ginsberg 1–18. Print.

———, ed. *Passing and the Fictions of Identity.* Durham, NC: Duke UP, 1996. Print.

Harris, Cheryl I. "Whiteness as Property." *Harvard Law Review* 106.8 (June 1993): 1710–91. Print.

Ho, Jennifer. "Ambiguous Movements: Paisley Rekdal's Passing Identity in *The Night My Mother Met Bruce Lee: Observations on Not Fitting In.*" *Women & Performance: A Journal of Feminist Theory* 15.1 (2005): 141–65. Print.

Howells, William Dean. *An Imperative Duty.* 1892. Ed. Edwin Cady. New York: Twayne, 1962. Print.

Jacobson, Robin Dale. *The New Nativism: Proposition 187 and the Debate over Immigration.* Minneapolis: U of Minnesota P, 2008. Print.

Johnson, James Weldon. *The Autobiography of an Ex-Colored Man.* 1912. Ed. William L. Andrews. New York: Penguin, 1990. Print.

Kawash, Samira. "*The Autobiography of an Ex-Coloured Man*: (Passing for) Black Passing for White." In Ginsberg 59–74. Print.

Kim, Claire Jean. "The Racial Triangulation of Asian Americans." *Politics and Society* 27.1 (1999): 105–38. Print.

Kim, Jinah. "Immigrants, Racial Citizens, and the (Multi)Cultural Politics of Neoliberal Los Angeles." *Social Justice* 35.3 (2008): 36–56. Print.

Kramer, Paul A. *The Blood of Government: Race, Empire, the United States, and the Philippines.* Chapel Hill: U of North Carolina P, 2006. Print.

López, Ian F. Haney. "Chance, Context, and Choice in the Social Construction of Race." *The Latino/a Condition*. Ed. Richard Delgado and Jean Stefancic. New York: New York UP, 1998. 9–16. Print.

Lowe, Lisa. *Immigrant Acts: On Asian American Cultural Politics.* Durham: Duke UP, 1996. Print.

Moran, Rachel F. "Demography and Distrust: The Latino Challenge to Civil Rights and Immigration Policy in the 1990s and Beyond." *La Raza Law Journal* 8.1 (Spring 1995): 1–24. Print.

Ngai, Mae. *Impossible Subjects: Illegal Aliens and the Making of Modern America.* Princeton: Princeton UP, 2004. Print.

Okihiro, Gary Y. "Colonial Vision, Racial Visibility: Racializations in Puerto Rico and the Philippines during the Initial Period of U.S. Colonization." *Racial Transformations: Latinos and Asians Remaking the United States*. Ed. Nicholas De Genova. Durham: Duke UP, 2006. 23–39. Print.

Omi, Michael, and Howard Winant. *Racial Formation in the United States: From the 1960s to the 1990s*. New York: Routledge, 1994. Print.

Ono, Kent A., and John M. Sloop. *Shifting Borders: Rhetoric, Immigration, and California's Proposition 187*. Philadelphia: Temple UP, 2002. Print.

Palumbo-Liu, David. *Asian/American: Historical Crossings of a Racial Frontier.* Stanford: Stanford UP, 1999. Print.

Pulido, Laura. *Black, Brown, Yellow, and Left: Radical Activism in Los Angeles.* Berkeley: U of California P, 2006. Print.

Roley, Brian Ascalon. *American Son*. New York: W. W. Norton, 2001. Print.

———. "*American Son* Epilogue." *Growing Up Filipino: Stories for Young Adults*. Ed. Cecilia Manguerra Brainard. Santa Monica: Palh, 2003. Print.

Song, Min-Hyoung. *Strange Future: Pessimism and the 1992 Los Angeles Riots.* Durham: Duke UP, 2005. Print.

Thomas, Piri. *Down These Mean Streets*.1967. New York: Vintage, 1997. Print.

Ty, Eleanor. "Abjection, Masculinity, and Violence in Brian Roley's *American Son* and Han Ong's *Fixer Chao*." *MELUS* 29.1 (2004): 119–36. Print.

Wald, Gayle. *Crossing the Line: Racial Passing in Twentieth-Century U.S. Literature and Culture.* Durham: Duke UP, 2000. Print.

White, Walter. *Flight*. 1926. Baton Rouge: Louisiana State UP, 1998. Print.

Wright, Richard. *Native Son*. 1940. New York: Library of America, 1991. Print.

Zhou, Min, and Yang Sao Xiong. "The Multifaceted American Experiences of the Children of Asian Immigrants: Lessons for Segmented Assimilation." *Ethnic and Racial Studies* 28.6 (2005): 1119–52. Print.

8

Race in the Marketplace

Postmodern Passing and Ali G

Ana Cristina Mendes

On September 21, 2006, the British newspaper *The Independent* ran a front page image of the blacked-up supermodel Kate Moss. Not only was her skin blackened, but also her lips were made bigger, her brows thicker, and her cheeks plumper. Both nose and cheekbones had been reshaped. "Not a Fashion Statement," the headline flashed, with the "not" strategically accentuated in red, while an inset at the bottom of the sidebar advertised a free poster of British photographer Nick Knight's startling image of Moss in the interior. The reaction in the media was fast—and close to injurious—to the picture, which had been commissioned by guest editor Giorgio Armani for this "Africa issue" whose "half of all revenues" would reportedly "help fight AIDS" in the continent.

An article published the following day in *The Guardian, The Independent*'s chief rival, under the ominous title "Return to the Dark Ages," questioned why the model featured on the front page of an issue dedicated to Africa could not have been black.[1] Cultural theorist Paul Gilroy, quoted in the scathing response, declared the picture to be nothing more than "empty nihilism." *The Guardian*'s journalist Hannah Pool further inquired: "What exactly is this picture of Moss-as-African-woman supposed to portray? I suppose it is meant to be subversive, but what does it say about race today when a quality newspaper decides that its readers will only relate to Africa through a blacked-up white model rather than a real-life black woman?"

The controversy surrounding the Moss picture was, one must presume, not unexpected, as Knight's image exhibits a representational complexity similar to Tibor Kalman's notorious visual works, which ran in the "What If . . ." issue of Benetton-sponsored *Colors* magazine in 1993, a series regarded by some as likewise deplorable and insulting.[2] These pictures included an Asian Pope John Paul II, a black Arnold Schwarzenegger, a white Spike Lee, and a black Queen Elizabeth II.[3] Pool might label Kalman, too, a callous bigot who should have used "a real-life black woman" as a model instead of manipulating a photograph of Elizabeth II. Another critic, however, might alternatively describe him as an artistic rabble-rouser who, while challenging traditional concepts of portrait photography, was also intent on forcing us to look at the markers of racial difference through a different lens. Notwithstanding the fact that Kalman's seductive and shocking work was part and parcel of the Benetton corporation's global and multiracial marketing strategy, his manipulated images effectively complicate an understanding of race as a monolithic category. By the same token, Knight's use of a highly identifiable supermodel such as Kate Moss, not only ensures popular and critical attention (and, even better for sales, controversy) but it also highlights the racial sleight-of-hand at work precisely through her easy recognizability as a white celebrity. Knight's disconcerting and rather bizarre picture also links issues of race to those of class: it is a picture of a privileged white woman masquerading as a disadvantaged black woman.

In this sense, blacking-up or masquerading as black (or white, or Asian) becomes a creative option in overtly re/presentational and technologically empowered visual mediums that can arouse debate, albeit with a touch of scandal, about identity power politics and, more specifically, Manichean racial distinctions. However, racial morphing—whether through technological image manipulation, blackface performance, racial masquerade, racial crossover, or passing—also embodies a double paradox: although it invokes notions of fluidity, it depends upon racial fixity, and it simultaneously depends upon antithetical feelings of empathy and alienation. Because the image of the blackened Moss embraces such extreme contradictions, it is no wonder critical response to it might travel in two opposite ways. One path might celebrate its subversive creative energies against an obsolete insistence on racial authenticity. The other perspective might look at it as an example of the rediscovery "of the boot polish," as Pool put it in *The Guardian,* acting as a demeaning form of racism and/or cultural theft for the profit of a stereotyping cultural industry, in other words, functioning as one of the newest forms of colonization.

What is important to note in these competing critical arguments is not in the discussion over Moss herself, but rather the paradox embodied in racial crossovers whereby they can act at the same time *for* and *against* stereotyping.

The concern of this essay is to use such recent critical disputes as a backdrop for examining how postmodern racial passing (as a form of racial morphing) in the visual media of film and television—with specific reference to the fictional character Ali G—frees racial stereotypes of their essentialist strength by *relying on* the widespread acceptance and familiarity of such stereotypes. That is, as the postmodern passer, Ali G subverts racial categories both graphically and linguistically in ways that highlight the mutability, multiplicity, and indeterminacy of those categories, even if the question still remains whether or not the character concurrently resets the same stereotypes that he attempts to destabilize. As opposed to earlier passers who "were" either "black" or "white," Ali G lacks a fundamental racial essence. Race is overtly constructed as performance, just as a photographic image can be easily altered to widen a nose or fatten a lip. Such visual cues, understood as biological because embodied, have come to signify racial categories. The postmodern audience, however, must understand the artifice: a race, like a face, can be constructed to signify in ways divorced from a biological "essence."

Imbalancing Power

Critics have pointed out the imbalance—or unidirectionality—of power in the tropes of passing and blackface. Despite Homi Bhabha's argument in his theory of mimicry that the contestatory power of mimicry is equivalent on both sides of the color divide (although with reference to a colonial context), the outcome does not seem to be quite the same for whites to pass as black, as for blacks to pass as white. Hence, even if the "whiteface" comedy *White Chicks* (2004)—a film where the black Wayans brothers put on blonde wigs, white makeup, and feminine clothing to satirize the Hilton sisters—might be seen as both an inversion and extension of the blackface minstrelsy tradition where white men played black men *and* women,[4] it cannot fully act as an exact counterpart to the performances of Sacha Baron Cohen, the white, Cambridge-educated, Jewish[5] comedian coming from an affluent North London family, who creates the racially indeterminate character Ali G. Unevenness in economic and sociocultural power dynamics will always imbalance racial passing/masquerade, since white individuals can cross to the other side of the color line without relinquishing hold of the privileges of whiteness, even if some might be perceived as underprivileged in terms of class and/or gender (Rehling 273). That is, Baron Cohen as a white man has access to cultural power that he voluntarily (and temporarily) forgoes in performance; he sojourns into the land of the oppressed but keeps his ticket stub for the ride back up. The Wayans brothers, in comparison, have *temporary* access to power, a state that is further mediated by the film's farcical mode and gender politics: they are never a real threat for the white audience, as their disguise is both hyper-evident and feminized.

The imbalance and ambivalence at the heart of racial crossovers extends, also, to different critical reactions: on the one hand, blacks who pass are regularly subject to accusations of treachery, greed, and complicity in oppressive power structures, while, on the other hand, whites who pass are often celebrated for their courageous, transgressive, self-sacrificing, and cathartic sojourns. The composite Baron Cohen/Ali G, however, offers a new postmodern model that resists easy categorization: *Baron Cohen* maintains his whiteness (which is noted in almost all media stories of him) when compared to blacks, although his whiteness is potentially destabilized by his Jewishness, and *Ali G*'s ethno-racial identity is overtly ever-shifting, so much so that critics variously report him to be Middle Eastern, black, Asian, and/or Jewish.[6] Furthermore, because Ali G originally passed as an authentic person (rather than being a fictional creation), audiences were encouraged to confuse or conflate *Baron Cohen* himself with his ambiguous creation.

Albeit artificially, it is possible to trace three stages in Ali G's development as a character, first as a hoax children's television presenter, then as a star interviewer, and at last as a film subject. He appeared originally on *The 11 O'Clock Show,* a late-night satirical comedy program first aired in 1999 on Britain's Channel 4. Masquerading as a children's television presenter, he interviewed leading figures in British politics, science, and religion in five-minute segments. His demeanor tended toward the unconventional and eccentric in, for instance, the overt embrace of gross materialism, ostentation, and hypersexuality, and in the blatant defense of his blackness, which was not at all observable by the personalities he interviewed. These early instances of nonconformity in terms of appearance and behavior were made to work for Ali G's advantage—having been drawn into the realm of popular culture, as Gilroy notes in his critical comments on the character, they add to the façade of his interviews as authentic media encounters. His technique (similar to interviews featured on two popular Comedy Central mock news shows, Jon Stewart's *The Daily Show* and Stephen Colbert's *The Colbert Report*) was to interview prominent people using a studied rude and/or naive line of questioning. In this way he profited from established media conventions which allowed him to trick his unsuspecting interviewees, despite his outlandish look and insolent manner, into answering absurd questions. In the end, by assuming the role of a recognizable media persona—that of a television presenter—he was able to pass as a true institutional representative.[7]

Satirizing "yoof TV" (Malik 104), the humor of Ali G resulted from manipulating and exposing the pretentiousness of those publicity-hungry celebrities who wanted to appeal to a "yoof" audience. As spoof television presenter and self-declared "voice of da yoof," most of the jokes were built on the gap between clichéd "street" and "establishment" positions (Weaver 2–3). Referring to these mock interviews and the ways in which they disavowed implicit media conventions, Gilroy celebrated Ali G's "carnivalesque contempt for the pompous and powerful people he [was] still able to ambush, manipulate and even humiliate" ("Ali G" 3), as well as "the density and complexity with which Ali's Rabelaisian idiom addresses the growing fissures in [British] public culture" (4). Such attributes, the critic argues, were what made him so engaging to youth audiences who, being fluent in Ali G's language, were able to understand the slang impenetrable to the representatives of the British establishment. These were the spoof interviewer satirical targets as, for example, on one occasion, when former British Labour Minister Roy Hattersley became so confounded that he was tricked into calling, by mistake, Prime Minister Tony Blair a "dong" (penis) (3–4).

Garnering immense popularity, Ali G progressed from performing five-minute slots on *The 11 O'Clock Show* to being given his own TV series in 2000—*Da Ali G Show*. Stirring up considerable debate as a talk show host eventually led to a comedy icon status: from spoof interviewer he was now a star interviewer, featuring in the original single-season series broadcast in the UK, and then in the second two-season series aired in the United States, a country where Ali G was virtually unheard of, with *Ali G in da USAiii* (2003). For the most part his technique in these shows consisted of posing a silly question, and, after receiving a sometimes perplexed answer from the interviewee, he proceeded to narrate an anecdote inspired by the topic under discussion starring his "homies," for instance, Ricky C and Dangerous Dave.

In this stage as a celebrity interviewer, the interviewees would have been well aware that he was a fictional character. The fact that Ali G was not an "actual" person was even underscored when he was cast as a motion picture character; because of his celebrity, the ambiguity surrounding his "real" identity was to some extent dispelled. His transition to the big screen began with the feature Hollywood film entitled *Ali G Indahouse: The Movie* (2002), a joint British-American production. With this film—whose plot contrasts Ali G with stuffy white MPs after getting himself elected for the British Parliament—it became progressively more difficult for Baron Cohen to maintain the racial indeterminacy of his character, and also to resume the disruptive portrayal of the values of the white status quo initiated in Ali G's original hoax interviews. Thus, protesters were present at the film's gala opening to accuse the comedian of "being a new Al Jolson, exploiting black culture and pimping it into the media mainstream where he, rather than the community to which it really belonged, could turn a profit from it" (Gilroy, "Ali G" 4). As Gilroy stated about this racially motivated confrontation, "The ideas of cultural ownership and experiential copyright on which that criticism depends are now anachronistic. But the resort to them tells us a lot about contemporary anxieties over the integrity of marginal identity and the value of minority culture" (4).

As cited above, demonstrators drew an analogy between Baron Cohen and the popular Jewish blackface performer Al Jolson (1886–1950), who used blackface as a form of passing or masquerade, as Richard Rodriguez notes: "The only way for a young Jewish man [Jolson] to sing from his heart on a stage, to be authentic to his private yearning, was to do so in blackface—a protective masquerade, also an emulation of the supposed freedom of black people" (71). The reference to Jolson should not surprise us. Although American readers might assume blackface minstrelsy was primarily an American phenomenon, its stage presence in England is well documented. For instance, archive records of blackface minstrelsy in England include the footage the Lumière brothers captured of blackface minstrels on a London street in 1896, at a time when the "Nigger Minstrel" was well established in the music-halls of the city. This entertainment tradition was restored on British television almost a century later with the variety show *The Black And White Minstrel Show,* broadcast by BBC Television for two decades, between 1958 and 1978. The main attraction of the program consisted of having performers don black wigs and blacked-up faces as well as shiny white lips and gloves, and sing and dance in what was assumed to be an impersonation of black American musicians of the nineteenth century. Despite its abusive depiction of black people—which led the Campaign Against Racial Discrimination to deliver a petition to the BBC in 1967 demanding that the program be discontinued—media critic Sarita Malik, writing on the Web site of the Museum of Broadcast Communications, makes a note of the importance of *The Black And White Minstrel Show* "because it outlines how racist representations became part of public debate and how performance was linked to social context." So, too, in the United States.

Both *The Black And White Minstrel Show* and the character of Ali G are rooted in historical backgrounds and socially structured milieus that do not only reflect power plays, but also critical debates about cultural belonging and the meaning of race. Even though the concept of white performers playing the role of black characters was in (over)due course understood as inappropriate, offensive, and racist, the 1990s and early 2000s witnessed a postmodern revival of the minstrel convention. Blacking-up has recently been used by both white and black artists in a self-proclaimed ironic way, that is, to ridicule the idea of blackface or minstrelsy. Black American performers such as the rapper Ludacris and standup comedian Dave Chappelle used blacking-up subversively, in a sort of hyper-blackface or blacked-up blackness, in an attempt to reappropriate the insulting legacy of blackface.[8] Recent examples of whites using blackface surface in the popular British comedy series *The League of Gentlemen,* where the regular character Papa Lazarou, with a cult following of his own, came out as a blacked-up circus owner, with white rings around the eyes like a minstrel. In a 2003 episode of *Little Britain,* the white comedy team Lucas and Walliams performed as two minstrels alarmed at the prospect of being sent back to "Minstrel Land" by the British Home Secretary (series 1, episode 1), and in the third season of the show (2005) white actor David Walliams blacked up and cross-dressed to play a character called Desiree, an overweight black woman. In this context of continuity of the minstrel heritage in popular cultural production, Malik puts forward the thorny question: What does it say "about the traditions of British television that a central tenet of its comedy programming has been so obsessed with, and dependent on, racist humour"? She adds:

> Comedy writers frequently pledge their commitment to irony or elevated liberal ideals to shield themselves and their comic creations from accusations of being anti-Black. This is a very British form of defence. Much of the British comedy tradition needs to be recognized as working within this culture of racism, while using the alibi of comedy to give the illusion of being outside it. (*Representing Black Britain* 106)

The critic illustrates her argument with, among others, the character of Ali G, a sexist, semiliterate, homophobic gang leader, who uses ill-defined street talk with repeated references to violence and drugs. In tune with what is considered to be the chauvinistic and misogynistic nature of hip hop culture, he cannot help but constantly mention the gigantic size of his penis. Ali lives in Staines, where he is the head of the "West Staines Massiv," a made-up suburban gang. He is obsessed by designer labels, and dresses in flashy shiny tracksuits and yellow-tinted wraparound sunglasses. On the DVD cover of *Ali G, Innit,* for instance, he ostentatiously displays heavy gold jewelry, chains and rings—"bling bling" in gangsta rap slang—and he always sports his trademark skullcap by white designer Tommy Hilfiger.

Tellingly, Tommy Hilfiger, whose market niche once consisted almost exclusively of so-called country club buyers, was adopted in the 1990s as some sort of official brand name gear by the American hip hop community due to the company's heavy investment in hip hop–influenced marketing. Naomi Klein depicts this Hilfiger marketing scheme as "selling white youth on their fetishization of black style, and black youth on their fetishization of white wealth" (76). The strategy of the clothing brand was to create a distinctive outward show of hip hop antihero coolness by allowing black inner-city teenagers to display their products. In so doing, well-off (e.g. white) consumers were eager to purchase Hilfiger's clothes—and with them an aura of black coolness—when they appeared in suburban shopping centers (75). The character of Ali G, always wearing his Hilfiger headgear, never failed to capitalize on this glamorized notion of "black style" combined with "white wealth." It is possible to discern, on Baron Cohen's part, a subversive response through semiotic appropriation—or, as Klein puts it, "culture jamming" (279–309)—to that trend promoted by the American clothing company. Ali G seemed then to act the part of a white victim of corporate capitalism's niche marketing strategies and their redeployment of black gangsta masculinity as commodity fetish. It was probably in this context that Spike Lee argued, in the DVD release of his film *Bamboozled* (2001), that "gangsta rap is a twenty-first-century version of minstrel shows," an association that might add a new layer of meaning to the comedian's performance.

Although Baron Cohen does not actually black-up to perform Ali G (and, hence, is like a passer), the character overplays stereotypical black affectations, slang, and fashion (as in blackface). He regularly refers to the ghetto and presents himself as black (Rehling 293). Indeed, his catchphrase—and almost ritual confrontation—was "Is it 'cos I is black?"

Instead, Ali G uses the performance characteristic of minstrelsy to perform more as a passer, although not an archetypal one. While passing presupposes the reality of race, even if just as an ontological category to be outdone and disposed of, it also ultimately challenges and undermines the very idea of race by rendering visible its discursive nature in its multiple constructed layers. Taking into account that the boundary between passing and posing is sometimes difficult to draw, it is a tricky question to answer whether the comedian succeeded in subverting stereotypes of black street youth, or whether he ended up reifying them. Malik notes precisely this ambiguity, echoing her earlier assessment of *The Black and White Minstrel Show* and its context-bound audience appeal, when considering similar performances:

> For some, those comedic expressions that are seen to deconstruct and challenge Black stereotypes by working through them (*No Problem!*, *Goodness Gracious Me*, Ali G) are seen by others as signs that we are now playing the essentialist game in order to get popular and mainstream profiles. The uncertainty is such that the "right targets" of comedy shift over time, are deemed (in)appropriate in different historical moments and are inescapably dependent on who delivers the joke, how the comedy is enunciated and the context within which it is read. (*Representing Black Britain* 106)

Adopting the trappings of black street culture, Ali G behaved as a *wigger,* a derogatory slang term combining the words *white* and *nigger,* used to describe a young, white person who emulates the peculiarities stereotypically associated with urban black Americans and hip hop culture in particular. The key to Ali G's identity that is put forward by most critics is that the character might be a satirical portrait of British suburban white boys who assert their empathy for black (American) culture (Howells 166). Baron Cohen could indeed be lampooning a current fascination with hip hop culture among British Asian youth: by "borrowing" street stylistic markers like American hip hop related slang and apparel in an allegedly ironic fashion, young British Asians have been attempting to redefine what it means to be Asian (Huq 202). Indeed, fixed racial categories are relentlessly disrupted and challenged by this group, as is illustrated by the recent publication of Gautam Malkani's novel *Londonstani* (2006) whose protagonist's desperate attempts to fit in a Housnlow-based gang of British Asian "rudeboys" entails that he take on a hip hop habitus and pass as someone of South Asian descent named "Jas." Throughout most of the novel, readers believe the name is short for Jasminder. In actuality, as the novel reveals near the end, the nickname is short for Jason Bartholomew-Cliveden.

Such racial dynamics resulting from an embracing of black American pop culture are also prominently played out in iona roseal brown's blackface series of paintings "a3 . . . black on both sides" (2002) whose subject matter is a specific Japanese appropriation of hip hop signifiers. Following a visit to Japan in 2001, brown embarked on this series of works featuring blacked-up Japanese characters, in what were meant be "afro-asiatic allegories," to assess how the exportation of American popular culture was impacting significantly on Japanese culture. The paintings are based on the subcultural practice of *ganguro,* which emerged during the early 1990s and was popular in metropolitan cities such as Tokyo: Japanese high school teens (primarily, but not exclusively, girls) who mimicked American hip hop icons by dramatically darkening their white skin. The *ganguro* subculture represented a severe rupture with Japanese traditions and set a direct conflict with traditional Japanese ideas of feminine beauty and sensuality. The girls' altered appearance, *de rigueur* for one seeking to emulate hip hop stars, departed drastically from the extreme white made-up face of the socially privileged and affluent geisha, thus confronting past conceptions of race and gender identity and playing with what were once definite boundaries. Flaunting extreme tans, achieved at tanning salons or through the use of heavy makeup, the followers of this trend put on white lipstick and eyeliner—in a way, reminiscent of white blacking-up in minstrel shows—dyed their hair blonde or brown, curled it into dreadlocks or weaved it into cornrows to show that they considered black culture "cooler" than their own.

brown revealed her mixed feelings about *ganguro* during an interview: "Being African-American, I'm flattered that our music and style is so influential. . . . But I have to say that I find the ganguro obsession with blackness pretty weird, and a little offensive. My paintings come out of trying to make sense of this appropriation" (qtd. in Gennocchio). Her work drew upon the conventions of seventeenth-century Japanese Ukiyo-e woodblock prints featuring subjects such as geishas and courtesans, but it was also informed by hip hop style and twenty-first-century popular youth culture in general. For instance, the painting "Blackface no. 43," exhibiting postmodern markers such as pastiche and parody, portrays a samurai after the traditional woodblock style, but brown's hip hop samurai is smoking a cigarette, dons a huge black afro instead of the elegant hairstyles portrayed by Japanese masters and, in place of a sword, is clutching a modern handgun, whereas his other formerly combat paraphernalia is substituted by copious bling. Other richly encoded paintings depict conventional kimonos joined up with trendy jeans, women sporting exaggerated acrylic nails, besides logos of international business conglomerates and record companies, and upmarket brand names such as Crystal Champagne, Burberry, and Adidas—analogous to Ali G's usage of his "Tommy gear"—that signal a lifestyle built around excessive spending and display of wealth.

Paralleling the politics of Baron Cohen's performance, brown's "a3 . . . black on both sides" borrowed from American hip hop culture and transposed it to a different context where it was rearticulated. In this way, brown's paintings prompt similar issues to Ali G: the current fascination with racial masquerade that can slip into racial passing, the impact of media imagery in the exportation of commodity-driven mass market icons, the circulation of hip hop as a global commodity, the "coolness" of black American culture and its subsequent fetishization by a consumer youth, as well as ostentation of recognizable brand name clothing and accessories. While not intending a simplistic comparison, it is almost inevitable to note the similarities between Baron Cohen's cultural sampling in Ali G and brown's reworking of *ganguro*. Both constitute hybrid assemblages of black American and Asian or British cultures brought about by the ongoing transnational spread of hip hop. Whereas brown is a black visual artist making use of a Japanese technique to represent Japanese teens fixated on black American culture, Baron Cohen is a white comedian who *might* be—the ambiguity here is key—lampooning white mimickers of that same culture. As in the character of Ali G, brown's paintings juxtapose a whole series of visual signifiers borrowed from black cultural forms in what could be regarded as narratives of racial passing.

Consistent with the strategy of morphing into other personas, Baron Cohen mixes up categories in Ali G: the character's accent is ambivalent throughout, a mixture of clichéd and, for the most part, overstated British African-Caribbean and hip hop slang; he is physically white but demands recognition as a black. It might also be possible to typify him as Asian or an Asian-wannabe-black if one takes into account references to his uncle, a curry-house owner named Jamal (Rehling 293), or as Middle Eastern, through his first name. The selection of the first name "Ali" was intentional according to Richard Howells who quotes original series producer Harry Thompson: "If he had a whiff of Islam about him, we thought people would be afraid to challenge him . . . if Muslims took offence, there was a plan to explain that the name was short for "Alistair [Leslie] Graham"

(166). There is, indeed, something subversive—or at least adventurous—in a Jew passing as a Muslim.[9]

To what racial (and ethnic, religious, and national, for that matter) "groups" does Ali G belong? The character (and Baron Cohen) deliberately works to keep this question unanswerable. In Baron Cohen's postmodern composite character, the fluid and multilayered nature of race is highlighted through an insistence on the discursive nature of racial belonging markers. He denounces the contention of difference used to fetishize racially othered groups and instead proposes an understanding of race as an unstable, "floating signifier" (Hall). At first glance, Ali G might seem as much about stabilizing race as destabilizing it by his reliance on stereotypes; however, by way of hyperbole, race is materialized and the black-white racial binary is deployed as ultimately a fiction, in existence only through performative reification. Thus, although the character temporarily seems to reify race, he finally transcends it by his self-reflective insistence on its mutability, multiplicity, and indeterminacy. In short, the hypervisibility of race in the Ali G character destabilizes race *after* relying on racial stereotypes and parameters to construct his critique. Although passing has been used in a variety of ways—in conservative or subversive fashion in different time periods and even within one time period—the standard passing narrative frequently works in the opposite direction: after exposing the constructedness of race, it tends to reinscribe race as essential.[10]

The character of Ali G was assembled as if calling up polarized debates on race springing both from an essentialist perspective grounded on a unitary and fixed concept of identity—the modeling of gestures and appearances regarded as characteristic of a specific racial group and dependent upon fixed racial classifications and ordering—and from a non-essentialist stance that problematizes identity in terms of cultural hybridity and "new ethnicities" (Hall 1996).[11] Drawing on these debates, Stuart Hall theorized two ways of reflecting on cultural identity: first, identity understood as a collective, shared history between individuals affiliated by race that is considered to be fixed or stable; and second, identity understood as unstable, metamorphic, and even contradictory—an identity marked by multiple points of similarities as well as differences. Such conflicting theories are particularly relevant to address the ways in which the British performer challenged totalizing notions of race.

In 1996, Hall suggested that a major shift had taken place in black cultural politics, "a change from a struggle over the relations of representation to the politics of representation itself" ("New Ethnicities" 165). His argument was that, shortly after the massive wave of immigration to the UK earlier in the century, the term *black* was used as an essential category to critique processes of exclusion and marginalization among highly differentiated racial communities; the "essential black subject" was therefore used as a counterhegemonic construction to contest white dominant practices of representation (163–64). By the 1990s, that heretofore unified framework shifted, according to the critic, to a new politics of representation, which entailed an "awareness of the black experience as a *diaspora* experience, and the consequences which this carries for the process of unsettling recombination, hybridization and 'cut-and-mix'—in short, the processes of cultural *diasporaization* . . . which it implies" (170; italics in original). In Hall's words, "we should think . . . of identity as a 'production' which is never complete, always in process, and always constituted within, not outside, representation" ("Cultural Identity and Diaspora" 234). Interwoven in Baron Cohen's performance are exactly this strong sense of the constructedness and fluidity of identity, of the multiple and overlapping forms of identification that constitute identity, and, as a result, a rejection of any sense of fixed identities or "essences." Not only does his composite character expose the structured markers of difference that racial thinking is predicated upon, but it also deconstructs those same markers. When Ali G requests, over and over again, that we "keep it real," he satirizes the obsession with authenticity which tends to downgrade the complexity of race. What is more, he shows his audience the seams and sutures implicated in the social construction of that category.

The strategy of reversing domination by establishing a "third space" is epitomized in the figure of the cultural hybrid—the modern racial passer—and rests at the core of Bhabha's claims for a new identity politics. In his view, this newfangled politics is only possible when one acknowledges that hybridity stands for an identity that is constructed out of open processes of negotiation and resistance. According to Bhabha, hybrid identities are not to be perceived as simple processes of accumulation that fuse different cultural forms into a homogenous whole—a view that Ali G shatters in his exaggerated juxtaposition of distinguishing features recognized by and large as pertaining to particular racial groups. On the contrary, "hybrid hyphenations," such as those effected by Ali G, "emphasize the incommensurable elements—the stubborn chunks—as the basis of cultural identifications" (219). These "stubborn chunks" are irreducible to fixed categorizations and thus create an interstitial space that allows for new worldviews. As Bhabha puts it:

> The theoretical recognition of the split-space of enunciation may open the way to conceptualizing an *inter*national culture based not on the exoticism of multiculturalism or the

> *diversity* of cultures but on the inscription and articulation of culture's *hybridity*. To that end we should remember that it is the "inter"—the cutting edge of translation and negotiation, the *in-between space*—that carries the burden of the meaning of culture. (38; italics in original)

In *After Empire* (2004),[12] Gilroy also articulates a dynamic concept of identity, underscoring notions of metamorphosis instead of fixity. In contemporary Britain, he notes, on the one hand, the "feral beauty of postcolonial culture" (157), and, on the other, the surfacing of "the cultural complex of postcolonial melancholia," the outcome of a refusal to come to grips with the breakup of Empire or, in the critic's own words, the result of a "cultural disorientation that accompanies the collapse of imperial certainties into postcolonial nihilism" (125). He describes here the effects of what Rushdie called in 1982 "The New Empire within Britain." Gilroy suggests the idea of "conviviality" to address this present British context of global transformation shaping politics and culture. By "convivial," he understands what is culturally "unkempt," "unruly," "unplanned," "chaotic," and "antic." As a way out of the political ineffectiveness of multiculturalism, the concept of conviviality allows us, according to Gilroy, to grasp more fully "the processes of cohabitation and interaction that have made multiculture an ordinary feature of social life in Britain's urban areas and in postcolonial cities elsewhere. . . . The radical openness that brings conviviality alive makes a nonsense of closed, fixed, and reified identity and turns attention toward the always-unpredictable mechanisms of identification" (xi). The convivial is an alternative to the reifying discourse of multiculturalism that maintains difference in order to promote the façade of political unity and liberalism.

If "[r]acial difference obstructs empathy and makes ethnocentrism inescapable," Gilroy maintains, "the powerful and pleasurable fantasy of transgressing that impassable boundary has started to circulate through the core of popular culture" (70). Following his line of argument, popular culture throws into question the reification of race, a necessary condition to fight racism *in effect* (167). Significantly, popular culture, via performers such as Baron Cohen, subversively "turn[s] the tables on all purity seekers" and "force[s] them to account for their phobia about otherness and their violent hostility" (167). Gilroy explores the potential of popular culture as a site of cultural healing and heralds Ali G as the epitome of such "chaotic pleasures of the convivial postcolonial urban world" (167), representing at once a threat to racial hierarchies and the potential to structure them anew. Expressions of popular culture such as this fictional character are then able to generate much-needed "emancipatory interruptions" (and here I reference Gilroy at length because of the complexity and relevancy of his work to my own):

> [T]here are other stories about "race" and racism to be told apart from the endless narrative of immigration as invasion and the melancholic blend of guilt, denial, laughter, and homogenizing violence that it has precipitated. Those emancipatory interruptions can perhaps be defined by a liberating sense of the banality of intermixture and the subversive ordinariness of this country's convivial cultures in which "race" is stripped of meaning and racism, as it fades, becomes only an aftereffect of long-gone imperial history. (166)

At this point the critic marks Baron Cohen's work as a response to a changing public sphere, as a practice committed to examining and charting the status quo:

> That unfixed and unstable Ali G might also have helped to break laughter's complicity with postcolonial melancholia and to locate new sources of comedy in a remade relationship with our heterogeneous selves, working through the aftereffects of empire in a self-consciously multicultural nation. That laughter does not intersperse loathing and self-hatred with manic elation. It helps instead to cultivate the everyday, ordinary virtue involved in managing healthier relationships with otherness that are not deformed by fear, anxiety, and violence. (149)

Gilroy explores an alternative idea of cosmopolitanism, described as "vulgar" or "demotic" cosmopolitanism, whose "value to the politics of multiculturalism lies in its refusal of state-centeredness and in its attractive vernacular style" (*After Empire* 75). He continues thus: "This cosmopolitan attachment finds civic and ethical value in the process of exposure to otherness. It glories in the ordinary virtues and ironies—listening, looking, discretion, friendship—that can be cultivated when mundane encounters with difference become rewarding" (75). In this context, irrespective of insidious or even racist meanings spawned by Ali G, the critic ends up deifying him as a boundary-straddling character (Weaver 12), involved in a "liberating project" (Gilroy, "Ali G" 5) which apparently reveals the multifarious nature of British convivial culture while promoting openness toward the other.

In an earlier analysis of Baron Cohen's character, entitled *Ali G and the Oscars* (2002), Gilroy drew on Zygmunt Bauman's conception of proteophobia, or fear of the multifarious, to explain critical and popular reactions to Ali G. Consistent with the critic's theorization of "the process of exposure to otherness," Bauman suggests in *Postmodern Ethics* the term *proteophobia* to describe "the apprehension aroused by the presence of multiform, allotropic phenomena which stubbornly elide assignment and sap the familiar classificatory grids" (181). The sociologist argues that if certain individuals generate anxiety because of their otherness—and whose status and role within society exhibit an "endemic ambivalence" (181), thus causing problems in the control of social spacing—specific strategies are mobilized to answer this predicament, but *not* to solve it completely. In this context, Bauman proposes the parallel concepts of "anthropophagic" and "anthropoemic," co-mechanisms of social spacing intent on neutralizing the threat of difference:

> The phagic strategy is *inclusivist,* the emic strategy is exclusivist. The first "assimilates" the strangers to the neighbours, the second merges them with the aliens [e.g. forcing them to exile]. Together, they polarize the strangers and attempt to clear up the most vexing and disturbing middle-ground between the poles of neighbourhood and alienness—between "home" and "abroad," "us" and "them." To the strangers whose life conditions and choices they define, they posit a genuine "either-or": conform or be damned, be like us or do not overstay your visit, play the game by our rules or be prepared to be kicked out from the game altogether. (180)

The anthropoemic strategy of making the strangers aliens is hence "aimed at the exile and annihilation of *the others*" (101), while the anthropophagic strategy of further removing aliens is "aimed at the suspension or annihilation of *their otherness*" (101). The stranger "posit[s] perennial problems of recycling and waste-disposal" (181), but the complementary and conflicting "phagic" and "emic" mechanisms of social spacing do not answer these problems, that is to say, they do not deactivate this disturbance within social spacing. Nevertheless, that apparent ineffectiveness is actually intentional since "[t]he administration of social space . . . *uses* proteophobia as its main resource, and willingly or inadvertedly, but constantly *replenishes* its stocks" (181).

Reactions to Ali G as stranger or alien seem to demonstrate Bauman's anthropoemic and anthropophagic strategies of managing the "other" within social space. As Simon Weaver notes, he is seen as "an ambivalent outsider who . . . disturbs the 'normal' methods of defining the content of cognitive space and so is in need of exile"—thus constituting a proteophobic response—or he is otherwise devoured "into the enjoyment of aesthetic space before he is similarly discarded" (7)—the result of a proteophilic attitude. In his praise of Baron Cohen's work, Gilroy eventually falls into the trap of overstating the proteophobic makeup of media debates on Ali G ("Ali G" 4–5)."[13] Using a characteristic celebratory tone, he views the off-putting responses to the comedic character the result of anxieties about "a larger process of dilution and mongrelisation in which the protective purity of largely racial cultures is being lost, leaving them vulnerable to unprotected encounters with difference that can only involve risk, fear and jeopardy" ("Ali G" 4). In other words, the critics' responses of hate, fear, and anxiety stem from Ali G's propensity for destabilizing, if not quite annihilating, the racial categories that undergird Britain's social system.

Indeed, what the proteophobic reactions selected by Gilroy seem to illustrate is that an image of a visibly or "clearly" black individual corresponds to an image of an unambiguous (and thus reassuring) identity, whereas an image of a white-to-black racial passer, an ambiguously raced character such as Ali G, is an impure, travesty image. He is not-quite-white, nor is he visibly black. Baron Cohen's creation, like Bauman's stranger, was not confusing and alarming only because he did not fit the categories of social spacing, but also—and perhaps chiefly—because he eluded classification by blurring the black-white racial binary, as well as exclusive conceptions of national and religious identities, irreversibly unsettling these discursive categories. The sight of Ali G's difference raised the specter of hybridity, carnivalization, and creolization, or, in Robert Young's phrasing, the "threat of degeneration and chaos incipient upon a 'raceless chaos' " (25).

With the comedian avoiding interaction with the media and remaining inscrutable over the "meaning" of the character—he hardly ever made media appearances out of character and gave only a small number of newspaper interviews—considerable debate on Baron Cohen's political intentions ensued, in particular following his entry into the mainstream. This caused a "semantic void" wherein the performer "is specifically *not* constructed as a celebrity and Ali G is reified or becomes the celebrity that Baron Cohen could have been" (Weaver 4). Added conjectures continued, promoting extra ambivalence which, according to Gilroy, was a positive outcome: "[A]n undecidable Ali is far preferable to the retreat involved in making him into the joker in the New Labour pack of ethnic happy families" ("Ali G" 5). Even though the comic character referenced himself as black, his ethnic identity remained ambiguous throughout his three stages, with commentators resisting this uncertainty surrounding Ali G's "real" identity and labeling him concurrently as (1) a black man; (2) a white man acting as an Asian pretending to be a black man; (3) an Asian wannabe black; (4) a Jew pretending to be an Asian wannabe rapper; (5) a white character blacked-up to mock a black person; (6) an impersonation of a white man who thinks he is black, and so on. Moreover, Baron Cohen's white middle-class Jewish background added to the complexity of his character, rendering him also as a North London white Jewish comedian lampooning an Asian youngster who sees himself as black. Even if, in Malik's words, Ali G is "[o]ne of the most contentious and popular comedic icons of Blackness" (103), Howells remarks that "[w]hat is much less clear . . . is whether Baron Cohen is actually pretending to be black at all" (166). In this respect, Gilroy argues that those somewhat failed efforts on the critics' part to put the character into fixed identity categories illustrate how they miss what is so subversive and invigorating about the performer's satire.

Not only was the possibility of Baron Cohen being a white man passing as black the major controversial issue in the public debate over the character of Ali G (rather than his political or cultural satire), but race itself was also a recurring *theme* in his comedic performance. For example, in a section dedicated to Wales in the film *Ali G, Innit,* the spoof interviewer—acting the role of the naive wise fool (Gilroy, *After Empire* 147)—is given a tour around a coal-mining museum by a former miner and jokes with pictures of what seem to him to be either blacked-up white miners or "brothers":

> Ali G: Hundreds of years ago, miners lived in here before they became human beings?
>
> Graham Gratton: They never *lived* within the mines; they only *worked* within the mines.
>
> AG: [peering into a shallow crawl-space] People worked under here?
>
> GG: Yes: 30 or 40 people worked here every day.
>
> AG: Dat is a crap job!

GG: No—that's a good job!

Up above ground level, the guide leads Ali into a more formal exhibition space:

> GG: Follow me and I'll just show you some photographs—
>
> [the camera cuts away to a historical photograph of a miner blackened with work at the coal-face]
>
> AG: So why is it mainly brothers who is workin' in the mine?
>
> GG: Brothers?
>
> AG: Aii: Why is it mainly the black man—that's a bit racialist innit?
>
> GG: Oh no! That's sweat and dirt, that is!
>
> AG: So why's he blacked himself up to pretend to be like a brother?
>
> GG: But he hasn't blacked himself up and he *hasn't* pretended to be like you say "a brother" . . . (transcribed in Howells 158–59)

In this skit, Baron Cohen bundles and satirizes the political, social, and economic discourses that create and maintain both race and class hierarchies. Or, in a skit using a similar type of intentional misconstruction around race and class, Ali G is interviewing Shawn Crawford, an ATF dog trainer.

> Crawford: Most of the dogs we get are black in color. We do get some yellows and, rarely, we get some chocolate colored ones too.
>
> AG: Ain that a bit racialist, getting mainly black dogs to do this?
>
> Crawford: No, not at all, that's just a part of the Labrador Retriever breeding.
>
> AG: Ay right.

> CRAWFORD: The black dogs are predominant.
>
> AG: But ain't it a bit racialist saying, ay right, this is dangerous work, let's get the brothers in to go find the bombs?
>
> CRAWFORD: No. That has nothing to do with it. (*Da Ali G Show* 2004)

Ali G uses these moments, couched in the absurd, to make what resonate as legitimate observations about continuing race-based inequities.

Consuming Race

"It is in many respects remarkable," Howells writes, that Ali G should have earned "such widespread acceptance among both the black community and the public at large" (163). The relevant (and problematic) questions to ask then about Baron Cohen's work seem to be inevitable: What accounted for such immense popularity? Why did the audience laugh? Who were they laughing at? What was indeed the exact source of Ali G's humor, or does this question make any sense at all? In this context, Malik notes the criticism Baron Cohen received from several black comedians who were outraged by what they perceived to be a vilification of black culture. While watching Ali G passing as black, audiences were at times uncertain of how to react, aware that by laughing they might be entering the domain of the politically incorrect (Rehling 293). In this respect, black comedian Felix Dennis states that Baron Cohen "[allowed] the liberal middle class to laugh at black street culture in a context where they can retain their political correctness" (qtd. in Kane). Apparently, not everyone laughing was really "getting the joke," but instead finding it amusing on the very terms the white comedian was professedly trying to critique. Raising charges of cultural theft and exploitation, what these artists condemned most of all was that Ali G passed as black not as a form of antiracist resistance, but because it was "cool" to act black. Moreover, many were upset at the character's success vis-à-vis black under-representativeness on British television, for instance, "Felix Dexter and Gina Yashere were critical of the media frenzy over 'Ali G.' compared to its marginalization of and lethargy towards 'genuinely' Black comedians, and comedian Curtis Walker compared Ali G to Al Jolson, feeling uncomfortable about the popularity of a 'Blacked up' performer in contemporary Britain" (Malik 104).

Probably one of the most disquieting characteristics of many postmodern analyses of power is the impotence in effectively locating resistance and acknowledging even a partial dismantling of power structures, notwithstanding the recurrent emphasis on opposition to that power. This sentiment, of an entire social space irredeemably shaped by "an implacable machine of power" (Hardt and Negri 323), is particularly rampant in the criticism of Ali G, and might account for the ambivalence in the reception of Baron Cohen's performance. For these black comedians, part of the character's success resulted from its scornful caricaturing of black people but, in a way, this charge revealed an underlying assumption wherein there are distinctive codes restricted to specific racial groups, regardless of sampling and appropriation by others, as if blackness were a coherent, stable category. Moreover, Baron Cohen's racial passing was heavily coded *as* performance. He arguably is passing *and,* simultaneously, parodying passing. For, if racial categories are empty, passing becomes impossible and the desire to appropriate an "other" identity hollow. Another element of defense is his own racial indeterminacy/multiplicity: his immediate ancestors were from Germany, Israel, Lithuania, and Wales. What race is he? What nationality? What ethnicity? What religion? What class? There are no easy answers.

Ali G is the modern-day passer—a fictional character who produces an intricate matrix of meanings at once. As postmodern passer, he can "pass" in full view. As a performer of racial masquerade, he can be a minstrel without blacking up. He can blur the color line, subverting racial categories by rendering visible their discursive nature. With his racial identity articulated outside of the dialectic binary of black-white, he presents an interesting case study for the examination of serious cultural issues: racism and the inequity, violence, and division it causes. Unfortunately, cross-identifications such as those performed—and caricatured—by the "white" comedian seem more likely to be mapped onto commodities (certainly Tommy Hilfiger has reaped financial reward from Baron Cohen's popularity, just as the image of a blacked-up Kate Moss sold newspapers) rather than political struggles over issues of racism and representation. However, although he is inescapably about mass consumption and entertainment *first*—as a comedian, he is selling a (performance) commodity—he is also capitalizing on (and critiquing) a long and complex history of racism, imperialism, exclusionism, and identity politics that gives his work a relevancy outside of the marketplace. In other words, as the phenomenal success of Baron Cohen's 2006 film *Borat: Cultural Learnings of America for Make Benefit Glorious Nation of Kazakhstan* suggests, a worldwide audience is still willing to buy what he is selling,[14] but his very popularity (including proteophobic reactions) evidences Western cultures' continued fascination with racial identities, the boundaries that demarcate those identities, and the transgressions we make daily across those boundaries. Thus, regardless of what we make of his convivial chaos, Baron Cohen reminds us that, in a postmodern world, we are all indeterminate, mutable, and multiple.

Notes

1. Here I will note that the British sense of the word *black* differs from its American use. In the UK, it is generally agreed upon that the term applies to individuals of African, Caribbean, and South Asian origin. The inclusive character of the term stems from a shared history of European imperialism, colonialism, and neocolonialism. There is some resistance by South Asian groups concerning the current use of this all-encompassing term given the diversity of South Asian cultural identities (such as, but not limited to, Indians, Pakistanis and Bangladeshis). Despite cultural nuances, the idea of "blacking up" generally translates from British to American culture, as do the types of racial play discussed throughout this essay.

2. Kalman (1949–1999) was an American graphic designer and founding editor-in-chief for *Colors* magazine.

3. American audiences will remember a similar type of racial morphing in Michael Jackson's 1991 video, "Black or White."

4. For an in-depth study on blackface minstrelsy, see Eric Lott's *Love and Theft: Blackface Minstrelsy and the American Working Class.*

5. The fact that Baron Cohen is Jewish is almost always mentioned in biographical accounts. The liminal and complex history of Jewish racial identity in relation to whiteness complicates and perhaps facilitates Cohen's ability to embody a racially mutable character. Even though a consideration of how Jews as an ethnic group became redefined as white would contribute to a further understanding of the multilayered nature of Cohen's performance, the complex nature of Jewish whiteness falls outside the scope of this chapter. For a detailed discussion of how Jews as an ethnic group became redefined as white, see Karen Brodkin's *How Jews Became White Folks* and Michael Rogin's *Blackface, White Noise: Jewish Immigrants in the Hollywood Melting Pot.*

6. The British Cohen further complicates his identity performance in later characters such as Borat Sagdiyev, a Kazakhstani journalist.

7. For an in-depth exploration of this type of interviewing on post-network satire television, see Jonathan Gray's *Satire TV: Politics and Comedy in the Post Network Era.* Gray argues that, as opposed to other satiric interviewers, such as Stephen Colbert or Jon Stewart, Ali G often makes himself rather than the interviewee appear stupid or misinformed, which bolsters rather than subverts the

public figure's image/agenda (155). Later, Gray argues that this is, however, not always so and the interview can also be used to highlight the interviewee's conservatism, racism, or sexism (156–57). Gray's argument, in either case, bolsters my own in that in his reading Ali G's performance as a "suburban gangsta wannabe" (154) is always foregrounded through his language, dress, and cultural references.

8. In *The Many Faces of Sacha Baron Cohen: Politics, Parody, and the Battle over Borat*, Robert A. Saunders discusses Cohen in relation to Chappelle and other comedians, as well as discusses in depth what he calls Cohen's "global minstrelsy" (4). Saunders offers a detailed reading of multiple Cohen characters—characters that combine various ethnic identities—and is thus an important resource for those interested in Cohen's work. Saunders's larger goal is to explore the "postmodern metamorphosis currently underway in satirical ethnic comedy, and how globalization and multiculturalism influence this shift" (4). In comparison, my specific goal here is to examine the character of Ali G through the trope of racial passing.

9. Although outside the scope of this essay, Cohen's engagement with Islam—particularly through later characters such as Admiral General Shabazz Aladeen of the 2012 film *The Dictator*—has caused controversy and has been called "Arab-faced minstrelsy" (Zayd) and a "modern-day minstrel show" (Obeidallah).

10. To understand the range of passing as a trope, see Ginsberg, Wald, Sanchez and Schlossberg, Wright and Glass, Dreisinger, and Moynihan. Arguably, the most common racial passing narrative is one in which a "mulatto" passes for white. The very act of passing highlights the performative nature of race. However, the passer often simultaneously feels as though she is betraying her race or that she is masquerading in a false identity, feelings that reaffirm race as an essential category. In the United States, one of the most widely known passing stories incorporating this standard narrative is the 1959 film *Imitation of Life*. In the film the light-skinned Sarah Jane passes as white, only to regret her actions and accept a black identity after the death of her black mother.

11. According to Hall, "new ethnicities" cannot be equated with the "old ethnicities" (e.g., Englishness or Americanness) which "could only survive by marginalizing, dispossessing, displacing and forgetting other ethnicities" ("New Ethnicities" 170).

12. Published in the United States by Columbia UP under the title *Postcolonial Melancholia* (2005).

13. Weaver addresses this limitation: "While Gilroy's account is productive to an extent, because he does not employ the concept of proteophilia, he overemphasizes the role of exclusionary tendencies in media descriptions of the character and is unable to properly describe less 'confrontational' or non-racist descriptions of Ali G" (11).

14. Cohen has since released two more films: *Brüno* (2009) is also based on an *Ali G* character. The reviews for *Brüno* were mixed, with some claiming the film rehashes rather than critiques homophobia and plays cheaply on stereotypes of gay men. The second, *The Dictator,* was released in 2012. Some reviews were

stronger than for *Brüno,* but did not reach the level of *Borat*; although others have objected to the film's characterization of Muslims (see note 9).

Works Cited

Ali G Indahouse. Dir. Mark Mylod. Universal Pictures, 2002.

Ali G in da USAiii. HBO, USA. 21 Feb. 2003-22 Aug. 2004.

Ali G, Innit. Channel Four, UK, 1999.

Ali G Show, Da. Channel Four, UK. 30 Mar. 2000-5 May 2000.

Bamboozled. Dir. Spike Lee. New Line, 2001.

Bauman, Zygmunt. *Postmodern Ethics.* Oxford: Blackwell, 1993. Print.

Bhabha, Homi K. *The Location of Culture.* New York: Routledge, 1994. Print.

Brodkin, Karen. *How Jews Became White Folks.* New Brunswick: Rutgers UP, 1998. Print.

Brüno. Dir. Larry Charles. Universal Pictures, 2009.

The Dictator. Dir. Larry Charles. Paramount Pictures, 2012.

Dreisinger, Baz. *Near Black: White to Black Passing in American Culture.* Amherst: U of Massachusetts P, 2008. Print.

Gennocchio, Benjamin. "For Japanese Girls, Black is Beautiful; Painting Hip-Hop as it Goes Geisha." *The New York Times.* 4 April 2004: 36. Print.

Gilroy, Paul. *After Empire: Melancholia or Convivial Culture?* London: Routledge, 2004. Print.

———. "Ali G and the Oscars." *openDemocracy.* 3 April 2002: 1–5. Web. 4 March 2008.

Ginsberg, Elaine K., ed. *Passing and the Fictions of Identity.* Durham: Duke UP, 1996. Print.

Gray, Jonathan, Jeffrey P. Jones, and Ethan Thompson. *Satire TV: Politics and Comedy in the Post-Network Era.* New York: New York UP, 2009. Print.

Hall, Stuart. "Cultural ldentity and Diaspora." *Theorizing Diaspora: A Reader.* Ed. Jana Evans Braziel and Anita Mannur. Oxford: Blackwell, 2003. 233–46. Print.

———. "New Ethnicities." *Black British Cultural Studies: A Reader.* Ed. Houston A. Baker Jr., Manthia Diawara, and Ruth H. Lindeborg. Chicago: U of Chicago P, 1996. 163–72. Print.

Hardt, Michael, and Antonio Negri. *Empire.* Cambridge and London: Harvard UP, 2000. Print.

Howells, Richard. " 'Is it Because I is Black?' Race, Humour and the Polysemiology of Ali G." *Historical Journal of Film, Radio and Television* 26.2 (2006): 155–77. Print.

Huq, Rupa. "Global Youth Cultures in Localized Spaces: The Case of the UK New Asian Dance Music and French Rap." *The Post-Subcultures Reader.* Ed. David Muggleton and Rupert Weinzierl. New York: Berg, 2003. 195–208. Print.

Imitation of Life. Dir. Douglas Sirk. Universal International Pictures, 1959.

iona rozeal brown a3 . . . black on both sides. 2004. Spellman College Museum of Fine Art. Web. 3 March 2008.

Kane, Pat. "Ali G: Da New White and Black Minstrel." *Sunday Herald*. 10 March 2002. Web. 3 March 2008.

Klein, Naomi. *No Logo: No Space, No Choice, No Jobs*. New York: Picador, 2002. Print.

League of Gentlemen, The. BBC, UK. 11 Jan. 1999-31 Oct. 2002.

Little Britain. BBC, UK. 16 Sept. 2003-31 Dec. 2006.

Lott, Eric. *Love and Theft: Blackface Minstrelsy and the American Working Class*. New York: Oxford UP, 1995. Print.

Malik, Sarita. *Representing Black Britain: Black and Asian Images on Television*. London: Sage, 2002. Print.

———. "The Black and White Minstrel Show." *The Museum of Broadcast Communications*. Web. 3 March 2008.

Malkani, Gautam. *Londonstani*. London: Fourth Estate, 2006.

Moynihan, Sinéad. *Passing Into the Present: Contemporary American Fiction of Racial and Gender Passing*. Manchester: Manchester UP, 2011. Print.

Obeidallah, Dean. "Sacha Cohen's Movie a Minstrel Show." *CNN*. Web. 11 May 2012.

Pool, Hannah. "Return to the Dark Ages." *The Guardian*. 22 Sept. 2006. Web. 3 March 2008.

Rehling, Nicola. "White Heterosexual Masculinity in Contemporary Popular Cinema." Unpublished PhD thesis, Aristotle U of Thessaloniki, 2005. Print.

Rodriguez, Richard. *Brown: The Last Discovery of America*. New York: Penguin, 2002. Print.

Rogin, Michael. *Blackface, White Noise: Jewish Immigrants in the Hollywood Melting Pot*. Berkeley: U of California P, 1996. Print.

Rushdie, Salman. "The New Empire Within Britain." 1982. *Imaginary Homelands: Essays and Criticism 1981–1991*. London: Granta, 1991. 129–38. Print.

Sánchez, Maria Carla, and Linda Schlossberg, eds. *Passing: Identity and Interpretation in Sexuality, Race, and Religion*. New York: New York UP, 2001. Print.

Saunders, Robert A. *The Many Faces of Sacha Baron Cohen: Politics, Parody, and the Battle over Borat*. Lanham, MD: Lexington Books, 2009. Print.

Wald, Gayle. *Crossing the Line: Racial Passing in Twentieth-Century U.S. Literature and Culture*. Durham: Duke UP, 2000. Print.

Weaver, Simon. "Comprehending Ambivalence: Ali G and Conceptualisations of the 'Other.'" *Connections* 4 (n/d): 1–16. Web. 3 March 2008.

White Chicks. Dir. Keenen Ivory Wayans. Columbia Pictures, 2004.

Wright, Susan Protho, and Ernestine Pickens Glass, eds. *Passing in the Works of Charles W. Chesnutt*. Jackson: U of Mississippi P, 2010. Print.

Young, Robert. *White Mythologies: Writing History and the West*. London: Routledge, 1996. Print.

Zayd, Daniel Ibn. "Sacha Cohen and Arab Minstrelsy." Dissident Voice: A Radical Newsletter in the Struggle for Peace and Social Justice. Web. 19 May 2012.

9

Passing for Black, White, and Jewish

Mixed-Race Identity in Rebecca Walker and Danzy Senna

Lori Harrison-Kahan

Danzy Senna's 1998 novel *Caucasia* narrates the coming-of-age story of a mixed-race protagonist named Birdie Lee. The offspring of a civil rights movement union between a black intellectual father and a white activist mother, Birdie appears white, but actively identifies with her dark-skinned sister Cole, openly embracing her African American heritage. Complicating the racial dynamics of traditional passing narratives, in which mixed-race protagonists seek the privileges afforded by their white appearance (even as this desire for whiteness is often fraught with ambivalence), Senna's novel reinvents the theme of passing for a multicultural, post–civil rights era: it presents us with a biracial female protagonist for whom blackness becomes the idealized racial identity, one that potentially yields more benefits than whiteness.

In the beginning of the novel, Birdie is depicted as passing for black, not white. At Nkrumah, the black power school she attends in Boston, she learns to speak Ebonics, wear her straight hair in tight braids to mask its texture, and accessorize with gold hoops, Sergio Valente Jeans, and Nike sneakers. Once initiated into "the art of changing" (62), Birdie—despite her skin color—is able to be black, accepted by the most popular girls at school. But Birdie's world is turned upside down by the dissolution of her parents' marriage, which fails to survive the political shift from the interracial cooperation of the integrationist civil rights movement to the separatism of black pride. Deck and Sandy Lee divvy up their daughters according to their color: Cole disappears with their father, who goes in search of a racial utopia in Brazil, while Birdie and her paranoid mother go underground, eventually recreating lives for themselves in white small-town New Hampshire. According to Birdie's mother, the fact that her daughter could now pass for *white* would allow them to elude the FBI, who are on her trail, she presumes, for her involvement with a radical activist group. As Birdie tells it, "The two bodies that had made her [mother] stand out in a crowd—made her more than just another white woman—were gone; now it was just the two of us. My body was the key to our going incognito" (128). Birdie must not only relabel herself as white, but must also confront a painful separation from the now-absent black body: her beloved sister Cole.

In describing Birdie's transformation into a white girl, Senna makes yet another important innovation in the traditional passing story, for whiteness is not represented as a monolithic category. Birdie must pass for a specific kind of white. Although Birdie, "a blank slate" (130), could be anything, her mother insists on inventing a Jewish identity and history for her. Once schooled on her black self at Nkrumah, Birdie is now schooled on a Jewish self. Her mother conjures an imaginary father for Birdie, a Jewish intellectual named David Goldman with a "mop of curly black hair, an afro, the way Jews have sometimes. . . . [H]e was pretty much an atheist even though he wanted you to know your history, your heritage. For him, Judaism was more like a cultural thing" (131). With this simple displacement of afro for "Jewfro," Birdie Lee is transformed into a half-Jewish girl named Jesse Goldman, passing as the daughter of an assimilated, secular Jew.

A significant contribution to the discourse on multiracialism that emerged in the 1990s, *Caucasia* is only one of a number of recent works of literature that either explicitly or implicitly invoke the concept of "passing" to examine the relationship among blackness, whiteness, and Jewishness. Last in vogue during the Harlem Renaissance, the theme of passing has been adopted and adapted by contemporary black and Jewish writers (as well as writers who could be identified as both black and Jewish). Jewishness was once an unstated, or understated, motif in narratives of passing; in popular novelist Fannie Hurst's 1933 *Imitation of Life,* for example, the experiences of Peola Johnston—the fair-skinned daughter who, in deciding to cross the color line, heartbreakingly forsakes her dark-skinned mother—might be read as a metaphor for the dilemma of

Jewish assimilation, especially given the author's vexed relationship to her Jewish identity.[1] Now, however, Jewishness has become integral to contemporary narratives in which characters negotiate—and ultimately, redefine—the color line. While this resurgence of interest in passing reflects the current trend to convey the social construction of race through the metaphorics of performance, novels such as *Caucasia* and Philip Roth's *The Human Stain* (2000), in which African American protagonists pass as Jewish, also shift the paradigm of the passing narrative, reinscribing the biracial binary of black and white in terms of more complex categories of identity: black, white, *and* Jewish.[2]

Black, White, and Jewish is, in fact, the title of a 2001 memoir by Rebecca Walker, the daughter of black feminist writer Alice Walker and Jewish civil rights attorney Mel Leventhal. Subtitling her book "autobiography of a shifting self," Walker describes how she transforms herself from a rebellious black adolescent living with her mother in the bohemia of San Francisco to an upper-middle-class Jewish girl living with her father and stepmother in the suburbs of Manhattan; the different identities she takes on in the course of her memoir attest to the fictions of identity itself. While most of the current scholarship on narratives of passing focuses on fiction, memoirs—and especially the rapidly proliferating genre of multiracial memoirs—are another important site for exploring what Sidonie Smith (borrowing from Judith Butler) calls "autobiographical performativity": the notion that the self does not preexist the act of narrating her or his life story, but rather comes into being through autobiographical acts and practices.[3]

By focusing on two texts—one novel and one memoir—in which Jewish identity is incorporated within the African American narrative of passing, this essay illustrates how Jewishness functions as a representation of multiplicity and ambivalence in contemporary multiracial literature. Adding a third term to the typically black-and-white schema of U.S. race relations, these contemporary texts deploy Jewishness to expose the social construction and plurality of whiteness as well as to challenge existing theories of mixed-race identity that rely on binary configurations. Occupying more than one position at once, Jewishness simultaneously signifies whiteness and racial otherness; furthermore, the confusion over whether the label "Jewish" refers to race, ethnicity, religion, or culture is emblematic of its complex meanings across categories of identity. As it appears in contemporary ethnic literature, the theme of "passing for Jewish" underscores the debate about whether Jewish identity should be aligned with a dominant whiteness or with the minoritarian position of racial otherness.

On the one hand, this theme places Jewishness within the framework of ethnic difference. While "passing" alone forces us to confront how identity has come to be defined socially and legally, the concept of "passing for Jewish" takes the challenge to essentialism one step farther since the theme evolved due to another construction that took place over the course of the twentieth century: the historical transformation of Jews from a racial minority into members of the white majority through the process of assimilation.[4] On the other hand, the theme of "passing for Jewish" depicts Jewishness *as* whiteness and thus as a part of the dominant culture. Once "almost white, but not quite," to play on Homi Bhabha's formulation,[5] Jews are now "almost ethnic, but not quite." Precisely because of its own multiple meanings—as "almost," as "both, but neither"—Jewishness plays a central role in representing and revealing the multiplicity in mixed-race identities.

The rocky relationship between Jews and blacks has been at the forefront of considerations of Jews in multicultural contexts, and, in many ways, it has come to stand in for the ambivalent status of Jewish difference. This strained relationship is largely the result of historical and political shifts in the second half of the twentieth century. During the mid-century civil rights movement, Jews and blacks formed what Nathan Glazer once called a "grand alliance" to fight for racial justice. In the 1970s, however, this alliance disintegrated as both groups began to express different interests.[6] Glazer attributes this split to the slowing of African American economic progress (in relation to Jewish success) and to the related onset of the Black Power movement, with its separatist impulse. Blacks also began to question the motivation behind Jewish involvement in civil rights. Today, while Jews are occasionally seen as another minority, sharing history and struggle with their African American brethren, they are more often viewed as benefiting from the racism of the United States. Cultural critics such as Michael Rogin have argued that Jews became white in relation to, and at the expense of, blacks. In "Rattling the Cage of Black-Jewish Relations," Jeffrey Melnick contends that this hierarchical relationship in which Jewish producers profit from their appropriations of black culture and narratives plagues the very notion of a black-Jewish dialogue: "As a recognizable rhetorical construct, 'Black-Jewish Relations' has largely been made by Jews" (50). Partially because of such contentions that this conversation is one-sided and unidirectional, I have chosen to examine the relationship between Jewishness and blackness in the work of writers who are usually identified—by themselves and by others—as black or multiracial. The fact that such minority writers are concerned with representations of Jewishness, however ambivalent, suggests that the construct of "black-Jewish relations" is more dialogue than monologue.

To rattle the cage of black-Jewish relations even further, this essay adds another complicating factor: gender. As commentators such as Melnick and Cornel West have pointed out, the black-Jewish dialogue has been "a male domain" (Melnick 59). Women's voices have rarely been heard in this heated debate about black-Jewish relations and cultural exchange. This study attempts to "de-patriarchalize" (West) the black-Jewish dialogue by focusing on two women writers, Rebecca Walker and Danzy Senna. Walker and Senna reimagine multiplicity in more complex terms not only because of their tendency to complicate current notions of mixed-race identities by adding Jewishness to the discussion, but also because of their additional concerns with sexual difference. While passing for Jewish may be a recent literary phenomenon,[7] earlier black women writers also included representations of Jewishness in their passing novels. In Jessie Fauset's *Plum Bun* (1928), for example, the secondary character of Rachel Salting, a Jewish woman who plans to marry a gentile man despite her parents' objections, serves as a double for the passing protagonist, Angela Murray, who similarly hopes to marry a white man, although it will permanently sever any remaining ties to her black family. In Nella Larsen's *Passing* (1929), Clare Kendry, who crosses the color line and succeeds in marrying a white man, empathizes with the seemingly ludicrous figure of Claude Jones, a black man who becomes a Jew.

In contrast to these earlier examples, Senna's and Walker's works do not make Jewishness secondary to the dilemmas of their passing protagonists. Instead, these texts feature female figures who perform blackness, whiteness, and Jewishness, thus bringing together all three identities within a single body. Despite the fact that both Senna and Walker give Jewishness a primary presence in their texts, their representations still retain uncertainty on the issue of whether or not Jewishness qualifies as whiteness. Tracing the ambivalence in contemporary representations of Jews and Jewish identity, this essay argues that Jewishness operates as a figure for multiplicity by illuminating other ethnic, racial, sexual, gender, and class identifications that compose subnarratives of these texts. Thus, Jewishness draws attention to the fact that multiplicity itself is, appropriately, multiple, since it refers both to the potential to transcend dichotomies, such as black and white, as well as to the need to account for the intersections of identities: the way that race, gender, sexuality, and class are interarticulated. In destabilizing categories of identity, Jewishness reveals identification to be an ambivalent process; it functions as a kind of ethnic "queerness," exposing the complexities of mixed-race identity in ways that resist simplistic and binary understandings of race.

Ambivalent Performances of Jewish Identity

Early in *Black, White, and Jewish,* Walker references the passing character in the cinematic adaptations of Hurst's *Imitation of Life* when she defines herself as a tragic mulatta: "Black. White. Nigger. Jew. That makes me the tragic mulatta caught between both worlds. . . . I am Mammy's near-white little girl . . . screaming, 'I don't want to be colored, I don't want to be like you!' in the film classic *Imitation of Life*" (12–13).[8] Although she lists "Jew" as part of her definition of "tragic mulatta," the ambiguous pronoun, "that," makes it somewhat unclear what aspects of her identity Walker views as contributing to this stereotypical construction of mixed-race subjectivity. Walker's Jewishness, in fact, seems to redeem her from tragedy. "I am not a bastard, the product of rape, the child of some white devil. I am a Movement Child," she writes, just before firmly declaring, "I am not tragic" (24). Walker's mixture of whiteness and blackness is not, after all, the result of a friction between oppressor and oppressed, as it is for the traditional mulatta figure; what keeps her father from being a "white devil" is his Jewishness. Portraying herself as a symbol of the civil rights movement alliance of blacks and Jews, Walker notes that she was conceived in love and political solidarity. Her parents' marriage—and her existence itself—is an act of protest not simply because it defies the taboo against interracial relationships, but also because it represents the united front of blacks and Jews against white racism.

Reacting against stereotypical, and binary, depictions of mixed-race identity, Senna, too, resists conforming to the feminized trope of the tragic mulatta.[9] Rather than succumb to a tragic fate, Birdie survives, "a little injured, perhaps, but alive" (393). *Caucasia* implies that part of the reason Birdie is able to survive is that she passes as Jewish instead of as white; that is, she does not completely renounce her minority identity. As her mother insists, Birdie "wasn't really passing because Jews weren't really white, more like an off-white. . . . [T]hey were the closest I was going to get to black and still stay white. 'Tragic history, kinky hair, good politics,' she explained. 'It's all there'" (140). Mourning for Cole and all that she and her name represent, Birdie is able to preserve some of the blackness she is forced to repudiate by taking on a Jewish identity. Thus, for the protagonists of *Caucasia* and *Black, White, and Jewish,* Jewishness (whether actual or assumed) functions importantly in their resistance to more traditional representations of mixed-race identity in which the inability to identify as either black or white leads often to death, literal or metaphorical.

However, whether or not Jewishness qualifies as whiteness remains a question for both Senna and Walker, in part because the story of Jewish assimilation in America can be read as a narrative of successful passing for white. In passing for Jewish, Birdie passes as the consummate passer since Jews were thought to have a chameleon-like ability to blend in with almost any group of people.[10] This paradoxical notion of Jewish mimicry as an essential trait highlights the ways that racial identity is constructed. When Birdie confronts her father at the end of the novel, revealing to him that she has lived as "a white girl, a Jewish girl" (391), he agrees with his wife that Birdie is not "really passing," but for a slightly different reason: "[T]here's no such thing as passing. We're all just pretending. Race is a complete illusion, make-believe. It's a costume. We all wear one" (391). The theme of passing as Jewish thus presents a double whammy for racial essentialism. Just as passing has often been used as evidence of the social construction of race, so too has the assimilation of Jews into whiteness. In passing for Jewish—in passing as one who passes—Birdie confirms that race is empty at its core.

Like other novels of racial passing, *Caucasia* exemplifies Butler's theory of gender performativity—the notion that masculinity and femininity are constituted through reiterated performances—by applying it to race. Having learned the lesson of black performativity at Nkrumah, Birdie similarly notes that her Jewishness is a "performance" (140): "We played up my Jewishness only some of the time; other times we nearly forgot about it. She had bought me a Star of David somewhere along the way, a cheap one from a pawn shop. It hung from a thick gold rope and left a vaguely greenish tint on the skin below my collarbone. Another time she bought me *The Diary of Anne Frank,* a book that had been Cole's favorite once upon a time. Sometimes, when she was feeling particularly paranoid in public places, she would call me her *meshugga nebbish* with exaggerated relish" (140). These acts reiterate and reinforce each other to create a Jewish identity for Birdie, transforming her into Jesse Goldman. Like her blackness at Nkrumah, Birdie's Jewishness rests on her ability to accessorize. However, the Star of David also represents Birdie's ambivalence about the identity she has taken on. In contrast to a Jewish girl at school whose Star of David "looked like real quality gold and had a diamond" (247), Birdie's necklace is not real, but a piece of costume jewelry, even if it does leave an indelible mark on her skin. The greenish tint connects Birdie to her fake immigrant past; Birdie, too, is a "greenhorn" in her New Hampshire environs. Birdie's fear that she will stand out as different in her new surroundings often manifests in terms of her concern that others will notice this green tint.

As Butler argues, identity is determined by language, which both initiates and forms part of these performances. Thus, Birdie's mother interpellates her daughter in Yiddish, even if "*meshugga nebbish*" does not make much sense as a term of endearment. In fact, Sandy eventually shortens the phrase to "mush," signifying its own meaninglessness, as well as Birdie's mixed identity. But, for the most part, Birdie's disguise works so well that she comes to believe it herself: "My father was fading on me. Not the Jewish father. I could see David Goldman clear as day . . . a yarmulke bobby-pinned precariously to his loose afro, as he bent over some ancient text" (188). Birdie's mourning for Cole and for blackness is transposed on to this mourning for her invented dead father and his Jewish past. Although Sandy had earlier insisted that Birdie's father was a secular Jew, David Goldman morphs into a Talmudic scholar. Having noted that one's Jewish identity, unlike blackness, can, at times, be "nearly" forgotten, Birdie seems to be looking backward down a line of imaginary fathers to the moment before Jews shed the telltale signs of their Jewishness and became "white folks." Furthermore, the afro, earlier displaced by "Jewfro," has reemerged in Birdie's imagination. The seeming incongruity of yarmulke and afro indicates that Deck Lee is not fading as quickly as Birdie thinks.

In *Black, White, and Jewish,* Walker experiences many of the same ambivalences about her Jewish identity. Walker, who is technically not Jewish according to Judaic laws of matrilineal descent, seems to become Jewish when she, like Birdie, is interpellated in Yiddish by her paternal grandmother. Calling her granddaughter "*bubbeleh, tchotchkeleh,*" her grandmother urges her not to forget that she is a Jew, no matter what her parents say (40). Walker's father may be even less observant as a Jew than the imaginary David Goldman, but the decisions he makes for his daughter force her to confront her Jewish identity, or lack thereof. When Walker is living with her father and stepmother, they send her to Fire Lake, a predominantly Jewish summer camp, where her favorite event is aptly Color War. While at Fire Lake, Walker describes how she must alter her clothes and her attitude to pass as Jewish. Like Birdie, Walker hopes that she will be labeled according to the labels she wears: "I wear Capezios and Guess jeans and Lacoste shirts, and I assume the appropriate air of petulant entitlement. And yet I never get it quite right, never get the voice to match up with the clothes, never can completely shake free of my blackness. . . . I heighten the characteristics I share with the people around me and minimize, as best I can, the ones that don't belong. At Fire Lake I am a Jap, but not one. I know *baruch atah Adonai Elohainu* and love Color War, but I don't own fifty Le Sportsacs or spend the week before camp starts on a Teen Tour in Israel. I move my body like I belong but I also hold it back" (177–78, 182–83).

On the one hand, Walker appears to be describing a Du Boisian double consciousness and thus the dilemma of her black American identity. "This sense of always looking at one's self through the eyes of others" (Du Bois 215) becomes even more evident when Walker describes herself as detached from her own body at camp: "I watch us play from someplace far away and safe. . . . I watch myself try to will my body into some kind of normal posture, into some semblance of ease and comfort to disguise my feeling of not belonging. I watch myself perform, shift, contort, sweat" (176). On the other hand, perhaps Walker does get "it" exactly "right" since the duality that she describes is a Jewish experience, too. Walker's own father, for example, is caught between his early involvement in the civil rights movement in Jackson, Mississippi, where his daughter's story begins, and his Jewish wife's dream of owning a house and a Volvo in Larchmont, New York (204).

While Walker invokes the Jewish American Princess to allude to the whitening of the Jews through the materialistic pursuit of the American dream, the stereotype notably differentiates Jews, and specifically Jewish women, from other white suburbanites or consumers: the J in JAP falsely suggests that Jewish consumption is a brand all its own.[11] Walker herself notes the ambivalence surrounding the JAP stereotype: "It [Jap] means something repulsive, gauche, flashy, and yet secretly we are proud to be Japs, to think of ourselves as spoiled by Daddy's money and Mom's overprotectiveness" (177). The stereotype highlights the borderline status of Jewish identity, simultaneously marking the success of Jewish assimilation and the separation of the Jews from other Americans through perceived tastes that relegate them to the realm of the *nouveau riche*.

Like Birdie, Walker finds her most successful identification with Jewishness through the story of Anne Frank. "While I read Anne Frank's diary, I become her," writes Walker. "I feel terror and loss and like nothing can save me from the same death as Anne's. I imagine the Gestapo is going to come to my house and take me and my father and stepmother. . . . and I will die just like Anne" (89). Haunted by the Holocaust, both Walker and Birdie identify as Jewish because they see themselves as victims and outsiders. Their specific identification with a Jewish girl coming of age in hiding also speaks to their own stories, even if their survival is not dependent on their disguises in the same way that Anne's was dependent on her seclusion. In contrast to Jews during the Holocaust who had to either hide themselves or their Jewish identities in order to survive (and often, both types of hiding failed to protect them), Birdie ironically sees her Jewishness as the "only way . . . to remain free" (189), since she believes that she and her mother are on the lam from the FBI. Once a dangerous sign of difference, Jewishness has come to represent a means of survival. Just as Jews had to be able to adapt, to disguise at least a part of themselves, Birdie, too, takes on this trait of malleability.

When Birdie most directly faces anti-Semitism, she decides to discard her Jewishness, although she does put it away for safe-keeping as she does with her black identity. *Caucasia* allegorizes the conversion of Jews into white folks (to paraphrase Karen Brodkin). Targeted by high school boys who throw pennies at her and call her a "kike," Birdie is momentarily confused, since she has come to see herself as a "New Hampshire girl" (244). Then, she "looked down . . . noticing my Star of David, thick and gleaming in the sunlight. I only realized then that they were throwing pennies at me because I was Jesse Goldman, daughter of David Goldman. I felt a pang of loyalty toward this imaginary father, and touched the necklace" (246). Although Birdie may experience a strong identification with Jews through this episode, the incident also leads her to remove the Star of David, concealing it in the bottom of her underwear drawer. She explains to her girlfriends that she is "not *really Jewish*. I mean, only my dad was, and he's dead. And to be really a Jew, you have to have a mother who is Jewish. It's like the religious law or something" (247). Birdie's own shifts of identity have called into question whether it is possible to be "really" anything; when the layers are peeled away, she is like a Russian nesting doll with an empty center. These layers of identity are most evident when biracial Birdie passes for a Jew who passes for white.[12]

Several scholars of African American literature have argued that the concept of passing upholds racial essentialism because the subject's "true" identity becomes defined in its very erasure. To further this argument, they point out that the passing figure often returns to her black roots, confirming that that identity must be the "real" one. In fact, the identity that is covered up can be just as fabricated as the one performed in its place, which is why so many passing narratives end ambiguously rather than with a wholehearted embrace of blackness.[13] Birdie's experience further proves that even a false identity can carry with it the stigma of seeming essentialism since she continues to be aware of her assumed Jewishness, even after she has shed its outward signs. The Star of David turns out to be one of the few items she takes with her when she runs away from her white existence in New Hampshire. Adding it to her box of "Negrobilia," which contains a collection of black power objects given to her by her father and sister before they disappeared, Birdie wryly jokes that if she were found dead in a dumpster, the necklace would be "the only object that seems to make any sense" (381). For Birdie, Jewishness makes more "sense" than blackness alone because of the contradictions it represents. The ambivalence of Jewish identity, as both marked and unmarked, explains Birdie's loyalty to her pretend Jewish self, which she thus feels the need to preserve, even if it is relegated to the recesses of her belongings.

While Walker and Senna both present ambivalent performances of Jewish identity, the two texts also diverge in their attitudes toward Jewishness, pointing to the different directions that such representations can take. Whereas Birdie sheds her Jewishness to conform, Walker eventually obscures her Jewish identity to rebel against conformity. She comments on the transformation of Jews into "white folks" when she changes her name, moving Leventhal to the "more obscure middle position" and adding "Walker to the end, privileging my blackness and downplaying what I think of as my whiteness" (310). Although Leventhal is an identifiably Jewish surname, Walker aligns it with white hegemony: "When I change my name I do so because I do not feel an affinity with whiteness, with what Jewishness has become, and I do feel an affinity with blackness, with an experience of living in the world with non-white skin" (311). Because she cannot pass—since skin color is not as easy to shed as a Star of David—Walker disidentifies with Jewishness on the grounds that it is passing into whiteness.

Walker's statement is a reminder of Brodkin's argument that Jews became white folks over the course of the twentieth century, but neither Walker nor Brodkin fully acknowledges that Jewishness transforms itself into whiteness across both time *and* space. In the beginning of her memoir, Walker depicts her father as a civil rights attorney in the South, defending his black and Jewish family from the Klan; in this context, Mel Leventhal is not white. In her somewhat stereotypical depiction of Northern upper-middle-class Jews, Walker neglects to note that whether or not Jewishness becomes whiteness depends not only on temporality, but also on geography. Yet, Walker is aware that her blackness signifies differently depending on location. When she spends a summer interning at the Museum of Modern Art in New York, she discovers that being black has a cachet in the downtown art world that it did not have elsewhere. Juxtaposed with blackness, Jewishness loses its status as a minority identity because of its ability, at least in some contexts, to offer the appearance of conformity with the dominant culture. While Anne Frank is an acceptable identification because, as Walker says, she has "an instant affinity with beings who suffer, whether they are my own, whatever that means, or not" (304), late-twentieth-century American Jewishness is a less desirable identification, due largely to the myth of the powerful Jew.[14] Walker repudiates her Jewishness based on her need to disidentify with power and instead align herself with the disenfranchised.

Even though *Caucasia* presents Jewishness more favorably, as the next best alternative to blackness, the vexed relationship between Jewishness and blackness is also addressed by Senna prior to Birdie's transformation into Jesse Goldman. A few rather covert references to Jewishness early in the novel recall arguments that Jews, and other immigrants, were Americanized and whitened in direct relation to blackness.[15] Visiting her Aunt Dot in Roxbury, Birdie observes that the house Dot lives in "once had belonged to a family of Hasidic Jews [who] fled Roxbury when it began to change colors" (12). On her first day at Nkrumah, Birdie similarly takes note of the "abandoned Jewish synagogue" next door to the school "with weeds growing out of the cracks of the stone" (42). These examples of so-called white flight allude to the movement of Jewishness from a minority identity into hegemonic whiteness. The whiteness of white flight is ex post facto; by leaving communities that were beginning to "change colors," Jews and other immigrants began to be seen as white.

However, another subtle example from *Caucasia* suggests that Jewishness, even if hidden from view, did not disappear completely. Confronted by the secretary at the Nkrumah school who offends Birdie by refusing to believe she and Cole are sisters, Birdie notices that "something smelled of food, and . . . glimpse[s] a foil wrapper with a half-chewed bagel and lox peeking out from under a newspaper" (43). The secretary eating a bagel and lox at the black power school serves as a reminder of a sort of reverse assimilation that took place, as aspects of Jewish culture have been integrated into mainstream American culture. Birdie's observation can also be read as alluding to a one-time affinity between blacks and Jews during a prior historical moment that has now been covered up by current events, represented by the newspaper that obscures the typically Jewish food from view. While the black power movement gave rise to an Afrocentric, sometimes anti-Semitic discourse that elided what one scholar has called the "unillustrious" civil rights movement alliance,[16] Birdie has sniffed out a reminder of this past; like her invented memory of her Jewish father in his yarmulke and afro, the detail suggests the inherent ambivalence in the Jewish transformation into whiteness.

Although both Birdie and Walker survive by shifting their identities, they question whether such assimilation is an adequate means of survival, worrying that the transformation one undergoes in passing can be too complete. As children, Birdie and her sister devise a secret language and utopian world called Elemeno: "The Elemenos . . . were a shifting people, constantly changing their form, color, pattern, in a quest for invisibility. . . . [T]heir changing routine was a serious matter—less a game of make-believe than a fight for the survival of their species. . . . [T]heir power lay precisely in their ability to disappear into any surrounding" (Senna 7). The description of the Elemenos sounds much like stereotypical notions of Jewish chameleonism: the uncanny ability to conform in appearance and behavior to the dominant culture. As Daniel Itzkovitz writes, "The Jew was most Jewish . . . when not Jewish at all" ("Passing Like Me," 43). Birdie, however, remains skeptical about whether invisibility is a desirable form of power: she asks, "What was the point of surviving if you had to disappear?" (Senna 8).

Despite their doubts about whether or not Jews have sold out and become white, neither Senna nor Walker fully equates Jewishness with whiteness. Although she may erase Leventhal from her name when she publishes her book, Walker's title, *Black, White, and Jewish,* asserts whiteness and Jewishness as separate categories. Yet, read another way, the title suggests the slippage between whiteness and Jewishness; if she saw her father's Jewish identity as distinct from whiteness, she would not need to include the second adjective at all. In *Caucasia,* Birdie repeatedly describes her assumed identity as "a white girl, a Jewish girl," as if they are separate parts of a single self. This view of Jewishness as almost white, but not quite—or "off-white," in the words of Birdie's mother—points to its many contradictions, making it an effective figure for the multiplicity and instability of identity.

Chosen Identities

Despite the continued debate about whether Jews are closer to minorities or to the mainstream, I argue that the cultural value of Jewishness in these contemporary texts lies precisely in its ambivalence. The theme of "passing for Jewish" calls into question existing notions of mixed-race identity that tend to rely on binary configurations. Drawing attention to the multivalence of whiteness, texts in which characters pass for Jewish, instead of passing for white, deemphasize racial duality. Jewishness becomes the chosen identity because of its status as a model minority—its capacity for assimilation, its closeness to whiteness—but it also functions as a figure for multiplicity due to its contradictions and because it is one of many racial and ethnic identities that offer themselves as viable alternatives. As Birdie indicates when she and her mother are inventing her new identity, she is a *tabula rasa* with seemingly endless possibilities. Her maternal grandmother has always reassured herself that Birdie's looks could make her "Italian. Or even French" (107), while a South Asian man seated next to her on a plane mistakes her for Pakistani, seeing "his home in [her] face" (379). Race appears to be in the eye of the beholder, reflecting the desires and identifications of the one who looks. But race can also reflect the desires and identifications of the one who is looked at. As David Hollinger argues, in "post-ethnic America," identities are chosen, rather than assigned, voluntary rather than involuntary. Since Jews can be viewed as a paradigmatic "community of choice" (Biale 31), Jewishness becomes an important trope in the work of contemporary multiracial writers whose work presents such willful performances of identity.

For Birdie, Jewishness is just one of many identities she can assume and thus it stands in for choice itself. Walker, on the other hand, comes to choose other identities in her attempt to repudiate her Jewishness. Still, it is her performance of a Jewish identity, her ability to alternate between blackness and Jewishness, that makes her aware that other options are available to her as well, ones that are not necessarily defined by "blood" in the way that these inherited identities are. Since she is, by her own account, at least patrilineally Jewish, Walker does not explicitly consider the playing up of her Jewish identity in terms of passing. Instead, her most obvious racial crossing occurs through her identification with her Puerto Rican neighbors. When Walker is living with her father and stepmother in Riverdale, she rebels against their bourgeois life, finding herself more comfortable among the working-class Hispanic population in the Bronx:

> My father and stepmother live just in Riverdale, but I live in Riverdale and the Bronx. Riverdale to me means Nanny and the Liebermans and shopping down on Johnson Avenue for challah for Friday-night dinner, to go with the chicken soup my stepmother makes. It means a little store that sells OshKosh

> overalls to my stepmother for my two-year-old brother, Ben, her firstborn son. It means walking around with my stepmother, this Sephardic-looking Jew who calls me her daughter around people who never question.
>
> The Bronx means saying hello respectfully to Mrs. Colón when I visit Loída or César. It means Dominican boys from JFK High School, Zulu Nation and Afrika Bambaataa, and fast girls getting pregnant young. The Bronx means being ready to fight. It means walking around with my friends Sam and Jesús and Theresa and Melissa and being seen as I feel I truly am: a Puertoriquena, a mulatta, breathed out with all that Spanish flavor. A girl of color with attitude. (197–98)

Among her Jewish friends in her suburban high school, Walker also takes on the identity of "a girl of color with attitude." When her best friend asks her "what am I, anyhow" (205), she replies that she is Spanish, intuiting that this is a more acceptable way to explain her difference. Like Birdie's Jewishness, which serves as a safer version of blackness, "Spanish" is the closest Walker can come to "Hispanic" while still retaining her insider status. By labeling herself "Spanish" and asserting that her Hispanic identity is who she feels she "truly" is (and how she is *seen*), Walker further questions notions of racial authenticity. Walker's cross-identification can be understood in terms of Gloria Anzaldúa's description of the "*mestiza* consciousness": "The new *mestiza* copes by developing a tolerance for contradictions, a tolerance for ambiguity. . . . She has a plural personality, she operates in a pluralistic mode—nothing is thrust out, the good the bad and the ugly, nothing rejected, nothing abandoned. Not only does she sustain contradictions, she turns the ambivalence into something else" (79). Instead of choosing between, or even straddling, two polar positions, Anzaldúa's "new *mestiza*" turns ambivalence into a "third element" (79), a more accurate representation of multiplicity. The question becomes why Jewishness, in all its own contradictions, does not serve the same purpose for Walker. Why does she repudiate her Jewish identity in favor of the *mestiza* consciousness?

Although Walker depicts herself as divided between two worlds, Riverdale and the Bronx, these spaces actually signify multiple positions. In racial or ethnic terms, a fourth adjective has been added to her memoir's title: black, white, Jewish, and Latina. However, her identity is also multiple because her identifications are not based on race alone. Her specific identification with Hispanic identity is as much rooted in a class consciousness as an ethnic one, which is why she ultimately defines her multiplicity through the representation of the "mestiza" rather than that of the Jew. Walker renounces her Jewishness in favor of being a "Puertoriquena" because, in the world she inhabits, the most visible Hispanic population is working-class and the most visible part of the Jewish population middle-class. When she is at the home of a Jewish friend, Allison Hoffman, for example, Walker describes feeling drawn to Maria, the Hoffmans' Latina maid in her black and white uniform: "I feel closer to Maria than I do to Allison, like I should call her Mrs. Somebody and I should go with her to the kitchen or wherever she's walking to, and not stay back here in the fancy front rooms" (208). Walker's descriptions of Riverdale and other Jewish milieu revolve around what is consumed there (challah, chicken soup, OshKosh overalls), and she laments that she is forced to choose her father's "totally bourgeois lifestyle" (206) with him. She feels more at home when she is visiting her friend Theresa: Theresa's house, "two boxy stories at the top of an uneven set of concrete stairs, hidden behind overgrown bushes and wild Bronx trees, reflects how I feel inside much more than the calm, collected, solidly middle-class world of my father and stepmother. . . . I am at home among the mess, the drama, the darkness of Theresa's house" (203).

In stating her preference for darkness, Walker expresses her desire for marked racial identity above unmarked difference. The "mess" and "drama" of the Puerto Rican Bronx fits more with her mixed-race background and her awareness of her performances of identity. Yet by substituting race for class instead of considering the ways that race and class are intertwined, Walker makes a historically dangerous association, conflating the "middle-class world" of her father's new family with Jewishness. Writing in the Jewish feminist periodical *Lilith,* Charlotte Honigman-Smith addresses this aspect of Walker's memoir: "Walker believes that their conformity and wealth was, and is, typically Jewish, and when writing about her life with the Leventhals she uses ugly, unabashed stereotypes about Jewish life and, in particular, Jewish women. . . . Walker's portrayal of Jews . . . is unexamined, irresponsible, and almost comically stereotypical" (16). In affirming her own multiplicity, Walker, ironically, ends up overlooking the multiplicity of Jewishness itself.

Just as Walker identifies more strongly with her Puerto Rican neighbors than her own flesh and blood, Birdie at times identifies more strongly with her invented self. Often more comfortable in their least authentic identities, both protagonists challenge the very notion of authentic identity. Even if Jewishness is the identification she is repudiating, Walker's previous performances of Jewish identity lead to her awareness that she can choose her racial and ethnic affiliations, culminating in her decision to change her last name from Leventhal to Walker. Similarly, for Birdie, her time spent as a Jewish girl leads her to recognize that, despite her deceptive white appearance, she can *choose* blackness. While this return to blackness often occurs at the end of passing texts and is sometimes understood as a reassertion of essential identity (and thus a validation of the law of hypodescent), Birdie's desire to return to blackness should not be mistaken for proof of her true identity, but rather as a testament to post-ethnic identity. Birdie flees her white, Jewish existence in order to go in search of her black self, but she ends up finding a more complex identity, and it is her assumption of Jewishness that leads her there.

Black, White, Jewish, and Queer

In *Black, White, and Jewish,* Walker tends to conflate Jewishness with the middle class rather than considering their intersections, but her memoir more successfully examines how race is constructed alongside sexuality. Although she does not make her sexual identity a primary focus of her memoir, the present-day scenes depict Walker looking back on her childhood as she lies in bed with her female lover. Yet, just as the Jewish press has addressed Walker's "anti-Semitism," linking it in particular to its negative portrayals of Jewish women, the gay press has criticized Walker for downplaying her sexual identity. An interview with Walker in *The Advocate* mentions "the absent fourth adjective in the book's title: bisexual" (Bunn 65). In response, Walker justifies her decision not to confront her sexual identity outright by, for example, incorporating a specific coming-out experience: "I was always bisexual and had a fairly fluid sexuality," she explains (qtd. in Bunn 65). *The Advocate* interviewer allows himself to have the final word in this matter: "After chapters overrun with boyfriends, Walker's 'fluidity' makes its first real appearance . . . 18 pages from the end. . . . There's a shyness, a sudden discretion, that emerges in these final pages that doesn't feel native to Walker, who is bold and unsparing elsewhere. . . . [I]t's hard not to feel that, at least for now, this one part of her shifting self has been negotiated right out of the conversation" (Bunn 65).

From her title alone, it does appear that Walker chose to privilege race over sexuality, perhaps even Jewishness over bisexuality. However, this criticism of Walker's memoir does not take into account how racial and sexual fluidity are implicated in one another. Like Anzaldúa, a Chicana lesbian, Walker posits a connection between queerness and the "*mestiza* consciousness." Her title's very resistance to a black and white duality through its addition of the third term, "Jewish," echoes Walker's own resistance to a strict binary of heterosexuality and homosexuality. Even choosing to declare herself bisexual would in many ways limit her to a binary configuration of sexual identity that depends solely on the sex of the object-choice. However, there is even a deeper complexity here since racial fluidity is not simply analogous to sexual fluidity in Walker's world. Instead, her memoir goes one step farther, revealing the ways that race and sexuality are mutually constitutive. Although the majority of the sexual encounters and liaisons Walker relates are with men, both white and black, her present relationship and her early sexual encounters are with other women of color. Significantly, she is initiated into the world of "heterosexual" romance by Debbie Perez, who teaches her to French kiss "right below a velvet painting of Jesus weeping under his crown of thorns" (Walker 40) and "how to slow dance by the light of dark red and green glass candles with the Virgin of Guadalupe painted on their slick sides" (Walker 39). Her lessons in ostensibly heterosexual desire are directly associated with the religious iconography of Hispanic culture, which may further explain her "*mestiza* consciousness."

Another scene of early sexual initiation with a black childhood friend, Malaika, reveals the ways that race and sexual desire are interarticulated:

> We are like sisters but I want to sleep naked next to Malaika, I like the warmth of our bodies flush against each other under the cool cotton of the blue sheets my stepmother puts on the bed for us in the guest room. In the dark there we twist this way and that, sometimes sweating from all of our rubbing. I like the color of Malaika's body, I like how brown she is, like Mama. When I look at her I feel the deep brown of her skin pour into me through my eyes and fill me up in a place that feels cold and empty, a place that I forget I have until I look at her naked body.
>
> On nights when I can convince her, Malaika plays Daddy and I play Mommy. I want to be the one who is touched more, the one who is done to, the one who is told what to do. Some nights we play with one of my father's old leather belts. I like the sound of it slapping my skin, the warm heat I feel when Malaika hits me, when Malaika plays Daddy. (Walker 96–97)

This attraction is specifically racialized since it is the darkness of Malaika, "sweet like chocolate" (95), that draws Walker. Walker's attraction to Malaika reflects not desire alone, but also identification: through Malaika, whose "deep brown . . . skin pour[s] into" her, Walker can identify with dark women such as her mother. Her desire to identify with blackness and femininity reminds the reader of her decision to disidentify with positions of power; she prefers to be on the "one who is done to, the one who is told what to do." The fluidity of gender and between gender and race becomes evident when Walker first sees Malaika as "brown . . . like Mama," but then reveals that she likes when Malaika "plays Daddy."

Walker's use of a nonnormative scene of sexual initiation reiterates the need to recognize nonnormative racial identities, both identities of color in general and mixed-race identities more specifically. While the gay press criticized Walker for failing adequately to address her sexual identity, other reviewers have criticized her for spending more time on her sexual exploits than issues of race; to them, her title is not missing a term, but fails to live up to its promised focus. Such critiques overlook the ways that race and sex are intimately intertwined as forms of power, as the scene with Malaika clearly illustrates. Any narrative of mixed-race identity is, of course, fundamentally, about race *and* sex, especially when interracial sex has been historically, and legally, taboo.

Like Walker's, Birdie's first sexual experiences involve same-sex encounters. When she and her mother are living on a commune, Birdie has a relationship with another girl, Alexis. Throughout the novel, she expresses a resistance to heterosexuality that is explicitly connected to race. As she becomes closer with her white neighbor, Nicholas, Birdie decides that she "would never be able to go all the way with a white boy. . . . Allowing a white boy inside of me would make my transformation complete" (274). When Birdie expresses the need for her identity to remain transitional, her fears are directly linked to her resistance to the fate of the tragic mulatta. She recognizes that the tragic mulatta is a racial *and* sexual stereotype when she observes another mixed girl at her school, Samantha, who develops a reputation for promiscuity, reaffirming the myth of the eroticized black woman. Because she does not want to be a "doomed, tragic shade of black" like Samantha, but "black like somebody else" (321), Birdie decides to leave New Hampshire and forgo her white, Jewish existence—a decision that directly coincides with the impending threat of her heterosexual initiation. Birdie's decision to run away from "Caucasia" is motivated by her desire for blackness, as well as her recognition that there is more than one way to be black.

Although *Caucasia,* as I stated at the beginning of this essay, privileges blackness over whiteness, the novel does not end with the act of "loving blackness" alone (hooks 9–20). Instead, *Caucasia* concludes with a validation of multiplicity. At the end of the novel, Birdie rediscovers her black self when she is reunited with Cole. The two sisters decide to make a new home together in the culturally diverse, liberal landscape of Berkeley, California, where multiracial children are "a dime a dozen" (Senna 412). In the last paragraph of the novel, Birdie indulges in her own fantasy of a racial utopia. Passing a school bus, she looks up at the faces of the students:

> They were black and Mexican and Asian and white, on the verge of puberty, but not quite in it. They were utterly ordinary, throwing obscenities and spitballs at one another the ways kids do. One face toward the back of the bus caught my eye, and I halted in my tracks, catching my breath. It was a cinnamon-skinned girl with her hair in braids. She was black like me, a mixed girl, and she was watching me from behind the dirty glass. For a second I thought I was somewhere familiar and she was a girl I already knew. I began to lift my hand, but stopped, remembering where I was and what I had already found. Then the bus lurched forward, and the face was gone with it, just a blur of yellow and black in motion. (413)

This scene directly echoes an earlier episode in which Birdie looked up at a school bus to catch her first glimpse of Samantha, the only other girl of color in her small New Hampshire town. In the earlier scene, Birdie described Samantha as "black like me—half, that is" (223). This time, Birdie may initially describe the girl she sees through the glass as "black like me," but in the next breath, she describes her as "mixed." In replacing "half" with "mixed," Birdie prioritizes the plurality of her identity over its duality. As the scene progresses, the different races represented by the "utterly ordinary" students on the bus—black, Mexican, Asian, and white—no longer remain distinct. They blend together as the bus moves forward, and the dark face that Birdie saw becomes a "blur of yellow and black in motion." In this description, whiteness disappears altogether: this is not Caucasia, but California.

Although Senna leaves Jewish faces off the bus and Walker conflates Jews with whites, in both texts, it is Jewishness that is largely responsible for making whiteness as a monolithic category disappear. Transforming the literary trope of passing for white into passing for Jewish, *Caucasia* and *Black, White, and Jewish* employ Jewishness as a figure for multiplicity, exposing the plurality of whiteness itself. Due to its ambivalent status, Jewishness serves as a category of mediation and transition, poised—or even passing—between whiteness and blackness. Both Walker and Birdie often comment that they are most comfortable not when assuming one of their various personae, but when they are in transition *between* identities. Birdie, for instance, feels "most safe" when she is "on a moving vehicle, rolling toward some destination but not quite there" (293), while Walker prefers airports to either of her parents' homes. When Walker refers to herself as "a Movement Child," she also employs the metaphor of motion. She refers not only to the civil rights union of her parents and her trips back and forth between coasts, but also to her "shifting" identities. In these contemporary works, Jewishness shifts, too; it takes on different meanings both within and between the texts. Through their depictions of contradictory and constantly shifting selves, Senna and Walker complicate our understanding of mixed race identity, affirming that race—including whiteness itself—is multiple and "in motion."

Notes

An earlier version of this essay was published as "Passing for White, Passing for Jewish: Mixed Race Identity in Danzy Senna and Rebecca Walker," *MELUS* 30:1 (Spring 2005): 19–48. I thank Julie Cary Nerad and the anonymous readers for assisting me in revising this essay.

1. On this point, see Itzkovitz "Introduction," and Harrison-Kahan 96–142. On Hurst's Jewish identity, see Antler 136–75.

2. For analyses of Jewishness in Roth's novel, see Freedman, chapter 4, and Glaser.

3. Like Walker, other contemporary writers interrogate "passing and the fictions of identity"—to use the title of Elaine K. Ginsberg's collection—through the form of the autobiography. In his combination of memoir and social commentary, *White Lies: Race and the Myths of Whiteness* (1999), Maurice Berger explores the ambivalence of his Jewish upbringing. While Berger's dark-skinned Sephardic mother cakes on layers of white powder to masquerade as white and refuses to fraternize with her black neighbors, his blond-haired, blue-eyed, liberal father strongly identifies with the plight of African Americans and would "have liked to pass for black himself" (109). Two memoirs published in 1996, James McBride's *The Color of Water: A Black Man's Tribute to His White Mother* and Jane Lazarre's *Beyond the Whiteness of Whiteness: Memoir of a White Mother of Black Sons,* feature Jewish women who cross the color barrier by marrying black men and

raising black children. At times, these women could be described as passing for black. In McBride's memoir, for example, the author's mother changes her name and leaves her Orthodox Jewish family behind to create a new identity for herself in Harlem, where she hides her Jewishness from her children for many years, explaining that she is "light-skinned." Other examples of the multiracial memoir that address race as a social and historical construction include Shirlee Taylor Haizlip's *The Sweeter the Juice: A Family Memoir in Black and White* (1994), Gregory Howard Williams's *Life on the Color Line: The True Story of a White Boy Who Discovered He Was Black* (1995), Bliss Broyard's *One Drop: My Father's Hidden Life—A Story of Race and Family Secrets* (2007), and Senna's own *Where Did You Sleep Last Night? A Personal History* (2009).

4. See Brodkin and Jacobson. For an especially nuanced account of this transformation, see Goldstein, who argues that Jews did not become white, but rather are continually in the process of negotiating their whiteness.

5. Bhabha describes the relationship of the colonized to the colonizer as "almost the same but not white" (89).

6. Recent scholarship questions the actual degree of this mythic harmony between blacks and Jews during the civil rights movement. See, for example, Salzman and West. For an excellent historical account of Jewish-black relations in twentieth-century America, see Greenberg.

7. One previous use of the theme of passing for Jewish occurred in Laura Z. Hobson's 1946 novel, *Gentleman's Agreement,* in which a gentile journalist passes as Jewish in order to write a series on anti-Semitism.

8. Hurst's novel was adapted to film twice: John Stahl's version premiered in 1934, one year after the novel's publication, and was remade in 1959 by Douglas Sirk with significant changes to the plot, including the names of characters as well as the profession of the white female protagonist.

9. On the intersections of race and gender in narratives of passing, see Valerie Smith.

10. See Itzkovitz, "Passing Like Me."

11. See Beck and Prell.

12. As Michael Lerner argues, Jews only became white by erasing their visibility as Jews. Yet, Lerner also questions how successful this transformation can be if it means rendering one's ethnic or religious identity invisible. In his dialogue with Cornel West, Lerner insists that Jews should not identify as white because "white-skin privilege [in the U.S.] is the privilege to renounce one's Judaism. By and large the way to get into this system is to take off your *kippah,* cut off your beard, hide your fringes; in other words, to reject your entire cultural and religious humanity. . . . To go out into the world was not obviously to go out into the world as a Jew. The inner dialogue amongst Jews is about whether or not this ability to pass is indeed true. Are we rather always going to be seen as Jews, and hence endangered?" (67–68). Like the fictional black intellectual, Deck Lee, Lerner appears to be arguing that there may be "no such thing as passing,"

although Lerner bases his argument on the fact that the stigma of essentialism will continue to pursue Jews who attempt to eradicate the visual signs of their identity.

13. Carole-Anne Tyler, for example, argues that passing results in the validation of the identity that one disavows. Barbara Christian notes that the passer often returns to her race. Despite arguments that the return home at the end of passing novels upholds racial essentialism, it is important to note, for example, the famous ambiguous ending of Larsen's *Passing* in which Clare Kendry mysteriously dies, just as she decides to return to Harlem and her black roots. In Fauset's *Plum Bun,* Angela Murray may appear to return to her roots when she confesses her black blood; however, in citing this incident as the narrative's conclusion, critics overlook the very end of the novel in which Angela leaves the United States for France, declaring that while abroad she will not "placard" herself as either black or white.

14. See Willis.

15. See Morrison.

16. See Phillips.

Works Cited

Antler, Joyce. *The Journey Home: Jewish Women and the American Century.* New York: Free Press, 1997. Print.

Anzaldúa, Gloria. *Borderlands/La Frontera: The New Mestiza.* San Francisco: Spinsters/Aunt Lute, 1987. Print.

Beck, Evelyn Torton. "From 'Kike' to 'JAP': How Misogyny, Anti-Semitism, and Racism Construct the 'Jewish American Princess.'" *Race, Class, and Gender.* Ed. Margaret Anderson and Patricia Hill Collins. New York: Wadsworth, 1998. 430–36. Print.

Berger, Maurice. *White Lies: Race and the Myths of Whiteness.* New York: Farrar, Straus, Giroux, 1999. Print.

Bhabha, Homi K. *The Location of Culture.* New York: Routledge, 1994. Print.

Biale, David. "The Melting Pot and Beyond: Jews and the Politics of American Identity." *Insider/Outsider: American Jews and Multiculturalism.* Ed. David Biale, Michael Galchinsky, and Susan Heschel. Berkeley: U of California P, 1998. 17–33. Print.

Brodkin, Karen. *How Jews Became White Folks.* New Brunswick: Rutgers UP, 1998. Print.

Bunn, Austin. "Walker, in Her Own Shoes." *The Advocate.* 27 Feb. 2001: 65. Print.

Butler, Judith. "Imitation and Gender Insubordination." *Inside/Out: Lesbian Theories, Gay Theories.* Ed. Diana Fuss. New York: Routledge, 1991. 13–31. Print.

Christian, Barbara. *Black Women Novelists.* Westport, CT: Greenwood, 1980. Print.

Du Bois, W. E. B. *The Souls of Black Folk.* 1903. In *Three Negro Classics.* New York: Avon, 1965. 207–390. Print.

Fauset, Jessie R. *Plum Bun: A Novel Without a Moral.* 1928. 2nd ed. Boston: Beacon Press, 1990. Print.

Freedman, Jonathan. *Klezmer America: Jewishness, Ethnicity, Modernity.* New York: Columbia UP, 2008. Print.

Ginsberg, Elaine K., ed. *Passing and the Fictions of Identity.* Durham: Duke UP, 1996. Print.

Glaser, Jennifer. "The Jew in the Canon: Reading Race and Literary History in Philip Roth's *The Human Stain.*" *PMLA* 123.5 (October 2008): 1465–78. Print.

Glazer, Nathan. "Jews and Blacks: What Happened to the Grand Alliance?" *Jews in Black Perspectives: A Dialogue.* Ed. Joseph R. Washington Jr. New Jersey: Fairleigh Dickinson UP, 1984. 105–12. Print.

Goldstein, Eric. *The Price of Whiteness: Jews, Race, and American Identity.* Princeton: Princeton UP, 2006. Print.

Greenberg, Lynn Cheryl. *Troubling the Waters: Black-Jewish Relations in the American Century.* Princeton: Princeton UP, 2006. Print.

Harrison-Kahan, Lori. *The White Negress: Literature, Minstrelsy, and the Black-Jewish Imaginary.* New Brunswick: Rutgers UP, 2011. Print.

Hobson, Laura Z. *Gentleman's Agreement.* New York: Simon and Schuster, 1946. Print.

Hollinger, David A. *Postethnic America: Beyond Multiculturalism.* New York: Basic Books, 2000. Print.

Honigman-Smith, Charlotte. "Portrayed, or Betrayed?" *Lilith* 26.2 (Summer 2001): 16–17. Print.

hooks, bell. *Black Looks: Race and Representation.* Boston: South End, 1992. Print.

Hurst, Fannie. *Imitation of Life.* Durham: Duke UP, 2004. Print.

Itzkovitz, Daniel. "Introduction." *Imitation of Life.* By Fannie Hurst. Durham: Duke UP, 2004. Print.

———. "Passing Like Me: Jewish Chameleonism and the Politics of Race." *Passing: Identity, and Interpretation in Sexuality, Race, and Religion.* Ed. Maria Carla Sánchez and Linda Schlossberg. New York: New York UP, 2001. 38–63. Print.

Jacobson, Matthew Frye. *Whiteness of a Different Color.* Cambridge: Harvard UP, 1998. Print.

Larsen, Nella. *Quicksand and Passing.* New Brunswick: Rutgers UP, 1986. Print.

Lazarre, Jane. *Beyond the Whiteness of Whiteness: Memoir of a White Mother of Black Sons.* Durham: Duke UP, 1997. Print.

Lerner, Michael, and Cornel West. *Jews and Blacks: A Dialogue on Race, Religion, and Culture in America.* New York: Penguin, 1995. Print.

McBride, James. *The Color of Water: A Black Man's Tribute to His White Mother.* New York: Riverhead, 1996. Print.

Melnick, Jeffrey. "Rattling the Cage of Black-Jewish Relations." *"Jewishness" and the World of "Difference" in the United States.* Ed. Marc Lee Raphael. Williamsburg: College of William and Mary, 2001. 50–64. Print.

Morrison, Toni. "On the Backs of Blacks." *Time*. 2 Dec. 1993: 57. Print.

Phillips, William M. Jr. *An Unillustrious Alliance: The African American and Jewish American Communities.* New York: Greenwood, 1991. Print.

Prell, Riv-Ellen. *Fighting to Become Americans: Assimilation and the Trouble Between Jewish Women and Jewish Men.* Boston: Beacon Press, 1999. Print.

Rogin, Michael. *Blackface, White Noise: Jewish Immigrants in the Hollywood Melting Pot.* Berkeley: U of California P, 1996. Print.

Salzman, Jack, and Cornel West, eds. *Struggles in the Promised Land: Toward a History of Black-Jewish Relations in the United States.* New York: Oxford UP, 1997. Print.

Senna, Danzy. *Caucasia.* New York: Riverhead Books, 1998. Print.

Smith, Sidonie. "Performativity, Autobiographical Practice, Resistance." *Women, Autobiography, Theory: A Reader.* Ed. Sidonie Smith and Julia Watson. Madison: U of Wisconsin P, 1998. 108–15. Print.

Smith, Valerie. "Reading the Intersection of Race and Gender in Narratives of Passing." *Diacritics* 24.2–3 (1994): 43–57. Print.

Tyler, Carole-Anne. "Passing: Narcissism, Identity, and Difference." *differences: A Journal of Feminist Cultural Studies* 6.2+3 (1994): 212–48. Print.

Walker, Rebecca. *Black, White, and Jewish: Autobiography of a Shifting Self.* New York: Riverhead, 2001. Print.

West, Cornel. "Foreword." *Fires in the Mirror.* By Anna Deavere Smith. New York: Anchor Books, 1993. xvii–xxii. Print.

Willis, Ellen. "The Myth of the Powerful Jew." *Strangers and Neighbors: Relations Between Blacks and Jews in the United States.* Ed. Maurianne Adams and John Bracey. Amherst: U of Massachusetts P, 1999. 720–28. Print.

10

Smiling Faces

Chameleon Street, Racial Passing/Performativity, and Film Blackness

Michael B. Gillespie

In 1985, an article in the *Detroit Free Press* ("Super Duper Imposter Says He Aided in Surgeries") recapped the exploits of William Douglas Street Jr., a black man and self-professed "Great Imposter" whose run of various criminal acts of impersonation began in the late 1960s. The article featured excerpts from a jailhouse interview with Street, who at the time was serving a prison term for unpaid loans he received while posing as a student at the University of Michigan.[1] Upon reading that article, Wendell B. Harris Jr. began researching for a film project based on Street's exploits that what would eventually become *Chameleon Street* (1989). Emblematic of the best sense of independent cinema and alternative financing, Harris raised a 1.5 million dollar budget with the help of his family and black businessmen in the Flint, Michigan, area. He spent three years visiting and corresponding with Street, writing the script, shooting the film, and completing post-production.[2] The film would go on to win the Grand Jury Prize at the Sundance Film Festival (1990). Harris, a Julliard-trained actor, stated how he identified with Street's masquerades in terms of acting:

> What I immediately saw when I read the first article on Doug was his ability to act, and act convincingly. That's the test of an actor: Does the audience believe? Part of the addiction

> that Doug has to the act of impersonation is the moment when he looks into somebody's eyes and he can see that he is pressing the right buttons to make them believe his performance. That's maybe the purest part of the high he gets from impersonating, because he certainly doesn't look for money. In fourteen years he made less than four thousand from the impersonations. (Moon 150–51)

Harris's noting of Street's ability to "act convincingly" suggests something of the way in which Street's impersonations operated to impress a belief and solicit a truth. But it is the measure of what constituted a "profit" for Street that remains a rich puzzle. After all, if the motivation for Street's impersonations was a kind of material profiteering that could be accounted for in terms of a net gain, then that might offer a satisfactory explanation. Yet, the return on Street's investment is not so immediately measurable. As the primary inspiration for *Chameleon Street,* the passing life of William Douglas Street Jr., the way he freely enacted multiple identity roles and negotiated with several cultural poses, signals something more than the curious adventures of a minor celebrity.

Street first received some measure of national attention in February 1971 due to a UPI story that was picked up by newspapers across the country. The story recounted Street's attempt to try out for a spot on the roster of the Detroit Tigers baseball team by passing himself off as Jerald Lee Levias, also known as Jerry Levias, an NFL wide receiver for the Houston Oilers. Street had tried out for the Detroit Tigers two summers earlier and had even attempted to make the roster of the Boston Red Sox while impersonating a sports reporter for *Time* magazine.[3] Street's 1971 ploy as Levias was initially successful. He portrayed himself as an athlete who had grown tired of the NFL and now wanted to play the sport he had always loved. Street as Levias was considered a star tryout by the Detroit Tigers organization to such an extent that they flew him down to training camp in Florida. Upon arriving, Street borrowed money from a Tigers player by claiming that his finances were still tied up with the Houston Oilers and that he would pay back the loan once he was on the team payroll. In spite of his less than stellar play in the field, Street's ruse was only discovered after the real Levias contacted the Tigers inquiring why the organization was circulating rumors about his NFL retirement. Street was not prosecuted. A few weeks after the Tigers ruse was exposed, Street was, however, prosecuted for passing bad checks at an Orlando hotel where the Minnesota Twins were staying. He claimed he was a member of the team.

Shortly after the Orlando misdemeanor, Street returned to Michigan and committed a crime far less amusing. On March 9, 1971, Street delivered a note to Gloria Horton, the wife of Willie Horton, a highly respected and admired Detroit Tigers All-Star. Claiming to have tapes, photographs, and documents in his possession that detailed her husband's criminal dealings, Street's note stated that he would turn over the incriminating material to the authorities unless Ms. Horton paid him $20,000. The note continued on to state that if she attempted to contact law enforcement, she, her husband, and their children would be killed. She did contact the police and Street was charged with extortion and underwent a court-ordered mental evaluation. He was eventually convicted and given a one to twenty year prison sentence. Over the course of the 1970s and 1980s Street served various prison stints as a result of his continued compulsion to pose. His masquerades included impersonating a physician, lawyer, medical student, and college football player.[4] As an adaptation of Street's history of passing, *Chameleon Street* indelicately provokes the tradition of racial passing in literature and film with a keen disregard for the political, cultural, and social equivocations about racial identity that organize the passing conceit.

Racial passing has often been considered in terms of an ontological violation, an instance whereby someone poses as something he or she is "not" with regard to racial identity. Of course, what is understood as fundamental aspects of racial personhood inevitably signifies something less than an indisputable or innate category and more a discourse meted by cultural, social, and political prescription. Street as character exemplifies what Elaine Ginsberg argues as the dialectical nature of passing: "[P]assing is about identities: their creation or imposition, their adoption or rejection, their accompanying rewards or penalties. Passing is also about the boundaries established between identity categories and about the individual and cultural anxieties induced by boundary crossing. Finally, passing is about specularity: the visible and the invisible, the seen and the unseen" (2). *Chameleon Street*'s protagonist thrives due to a proficient quarreling with the power, privilege, and regulation of boundary crossing. In this way, the film depicts the strategic opportunities generated by the discounting of race's categorical immanence.

The film details the wielding of race as constitutive cultural fiction, re-purposing the racial passing tradition with the cruel play of a rebel cipher. As a result, the film explores the limits of racial passing narratives with a disinterest in the more melodramatic tendencies of the mode that tacitly infer regulation and prohibition. As morality tales, these passing fictions devote a great deal of attention to how the racial passer suffers in his/her access to privileges previously denied. Thus, the classic passing narrative is replete with a clustered offering of the familiar and tragic melodies of "passing as betrayal, blackness as self-denial, whiteness as comfort" (Smith, Valerie 45).[5] As a result, questions of power and knowledge are defused because the racial passer acts as the foregrounded object of pity and scorn with racial hegemonies further naturalized and obscured. In this way, Street as film protagonist irreverently re-signifies the core impulses of the racial passing narrative.

Chameleon Street's resemblance to the passing film is made evident by the film's element of race and thematic anxieties around masquerade and authenticity, but the driving tenor of the film obviously considers the substance of blackness and the passing tradition in ways not dependent on self-loathing or racial dispossession. Furthermore, Street as film protagonist does not exhibit any interest in the disavowal of blackness for the lure of whiteness. As Cherise Smith comments, "To pass successfully, one must suppress one's own difference from, and perform the behaviors of, members of the dominant culture in order to appear like them" (13). The tenor of Street's success occurs with a seditious impression of this suppression/emulation impulse. His passings transpire as epistemological challenges that distinctly amplify the way racial passing potentially displaces "the relationship between inside and outside, truth and appearance, identity and identity politics" (Robinson 250). This is what makes watching the film like a spectatorial litmus test, for whatever judgment we make of Street's passings reveals the extent to which we concede authority to the conditional categories implicated in his masquerades.

How does one discuss a racial passing film whose protagonist has no allegiance to the more diagnostic conjecture of racial passing? How does one discuss a film whose protagonist demonstrates a deep disregard for the one-drop speculations of visuality and racial masquerade? The film's accreting lack of correspondence to the deracinated longings of the racial passing tradition features a black subject enacting various impersonations of being in a manner that significantly unhinges passing from its classical moorings. Considered in this way, *Chameleon Street*'s narrativization of racial passing moves beyond the rhetoric of racial phenotype and permanence by demonstrating the discursivity of race itself. The film represents a *raced* passer compelled by a desire to be convincing, successful, and exceptional. *Raced* functions as a term for Street's modulating acts of identity as a measured motion or rhythm that is affectively attuned to place, race, and being.

Street's capacity to pass is effected as a raced subject whose blackness modifies the idea of race with each of his passing episodes. For the purposes of a racial passing narrative, Street's blackness construes more than the ability to demonstrate expertise with a trade or occupation. This is because *Chameleon Street* insists on a shift from racial fidelity to identitarian disloyalty, racial passing to racial performativity. In other words, *Chameleon Street* as an enactment of film blackness reveals the speculative and creative possibilities of the idea of black film. With a contextual regard for black visual and expressive culture, *Chameleon Street* proposes more than a mimetic corroboration of the social category of race.[6]

Supplementing Judith Butler's proposal of gender identity as a performative act rather than inert category of being, Debby Thompson questions whether race is a trope. Thompson focuses on how Anna Deavere Smith's performance art complicates the idea of race as strictly a static category of social being. As Thompson suggests,

> When an assigned identity is not re-cited and re-performed perfectly, then that identity can shift. Resistant or subversive performative repetitions, always done, of course, under surveillance and the threat of potentially severe punishment, are nevertheless possible. The subject produced through performative reiteration of norms can also somewhat re-perform those norms with a difference, and even, potentially constitute performative identities not yet normalized or even scripted or embodied. (132)

Street deftly models disobedient craft as a refusal to comply. In *Chameleon Street,* racial passing becomes a performative act that consequently re-signifies and interrogates the visual and textual logic of race, "the constructed, instable, reiterated, and citational discursivity of race" (Harris 27). As an enactment of film blackness, the film indexes racial passing through multiple strategies of black performativity. This essay will focus on four interdependent features of disobedience in the film, four strains of dispute resulting from the film's enactment of racial performativity: the diagnostic dispute, the menace of mimicry, the black modernist, and improvisational chaos.

Think Twice

> The film you are about to see and hear is based on the life experiences of William Douglas Street, Jr. and Erik Dupin. Many of the characters appear as themselves, while others assume fictional personae.[7]

At its start, the film forecasts a thesis preoccupied with race and performativity. Following the opening disclaimer of the scripted veracity to come, the first image of the film features an over-the-shoulder shot of a black man in a medical robe sitting in front of a desk. Seated behind the desk and facing the robed figure is an official-looking white man in a suit. The official, a prison counselor, addresses the black man, and yet to be revealed protagonist, with a question: "Have you thought about what you're going to do on the outside?" The question seeks to substantiate whether this prisoner has been rehabilitated enough to be released. Indifferent to the formalities of the debriefing, the black man responds:

> STREET: Umm.
>
> COUNSELOR: Let me put it this way. Once you get out, will there be any more of these? [He picks up a newspaper article from a full folder and shakes it at Street].
>
> STREET: No, no. I'm through, no more.
>
> COUNSELOR: No more impersonations.
>
> STREET: No, enough is enough.
>
> COUNSELOR: I don't believe you.
>
> STREET: Would I lie?
>
> COUNSELOR: I don't think you're necessarily lying. I don't think you're in control of what you do or say. I think you behave in complementarity.
>
> STREET: Okay.

COUNSELOR: Do you know what that means?

STREET: No.

COUNSELOR: That means you intuit what another person needs and then you become that need. Like right now you know that my job is to diagnose neurosis.

STREET: Neurosis are red. Neurosis are blue.

Street's pun serves as an aural cut to the beginning of the title sequence. The sequence features a series of jump cuts comprised of four close-ups of his face. Set in an indistinct space that suggests an underneath or a hole, each shot shows the face bisected by the illumination and shadow of high contrast lighting that intimates a caul or the Du Boisian Veil. His countenance ranges from agitated, bored, smug, to solemn. Throughout, the soundtrack features a voice at various speeds of indecipherability. The hailing of "Sit Down," "Shut Up," "Don't cross me," and "Look at him" are the only discernible phrases amid the aural buzz. The soundtrack then settles on a normal speed during the final portion of the title sequence with the following prose: *The chameleon is about to invest/I think, therefore I scam.* This final portion shifts to flashes of color that pulse from red to blue to yellow with the title *Chameleon Street* flashing in a contrasting color within the frame blocks as the prose continues: *I think the air is sweet/I know not what I am/I am chameleon street.* At the close, there is the sound of a heartbeat before the film starts with a voiceover: "Autumn 1978."

The opening sequence pivots on an abstracted address of behavioral psychology with the complementarity diagnosis. As a term for the way that social beings desire to be enhanced by another, complementarity suggests that individuals seek those who possess attributes that ultimately complete one's own self. The montage that follows the interview poses a clever response to the complementarity diagnosis. The prefacing of the primary colors by a black face generates a distinct hermeneutic triggering of the eye's physiological register of color. The diacritical encounter of the primary colors and a racial signifier acts as black visual rhetoric (the black, red, yellow, and blue).[8]

Significantly, this compositional shifting between color and colored converges around the reference to the Cartesian subject. "I think therefore I scam" puns Rene Descartes's "I think, therefore I am." Descartes's maxim illustrates a belief in the fundamental self-evidence of an individual's truth of existence, the capacity to think. But, for Charles Mills, the Cartesian ideal engenders a normativity synonymous with the white existential condition while the non-Cartesian sum signifies a philosophical dispute and initiation of an African American or Africana philosophy attendant to the black existential condition: "So it will be a *sum* that is metaphysical not in the Cartesian sense but in the sense of challenging a *social* ontology; not the consequent of a proof but the beginnings of an affirmation of one's self-worth, one's reality as a person, and one's militant insistence that others recognize it also" (Mills 9). Thus, the black face, the new standard of color, in conjunction with the scam pun, suggests a sense of raced self-evidence, a viciously signifying sum. Street's militant insistence operates as a protean joke that rebukes the perception/conception of his blackness.[9] Mercurial, unstable, and improvisational, Street as intuitionist encounters the Cartesian ideal as a raced passer devoted to self-evidenced truth as performative.

Street's sum and joke grows heavier with the last line of the prose: "I am chameleon street." The film's opening announces anonymity and expressivity in an autobiographical mode. The authoring of "I am Chameleon Street" shares an affinity with another subterranean utterance, "I am an invisible man." Like the opening line of Ralph Ellison's *Invisible Man* (1952), the film's declaration represents "the encounter with a self that is only the presentation of its own mask and that does not exist outside of the unfolding autobiographical act" (Griffiths 321–22). Yet, in the instance of *Chameleon Street,* the speculative tendency of the biopic becomes an examination of the mask with no illusions of an ontological self that lies beneath.

Chameleon Street's first half closely follows the real life exploits of Douglas Street's passing escapades. The postindustrial Michigan setting lends a disquieting motivation for Street's compulsions. In particular, the Flint locations lend a quality of dispossession to the film with an urban setting marked by the trickle-down promises of Reaganomics, blight, economic recession, white flight, and the grinding down of the underclass. Beginning with the Willie Horton blackmail scheme and the subsequent celebrity attempt to procure a tryout with the Detroit Tigers, Street ultimately fails to charm fully the press and public.[10] Falsifying his press credentials, he lands an exclusive interview with USC basketball star Paula McGee (played by herself). Neither Clifford Irving nor Jayson Blair, Street's journalism pass is short-lived. He then moves on to pass as a Harvard medical student who transfers his residency to Wayne State

Medical School. Using a medical textbook tucked in his pants, Street quickly becomes recognized in the hospital as the "Harvard man" who can do no wrong. Only after a random background check does the ruse end and Street is arrested.[11]

"I've got to get a new identity." Only once in the film does Street refer to his passings as a matter of identity. Tellingly, the line comes during the film's sporadically used transitional bridge of intercutting to the next scene with an unrelated scene: a shot of a train with the rattling sounds of acceleration on the tracks. The linking of Street's performative rigor to the rails and momentum suggests escape velocity. Street's train re-mediates Paul Gilroy's chronotopic sense of the train's function in African American literature as trope of black modernism and the themes of "movement, relocation, displacement, and restlessness" (133).[12] The film's sense of propulsion is organized by sardonic brilliance as Street's spatiotemporal flow represents the poignant and unruly mapping of blackness as a dynamic system and not strictly a noun in the sense suggested by Nathaniel Mackey: "To see being as a verb rather than noun is to be at odds with hypostasis, the reification of fixed identities that has been the bane of socially marginalized groups" (20). In other words, Street's passings are dynamic acts of narrative that defy antidiagnostic renderings of blackness.

The Spook Who Sat by the Door

> Yes, I know your little secrets now.
> And I insist upon being not one of your clowns, but one of you.
> And I shall stay with you, if I'm permitted to for a little while.
> That's up to you of course.
>
> —Nina Simone, *Live at Montreux* (1976)

A scene from later in the film illustrates another distinct strain of Street's performative disobedience. Street sits in the living room as his wife does their daughter's hair. The daughter's demand for new toys quickly escalates and Street picks up one of her Barbie dolls. Daydreaming of a lover, Street picks up an aerosol can and sprays the doll's face with black paint. Finishing the gesture, Street tosses the doll across the table: "There you go. Black Barbie." The gesture contemptuously evokes 'black versioning' but in terms of *Chameleon Street*'s passing conceit, the gesture also evokes Ralph Ellison's sense of blackness and the mask. As Ellison instructs, "America is a land of masking jokers. We wear the mask for purposes of aggression as well as for defense; when we are projecting the future and preserving the past. In short, the motives hidden behind the mask are as numerous as the ambiguities the mask conceals" ("Change the Joke" 55). Ellison's conception of the mask's ability to navigate the antiblack core values of America entails a distinct sense of time management. In the context of Street's performativity, the negotiation of the past ("preservation") and the future ("projection") resonates with the vigilant sense of the present that Street must always regulate in order to succeed.

Rather than the black on the outside/white on the inside rhetoric of black lack and oreo envy, the Barbie scene absurdly highlights Street's menace in the land of jokers and cowards.[13] This section focuses on the how Street's performative impulse fumes with a disdain for whiteness and antiblack standards of normativity. *Chameleon Street*'s measure of the mask at times encounters the way racial passing often acts as "a model for the cultural production of whiteness" (Mullen 72). Yet, Street as a raced performant assumes an attitude of menacing mimic.

"The *menace* of mimicry," as Homi Bhabha writes, "is its *double* vision which in disclosing the ambivalence of colonial discourse also disrupts its authority" (88). For Bhabha, the menace of mimicry is generated by the provocation of the colonial authority's culture as the normative standard. The colonial subject's repetition and mimicry of this cultural standard is done as "*a subject of a difference that is almost the same, but not quite.*" Mimicry does not ask the colonial subject to stop being a subject of the authority's rule. Mimicry asks the colonial subject to desire the discipline of subjection. The menace arises from the ambivalence necessary for the possibility of mimicry. The invitation to emulate deauthorizes the colonial authority's culture as either innate or natural. The capacity of this menace to subvert authority always exists for the colonial subject remains suspended between presence and absence, similar and dissimilar.

Chameleon Street's menace inflection evolves as Street's performativity disputes compulsory measures of class, privilege/power, and access to knowledge. Street's deauthorization intent fuels his acumen and desire for the privileges of the authority he assumes. As Ed Guerrero writes, "Street masquerades as a doctor, lawyer, journalist, and thus rebels by infiltrating exclusive zone of elite professional castes kept out of the practical reach, and aspirations, of most black men" ("The Black Man" 187). While class aspirations and "the criteria of distinction" obviously inform Street's performative impulse, this impulse also strongly exhibits a signifying contempt for whiteness.[14] In this way, his institutional gambits feature a shuttling between exceptionalism and disdain for whiteness as standard. Street's acts demonstrate a query: What is the point in being an ethical black subject in an unethical, antiblack world? The film conveys a great deal of ambivalence toward an identity politics that would ultimately reinscribe race as a stasis of being. Street remains irreconcilable. While James Weldon Johnson's "ex-colored man" eventually stopped considering his passing as a game but as the betrayal of a birthright, Street's Talented Tenth dissident pose appears removed from the stakes of a "mess of pottage." Street manically shifts the codes of embodiment and deflects prevarications of his blackness.

One scene that exemplifies the film's evasiveness begins with Street cantankerous and bored while sitting on the couch with his daughter in his living room. Reaching above the couch, he removes a mask hanging on the wall next to a map of Africa. Street dons the mask, pulls out a knife, and calls his daughter to come and play. Circling around the room, Street creeps behind her with knife in hand. Eventually, with his daughter in his lap, she asks him whether something is wrong. Street mutters, "I'm insane," and begins cutting his arm with the knife. As his daughter passively looks on he runs the blade over her body before settling on her throat asking, "Does this tickle?" Escalating the tickling with the blade, Street cuts her throat. She screams as Gabrielle, Street's wife, rushes into the room and says, "Doug what have you done?" The daughter yells, "Mommy, you ruined the game!" When Street's wife complains about how difficult it is to remove the bloodstains, he replies that the fake blood is supposed to wash out. It was just a game.

Bitter artifice informs the psychotic-driven-to-filicide premise from the start. Positioned next to the map, the mask metonymically stands in for the dark continent of Africa. Yet, the mask is not a tribal one, it is a comedy mask unaccompanied by its tragedy counterpart as theatricality abounds nonetheless. His donning of the mask and the play that follows evokes the tokenism of Diouana's mask in Ousmane Sembene's *Black Girl* (1966). In *Black Girl,* the mask functions as symbol of dispossession and objectification. It later serves as an emblem for the conditional madness of the postcolonial subject and also the haunting presence of the dead/improperly buried. The ritualized play of Street's mimed psychosis parodies the pathologization of a savage continent. Neither cannibal nor Trueblood, Street's taboo of choice is killer of sheep as the exquisite jokes keep coming.

While serving another prison stint, Street bristles within another psychiatric scene:

COUNSELOR: Has anyone ever told you your sense of sarcasm is extremely strong?

STREET: Oh yeah. Has anyone ever told you that white people who get caught in the rain smell exactly like wet dogs? This is fact. Believe or not.

COUNSELOR: I beg your pardon.

STREET: Have you ever been standing in a crowd of white people and all of a sudden it starts to rain? It's a very particular odor, extremely aromatic.

COUNSELOR: You like to use humor as a smokescreen.

STREET: Look, I'm so far ahead of you. I know what you're about to say. I know what you're thinking. I know what you're writing on those evaluation papers. I know that you're wearing an incredibly cheap toupee. I mean I can sit here and punch all the right buttons and make you think that you're a genius for correctly analyzing this complex, exotic, notorious negro but—"notorious negro." That would be a good name for my autobiography. I've started writing my life story. . . . But, you're not so far off. I give people what they want. When I meet somebody, I know in the first two minutes who they want me to be and I just cut the emotional cloth of my personality to fit the emotional clothing of whoever I'm—

COUNSELOR: Conning?

The Autobiography of a Notorious Negro could very well have been the film's alternate title. The title alludes to pulp engineering, a noir inflection that appropriately touches on how "the passing genre reads like the detective genre without the detective" (Huh 570).[15] *Chameleon Street*'s staging of the noir modal suspends the classical conception of crime/punishment and the sanctity of the law. The non sequitur of a vernacular snub that white people smell like wet dogs acts as a distinct racialized variant of people who believe "their shit doesn't stink." Overall, Street responds to his counseling session as a mimic grown bored with his diagnosis. As "notorious negro" (more Cross Damon than Bigger Thomas), Street straddles the classical division accorded to the black male in visual culture: "This schizophrenic way of representing black males as concentrated at the poles of celebrity and pathology leads to a dangerous array of perceptions and assumptions" (Guerrero, "The Black Man" 183). As the legacy of Richard Pryor attests to, "that nigger's crazy" never had anything to do with mental state (Harris, Keith). Conceding to the diagnosis means recognizing an authority and sanctioning a script. Of course, to do so would be anathema to Street's insistence on the improvised incarnations of his blackness. His mimic impulse as schizoid fury broaches being as a matter of anticipation and adaptation.

In a later sequence, Street passes as an attorney with the Detroit Human Rights Commission. Street's legal mimicry results in the successful negotiation of city contracts with four white corporate lawyers. During the celebratory dinner, the fantastical and the pathological again converge. Overhearing a conversation about tanning salons, Street begins to question the lawyers about the tanning service. One of the white lawyers nervously asks him about his interest and Street responds that it is for research purposes. When pressed further by the lawyers about what kind of research, Street replies, "White people." Street continues: "It amazes me that whites avidly seek after all the accouterments of black style. You pickle your bodies in gallons of tanning lotion. You broil your pale flesh brown in the tanning spas at great expense and all the while maintaining such a marvelous contempt for black people. You wily Caucasians." Finishing his monologue, Street raises his glass to toast them. The absence of a reaction from them, as if he had never said a word, reveals the monologue to be his interior voice in the sense of "thinking out loud."[16]

As menacing mimic, Street's wily comment alludes to the ways of "racechange" and crossracial mutuality.[17] Moreover, the "marvelous contempt" thesis relates to what Greg Tate identifies as "the long-standing, ongoing, and unarrested theft of African-American cultural properties by thieving, flavorless whitefolk" that desire "everything but the burden" (2). *Chameleon Street* tendentiously serves a sharp and performative address of race and desire. Masterfully versed in the ways of white folk, Street works hard at outmaneuvering racial privilege with the scorn of an independent scholar hidden in plain sight. The impudent verve of his refined pose reflects an ability to sustain a stature as the most deserving recipient of privilege. Street does not like people, white folk in particular. His performative sweep takes a distinct relish in showing up and ridiculing the sway of whiteness as the standard. Instead, Street as menacing mimic gleefully circulates as a raced heretic genius.

The Young Mod's Forgotten Story

> THE FORGER: You've seen my big Cézanne at the Metropolitan? Is that just a forgery, my friend? Is it not also a painting?
>
> —*F For Fake* (Orson Welles, 1974)

> Are we in the embraces of a charming rogue? . . . The play of meanings thickens. There is the battle of wits against any authorized set of assumptions. But then there is the segue into his loving the game for its own sake, his desire to pull off a *masterpiece* of illusion.
>
> —Clyde Taylor, "Two Way Street"

> People ask me all the time, "What are we listening to?" I play the classics: Vivaldi, Hendrix, Debussy, Sly Stone, Sex Pistol, Ipso Facto.
>
> —William Douglas Street Jr.

Street's performative raison d'être is mediated by an aesthetic ambition for what Clyde Taylor describes as *masterpieces*. Likened to a well-executed craft or a perfect art, the success of Street's masquerades communicates the substance of the above line from *F For Fake*. At the close of the film, Welles tells a story about an encounter between Pablo Picasso and a dying Hungarian man who is a legendary art forger, a rumored "ghost" of the art world. At one point in the exchange between the two men, the Hungarian exclaims, "Do you think I should confess? For what? For committing masterpieces." Street's masquerades ignore the distinctions between art and forgery, there is the normative and there is glory. His brand of outsider art consistently tends toward an acculturated tact of performativity.

Street enlists blackness as a discursive interlocutor. His insistence on elegance, style, and wit demonstrates the adaptability and cosmopolitanism that characterizes chameleonism. In this way, the phenomenon of black dandyism helps appreciate the proficiency of the film's protagonist, a savvy aesthete who does more than merely recycle conceits but practices passing as an art of racialization. "Black dandyism in the early 20th century," Monica L. Miller notes, "emerged as a sign that Black people now considered themselves modern, cosmopolitan, urban, part of a debate on how to reform, worldwide, conceptions of blackness and black people of the diaspora" (221). With the sartorial ways of the so fresh and so clean in mind, Street appreciably acts as a cross-racial and intercultural auteur who fashions being as the performative craft of a black renegade chic.

The film's conceptualization of the black modernist pursuit touches on what Henry Louis Gates Jr. notes about the passing life of Anatole Broyard, "The thematic elements of passing—fragmentation, alienation, liminality, self-fashioning—echo the great themes of modernism" (200). Therefore, the life of Anatole Broyard requires an acknowledgment of the consequences of passing less ethically motivated for "it was not so much that Broyard *lived* a lie as that he *refused* to live a conventional fiction" (Caughie 387). Street's refusal of a conventional fiction exists as an aesthetic ambition that ultimately informs his dandy pursuit. This pursuit bears out the struggle against the antiblack permutations of anonymity in the sense of all black people essentially being the same, indistinguishable from one another.[18]

While out having dinner with his wife, Street encounters a drunken white man who presumes that Street's wife is a prostitute and available for purchase. When Street pushes him away, the white man throws his drink in Street's face while yelling, "Nigger! Get your nasty black hands off of me! Fuckin' let go!" Flustered and upset, Street regains his composure and addresses the drunk:

> You know that's a very nasty word. But you know what's, pardon the expression, fucked-up is your grammar. *Fuckin' let go.* You can't say that. The rules of grammar apply to profanity as well. "Fuck" comes from the German root, *ficum,* which means to strike. It's a verb and it can be used in a variety of ways both transitive and intransitive. [Street proceeds to mime how fuck can be used to express simple aggression, confusion, apathy, ignorance, defiance, and authority.] See these are all the things you could have used if you weren't so unbelievably coarse and crude and countrified. [Street looks at his wife.] That's alliteration, Babe. Remember peckerwood, profanity is the last refuge of the ignorant, the insensitive, and the illiterate but if you're going to use it, and I see you are, at least get the fucking grammar right, moron.

Street's dressing down of this white man occurs with an intertextual nod to Edmund Rostand's *Cyrano de Bergerac* (1897) and Cyrano's humiliation of a defaming stranger through a consideration of what would be more original and less obvious insults regarding his nose. Like Cyrano, Street attempts to defuse the humiliation of a slight with words. Unlike Cyrano, Street as the sophisticated gentleman has less than remarkable swordsmanship and is beaten unconscious. Street's invocation of Cyrano refuses the hailing of the white man's nigger declaration. Importantly, Street does not speak to the "nigger-naming" but to the use of "fuck." The scene redirects antiblack racist speech as a matter of poor diction that requires elocution training. "The rain in Spain stays mainly in the plain."

The longest impersonation sequence of the film entails Street's escapades at Yale University following his escape from a Michigan prison. During this sequence, the allusive and intertextual measure of Street's aesthete tendency is most evident. Arriving in New Haven, Street models himself as a buppie collegiate before settling on the identity of a French-speaking exchange student from Martinique named "Pépé le Mofo." The rude hilarity of the name is a nod to Julien Duvivier's *Pépé le Moko* (1936), a Morocco-set film that centers on a Parisian jewel thief and bank robber (Jean Gabin) who must pass as an Algerian and reside in the "teeming anthill" of the Casbah to escape capture by the authorities. The connection to Duvivier's film also touches on the previous point of the menace of mimicry for, as Ella Shohat and Robert Stam remark, Duvivier's film "illustrate[s] perfectly Fanon's description of the imperial vision" (251). In *Chameleon Street,* the narrative codes of passing are remediated to suggest an adaptation that stages Pépé passing as Jean Gabin, the menace of the gentleman other. An enchanting cinéphile, Street bypasses merely citational intention as he embodies these cinematic roles as an accredited black artist of being.

Street practices French by viewing Edith Piaf videos, reading Rimbaud, and, by what he calls "getting my mind right," watching *Beauty and The Beast* (Jean Cocteau, 1946). For a short time, he even convinces a group of French students at a party of his pedigree by comically rephrasing Emile Zola's indictment of the Dreyfus affair. He simply says, "J'accuse . . . ," and then randomly adds an object.

Street's dandy pursuits build to the grand fruition of a French Revolution–themed costume ball. He attends the affair immaculately attired as Cocteau's "Beast." As Beast, Street critiques the white crowd's chants ("Marat!") as a sign of their ignorance and lack of refinement. This black Beast throws shade and becomes ennobled amid the swirl of white dilettantes, repurposing the reductive binaries of savagery and race, beast and aristocrat. Gabrielle, Street's wife, arrives at the ball conveniently dressed as "Beauty." She does not immediately recognize him and only discovers that it is her husband once their names are announced as the winning costumed couple. Basking in his "moment" on stage, the middle shot cuts to a wide-angle, close-up of his face. The black Beast smiles wide and his canines sparkle. The majesty of Street's Beast turns grotesque as the tightness of the close-up produces an unsettling fishbowl effect with the elongation of the image turning the salon setting into a funhouse. Gabrielle, hearing his name announced, rips the mask from his face, exposing his "true" identity to the Michigan authorities waiting in the crowd. Once unmasked, Street's makeup-smeared face appears as disfigured and profane as Dorian Gray's portrait.[19] Though the regalness of Street as The Beast ultimately repurposes the moral of the fairy tale, there is no truth inside, the cover is the thing.

Street's aesthete aspirations mirror the art cinema designs of the film itself. In particular, one sequence from the film symbolically illustrates the consequences of the film's auteurist manner. Shot from Street's point of view, Street considers selling drugs and discusses the entrepreneurial benefits of selling drugs. Mulling over the dealer's pitch, Street asks, "The question is do I have to sell drugs, in order to make money?" The supplier replies, "Look, brother. Do you want to philosophize or do you want to make some money?" The drug dealing consideration gestures toward the more popular permutations of the idea of black film at the time of the film's release. Of course, the film's preference lies with philosophy over the "keeping it real" profiteering of black cinema in the early 1990s. Thus, the film's inability to benefit from the new black cinema moment of the early 1990s illustrates the central problem of the industrial and academic collusion that produced a delineation of black film that was not necessarily distinguished from the social category of race itself.

As Russell Schwartz of Miramax Distributors noted on *Edge* (1991), "It [*Chameleon Street*] is not obviously a black picture, per se. Which is also one of the good things about it. If it had any potential, it could work as a crossover picture."[20] A review of the critical reception of the film's commercial run (New York City, April 1991 to Boston, January 1992) illustrates a compelling narrative of the categorical failure hinted at by Schwartz. The film experienced what was seemingly a cumulative failure to be convincingly understood or circulate as an art film, independent film, American film, or even a black film. It suffered a disappointing run as a result of a clustering of factors that included critical inattentiveness or misunderstanding, poor distribution, independent film cronyism, unfortunate programming choices by exhibitors, antiblack racism, and more generally, the film's lack of compliance with popular perceptions of the idea of black film advanced by academics, the film industry, and the general moviegoing audience.

Chameleon Street was lost and disavowed as an uppity, weird, black, arty thing lacking real value, as if a forgery. As Armond White wrote in the wake of a revival screening of the film at the American Museum of the Moving Image (February 1992), "*Chameleon Street* is a seriously talented person's attempt to find a means of expression he can call his own. And that, in the popular arts, is a heroic endeavor. It risks being unpopular, it risks not being distributed, and risks being misunderstood" (White 282).[21] The film was met with a consistent refusal to rethink the idea of black film and in many cases experienced hostile criticism as though the film was Street incarnate. In other words, the film was treated in many instances as though it embodied a categorical trespasser and thus endured a punishment spectacle like a passer exposed.

Wolf Like Me

> Can it be, I thought, can it actually be? And I knew that it was. I had heard of it before but I'd never come so close. Still, could he be all of them: Rine the runner and Rine the gambler and Rine the briber and Rine the lover and Rinehart the Reverend? Could he himself be both rind and heart? What is real anyway? But how could I doubt it? He was a broad man, a man of parts who got around. Rinehart the rounder. It was true as I was true. His world was possibility and he knew it. . . . The world in which we lived was without boundaries. A vast seething, hot world of fluidity, and Rine the rascal was at home. . . . It was unbelievable, but perhaps only the unbelievable could be believed. Perhaps the truth was always a lie.
>
> —Ralph Ellison, *Invisible Man*

The final sequence of *Chameleon Street* begins with Street in his law office at the Detroit Human Rights Commission. A co-worker comes in as Street begins a monologue that recaps his own folklore:

> William Douglas Street Jr. Born in a log cabin in the backwoods of Kentucky, young Douglas soon elevated himself from field hand to Tiger, from Tiger to reporter, from reporter to doctor, from doctor to co-ed, from co-ed to attorney, from attorney to congressman, from congressman to President. I could play President.

The shot/reverse shot rally between Street and his co-worker provides a survey of Street's office. His office walls are decorated with drafts of

America's most significant expression of the social contract, posters of various ratifications of the U.S. Constitution. The co-worker nervously interrupts Street's from slavery to the White House narrative with news that U.S. Marshals and thirty armed policemen wait outside the office door. The co-worker whispers, "The fire escape." Rather than run, Street instead raises his hand to his throat and motions a slash across his neck; the jig is up. The authorities arrive and he discovers that his wife Gabrielle turned him in.

Led outside in handcuffs, flanked by marshals on either side, the film shifts to slow motion as Street walks through a gauntlet of officers to a waiting car. The final shot of the film is from the side of an escorted Street. The spectacle of his punishment, his "perp walk," becomes magnified by the temporal elongation and winding down of the slow motion effect. Before exiting the frame all together, he looks directly at the camera and smiles. Cheeky until the end, Street raises his shoulders ("I yam what I yam") as the shot becomes a freeze frame. Once a performant of fluidity and improvisational momentum, the freeze frame leaves Street a fixed and secured body.

The end credits scroll alongside a montage comprised of actors from the film. Their voices and visages are spliced together in a collective reciting of the story of "The Scorpion and The Frog." Caught in a storm, The Scorpion rides across a rising river on The Frog's back after convincing The Frog he will not sting him. The Frog works his way through the swelling water and, nearing the end, feels The Scorpion's sting on his back. Succumbing to the poison, The Frog turns to ask why the Scorpion would sting him, condemning them both to die. The montage recitation closes on a shot of Street in his prison cell who indifferently offers the closing explanation from within a cloud of cigarette smoke: "Well, because it's my character."

Character connotes personality, portrayal, and in the case of *Chameleon Street,* a racial performant's prerogative. A self-critique, an intertextual nod to auteurist designs, and a psychoanalytic and philosophic rendering of the black existential condition, the collision of meanings attributable to the significance of the tale's place in the film evinces the contradictions and intricacies of an extraordinary performant.[22]

In the film's final shot as Street delivers his "character" line, he stands with his back to the barred window of his prison cell. Strongly backlit by the light pouring through and cloaked in smoke, the sight of Street is completely blown out and obscured. The sight of his vacancy resembles an indecipherable spot, a black hole. Then again, he has always been that way. In the end, the immaterial, if not ectoplasmic, Street becomes a pure black space.

His literal and metaphoric imperceptibility suggests what Ralph Ellison characterized as Rinehartism, a term derived from the never-seen performant in *Invisible Man*: "Rinehart is my name for chaos. He is also intended to represent America and change. He has lived so long with chaos that he knows how to manipulate it" ("The Art of Fiction" 181). The final shot of the film parallels the unfinalizability of Rinehart alluded to by Ellison. Street exercises a particular brand of improvisational chaos, a Rinehart-inflected sense of "myth and dash, being and non-being" (Jackson 84).[23] Street's adroit refusal to be named and quantified exposes the plasticity of racial taxonomies of being (Benston 161). With the black hole summation of the film, the sight of Street acts as a vision of pure alterity horror.

This essay has detailed some of the ways that Chameleon Street stages racial passing in the key of racial performativity. Clever and rigorous, the film generously provides a compelling example of film blackness with attention to the indexing of race's relational and affective quality. By enlivening the racial passing tradition with the force of racial performativity, the film accounts for the art of blackness in productively challenging ways.

Notes

I am grateful to Gary Holcomb, Lokeilana Kaimana, and Dana Seitler for their suggestions and critical insights. I owe special thanks to Julie Cary Nerad for her invaluable editorial guidance. I also owe special thanks to Robert Sklar (1936–2011) for encouraging me to write on *Chameleon Street*. Finally, special appreciation is due to Wendell B. Harris Jr. for *Chameleon Street*.

1. See Edmonds.

2. In September 1989, *Chameleon Street* premiered in Venice at the Venice Film Festival and was screened shortly afterward in Toronto at the Toronto International Film Festival. The film did not premiere in the U.S. until April 1990 at the Sundance Film Festival. Most of the production information in this essay is culled from conversations with Wendell Harris (telephone interview, 1996, e-mail interview 2011) and Moon and Weiner.

3. Posing as a Red Sox official, Street would later attempt to get a Red Sox World Series ring from the team's 1975 run.

4. Douglas Street was released from prison not long before *Chameleon Street* was screened at the Venice and Toronto film festivals in late 1989. Wendell Harris and Street appeared together on an episode of *The Geraldo Rivera Show*

devoted to con men. Not long after the broadcast, Street began serving his sixth stint in prison for check forgery.

5. In "Reading the Intersection of Race and Gender in Narratives of Passing," Valerie Smith examines the passing narrative in literature [e.g., James Weldon Johnson's *Autobiography of an Ex-Coloured Man* (1912), Nella Larson's *Passing* (1929), Jessie Fauset's *Plum Bun* (1928)] and film [John Stahl's (1934) and Douglas Sirk's (1959) adaptations of Fannie Hurst's *Imitation of Life* (1933), and Julie Dash's *Illusions* (1982)]. Smith's discussion of "contemporary revisions of the passing plot" includes an address of *True Identity* (Charles Lane, 1991). The film offers an additional complication to the revision impulse due to the lead actor, Lenny Henry. Henry's 'Miles Pope' must pass as an Italian hitman sent to murder him. While passing as his own assassin, Pope is cast as James Earl Jones's understudy in a production of *Othello*. Significantly, the film's fatal weakness is a result of the Black British Henry's performance of an African American. Thus, the film's extradiegetic issue of cross-cultural casting undercuts the success of the diegetic conceit.

6. As I have argued elsewhere, "As a craft and a process, black film is an idea that represents a visual negotiation, if not tension, between film as art and race as a constitutive, cultural fiction. This means that rather than addressing black film as a stable category, genre or mimetic corroboration of the black experience, this chapter engenders a deliberate shift. Such a shift distinguishes between the idea of race and the social category of race. Furthermore, this shift disputes the fidelity considerations of black film; the presumption that this brand of American cinema has an extradiegetic responsibility to embody the black lifeworld or provide answers in the sense of social problem solving. Black film must be understood as art, not sociological prescription or tenable to an ethics of positive and negative representation that tacitly encourages the idea of film as cultural policy" (Gillespie 56).

7. The source material of *Chameleon Street* was gathered from interviews of Douglas Street conducted by Wendell Harris and several long, handwritten letters Street wrote to Harris between 1985 and 1988. Adhering closely to Street's confessions, Harris has stated that much of the film's dialogue is directly from Street. As a way of acknowledging the derivation from the "true story" and as a sign of Harris's creative license, the pseudonym of "Erik Dupin" was used (Harris, e-mail interview 2011).

8. The presence of the primary colors or painter's primaries expresses an affinity for Jean-Luc Godard, modernist art, and art cinema. For a fuller explanation of the cinematic legacy of the painter's primaries, see Branigan.

9. As Charles Johnson argues, the question of black embodiment entails an address of the phenomenological imperative of racial perception. As Johnson summarizes, "To perceive a content is to conceive that content" (603).

10. The film adaptation opts to portray Street's blackmail note as an attempt to get a tryout with the Tigers. There is no reference to the death threat.

11. While the film comically details Street's one surgery, a hysterectomy, the real Street performed several successful hysterectomies before being exposed as an impersonator.

12. Also, see Dinerstein, Massood, Kun.

13. In a speech given to the Justice Department staff as part of Black History Month (February 18, 2009), Attorney General Eric Holder made observations of America that I have appended to Ellison's masking jokers comment, "Though this nation has proudly thought of itself as an ethnic melting pot, in things racial we have always been and continue to be, in too many ways, essentially a nation of cowards."

14. As Rouse notes, *Chameleon Street* "addresses the growing sense that signs of professional and social savoir-faire that now mark the boundaries between the bottom of the class structure and its upper reaches are so readily simulated that they cannot act as effective criteria of distinction" (391).

15. Furthermore, the noir-inflection of the voiceover narration greatly enables the film's autobiographical conceit. This is to say that *Chameleon Street*'s voiceover bears a resemblance to the general division of body and voice that has characterized the use of voiceover narration in film noir. The disconnection between the voice and the body of the noir protagonist engages as a battle for authority that propels and structures the narrative toward resolution and unification (Hollinger). The disembodiment crisis of the noir protagonist in general explores the question of a complete persona as a central conceit of noir: "The noir convention is that the separation between the voice and body gradually disappears as the film comes to the end, when we are gradually brought to the present of the narrative and to the reunion of the voice and the body of the detective, whose complete persona we see end the film" (Oliver and Trigo 169).

16. This sequence is one of the many Walter Mitty moments of film blackness, scenes involving black characters that lack obvious cues of interiority and instead pose sharp wit and/or fantastical vengeance. They include Dorothy cracking a bottle over the head of her social worker in *Bush Mama* (Haile Gerima, 1976), Malcolm Little smearing cake in the faces of condescending white patrons while working on the train in *Malcolm X* (Spike Lee, 1992), and Pierre Delacroix's accelerated slapping of Thomas Dunwitty in *Bamboozled* (Spike Lee, 2000). Also, see *Top of the Heap* (Christopher St. John, 1972) and *Hollywood Shuffle* (Robert Townsend, 1986).

17. As Susan Gubar puts forward, "[Racechange] is meant to suggest the traversing of race boundaries, racial imitation or impersonation, cross-racial mimicry or mutability, white posing as black passing as white, pan-racial mutuality" (5).

18. See Gordon.

19. Wendell Harris: "The evening of the fourth day when the beast mask was taken off my face by the make-up man, it unfortunately also started taking off layers of skin. The adhesives used to make the mask adhere to my skin was as damaging to the face as what they put on to take it off. I went home that

night and looked in the mirror and thought my face looked like the final *Portrait of Dorian Grey*" (Moon 157).

20. In 1991, *Chameleon Street* and Wendell Harris were profiled in a segment penned by Elvis Mitchell for PBS's *Edge,* a short-lived show billed as a monthly television magazine devoted to American culture. Mitchell questioned the sincerity of Hollywood's openness to the then-current iteration of a new black cinema in light of the problems experienced by *Chameleon Street.* He posed that the critical resistance to the film's content and form, coupled with the distribution problems experienced by the film, represented the sign of a ceiling on black cinema. In particular, the piece lingered on the issue of Warner Brothers' purchase of the indefinite remake rights of the film. The remake practice is usually reserved for adapting a foreign source, not a domestic one. Mitchell pointed out that the remake proposition was emblematic of the way *Chameleon Street* was ultimately perceived as outside the American film canon, and thus foreign. As Ed Guerrero reasons, "Street's fantasy life . . . his frustrated ambition and intelligence, his dissembling in the face of white professional class so eager to disavow its reflex feelings of racial superiority that it uncritically accepts him, all culminate in a dialectically shocking metaphor for the double consciousness, masked anger, and constant pretending that all blacks, to some degree, must deploy to live in a persistently racist society. And, of course, here resides the dark, troubled core of the film. Embellished by Harris's arty, *avant-garde* style and sardonic voiceover monologue, this is the unspoken and unspeakable truth that will forever keep *Chameleon Street* out of dominant cinema's mass entertainment markets" (*Framing* 174). Also, see Chin.

21. At the close of its commercial run, *Chameleon Street* was sporadically shown over the years at Black History Month festivals around the country before being picked up for a season run on the Independent Film Channel and later for a season on the African Heritage Movie Network. The expression "not another *Chameleon Street*" circulated in the trade press coverage of Sundance over the years. Harris wrote a screenplay entitled *Negropolis* with the idea of it becoming a Spike Lee project and was in talks with Milos Forman over a proposed Joe Louis biopic/project. Neither came to fruition. He has appeared in two films since his own *Chameleon Street,* as a Detroit detective in *Out of Sight* (Steven Soderbergh, 1998) and a philosophy professor in *Road Trip* (Todd Phillips, 2000). Through his Prismatic Productions, Harris has been working to complete a UFO-themed drama, *Arbiter Roswell.* In 2007, Harris was honorable mentioned on the British Film Institute's list of 100 Black Screen Icons. Long out of print, the film was released on DVD in 2007. In 2009, *Chameleon Street* and Harris were invited back to The Sundance Film Festival as part of the twenty-fifth anniversary of the festival and the film's inclusion in the Sundance Collection, a film preservation project established with the UCLA Film and Television Archive. Ironically, the film has been covertly circulated for some time through hip hop. A sampling of dialogue from the film by producer J. Rawls acts as the intro to "Brown Skin

Lady" on *Mos Def and Talib Kweli are Black Star* (1998): "I'm a victim of four hundred years of conditioning. The Man has programmed my conditioning. Even my conditioning has been conditioned!"

22. The fable's place in *Chameleon Street* most immediately acts as a citation of a scene from *Mr. Arkadin/Confidential Report* (Orson Welles, 1955). In this scene, Mr. Arkadin (Orson Welles) tells the parable to guests gathered at his Spanish castle. Once finished with the recitation, Mr. Arkadin raises his glass and toasts, "Let's drink to character." Considering Orson Welles's conflicted comments on morality and judgment, Gilles Deleuze puts Welles in conversation with Nietzsche. As Gilles Deleuze notes, "Nietzsche said: behind the truthful man, who judges life, there is the sick man, sick with life itself. And Welles adds: behind the frog, the epitome of the truthful animal, there is the scorpion, the animal sick with itself. The first is an idiot and the second is a bastard" (141). Moreover, the tale serendipitously addresses Richard Wright's re-fabulation of the Nietzschean "frog perspective" as emblematic of the psychology of the oppressed. In *White Man Listen!,* he writes, "This is a phrase that I've borrowed from Nietzsche to describe someone looking from below upward, a sense of someone who feels himself lower than others. The concept of distance involved here is not physical; it is psychological. It involves a situation in which for moral or social reasons, a person or a group feels that there is another person or group above it. Yet physically they all live on the same general, material plane. A certain degree of hate combined with love (ambivalence) is always involved in this looking from below upward and the object against which the subject is measuring himself undergoes constant change. He loves the object because he would like to resemble it; he hates the object because his chances of resembling it are remote, slight" (Wright 6). Wright's visualization of the black existential condition in the terms of the frog perspective links the philosophical with the experiential to identify a perspectival nexus, a "dreadful objectivity" (Gilroy 171).

23. To pursue the point further, Kevin Bell's comments about Rinehart's free circulation further draws a connection to *Chameleon Street*'s protagonist. As Bell writes, "Irreducible to any single role, or to any identifiable motives such as money, power, or sex, in his [Rinehart's] embrace of multiple modes of identification, he abandons all, freeing himself to align with the fluid and shifting forces of a life 'underground' in plain sight. . . . Rinehart embodies multiplicity in ceaseless motion, undermining every certitude, destabilizing every authority, *concealing* the 'truth' of his character *by performing* its proliferation in public" (168).

Works Cited

Bamboozled. Dir. Spike Lee. Forty Acres and a Mule Filmworks, 2000.

Bell, Kevin. *Ashes Taken for Fire: Aesthetic Modernism and The Critique of Identity.* Minneapolis: U of Minnesota P, 2007. Print.

Benston, Kimberly. "I Yam What I Am: The Topos of Un(naming) in Afro-American Literature." *Black Literature and Literary Theory*. Ed. Henry Louis Gates Jr. New York: Methuen, 1984. 151–72. Print.

Bhabha, Homi K. "Of Mimicry and Man." *The Location of Culture*. New York: Routledge, 1994. 85–92. Print.

Black Girl. Dir. Ousmane Sembene. 1966. New Yorker Films, 2006.

Branigan, Edward. "The Articulation of Color in a Filmic System: Deux ou trois choses que je sais d'elle." *Color: The Film Reader*. Ed. Angela Dalle Vacche and Brian Price. New York: Routledge, 2006. 170–82. Print.

Bush Mama. Dir. Haile Gerima. 1976. DVD. Mypheduh Films, Inc., 2009.

Caughie, Pamela. "Passing as Modernism." *Modernism/Modernity* 12.3 (2005): 385–406. Print.

Chameleon Street. Dir. Wendell B. Harris. Gethsemane 84, Inc./ Prismatic Images, Inc., 1989.

Chin, Daryl. "Multiculturalism and Its Masks: The Art of Identity Politics." *Performing Arts Journal* 14.1 (1992): 1–15. Print.

Deleuze, Gilles. *Cinema: The Time Image 2*. Trans. Hugh Tomlinson Robert Galeta. Minneapolis: U of Minnesota P, 1989. Print.

Dinerstein, Joel. *Swinging the Machine: Modernity, Technology, and African American Culture Between the World Wars*. Amherst: U of Massachusetts P, 2003. Print.

Duvivier, Julien, dir. *Pépé le Moko*. 1937. DVD. The Criterion Collection, 2004.

Edge. "Episode 102." PBS. WNET, New York City. 6 Nov. 1991. Television.

Edmonds, Patricia. "Super Duper Imposter Says He Aided in Surgeries." *Detroit Free Press*. 16 March 1985: 1A. Print.

Ellison, Ralph. "The Art of Fiction: An Interview." *Shadow and Act*. New York: Vintage, 1953. 167–83. Print.

———. "Change the Joke and Slip the Yoke." *Shadow and Act*. New York: Vintage, 1953. 45–59. Print.

———. *Invisible Man*. 1951. New York: Random House, 1972. Print.

F for Fake. Dir. Orson Welles. 1974. Specialty Films, 1975.

Gates, Jr., Henry Louis. "The Passing of Anatole Broyard." *Thirteen Ways of Looking at a Black Man*. New York: Random House, 1997. 180–214. Print.

Gillespie, Michael B. "Reckless Eyeballing: *Coonskin*, Film Blackness, and the Racial Grotesque." *Contemporary Black American Cinema: Race, Gender, and Sexuality at the Movies*. Ed. Mia Mask. New York: Routledge, 2012. 56–86. Print.

Gilroy, Paul. *The Black Atlantic: Modernity and Double Consciousness*. Cambridge: Harvard UP, 1993. Print.

Ginsberg, Elaine K. "Introduction: The Politics of Passing." *Passing and the Fictions of Identity*. Ed. Elaine K. Ginsberg. Durham: Duke UP, 1996. 1–18. Print.

Gordon, Lewis. "A Questioning Body of Laughter and Tears: Reading *Black Skin, White Masks* through the Cat and Mouse of Reason and a Misguided Theodicy." *parallax* 8.2 (2002): 10–29. Print.

Griffiths, Frederick T. "Copy Wright: What Is an (Invisible) Author?" *New Literary History* 33 (2002): 315–41. Print.

Gubar, Susan. *Racechanges: White Skin, Black Face in American Culture.* New York: Oxford UP, 1997. Print.

Guerrero, Ed. *Framing Blackness: The African-American Image in Film.* Philadelphia: Temple UP, 1993. Print.

———. "The Black Man on Our Screens and the Empty Space in Representation." *Black Male: Representations of Masculinity in Contemporary American Art.* Ed. Thelma Golden. New York: Whitney Museum of American Art, 1994. 181–90. Print.

Harris, Keith M. " 'That Nigger's Crazy': *Richard Pryor,* Racial Performativity, Cultural Critique." *Richard Pryor: The Life and Legacy of a "Crazy" Black Man.* Ed. Audrey Thomas McCluskey. Bloomington: Indiana UP, 2008. 23–38. Print.

Harris, Wendell B. Telephone interview. 10 March 1996.

———. E-mail interview. 4 December 2011.

Holder, Eric. "Attorney General Eric Holder at the Department of Justice African American History Month Program." The Department of Justice, Washington, DC. Web. 18 Feb. 2009.

Hollinger, Karen. "Film Noir, Voice Over, and the Femme Fatale." *Film Noir Reader.* Ed. Alain Silver and James Ursini. New York: Limelight Editions, 1996: 243–59. Print.

Hollywood Shuffle. Dir. Robert Townsend. The Samuel Goldwyn Co, 1987.

Huh, Jinny. "Whispers of Norbury: Sir Arthur Conan Doyle and the Modernist Crisis of Racial (Un)Detection." *Modern Fiction Studies* 49.3 (2003): 550–80. Print.

Jackson, Lawrence. "Ralph Ellison, Sharpies, Rinehart, and Politics in *Invisible Man.*" *The Massachusetts Review* 40.1 (1990): 71–95. Print.

Johnson, Charles. "A Phenomenology of the Black Body." *Michigan Quarterly Review* 32.4 (1993): 595–614. Print.

Johnson, James Weldon. *The Autobiography of An Ex-Coloured Man.* 1912. New York: Hill and Wang, 1960. Print.

Kun, Josh. *Audiotopia: Music, Race, and America.* Berkeley and Los Angeles: U of California P, 2005. Print.

Mackey, Nathaniel. *Discrepant Engagement: Dissonance, Cross-Culturality, and Experimental Writing.* Cambridge: Cambridge UP, 1993. Print.

Malcolm X. Dir. Spike Lee. Forty Acres and a Mule Filmworks, 1992.

Massood, Paula. *Black City Cinema: African American Urban Experiences in Film.* Philadelphia: Temple UP, 2003. Print.

Miller, Monica L. *Slaves to Fashion: Black Dandyism and the Styling of Black Diasporic Identity.* Durham: Duke UP, 2009. Print.

Mills, Charles W. "Non-Cartesian Sums: Philosophy and the African-American Experience." *Blackness Visible: Essays on Philosophy and Race.* Ithaca: Cornell UP, 1998. 1–20. Print.

Moon, Spencer. *Reel Black Talk: A Sourcebook of 50 American Filmmakers*. Westport, CT.: Greenwood, 1997. Print.

Mullen, Harryette. "Optic White: Blackness and the Production of Whiteness." *Diacritics* 24.2/3 (1994): 71–89. Print.

Nina Simone: Live At Montreux. Dir. Raymond Jaussi. 1976. Eagle Rock Entertainment, 2006.

Oliver, Kelly, and Benigno Trigo. *Noir Anxiety*. Minneapolis: U of Minnesota P, 2003. Print.

Out of Sight. Dir. Steven Soderbergh. Universal Pictures, 1998.

Road Trip. Dir. Todd Phillips. Dream Works, 2000.

Robinson, Amy. "Forms of Appearance of Value: Homer Plessy and the Politics of Privacy." *Performance and Cultural Politics*. Ed. Elin Diamond. New York: Routledge, 1996. 237–60. Print.

Rostand, Edmund. *Cyrano de Bergerac*. 1897. Trans. Anthony Burgess. New York: Applause Books, 1998. Print.

Rouse, Roger. "Thinking through Transnationalism: Notes on the Cultural Politics of Class Relations in the Contemporary United States." *Public Culture* 7 (1995): 353–402. Print.

Shohat, Ella, and Robert Stam. *Unthinking Eurocentrism: Multiculturalism and the Media*. New York: Routledge, 1994. Print.

Smith, Cherise. *Enacting Others: Enacting Others: Politics of Identity in Eleanor Antin, Nikki S. Lee, Adrian Piper, and Anna Deavere Smith*. Durham: Duke UP, 2011. Print.

Smith, Valerie. "Reading the Intersection of Race and Gender in Narratives of Passing." *Diacritics* 24.2–3 (1994): 43–57. Print.

Tate, Greg. "Nigs R Us, or How Blackfolk Became Fetish Objects." *Everything But The Burden: What White People Are Taking From Black Culture*. Ed. Greg Tate. New York: Broadway Books, 2003. 1–14. Print.

Taylor, Clyde. "Two Way Street." *Black Film Review* 1.6 (1990): 8–9. Print.

Thompson, Debby. "'Is Race a Trope?': Anna Deavere Smith and the Question of Racial Performativity." *African American Review* 37.1 (2003): 127–38. Print.

Top of the Heap. Dir. Christopher St. John. The Fanfare Corp, 1972.

Weiner, Rex. "One Way Street." *Variety*. 22 Jan. 1996: 13. Print.

White, Armond. "Apostasy: Anti-hype in Four Steps." *The Resistance*. Woodstock, NY: Overlook, 1995. 278–82. Print.

Wright, Richard. *White Man Listen!* 1957. New York: Anchor Books, 1964. Print.

11

Consuming Performances

Race, Media, and the Failure of the Cultural Mulatto in *Bamboozled* and *Erasure*

Meredith McCarroll

> The ultimate condition of production is therefore the reproduction of the conditions of production.
>
> —Louis Althusser, "Ideology and Ideological State Apparatuses"

> For I found the greatest difficulty for a Negro writer was the problem of revealing what he truly felt, rather than serving up what Negroes were supposed to feel, and were encouraged to feel.
>
> —Ralph Ellison, *Shadow and Act*

In "The New Black Aesthetic" (1989), novelist and scholar Trey Ellis writes about "cultural mulattoes" who are phenotypically black but are culturally white enough to "navigate easily in the white world" (189).[1] Employing terms at home in the concurrently rising multiracial movement, he writes: "Just as a genetic mulatto is a black person of mixed parents who can often get along fine with his white grandparents, a cultural mulatto, educated by a multiracial mix of cultures, can also navigate easily in the white world. . . . We no longer need to deny or suppress any part of our complicated and sometimes contradictory cultural baggage to please either white people or black" (235). Central to Ellis's optimism regarding cultural mulattoes is his presumption of agency from within a hybrid borderland of black and white. The new cultural mulatto, unlike mulattoes of the past, would arguably have the ability to cross borders and speak freely from, as Arjun Appadurai phrases it, an "imagined world." They would function as—in Ellis's terms—"thriving hybrids" instead of "neutered mutations" (201) that history had made them to be. They would, in other words, easily inhabit the transgressive realm of a "third race."[2] Over the last few decades, theorists such as Paul Gilroy, Arjun Appadurai, Gloria Anzaldúa, and Donna Haraway have imagined such a transgressive space between boundaries as well as a subject position from within the margin that maintains sufficient agency and vocality to disrupt the seemingly natural dichotomy in which two sides (here, black and white) depend upon one another to exist.[3] However, although these cultural mulattoes would define themselves outside of the traditional binaric racial system, they would not—as the term itself suggests—fall outside of the history of race in the United States.[4] Indeed, even to use the phrase "cultural mulatto" is to evoke the history of (genetic) mulattoes in America, and to reclaim their often tumultuous social position(s).[5]

In its echoing of the term *tragic mulatto,* the cultural mulatto also awakens the never-quite-sleeping monster of miscegenation and, along with it, the troublesome issue of racial passing. Racial passing, of course, has a long and varied history. In her reading of Charles W. Chesnutt's "The Passing of Grandison," Martha J. Cutter summarizes this history nicely: "[F]rom a historical perspective the term 'passing' has such plasticity of meaning that it can connote a whole range of behaviors and ideologies that may be complicit or subversive, enslaving or freeing, hegemonic or transgressive" (note 1, 48). A more specific, if generic, understanding of the term, however, situates it within the historical black/white racial dichotomy: " 'Passing' is used most frequently, however, as if it were short for 'passing for white,' in the sense of 'crossing over' the color line in the United States from the black to the white side" (Sollors 247).[6] In this most common form, passing relies on both the subject's intent and the audience's reception. That is, the passing subject needs both the phenotypic *ability* and, in any intentional act of passing, the *desire* to be read as white, while the audience must *read* or interpret that person's performance as an embodiment of whiteness, usually without being aware that an act of interpretation has even occurred. The interpretation of the performance relies upon a belief in essentialized blackness and whiteness, categories separated by a racial line that *can be* crossed, regardless of whether that crossing is understood as a transgression, a betrayal, a crime, a joke, or a liberation. Because of Jim Crow segregation, passing from black to white often historically provided literal access to de jure white (physical and cultural) spaces; however, in exchange, passers usually forfeited their association with blackness and with black spaces for that access.[7] Theoretically, post–Jim Crow, entering into a once racially sanctioned space is easier: without a "whites only" sign on the door, anyone should be able to walk right in. Thus, passing would become anachronistic. The trope of passing, however, is still with us. Although more traditional passing narratives such as Philip Roth's *The Human Stain* (2000) are still being produced, passing also survives, I argue, through the construct of the cultural mulatto.

As for earlier passers, the kind of postsegregation, post-soul passing called up by the concept of the cultural mulatto relies on a similar (white) control of and (black) desire for access into sanctioned spaces, but those spaces are now demarcated primarily as metaphorical cultural spaces. Despite the rise of multiracialism in the 1990s, these cultural spaces continue to be policed in exclusionary ways that arise from and reify a specific understanding of racial identities, one built in part on the belief that there is an authentically black or authentically white way of behaving/being that (usually) corresponds to skin color but is about larger claims to racialized-cultural properties. Thus, postmodern passing presses the fault line between *looking* and *acting* "black" or "white."[8] Mirroring the move toward cultural space and away from the physical, this type of postmodern passing is also divorced from the (shade of the) body and is shifted more fully onto the performance of a cultural whiteness or blackness. In other words, some of these postmodern passers are not light-skinned blacks who "look white." For them, a performance of whiteness is not one that depends upon skin color. Indeed, the term "look" shifts: instead of being the object of the gaze, they become the one who looks through a "white" or "black" lens. The postmodern passer's fracturing of (racial) identity from the body foregrounds the role of knowledge and performance in the perpetual creation of the self. However, the communities around these passers continue to insist on mapping race—and particularly blackness—visually, exclusively, and stereotypically, sometimes even to the point of absurdity, which is why the individual is still *passing* rather than just "thriving." The failure of the cultural mulatto thus reminds us that racialized communities continue to maintain the borders that "hybrids" threaten. This policing, furthermore, is still directionally weighted. That is, although certainly post-soul/post–civil rights blackness insists on its own value, the residual effects of segregation remain: the still-dominant white society allows passage into blackness but guards entry into whiteness, maintaining its reputed purity as well as its cultural and economic power. What Homi Bhabha calls the "hybridity of imagined communities" cannot stand against what George Lipsitz calls the "possessive investment in whiteness."

This essay examines such postmodern passers in two texts by of burgeoning black artists of the 1980s and 1990s—Spike Lee and Percival Everett—to explore the matrix of racial investment and production that remained operative in the post-soul United States despite the optimism that generated the concept of the cultural mulatto. Spike Lee's film *Bamboozled* (2000) and Percival Everett's novel *Erasure* (2001) are experimental and postmodern in both form and narrative content. While *Bamboozled* is a film about a television show and *Erasure* is a novel about a novel, the genre differences are not crucial for my purposes here. Although certainly form affects the possibilities of representation and, potentially, the effect on readers, what drives this analysis are these texts' engagements with shared concepts: In both, the protagonists are cultural mulattoes—black men who are comfortable in and influenced by "white" spaces. Also, in both, although the protagonists do cross the cultural color line, they find themselves unable to occupy the type of liminal or hybrid space that Ellis and other cultural critics imagine. For Lee's and Everett's protagonists, liminality fails to provide an adequate site of identification due to pressures that are both internal (how one sees oneself) and external (how others see you).[9] Although the texts highlight "the interplay of self-deception and self-awareness" necessary in any effective performance of identity or race (Lucia 10), they also suggest that individuals are still constrained by a largely binaric racial system, one that is continually reproduced through the media and mediated through a system of exchange. Indeed, the protagonists' inability to inhabit a third race evinces the continued essentialization of racial identity policed through mutually exclusive racial roles that sustain a racialized economic and social hierarchy. Ultimately, Lee's and Everett's cultural mulattoes—unlike Ellis's—seem alternately to *pass* as black and/or as white in attempts to negotiate a (racial) identity in an America still clinging tenaciously to racial performances that reify (even to the point of caricature) a racial hierarchy that produces and maintains the cultural supremacy of whiteness. More specifically, both Lee and Everett problematize the cultural mulatto by revealing that racial producers and consumers are part of a hegemonic capitalist power structure that is designed for profit and embedded in a culture of racial hierarchy. They thus push us to question our own continued complicity in the reproduction of race, and suggest that "navigating the white [media-driven] world" at the turn of the twenty-first century continues to be a challenging enterprise for anyone who is not seen as authentically white.

Racial (Ex)Change

In *Bamboozled,* protagonist Pierre Delacroix (Damon Wayans) is a phenotypically black television writer whose affected diction, sharp dress, and distance from "ghetto"-blackness mark him (satirically) as culturally white. As his network's only African American writer, however, he is expected to create television shows that are authentically "black." *Erasure* centers on Monk Ellison, a phenotypically black novelist and scholar whose interests in woodworking and semiotics are deemed "too white" by his publisher for his prospective audience. The *way* that these two men inhabit their black bodies threatens the culturally sanctioned ideal of a pure, distinct, differentiated, and natural whiteness in that *their* blackness looks and sounds too much like whiteness. In response, white figures around and above these two men force them—if, that is, the two men want to succeed economically—to perform a particular type of stereotyped and ghettoized blackness, a blackness whose value paradoxically lies in its devaluation of blackness. Delacroix and Ellison respond similarly—each writing a parody of blackness. In *Bamboozled,* Delacroix schemes a way to break his contract and make a political statement by pitching *Mantan: The New Millennium Minstrel Show,* complete with the most racist roles retrieved from minstrel shows of the late nineteenth and early twentieth centuries. To his shock, the show is picked up and becomes an overnight success. To capitalize on this success, Delacroix shifts from being too culturally white to being stereotypically black. In *Erasure,* Ellison writes *My Pafology,* an absurdist take on Richard Wright's *Native Son* which is so "ghetto" and so "hardcore" that he eventually changes the book's title to *Fuck.* Ellison writes this text under a pseudonym and watches the novel not only make it to publication, but also to become an award-winning best seller heralded for its honesty.[10] Ellison begins to play the role of the imaginary novelist of *Fuck,* and vacillates between being the too-white black writer or the ghetto-black black writer.

The texts within the texts—*Mantan* and *Fuck*—clearly function as precipitating causes for the protagonists' shift in racial performance (reversing the traditional black-to-white passing scenario, they provide financial reasons for the two men to "pass" as black). But, as importantly, they propel us (as meta-audience) directly into issues of agency and/in the production of knowledge, and reframe the act of passing—or even (racial) identity itself—as an exchange of production and consumption performed but not proscribed by the body. The postmodern nature of both texts, with Everett's self-reflexive narration and fragmented experimentation with form and Lee's similar first-person narration and cinematic techniques, assault the reader/viewer with reminders that they are watching/consuming representations. Not only does *Erasure*'s Monk write a satirical novel that is embedded in the text, Everett includes a presentation from an academic article that challenges Roland Barthes's *S/Z*. Each of these fragments draws the reader's attention to the process of production. Similarly, Lee makes use of handheld cameras, as well as reaction shots from onlookers, to remind the reader of the presence of the producer of a text and the element of performance that is key on and off screen of Delacroix's satirical television show.

What the texts highlight is that individuals produce "race" through a performance that is consumed by an audience, a community that authorizes or validates the individual's "race" through that act of consumption. If they "don't buy" the performance, then the individual cannot "be" white (or black). According to Louis Althusser, power remains with the producer of images, which is, however, notably not the same as the artist him/herself but is rather linked to the system of production—in the case of Lee's protagonist, it is the television network, and in the case of Everett's protagonist, the publishing world. In his reading of Marx, Althusser aligns the consumer of images with the masses who are interpellated into a particular subject position and passively respond according to how they are hailed and how they understand themselves within that particular moment and structure. However, depending on one's perspective, a viewer might also be an agent in determining what is considered fashionable or offensive. Reader response theorists (e.g., Jonathan Culler, Roland Barthes, Stanley Fish) have argued that the reader (here, the consumer) has power to interact with and shift the meanings of texts. *Bamboozled* and *Erasure* acknowledge this *active* power of the consumer, asserting that the consumer of images (the reader/audience) participates in making the meaning of those images, *as well as* Althusser's perspective, which grants power to the producer. Put within the context of racial production, both the consumer and the producer are situated within a racial hierarchy that privileges whiteness and depends upon blackness as its Other, and race itself is created in the exchange between the two entities. The questions then become what are we, as the audience of Lee's and Everett's texts, consuming? We participate in the (re)construction/production of race when we laugh—whether with or at—the textual audience: the texts have reproduced the conditions of production even in an attempt to challenge them. The embedded texts turn our attention to the *process* of racial production, as well as the *products,* yet the protagonists' inability to form a stable identity outside of this system of production highlights how embedded in a binaric racial system U.S. culture continues to be.

Racial Performance as Cultural Property

Erasure's protagonist and narrator, Thelonious "Monk" Ellison, introduces himself to readers by saying, "I don't believe in race" (2). However, he goes on to describe his racial heritage and phenotype, noting that he has "dark brown skin, curly hair, a broad nose" and that "some of [his] ancestors were slaves" (1). His very name, "an obvious composite of the jazz innovator and the author of *Invisible Man,*" evokes blackness (Russet 364–65). His Du Boisian "double consciousness" makes him acutely aware that the society in which he lives sees him as black and expects him to perform a particular blackness, an expectation which he resents. Perhaps in resistance, he goes by "Monk," the one part of his name which—thrown out of context by the erasure of "Thelonious"—evokes an image of whiteness and austerity. His interests also mark him as "white": he is a woodworker whose novels are set in Greece and whose scholarship is grounded in European poststructuralism.[11] Monk explains that he "graduated summa cum laude from Harvard" and that his "family [of doctors] owned a bungalow near Annapolis" (1–2). Although he sees these aspects of his past as having to do more with class than with race, others deem them, too, as "too white," and he is frequently accused of passing as white, an accusation which he rejects.

Monk is aware both of the expectation for him to enact blackness—to enact a cultural identity that matches his phenotype—and of the resistance to the way he enacts a white cultural identity. However, he refuses to accept such easy cultural readings of black and white as grounds for his self-definition and attempts subtly to embody the marginal space of a cultural mulatto. This attempt exposes as ludicrous the racial dichotomy, which has no space for Monk, and calls into question the very meaning of "black" and "white." Thus, early in the novel, Everett explores the potential for racial transgression despite the pressure to conform to an exclusive racial category.

In Spike Lee's *Bamboozled,*[12] the protagonist also defines himself outside of stereotypical blackness, albeit through what the audience recognizes as a satiric performance of class and educational pedigree stereotypically associated with whiteness. Pierre Delacroix introduces himself to the audience in French with exaggerated enunciation that film scholar Cynthia Lucia calls an "odd Grace-Kelly-meets-James-Earl-Jones accent" (10). His past—he was born Peerless Dothan to a working-class family—motivates the performance that opens the film. Along with his Harvard degree, Peerless took another name, accent, attire, and attitude—a creation that inspires his own father to ask, "Nigger, where the fuck did you get that accent?" Like Monk, Pierre is considered (especially by whites, but also by blacks, as his father's dressing-down of him suggests) to be (culturally) too white. Unlike with Monk, however, Pierre's whiteness is clearly (for Lee's audience) an intentional performance, his voice a practiced caricature that black comedians have long used to imitate "crackers." Judith Butler explores the transgressive potential of imitation, asking of gender performativity, "Is drag the imitation of gender, or does it dramatize the signifying gestures through which gender itself is established?" (viii). One might read Pierre as applying the concept of drag as imitation to racial performativity. His cultural passing, as overt performance, might "dramatize the signifying gestures" of racial construction in order to destabilize race altogether and allow for a more liberated embodiment of a self free of racial expectations. In other words, such a playful performance of race might disrupt the black/white binary, much as Butler suggests that a playful performance of gender can disrupt the gender binary. However, because Pierre is the token black man at work, such play is particularly ignored or, alternately, denounced. He is expected to perform and produce blackness while representing the black race—the same race from which he seems to be racing.

Their peers read both Monk and Pierre as disingenuous in their embodiments of race, especially as artists who are expected to create art that speaks to the "black community" and who are—or should be—writing out of what Pierre's boss, Dunwitty, calls his "pain as a Negro." Monk's editor, Yul, insinuates that Monk's novels are "not black enough" and that if Monk wrote more authentically, his work would be more black. Similarly, Dunwitty challenges Pierre to create "real" black television shows. When Pierre questions the expectations placed on black art, Dunwitty calls him out, saying, "Brother man, I'm blacker than you. I'm keepin' it real. You're just frontin' tryin' to be white." Yul and Dunwitty, both white, encourage Monk and Pierre to "keep it real," so long as "real" meets their expectations of blackness and steers clear of whiteness. In this, they represent what Theodor Adorno and Max Horkheimer refer to as the "circle of manipulation" operating in the culture industry (33). Discussing television, they explain that "there is the agreement—or at least the determination—of all executive authorities not to produce or sanction anything that in any way differs from their own rules, their own ideas about consumer, or above all themselves" (34). Within the texts, the white executives in power deem the art that Monk and Pierre create to be too white—too white to come from black men, at least. For them and, by extension, their audiences, white writers should create "white" shows, and black writers, "black" ones. They won't "buy" anything else because they don't believe it will sell. Their creative color line grows from a belief in racial "authenticity" that maps racial identity (read on the body) onto racial performance—a blending of Jim Crow and black power that continues to slot people into proscribed cultural spaces based on phenotype. Lee and Everett highlight here the media's role in the (re)production of racial identity and, more specifically, a racial hierarchy with whiteness enthroned at the top, through the media's power over the production of images, be they in novels or, more visually, on television.

Consuming Images; Failed Satires

Within the texts, whites and blacks enthusiastically consume images of blackness that belittle, marginalize, and disempower African Americans. By extrapolation, then, the texts also ask us to reflect on our own practices of consumption and complicity in the media's production of race and a racial hierarchy. Playing on misreadings of black culture and the performative nature of blackness (and whiteness), both Pierre and Monk create outrageous satires in order to force their white employers to acknowledge the media-driven culture's limited conceptualizations of blackness.[13] Pierre and Monk intend to access a history of damning representation of blacks and emphasize the continued production of white-imagined stereotypes of blackness in culture. In both cases, however, their experiments backfire dramatically. The satires' (unintended) commercial success reifies rather than dismantles what they seek to critique. Their success also serves to highlight the complicity of African Americans in an economic system of cultural representation that reproduces the conditions of oppression. Indeed, for Everett and Lee to make their points, their protagonists' satires must be commercial successes.[14] That is, *Mantan* and *Fuck* must fail as satire (for the external/real audiences, if not for the internal ones) in order for *Bamboozled* and *Erasure* to be effective in their critiques of contemporary culture.

In *Bamboozled,* Pierre satirizes his imaginings of the culture's expectations of black art and black identity, dreaming up a show that "will be so negative, so offensive and racist" that everyone will soon understand that "the network does not want to see Negroes on television unless they are buffoons." Lee overtly evokes racial performativity by revising late-nineteenth and early-twentieth-century minstrel shows which featured black and white performers donning blackface, acting out racist skits, and dancing and singing for the enjoyment of white—and later black—audiences.[15] Set in a watermelon patch, *Mantan: The New Millennium Minstrel Show* stars Mantan (Savion Glover) and Sleep-n-Eat (Tommy Davidson)—"two real coons" who are "ignorant, dull-witted, lazy and unlucky," playing on centuries of damning black representation. As Donald Bogle and others[16] have shown, representation of the "coon" served an imperative purpose in the social positioning of blacks as nonthreatening and undeserving of full access to citizenship and civil rights. Lee accesses this history and, more specifically, reflects on the irreconcilability of Pierre's own position as a cultural mulatto, all while highlighting the similarity in various types of racial performance: blackface, passing, and "keepin' it real."

While Pierre in *Bamboozled* sets his satire in an antebellum rural setting—Mantan and Sleep-n-Eat shuffle along stealing chickens—Monk sets his story in an urban location. His satire is inspired by Juanita Mae Jenkins, a black woman who writes *We's Lives in Da Ghetto* as an insider, but who is actually a midwesterner who spent "a couple of days" visiting relatives in Harlem. Nevertheless, she feels justified to write "our stories" from that "insider" knowledge (53). Monk describes Jenkins's book in terms reminiscent of the minstrel show: reading it was like "strolling through an antique mall, feeling good, liking the sunny day and then turning the corner to find a display of watermelon-eating, banjo-playing darkie carvings and a pyramid of Mammy cookie jars" (29). Monk rejects Jenkins's stereotypes, just as he bemoans the popularity of "ghetto literature" that relies upon contemporary caricatures of urban black poverty in order to sell books. In protest, under the pseudonym Stagg R. Leigh,[17] Monk writes a contemporary satire of Richard Wright's 1940 novel *Native Son,* originally entitled *My Pafology*.[18] The novel centers on a young black narrator, Van Go Jenkins, who enacts contemporary stereotypes of black ignorance and apathy. He says, for instance, "My name is Van Go Jenkins and I'm nineteen years old and I don't give a fuck about nobody, not you, not my Mama, not the man. The world don't give a fuck about nobody, so why should I?" (66). Go's attitude recalls Wright's protagonist Bigger Thomas's, but his employment with the wealthy *black* Daltons is a significant change from Wright's novel in which the *white* Daltons employ Bigger. This revision is one of the novel's critiques of African American complicity in the maintenance of an oppressive racial system, a critique surfacing in *Bamboozled* through the black audience's reception—and acceptance—of *Mantan*.

At the taping of the pilot of *Mantan*, Pierre braces for the riotous response he expects from the mixed-race audience, eager to prove to Dunwitty and the other executives that America will not condone the racist work that he has been asked to produce. The scene opens with a pan of the audience and breaks down into medium close-ups on individuals of various races. Cutting alternately to Pierre in the sound booth watching the audience, to quick takes of the audience watching the stage, and finally to Mantan and Sleep-n-eat on the stage, the power triumvirate of producer/text/audience is captured through reaction shots making clear the transition from uncertainty to approval, which is driven by the audience. Instead of a riot, after stalled applause and uncomfortable silence, the white audience members take their performative cue from the black audience members shown through medium close shot and reverse shot of black and white audience members who end the taping with a standing ovation. Lee points to this moment as a key scene of the film, in which "the white people look around to see if black people are laughing, because if they are, then it's sanctioned, and it's OK for them to laugh, too" (Crowdus and Georgakas 6). In this moment of reception, the agency is located within the consumptive (black) audience.

In *S/Z,* Roland Barthes asserts that writerly texts empower particular readers to transform from the position of consumer to producer.[19] The text does not exist until it is read, and thus depends upon the reader to "actualize" its potential meaning. A satire, especially, may be called a writerly text which depends upon an adroit reader to decode the text and make meaning of it. The failure of an audience appropriately to read satire or to be appropriately interpellated by satire is recorded as early as 1704 by Jonathan Swift who wrote, "Satire is a sort of glass wherein beholders do generally discover everybody's face but their own, which is the chief reason for the kind of reception it meets in the world, and that so very few are offended with it" (*The Battle of the Books*). Just so here. The meaning made through the audience's acceptance and applause undergirds the racist images that their authors sought to transgress and instead "reproduce[s] . . . the conditions of production," highlighting black complicity in its own subjugation and reassuring whites that their own racism is inoffensive, at best, and sanctioned, at worst.

However, the moment of reception—and of production—here also leaves open the possibility that the politics of that cultural production is more complicated. The audience's agency within the text, we perhaps are to recognize, is conditioned by cultural and historical factors. For instance, the awkward moment before the laughter arguably suggests that the African American audience recognizes *Mantan*'s racism and makes a choice. Their pause is laden with the burden of history: Are they ready to confront racism openly? Are they ready to riot? And, by extension, are we as the audience of *Bamboozled*? Speaking of the film's weak reception, Lee acknowledges that the final montage is difficult to watch, but, he adds, "so is the footage from the Auschwitz concentration camp, but you have to look at it. This stuff cannot be swept under the rug" (Crowdus and Georgakas 9). Within the film, Pierre similarly notes to his assistant, Sloane (Jada Pinkett-Smith): "The good Reverend Dr. Martin Luther King did not enjoy seeing his people beaten on the six o'clock news. However, white America needed to see that in order to move this country to change. They need to see this show for that exact reason." Pierre's audience, however, proves itself unready to change, which potentially prompts *Lee's* audience to question its own complicity in the production of racial stereotypes. Did they laugh, too?

Where *Mantan* maintains a safer distance by drawing on historical racial stereotypes, Monk's composite of contemporary negative stereotypes hits closer to (temporal) home. The protagonist Go is the epitome of apathy and the embodiment of the myths of Generation X, angry black men, and welfare recipients combined. The novel is so outrageous that Monk awaits the publishers' shock, much like Pierre does at the taping, anticipating the freedom to follow the white enlightenment he enables. After reading the book, however, Monk's editor Yul remains bound by commercial pressure and says, "I appreciate your position and I even admire the parody, but who's going to publish this?" (132). In frustration, Monk tells Yul to send the book "straight," without qualifying it as a parody: "If they can't see it's a parody, fuck them," Monk says (133). "They" indeed don't see it as a parody. And "they" love the book. Random House offers $600,000 for rights, calling it—and echoing President Woodrow Wilson's response to *The Birth of a Nation*—"true to life" and "magnificently raw and honest" (136).[20] Both black and white readers, ranging from the black Oprah Winfrey–inspired talk show host Kenya Dunston to white publishers and panelists for an esteemed book award, praise the book's realism. Once again, *Erasure*'s message hinges on the failure of the internal audience to read the embedded text as satire. The internal audience buys (both ideologically and literally) the novel as an authentic (re)production of racial identities, thus reproducing race itself, without recognizing its own agency or its own interpellation into the system of production. That is, the community/audience/consumer is unarmed—or unwilling—to read critically, and rather passively assumes their positions of power like programmed proletariat in a capitalist scheme.

In "Signing to the Blind," Everett acknowledges the agency of the reader and advocates a more informed and critical readership: "I do not believe that the works we produce need to be any different; the failing is not in what we show but in how it is seen" (10). As Everett concludes the essay, his tone is defeated and exhausted: "We have no audience. At least, no audience that reads with political empowerment. And so our work becomes a matter worse than preaching to the choir. It is more like we are standing in the dark signing furiously to the blind" (11). Both Pierre and Monk similarly seem to be signing to the blind, as their messages go unrecognized and their artistic productions work to produce the very thing they attempt to dismantle. Indeed, much of the remainder of the texts focuses on the costs of the system of racial (re)production. At the failure (or commercial success) of their satires, Pierre and Monk let pass their opportunities to claim their works as satirical and passively observe the intersection of text and audience—awed by the reception and the (re) making of meaning. They then begin to affect the very embodiment of blackness they attempted to satirize, to pass as (stereotyped) black.

As noted above, early in the texts, Pierre and Monk are both criticized for trying to pass as white. When they craft caricatured black racial performances, however, they are accepted and even (literally) applauded. Lee and Everett, through their characters passing alternatively as white *and* as black, thus illuminate the important directional differences in trespassing into whiteness and trespassing into blackness. Entry into blackness is less guarded than entry into whiteness: while blacks who "front" as white cause discomfort and even anger, blacks who absurdly "front" as ghetto-black by assuming the most outrageous stereotypes available are praised for their honesty, stabilizing an essentialist notion of race and its characteristics. Pierre and Monk recognize the workings of the racial system and attempt to expose its ludicrousness. They both, however, overestimate the tenacity of the one-drop rule that remained largely unchallenged by the civil rights movement and that continues to police the boundaries of racialized cultural property in ways that maintain a cultural hierarchy with whites on top.

Monk begins to live part of his life as Stagg R. Leigh, with "black shoes, black trousers, black turtleneck sweater, black blazer, black beard, black fedora" (245), acting aloof, inarticulate, and rude, and dressing in a uniform of black militants from three decades past. He also alternately continues to pass (culturally) as white, living as Monk in his family's Annapolis cottage and dating a white woman. For a time, Monk is able to maintain a balance. Far from Ellis's imagined ideal of a cultural mulatto, however, Monk does not live in a liminal or in-between space; his performances are both geographically and physically distinct. Monk reflects, in a splintered recognition, "So, I had managed to take myself, the writer, reconfigure myself, then disintegrate myself, leaving two bodies of work, two bodies, no boundaries yet walls everywhere" (257). Ultimately, Monk's performance of Stagg takes over his "real personality" (365), the one posited at the beginning of the novel as hybrid and potentially transgressive. In the place of the multifaceted writer/son/lover/scholar, Monk becomes a monolithic stereotype. He is last seen claiming authorship of *Fuck,* although the audience does not understand. He steps forward to claim the award, but the committee and the general audience assume that he is delivering a message for Stagg, without understanding that he *is* Stagg. He morphs, finally, into Van Go Jenkins, the character of his parody, signifying on Van Go's final line of *Fuck* by saying, "Egads, I'm on television" (265). Monk has been lost, the damage of his satire has been done, and any hope of exposing or critiquing the expectations placed upon him as a black writer has been replaced by his total absorption into the performance of Stagg and, finally, Van Go.

In *Bamboozled,* Pierre also begins passing as stereotypically black, collecting black artifacts and embracing his position as a black man in the eyes of those around him. What begins as a gift of warning—a "jolly nigger bank" from his assistant Sloane—inspires an obsessive collection of racist artifacts. As with the television show, no one knows quite how to take these artifacts at first. Pierre himself seems both drawn to and repulsed by them. Pierre ends the film, in blackface, surrounded by the derogatory artifacts, watching in terror as extremist black protestors kidnap Mantan. This dysfunctional militant group, whose members see Pierre as an "Uncle Tom" even while the majority of America celebrates his creation, eventually execute Mantan in front of a live television audience. Sloane, always mindful of and resistant to the impact of Pierre's creation, shoots and kills Pierre just as the protestors are killed by the police. The mass violence, all enacted against blacks, serves as a scathing indictment on the power of the media and responsibility of both producers and consumers of black art—and blackness.

In their performance of a stereotyped blackness, Monk and Pierre move out of identities built from their lived experiences to pass as something that is a product of the U.S. racial system. However, they both produce and are consumed by that system—a process exaggerated in their satiric artistic productions. Monk's performance of Stagg R. Leigh becomes his primary performative identity, while Pierre begins to blacken his face in the tradition of minstrel actors. The men who were once accused of passing as culturally white have now passed into stereotypical blackness at a huge cost. Both performances of "blackness" are determined and supported by whites. Pierre is last seen in blackface while Monk is last seen costumed as Stagg—both images reifying negative constructions of blackness. The racial dynamics affect not only these two men who seem to be consumed by their own performances, but also empower whites. By disallowing Monk and Pierre access to the space of cultural "whiteness," by interpellating them as "niggers" who should write about their black pain, whiteness is reproduced as an elite space into which a black man—or even a cultural mulatto—cannot enter.

In a review of *Bamboozled* included in a symposium on the work published in *Cineaste* film journal, Greg Tate asks whether it is "possible to perform blackness and not be coonin' " (16). For Pierre, who shapes and markets *Mantan,* and for Monk, who creates Van Go *and* Stagg R. Leigh, the answer is no. To perform blackness is to give in to a cultural (white) imagining of blackness, which demeans and underestimates an entire race on the basis of a narrowly performed role: anything else is "acting white." All elements of parody and subversion are lost on the white (and sometimes black) audiences who "blacken up"—either literally as in *Bamboozled* or figuratively as in *Erasure*—as they consume the black performance without realizing that it is, in fact, a performance. Thus, in both texts, the white establishment urges the cultural mulatto out of the "third race" into a (caricatured) performance of blackness. White viewers and fans of *Mantan* revitalize the once demeaning act of wearing blackface without revising its significance. More subtly, white reviewers of *My Pafology* awkwardly effect ghetto-blackness by saying "it's a black thang" without interrogating the essentialism of the mere existence of "a black thang" or questioning their own access to that racial performance (260). The blackness that Stagg and post-*Mantan* Pierre enact makes whites far more comfortable than the supposed whiteness that Monk and pre-*Mantan*

Pierre enacted. To be read as black, these works show, is to be expected to "shuck and jive." Other roles aligned with the property of whiteness—writer of experimental novels, appreciator of opera, woodworker, fisherman, or Harvard alumnus—make audiences assume that the cultural mulatto acts out of imitation rather than from a space of authenticity. The audience remains in the dark, missing the "furious" signs coming from Pierre and Monk—misidentifying themselves in the mirror of the satire.

The Failure of the Cultural Mulatto

Postcolonial theorists have attempted to challenge the Marxist assertions of early cultural studies theorists, hoping to answer affirmatively Gayatri Spivak's question: "Can the Subaltern Speak?" by envisioning a space that crosses borders and whose inhabitants point to the performative construction of the seemingly natural—in this case, racial identity. Trey Ellis, on the brink of what he envisioned as a renaissance in black art which could embrace what Greg Tate calls a "post-liberated aesthetic," joined the ranks of postcolonial thinkers to empower those inhabiting the liminal space in an effort to disrupt the socially constructed dichotomy of race in American culture (Ellis, "The New Black" 190). With "optimism and desire" that Eric Lott said "burst so infectiously from [the] essay," Ellis imagines an unprecedented agency for the cultural mulatto (Lott, "Response" 244). In response to Spivak, Ellis answers "yes," and promises that the speaking subaltern are varied in their voices.[21] However, other texts—such as *Bamboozled* and *Erasure*—both reflective and productive of the culture, suggest that if the subaltern speak, it is with borrowed voices.

Writing at the cusp of the multiracial movement, Ellis envisions the New Black Aesthetic as a hopeful new generation freed entirely from the debate over the responsibility of the "Negro Artist" that harkens back at least to the Harlem Renaissance.[22] For Ellis, the cultural mulatto offers a freedom from racial expectations that have long limited the artistic expressions of those that society calls "Negro" or "Black" or "African American." Tied for generations to a need to prove one's humanity *and* change one's conditions, Ellis imagines a new day in which New Black Aesthetic artists, through their "unshakable belief that our youthful black power can perfect society and perfect the soul" do, in fact, change the world—one novel or film or album at a time. Ellis's dream is that the masses who find themselves in the position of neither/nor "go out and create (their) own" world rather than being torn between the two. This hybrid movement reveals to Ellis glimpses of the potency and agency of black art that could blossom into "one of the most fertile periods black culture has ever known" (202).

What Ellis sees as expansive freedom without the political pressures of the past, however, some critics read with less enthusiasm. In *Black Intellectuals,* William M. Banks worried that the artists Ellis identified have no "common theme or set of artistic values" (219). Eric Lott points to the absence of politics in the movement and the classism of Ellis's definitions of the NBA artists ("Response" 244). Ultimately, Lott calls Ellis naive in his portrayal of a new movement, worrying that "what finally undercuts the optimism of Ellis's essay is the gap between the hope for such institutions [which will offer support to black artists] and their actual paucity" ("Response" 246). Ellis, who was further attacked for his sexism (Tera Hunter) as well as his classism (J. Martin Favor), offers a rebuttal by reiterating his belief in the transgressive space of the cultural mulatto through what he calls an "anti-aesthetic."[23] He clarifies his vision for the movement:

> It is important to remember that the New Black Aesthetic I try to define is really an anti-aesthetic that defies definition. The NBA is an attitude of liberalism rather than a restrictive code. . . . I was trying to argue that today we can be more honest and critical of ourselves than ever before, and this open-minded far-sightedness may very well produce some of the greatest works of art the world has ever known. (251)

Ellis maintains his idealism about freedom from limits and the ability to "navigate" in both black and white worlds. Despite its optimism, the New Black Aesthetic fails to address the sociopolitical and economic function of racial boundaries and the "predominantly white-crafted myth of absolute racial difference" required to maintain white privilege in America (Hale 30).

Lee and Everett are much less optimistic than Ellis in their explorations of what life as a cultural mulatto is like. In *Bamboozled* and *Erasure,* the fictional cultural mulattoes fail to sustain "thriving hybrid[ity]" when the intersection of text and consumer grants agency to the consumer to make meaning—and that meaning is born of a climate in which (re)production through performance is taken as reality and race is still inscribed on the body. Indeed, *because* the texts try to move race outside of the body—because they begin from the space of a third race—they risk failing to destabilize race and racial categories: because the audience still "sees" a black body, Pierre's and Monk's performances of whiteness translate into mere masquerade, "playing the races," or even blackface, overt performances, which historically have been used to reify rather than dismantle race (a danger that both texts specifically engage through the failed satires of their embedded texts). In *Playing Indian,* Philip Deloria asserts that when whites "play" Indian, whether white protesters at the Boston Tea Party or mascots at a sporting event, they are allowed brief access to another race without losing the privilege of their own racial identity. This sort of playing is not meant to convince anyone, but rather to allow a safe, because controlled, entry into another perspective. When playing a race, as is the case with blackface, convincing and realistic costuming or behavior is not essential. Instead, there is the sense that one is only stepping into this world in order to be able to step back into his or her own "real" world. If audiences see Lee's and Everett's protagonists' occupation of whiteness as such masquerade, and, complementarily, their latter occupation of blackness as real (if admittedly caricatured)—rather than recognizing the texts' quite complicated postmodern critique of the racial system in the United States—then both texts ultimately reify the very system they seem to be critiquing (the much-examined paradox of the passing narrative itself). More generously, perhaps that (potential) failure is yet another layer of the texts' metanarrative critique: we are blind to our own blindness.

Notes

1. Trey Ellis began "The New Black Aesthetic" as a midterm paper at Stanford, which he expanded when *New York Times Magazine* approached him to write a "hip and young and cutting edge" piece (xii). For this assignment, Ellis traveled across the United States interviewing young black artists such as Fishbone, Spike Lee, Living Colour, Chris Rock, and the Hudlin Brothers, who were then all unknown artists who would go on to reach celebrity. Nearly two decades later, Ellis's assessment of his generation stands as a poignant and controversial snapshot of a transitional moment in black artistic representation and expression.

2. My term *third race* signifies on Homi Bhabha's "Third Space," a concept that suggests a productive blending that challenges a homogenous understanding of culture or race.

3. For Gilroy, it is the fluidity of transnational identity that allows for what Appadurai describes as "imagined worlds" created by globalization, which can "contest and sometimes even subvert" the dichotomies that call for a border in the first place (222). Anzaldúa and Haraway relish the spaces between as

reproductive sites ripe for "recoupling" the once contentiously separated sides of a dichotomy—Mexico/America or Machine/Organism. For more on these ideas, see Gilroy, *The Black Atlantic* (1994), Appadurai, "Disjuncture and Difference in the Global Cultural Economy" (1986), Anzaldúa, *Borderlands/La Frontera* (1987), Bhabha, *The Location of Culture* (1994), and Haraway, "The Cyborg Manifesto" (1991).

4. Similarly, Ellis's "New Black Aesthetic" is itself a historically loaded term. The term signifies on both the conversations around the New Negro in the 1920s and the Black Aesthetic in the late 1960s, thus positioning contemporary works within a larger aesthetic and political dialogue. However, unlike the debate that unfolded in the pages of *The Nation* around the promise of the New Negro and unlike the reactive New Black Aesthetic movement of the next generation, Ellis's manifesto is unique in its promise to *subvert* racial categories. Rather than creating finite definitions of blackness—which in both the New Negro and the Black Arts models were established in opposition to whiteness—Ellis imagines blackness as infinite. Ellis hopes that these New Black Aesthetic artists, diverging from the two earlier movements, will be free to create art without the pressure of politics or the boundaries of race.

5. For more about the history of mulattoes in the United States, see Werner Sollors's *Neither Black Nor White, Yet Both*; Stephan Talty's *Mulatto America: At the Crossroads of Black and White Culture: A Social History*; and Elise Lemire's *"Miscegenation": Making Race in America*.

6. See Sollors, 247–83, for an extended discussion of the term.

7. Many passing narratives (although certainly not all), such as Nella Larsen's *Passing* (1929) and Jessie Redmon Fauset's *Plum Bun* (1928) to name just two, emphasize this necessary disconnect from blackness associated with passing as white.

8. Although outside the scope of this discussion, the ongoing debates surrounding white Hip Hop artists such as Eminem, who has been and is regularly accused of "acting black," or African American students who excel in academics who are accused of "acting white" neatly illustrate the United States' cultural obsession with maintaining racial identities through performance or possession of cultural (racial) "property."

9. Another similar text is Paul Beatty's *White Boy Shuffle* (1996), which offers an absurdist satirical look at a cultural mulatto in the character of Gunnar Kaufman. Beatty demonstrates the binaric black/white worlds of Los Angeles, caricaturing both. Kaufman, like the fictional cultural mulattos discussed here, finds himself limited by outside definitions and expectations and eventually commits suicide.

10. The raw "honesty" that is assumed of Ellison's parody evokes questions of both the role of art and the responsibility of a viewer. Reviewers express that *Fuck* is simultaneously horrific and true, and celebrate it as cultural outsiders whose positions of privilege are maintained through the "real" story they applaud.

11. Percival Everett himself has been pressured to be a more authentically black writer. Even in an attempt to work outside of that racial boundary, reviewer David McGoy first acknowledges Everett's race in his comment that publishers selected for the book's cover: "This is not a good book by a Black writer, nor is it a Black book by a good writer; it is a remarkable work of fiction that transcends labels." Even if it transcends labels, McGoy first draws attention to those labels.

12. Spike Lee, like the characters that he writes in his film, is largely bound by the label of race. That he owns his production company and is well established both serves Lee and types him—many consider Lee *the* figurehead of black filmmaking. Criticism of Lee centers on his treatment of race even though many of his films (*Summer of Sam, 25*th *Hour*) are not primarily "race films." Lee is alternately "a mediator between the African-American community and the white establishment" (Pouzoulet 32) and "the quintessential buppie" (Baraka, "Spike Lee" 146) whose " 'crafty' houseslave, is [the only black character] *dignified*" in his films (145). In *Bamboozled,* Lee addresses issues of racial performance and expectations of blackness like those that he has confronted in his own career.

13. That both texts are satires may further empower the texts' ability to reflect on the cultural conditions that real people must negotiate. For the effectiveness of satire in cultural critiques, see Stephen E. Kercher's *Revel with a Cause: Liberal Satire in Postwar America*; Jonathan Gray, Jeffrey Jones, and Ethan Thompson's *Satire TV: Politics and Comedy in the Post-Network Era*; and Steven Weisenburger's *Fables of Subversion: Satire and the American Novel, 1930–1980.*

14. In her dissertation "Buggy Jiving: Comic Strategies of the Black Avant Garde" (2010), Danielle Heard argues that comedy, in the second half of the twentieth century, was a sort of activism. In her final chapter on Lee and Everett, she points to the possibilities and limitations of contemporary comedic positioning in satire.

15. For discussion on blackface and minstrel shows, see Lott's *Love and Theft.*

16. See also Cripps, and Leab.

17. Stagg R. Leigh refers to the figure of Stagger Lee or Stagolee, whose mythic status as a black man unafraid of standing up to the white man is based upon an 1895 murder in which Lee, a cab driver and pimp, killed William Lyons over a Stetson hat. Mississippi John Hurt popularized the ballad in 1928, though it has been revised throughout music history. See Cecil Brown's *Stagolee Shot Billy.*

18. I use the word *satire* here, although *parody*—as a form of "satirical mimicry"—might be a more appropriate term. Certainly, *Fuck* is a parody of *Native Son,* while *Mantan* signifies accordingly on a composite of minstrel shows of the late nineteenth and early twentieth centuries. I settle upon "satire" primarily because Spike Lee begins *Bamboozled* by defining satire, which suffices in this essay as the broader category.

19. Importantly, Everett signifies not only on Richard Wright, but also on Barthes's *S/Z.* Within the novel, Monk writes a conference paper that responds to *S/Z* and causes a riot. Everett is from both traditions and playfully rewrites both within the text of *Erasure.*

20. D. W. Griffith's film, *The Birth of a Nation* (1915), was shown to Wilson in a private screening at the White House. Upon completing the 187-minute film based upon Thomas Dixon's novel *The Clansman,* which chronicles the Reconstruction South through damning representations of blackness, Wilson is quoted as saying, "It is like writing history with lightning. And my only regret is that it is all so terribly true." For a discussion (and list of sources) of the black response to the film, see Wright.

21. Ellis's own novel, *Platitudes* (1988), not surprisingly, explores a fictional embodiment of cultural mulattoism. Ellis creates a metanovel with a character, Earl, who challenges the stereotypes of blackness but struggles to navigate black and white worlds. The figure of Dorothy offers an example of a satisfied cultural mulatto, and the union of Earl and Dorothy (mirrored by the characters of the story's frame) offers the promise of a productive merging of black and white culture.

22. In his 1925 essay, "The New Negro," Alain Locke is invigorated to see new voices bursting forth from his "New Negro" which he locates "between defiance and appeal, midway almost between cynicism and hope" (990–91). The following year, George Schuyler challenged Locke's perception of Negros and their art in "The Negro-Art Hokum," published in *Nation* in June 1926, arguing that there is no artistic movement among Negros, whom he calls "lampblacked Anglo-Saxon" (1222). Langston Hughes rebuts Schuyler's denial of racialized art in "The Negro Artist and the Racial Mountain," equating the desire to ignore race in the name of art with "the race toward whiteness, the desire to pour racial individuality into the mold of American standardization, and to be as little Negro and as much American as possible" (1311).

23. In her piece entitled "'It's a Man's Man's Man's World': Specters of the Old Re-Newed in Afro-American Culture and Criticism," Tera Hunter takes issue with Ellis's choices to highlight mostly male and often antifemale black artists. J. Martin Favor, in "'Ain't Nothin' Like the Real Thing Baby': Trey Ellis's Search for New Black Voices," argues that "Ellis's NBA is a class-conscious manifesto concerned with the repositioning of certain types of epistemological power" (704).

Works Cited

Adorno, Theodor, and Max Horkheimer. "The Culture Industry: Enlightenment as Mass Deception." In During 31–41. Print.

Althusser, Louis. "Ideology and Ideological State Apparatuses (Notes towards an Investigation)." *Lenin and Philosophy and Other Essays.* New York: Monthly Review, 2001. 127–86. Print.

Anzaldúa, Gloria. "Borderlands/La Frontera." *Literary Theory: An Anthology.* Ed. Julie Rivkin and Michael Ryan. Malden, MA: Blackwell, 1998. 887–902. Print.

Appadurai, Arjun. "Disjuncture and Difference in the Global Cultural Economy." In During 223–32. Print.

Banks, William. *Black Intellectuals.* New York: Norton, 1996. Print.

Baraka, Amiri. "Spike Lee at the Movies." *Black American Cinema.* Ed. Manthia Diawara. New York: Routledge, 1993. 145–53. Print.

Barthes, Roland. *The Barthes Reader.* New York: Hill and Wang, 1982. Print.

———. *S/Z.* New York: Farrar, 1974. Print.

Beatty, Paul. *White Boy Shuffle.* New York: Houghton Mifflin, 1996. Print.

Bhabha, Homi K. "The Postcolonial and the Postmodern: The Question of Agency." In During 189–208. Print.

———. *The Location of Culture.* New York: Routledge, 1994. Print.

Bogle, Donald. *Toms, Coons, Mammies, Mulattoes and Bucks: An Interpretive History of Blacks in American Film.* New York: Continuum, 1991. Print.

Brown, Cecil. *Stagolee Shot Billy.* Cambridge: Harvard UP, 2003. Print.

Butler, Judith. *Gender Trouble.* New York: Routledge, 1990. Print.

Cripps, Thomas. *Slow Fade to Black: The Negro in American Films.* New York: Oxford UP, 1993. Print.

Crowdus, Gary, and Dan Georgakas. "Thinking About the Power of Images: An Interview with Spike Lee." *Cineaste* 26.2 (2001): 4–9. Print.

Cutter, Martha J. "Passing as Narrative and Textual Strategy in Charles Chesnutt's 'The Passing of Grandison.'" In Wright and Glass 39–50. Print.

Deloria, Philip. *Playing Indian.* New Haven: Yale UP, 1999. Print.

Dixon, Thomas. *The Clansman.* 1905. Lexington: U of Kentucky P, 1970. Print.

During, Simon, ed. *Cultural Studies: A Reader.* London: Routledge, 1993. Print.

Ellis, Trey. "The New Black Aesthetic." *Callaloo* 12.1 (1989): 185–203. Print.

———. *Platitudes.* 1988. Lebanon, NH: Northeastern UP, 2003. Print.

Ellison, Ralph. *Shadow and Act.* New York: Vintage, 1953. Print.

Everett, Percival. *Erasure.* New York: Hyperion, 2001. Print.

———. "Signing to the Blind." *Callaloo* 14.1 (1991): 9–11. Print.

Favor, J. Martin. "'Ain't Nothin' Like the Real Thing, Baby': Trey Ellis' Search for New Black Voices." *Callaloo* 16.3 (1993): 694–705. Print.

Gates, Henry Louis Jr., and Nellie Y. McKay, eds. *Norton Anthology of African American Literature.* New York: W. W. Norton, 2004. Print.

Gilroy, Paul. *The Black Atlantic: Modernity and Double Consciousness.* Cambridge: Harvard UP, 1993. Print.

Gray, Jonathan, Jeffrey P. Jones, and Ethan Thompson. *Satire TV: Politics and Comedy in the Post-Network Era.* New York: New York UP, 2009. Print.

Hale, Grace Elizabeth. *Making Whiteness: The Culture of Segregation in the South, 1890–1940.* New York: Vintage, 1998. Print.

Haraway, Donna. "A Cyborg Manifesto: Science, Technology, and Socialist Feminism in the Late Twentieth Century." *Simians, Cyborgs, and Women: The Reinvention of Nature.* New York: Routledge, 1991. 149–81. Print.

Heard, Danielle Christine. "Buggy Jiving Comic Strategies of the Black Avant-Garde." Diss. Cornell U., 2010.

Hughes, Langston. "The Negro Artist and the Racial Mountain." In Gates and McKay 1311–14. Print.

Hunter, Tera. " 'It's a Man's Man's Man's World': Specters of the Old Re-Newed in Afro-American Culture and Criticism." *Callaloo* 38 (1989): 247–49. Print.

Kercher, Stephen E. *Revel with a Cause: Liberal Satire in Postwar America*. Chicago: U of Chicago P, 2006. Print.

Leab, D. J. *From Sambo to Superspade: The Black Experience in Motion Pictures*. Boston: Houghton Mifflin, 1975. Print.

Lee, Spike, dir. *Bamboozled*. 2000. Forty Acres and a Mule Filmworks.

Lemire, Elise. *"Miscegenation": Making Race in America*. Philadelphia: U of Pennsylvania P, 2002. Print.

Lipsitz, George. "The Possessive Investment in Whiteness: Racialized Social Democracy and the White Problem in American Studies." *American Quarterly* 47 (Sept.1995): 369–87. Print.

Locke, Alain. "The New Negro." In Gates and McKay 984–92. Print.

Lott, Eric. *Love and Theft: Blackface Minstrelsy and the American Working Class*. New York: Oxford UP, 1995. Print.

———. "Response to Trey Ellis's 'The New Black Aesthetic.'" *Callaloo* 12.1 (1989): 244–46. Print.

Lucia, Cynthia. "Race, Media, and Money: A Critical Symposium on Spike Lee's *Bamboozled*." *Cineaste* 26.2 (2001): 10–17. Print.

Pouzoulet, Catherine. "The Cinema of Spike Lee: Images of a Mosaic City." *Spike Lee's* Do the Right Thing. Ed. Mark A. Reid. New York: Cambridge UP, 1997. 31–49. Print.

Roth, Philip. *The Human Stain*. Boston and New York: Houghton Mifflin, 2000. Print.

Russet, Margaret. "Race Under *Erasure*." *Callaloo* 28.2 (2005): 358–68. Print.

Schuyler, George. "Negro Art-Hokum." In Gates and McKay 1221–23. Print.

Sollors, Werner. *Neither Black Nor White Yet Both: Thematic Explorations of Interracial Literature*. New York: Oxford UP, 1997. Print.

Spivak, Gayatri Chakravorty. "Can the Subaltern Speak?" *Marxism and the Interpretation of Culture*. Ed. Cary Nelson and Lawrence Grossberg. London: Macmillan, 1988. 271–313. Print.

Swift, Jonathan. *The Battle of the Books*. Lenox, MA: Hard Press, 2006. Print.

Talty, Stephan. *Mulatto America: At the Crossroads of Black and White Culture*. New York: Harper, 2003. Print.

Weisenburger, Steven. *Fables of Subversion: Satire and the American Novel, 1930–1980*. Athens: U of Georgia P, 1995. Print.

Wright, Richard. "Blueprint for Negro Writing." In Gates and McKay 1380–88. Print.

———. *Native Son*. 1940. New York: Perennial, 1987. Print.

Wright, Susan Prothro. "In the Wake of D. W. Griffith's *The Birth of a Nation* Chesnutt's *Paul Marchand, F.M.C.* as Command Performance." In Wright and Glass 67–83. Print.

———, and Ernestine Pickens Glass, eds. *Passing in the Works of Charles W. Chesnutt*. Jackson: U of Mississippi P, 2010. Print.

Bibliography

"2010 Census Shows America's Diversity." *U.S. Census 2010 News Releases*. U.S. Census Bureau. 24 Mar. 2011. Web. 12 June 2012.

Abbott, Stacey. *Angel*. Detroit: Wayne State UP, 2009. Print.

Abrams, Joseph. "Black Like Whom? Obama vs. the Leaders." Web. 16 Jan. 2008. *National Review Online*. 12 Oct. 2008.

"Absalom." *Without a Trace*. CBS. WJZ. Baltimore. 15 Nov. 2007.

Adorno, Theodor, and Max Horkheimer. "The Culture Industry: Enlightenment as Mass Deception." In During 31–41. Print.

"An African American History Month Special: A Look at 'The Wind Done Gone,' a Parody of 'Gone With the Wind' Told From a Slave's Perspective. 21 Feb 2002. Web. 22 Dec. 2008.

"African American Lives 2: Bliss Broyard." *African American Lives 2 With Dr. Henry Louis Gates, Jr.* PBS. New York. 6 Feb. 2008.

Airplane. Dirs. Jim Abrahams, David Zucker, and Jerry Zucker. Paramount, 1980.

Ali G Indahouse. Dir. Mark Mylod. Universal Pictures, 2002.

Ali G in da USAiii. HBO, USA. 21 Feb. 2003-22 Aug. 2004.

Ali G, Innit. Channel Four, UK, 1999.

Ali G Show, Da. Channel Four, UK. 30 Mar. 2000-5 May 2000.

Allen, Sarah A. "The Test of Manhood, A Christmas Story." *Colored American Magazine*. Dec. 1906. Print.

Allen, Theodore W. *The Invention of the White Race: The Origin of Racial Oppression in Anglo-America*. New York: Verso, 1997. Print.

Althusser, Louis. "Ideology and Ideological State Apparatuses (Notes towards an Investigation)." *Lenin and Philosophy and Other Essays*. New York: Monthly Review, 2001. 127–86. Print.

"AMEA's History." *AMEA: Association of Multiethnic Americans*. Web. 18 June 2012.

"Angel." *IMDb*. IMDb.com, Inc. n.d. Web. 10 Aug. 2011.

Antler, Joyce. *The Journey Home: Jewish Women and the American Century*. New York: Free Press, 1997. Print.

Anzaldúa, Gloria. "Borderlands/La Frontera." *Literary Theory: An Anthology*. Ed. Julie Rivkin and Michael Ryan. Malden, MA: Blackwell, 1998. 887–902. Print.

———. *Borderlands/La Frontera: The New Mestiza*. 1987. San Francisco: Aunt Lute Books, 1999. Print.

Appadurai, Arjun. "Disjuncture and Difference in the Global Cultural Economy." *Cultural Studies: A Reader*. In During 223–32. Print.

Appiah, K. Anthony, and Amy Gutman. *Color Conscious: The Political Morality of Race*. Princeton: Princeton UP, 1996. Print.

"Are You Now or Have You Ever Been?" *Angel*. Warner Brothers Network. 3 Oct. 2000.

Argall, Nicole. "A Rib from my Chest: Cynara's Journey as an Africana Womanist." *CLA Journal* 47.2 (2003): 231–43. Print.

Babb, Valerie. *Whiteness Visible: The Meaning of Whiteness in American Literature and Culture*. New York: New York UP, 1998. Print.

Bagdikian, Ben. H. et al. "Letter of Support." 10 April 2001. Web. 19 Dec. 2008.

Balshaw, Maria. " 'Black Was White': Urbanity, Passing, and the Spectacle of Harlem." *Journal of American Studies* 33 (1999): 307–22. Print.

Bamboozled. Dir. Spike Lee. Forty Acres and a Mule Filmworks, 2000.

Band of Angels. Dir. Raoul Walsh. 1957. DVD. Warner Home Studios, 2007.

Banks, William. *Black Intellectuals*. New York: Norton, 1996. Print.

Baraka, Amiri. "Spike Lee at the Movies." *Black American Cinema*. Ed. Manthia Diawara. New York: Routledge, 1993. 145–53. Print.

Barrington, Judith. *Writing the Memoir: From Truth to Art*. Portland, OR: The Eight Mountain Press, 2002. Print.

Barthes, Roland. *The Barthes Reader*. New York: Hill and Wang, 1982. Print.

———. *S/Z*. New York: Farrar, 1974. Print.

Bartholomew, Anne. Promotional comment on *Rhett Butler's People*. 9 Jan. 2009. Web.

Baschirotto, Corinna. " 'I want to be the rule itself, not the exception that proves it' *The Wind Done Gone*: Rewriting *Gone With the Wind*." *The 49th Parallel: An Interdisciplinary Journal of North American Studies* 14 (2004): np. Print.

Bauman, Zygmunt. *Postmodern Ethics*. Oxford: Blackwell, 1993. Print.

Beatty, Paul. *White Boy Shuffle*. New York: Houghton Mifflin, 1996. Print.

Beck, Evelyn Torton. "From 'Kike' to 'JAP': How Misogyny, Anti-Semitism, and Racism Construct the 'Jewish American Princess.' " *Race, Class, and Gender*. Ed. Margaret Anderson and Patricia Hill Collins. New York: Wadsworth, 1998. 430–36. Print.

Beck, Joseph M. "Copyright and the First Amendment after *The Wind Done Gone*." *Vanderbilt Journal of Entertainment Law and Practice* 5.2 (2003): 1–10. Print.

Beck, Warren, and Myles Clowers. *Understanding American History Through Fiction*. New York: McGraw-Hill, 1975. Print.

Bell, Kevin. *Ashes Taken For Fire: Aesthetic Modernism and The Critique of Identity*. Minneapolis: U of Minnesota P, 2007. Print.

Bellafante, Gina. "*Black.White.*: Reality TV for Those Infatuated with Passing." *New York Times*. 8 March 2006: E8. Print.

Belluscio, Steven J. *To Be Suddenly White: Literary Realism and Racial Passing*. St. Louis: U of Missouri P, 2006. Print.

Bennett, Juda. *The Passing Figure: Racial Confusion in Modern American Literature*. New York: Peter Lang, 1996. Print.

———. "Toni Morrison and the Burden of the Passing Narrative." *African American Review* 35 (2001): 205–17. Print.

Benston, Kimberly. "I Yam What I Am: The Topos of Un(naming) in Afro-American literature." *Black Literature and Literary Theory*. Ed. Henry Louis Gates Jr. New York: Methuen, 1984. 151–72. Print.

Berger, Maurice. *White Lies: Race and the Myths of Whiteness*. New York: Farrar, Straus, Giroux, 1999. Print.

Berzon, Judith R. *Neither White Nor Black: The Mulatto Character in American Fiction*. New York: New York UP, 1978. Print.

Bhabha, Homi K. *The Location of Culture*. New York: Routledge, 1994. Print.

———. "Of Mimicry and Man." *The Location of Culture*. New York: Routledge, 1994. 85–92. Print.

———. "The Postcolonial and the Postmodern: The Question of Agency." In During 189–208. Print.

Biale, David. "The Melting Pot and Beyond: Jews and the Politics of American Identity." *Insider/Outsider: American Jews and Multiculturalism*. Ed. David Biale, Michael Galchinsky, and Susan Heschel. Berkeley: U of California P, 1998. 17–33. Print.

Black Girl. Dir. Ousmane Sembene. 1966. New Yorker Films, 2006.

Black.White. Dir. R. J. Cutler. fX Networks, 2006.

Bland, Sterling Lecater Jr. *Voices of the Fugitives: Runaway Slave Stories and their Fictions of Self-Creation*. Westport: Greenwood, 2000. Print.

"Blood." *Law & Order*. NBC. LEX18. Lexington, KY. 19 Nov. 1997.

Bogle, Donald. *Toms, Coons, Mammies, Mulattoes, and Bucks: An Interpretive History of Blacks in American Film*. New York: Continuum, 1991. Print.

Bone, Robert. *The Negro Novel in America*. 1958. Rev. ed. New Haven: Yale UP, 1970. Print.

Border Fence Environmental Planning. U.S. Army Corps of Engineers/U.S. Customs and Border Protection. Web. 28 June 2009.

Bowman, Elizabeth Atkins. *Dark Secret*. New York: Forge, 2000. Print.

Boyle, James. *The Public Domain: Enclosing the Commons of the Mind*. New Haven: Yale UP, 2010. Print.

Branigan, Edward. "The Articulation of Color in a Filmic System: Deux ou trois choses que je sais d'elle." *Color: The Film Reader*. Ed. Angela Dalle Vacche and Brian Price. New York: Routledge, 2006. 170–82. Print.

Brodie, John. "Diesel Power: Vin Diesel Muscles His Way to Stardom." *Gentlemen's Quarterly*. Aug. 2002. 109–13, 179. Print.

Brodkin, Karen. *How Jews Became White Folks*. New Brunswick: Rutgers UP, 1998. Print.

Browder, Laura. *Slippery Characters: Ethnic Impersonators and American Identities.* Chapel Hill: U of North Carolina P, 2000. Print.

Brown, Cecil. *Stagolee Shot Billy.* Cambridge: Harvard UP, 2003. Print.

Brown, John Gregory. *Decorations in a Ruined Cemetery.* 1994. New York: Mariner Books, 2001. Print.

Brown, Nancy G., and Ramona E. Douglass. "Making the Invisible Visible: The Growth of Community Network Organizations." *The Multiracial Experience: Racial Borders as the New Frontier.* Thousand Oaks, CA: Sage, 1996. Print.

Brown, Wesley. *Darktown Strutters.* Amherst: U of Massachusetts P, 1994. Print.

Brown, William Wells. *Clotel; or, the President's Daughter.* 1853. *Three Classic African American Novels.* Ed. Henry Louis Gates Jr. Vintage Classics. New York: Random House, 1990. 3–224. Print.

Broyard, Anatole. "Portrait of the Inauthentic Negro." *Commentary* (July 1950): 56–64. Print.

Broyard, Bliss. *One Drop: My Father's Hidden Life—A Story of Race and Family Secrets.* New York: Little Brown, 2007. Print.

Brüno. Dir. Larry Charles. Universal Pictures, 2009.

Bunn, Austin. "Walker, in Her Own Shoes." *The Advocate.* 27 Feb. 2001: 65. Print.

Bush Mama. Dir. Haile Gerima. 1976. DVD. Mypheduh Films, Inc., 2009.

Butler, Judith. *Gender Trouble.* New York: Routledge, 1990. Print.

———. "Imitation and Gender Insubordination." *Inside/Out: Lesbian Theories, Gay Theories.* Ed. Diana Fuss. New York: Routledge, 1991. 13–31. Print.

Catonese, Brandi Wilkins. *The Problem of the Color[blind]: Racial Transgression and the Politics of Black Performance.* Ann Arbor: U of Michigan P, 2011. Print.

Caughie, Pamela L. *Passing and Pedagogy: The Dynamics of Responsibility.* Urbana: U of Illinois P, 1999. Print.

———. "Passing as Modernism." *Modernism/Modernity* 12.3 (2005): 385–406. Print.

Chameleon Street. Dir. Wendell B. Harris. Gethsemane 84, Inc./ Prismatic Images, Inc., 1989.

Chesnutt, Charles W. "The Future American: What the Race is Likely to Become in the Process of Time." *MELUS* 15.3 (1988): 95–107. Web. 23 March 2011.

———. *The House Behind the Cedars.* 1900. New York: Penguin, 1993. Print.

———. *Mandy Oxendine.* Foreword Williams L. Andrews. Intro. Charles Hackenberry. Urbana and Chicago: U of Illinois P, 1997. Print.

———. *Paul Marchand, F.M.C.* Intro. Matthew Wilson. Jackson: UP of Mississippi, 1998. Print.

———. *The Quarry.* Intro. Dean McWilliams. Princeton: Princeton UP, 1999. Print.

Cheung, King-Kok. "(Mis)Interpretations and (In)justice: The 1992 Los Angeles 'Riots' and the 'Black-Korean Conflict.'" *MELUS* 30.3 (Fall 2005): 3–40. Print.

Chin, Daryl. "Multiculturalism and Its Masks: The Art of Identity Politics." *Performing Arts Journal* 14.1 (1992): 1–15. Print.

Christian, Barbara. *Black Women Novelists*. Westport, CT: Greenwood, 1980. Print.

"Civil Rights Act of 1990." *Govtrack.us*. 22 June 2012. Web.

"Civil Rights Act of 1991." *EEOC 35th Anniversary*. 22 June 2012. Web.

Cooper, J. California. *Family*. New York: Anchor Books, 1991. Print.

Cooper, James Fenimore. *The Last of the Mohicans*. 1826. Ed. and Intro. Paul C. Gutjahr. Ontario: Broadview, 2009. Print.

Couch, Greg. "Woods: I'm More than Black." *Chicago Sun Times*. 22 April 1997, late sports final ed.: News 1. *Lexis-Nexis*. Web. 2 Dec. 2004.

Crafts, Hannah. *The Bondswoman's Narrative*. ca. 1857. Ed. Henry Louis Gates Jr. New York: Warner Books, 2002. Print.

Crenshaw, Kimberlé. "Demarginalizing the Intersection of Race and Sex: A Black Feminist Critique of Antidiscrimination Doctrine, Feminist Theory, and Antiracist Politics." *University of Chicago Legal Forum* 139 (1989): 139–67. Print.

Crews, Chip. "More Than Skin Deep: FX's *Black.White*." *The Washington Post*. 8 March 2006: C08. Print.

Cripps, Thomas. *Slow Fade to Black: The Negro in American Films*. New York: Oxford UP, 1993. Print.

Crowdus, Gary, and Dan Georgakas. "Thinking About the Power of Images: An Interview with Spike Lee." *Cineaste* 26.2 (2001): 4–9. Print.

Cutter, Martha J. "Passing as Narrative and Textual Strategy in Charles Chesnutt's 'The Passing of Grandison.'" In Wright and Glass 39–50. Print.

———. "Sliding Significations: Passing as a Narrative and Textual Strategy in Nella Larsen's Fiction." In Ginsberg 75–100. Print.

DaCosta, Kimberly McClain. *Making Multiracials: State, Family, and Market in the Redrawing of the Color Line*. Stanford: Stanford UP, 2007. Print.

Dalmage, Heather. *The Politics of Multiracialism: Challenging Racial Thinking*. Albany: State U of New York P, 2004. Print.

Daniel, G. Reginald. *More Than Black? Multiracial Identity and New Racial Order*. Philadelphia: Temple UP, 2001. Print.

Darder, Antonia. "The Politics of Biculturalism: Culture and Difference in the Formation of *Warriors for Gringostroika* and *The New Mestizas*." *The Latino Studies Reader*. Ed. Antonia Darder and Rodolfo D. Torres. Malden, MA: Blackwell, 1998. 129–42. Print.

Davis, F. James. *Who is Black? One Nation's Definition*. Tenth Anniversary Ed. University Park: Pennsylvania State UP, 2001. Print.

Davis, Rebecca Harding. *Waiting for the Verdict*. 1867. Ed. Donald Dingledine. Albany: NCUP, 1995. Print.

Dawkins, Laura. "Black Babies, White Hysteria: The Dark Child in African-American Literature of the Harlem Renaissance." *The American Child: A Cultural Studies Reader*. Ed. Caroline F. Levander and Carol J. Singley. New Brunswick: Rutgers UP, 2003. Print.

Deleuze, Gilles. *Cinema: The Time Image 2*. Trans. Hugh Tomlinson and Robert Galeta. Minneapolis: U of Minnesota P, 1989. Print.

Deloria, Philip. *Playing Indian.* New Haven: Yale UP, 1999. Print.
Devil in a Blue Dress. Dir. Carl Franklin. TriStar Pictures, 1995.
Dickerson, Debra. "Colorblind." *Salon.* 22 Jan. 2007. n.p. Web. 5 Jan. 2009.
The Dictator. Dir. Larry Charles. Paramount Pictures, 2012.
Dinerstein, Joel. *Swinging the Machine: Modernity, Technology, and African American Culture Between the World Wars.* Amherst: U of Massachusetts P, 2003. Print.
Dixon, Thomas. *The Clansman.* 1905. Lexington: U of Kentucky P, 1970. Print.
Dominguez, Virginia. *White By Definition: Social Classification in Creole Louisiana.* Piscataway: Rutgers UP, 1994. Print.
Donaldson, Susan V. "Telling Forgotten Stories of Slavery in the Postmodern South." *Southern Literary Journal* 40.2 (2008): 267–83. Print.
Dovey, Jon. *Freakshow: First Person Media and Factual Television.* Berkeley: U of California P, 2000. Print.
Dreisinger, Baz. *Near Black: White to Black Passing in American Culture.* Amherst: U of Massachusetts P, 2008. Print.
Du Bois, W. E. B. *The Souls of Black Folk.* 1903. New York: Dover, 1994. Print.
Durham, Robert Lee. *The Call of the South.* Boston: L.C. Page, 1908. Print.
During, Simon, ed. *Cultural Studies: A Reader.* London: Routledge, 1993. Print.
Duvall, J. Michael, and Julie Cary Nerad. " 'Suddenly and Shockingly Black': The Atavistic Child in Turn-into-the-Twentieth-Century American Fiction." *African American Review* 46.1 (2007): 51–66. Web.
Dyer, Richard. *White.* London: Routledge, 1997. Print.
Edge. "Episode 102." PBS. WNET, New York City. 6 Nov. 1991.
Edmonds, Patricia. "Super Duper Imposter Says He Aided in Surgeries." *Detroit Free Press.* 16 March 1985: 1A. Print.
Elam, Michele. "Passing in the Post-Soul Race Era: Danzy Senna, Philip Roth, and Colson Whitehead." *African American Review* 41 (2007): 749–68. Print.
———. *The Souls of Mixed Folk: Race, Politics, and Aesthetics in the New Millennium.* Stanford: Stanford UP, 2011. Print.
Ellis, Trey. "The New Black Aesthetic." *Callaloo* 12.1 (1989): 185–203. Print.
———. *Platitudes.* 1988. Lebanon, NH: Northeastern UP, 2003. Print.
Ellison, Ralph. "The Art of Fiction: An Interview." *Shadow and Act.* New York: Vintage, 1953. 167–83. Print.
———. "Change the Joke and Slip the Yoke." *Shadow and Act.* New York: Vintage, 1953. 45–59. Print.
———. *Invisible Man.* 1951. New York: Random House, 1972. Print.
———. *Juneteenth: A Novel.* Ed. John F. Callahan. New York: Random House, 1999. Print.
———. *Shadow and Act.* New York: Vintage, 1953. Print.
Erasure. Dir. Percival Everett. Hyperion, 2001.
Everett, Percival. "Signing to the Blind." *Callaloo* 14.1 (1991): 9–11. Print.
F for Fake. Dir. Orson Welles. 1974. Specialty Films, 1975.
Fabi, M. Giulia. *Passing and the Rise of the African American Novel.* Urbana: U of Illinois P, 2001. Print.

Fanon, Frantz. *Black Skin White Masks*. 1952. Trans. Charles Lam Markmann. New York: Grove, 1967. Print.

Faulkner, William. *Light in August*. 1932. New York: Vintage International, 1990. Print.

Fauset, Jessie R. *Plum Bun: A Novel Without a Moral*. 1928. 2nd ed. Boston: Beacon Press, 1990. Print.

Favor, J. Martin. "'Ain't Nothin' Like the Real Thing, Baby": Trey Ellis' Search for New Black Voices." *Callaloo* 16.3 (1993): 694–705. Print.

Freedman, Jonathan. *Klezmer America: Jewishness, Ethnicity, Modernity*. New York: Columbia UP, 2008. Print.

Galindo, Elaine. *Beyond Passing*. Bloomington, IN: Xlibris, 2011. Print.

Gallego, Mar. *Passing Novels in the Harlem Renaissance: Identity Politics and Textual Strategies*. Hamburg: Lit Verlag, 2003. Print.

Gates Jr., Henry Louis. "The Passing of Anatole Broyard." *Thirteen Ways of Looking at a Black Man*. New York: Random House, 1997. 180–214. Print.

———, and Nellie Y. McKay, eds. *Norton Anthology of African American Literature*. New York: Norton, 2004. Print.

Gennochio, Benjamin. "For Japanese Girls, Black is Beautiful; Painting Hip-Hop as it Goes Geisha." *The New York Times*. 4 April 2004: 36. Print.

Gillespie, Michael B. "Reckless Eyeballing: *Coonskin*, Film Blackness, and the Racial Grotesque." *Contemporary Black American Cinema: Race, Gender, and Sexuality at the Movies*. Ed. Mia Mask. New York: Routledge, 2012: 56–86. Print.

Gilroy, Paul. *After Empire: Melancholia or Convivial Culture?* London: Routledge, 2004. Print.

———. "Ali G and the Oscars." *openDemocracy* 3 April 2002: 1–5. Web. 4 March 2008.

———. *The Black Atlantic: Modernity and Double Consciousness*. Cambridge: Harvard UP, 1993. Print.

Ginsberg, Elaine K. "Introduction: The Politics of Passing." In Ginsberg 1–18. Print.

———, ed. *Passing and the Fictions of Identity*. Durham: Duke UP, 1996. Print.

Glaser, Jennifer. "The Jew in the Canon: Reading Race and Literary History in Philip Roth's *The Human Stain*." *PMLA* 123.5 (October 2008): 1465–78. Print.

Glazer, Nathan. "Jews and Blacks: What Happened to the Grand Alliance?" *Jews in Black Perspectives: A Dialogue*. Ed. Joseph R. Washington Jr. New Jersey: Fairleigh Dickinson UP, 1984. 105–12. Print.

Goldberg, David Theo. *The Racial State*. Malden, MA: Blackwell, 2002. Print.

Goldstein, David S., and Audrey B. Thacker, eds. *Complicating Constructions: Race, Ethnicity, and Hybridity in American Texts*. Seattle: U of Washington P, 2007. Print.

Goldstein, Eric. *The Price of Whiteness: Jews, Race, and American Identity*. Princeton: Princeton UP, 2006. Print.

"*Gone With the Wind Done Gone*: 'Re-Writing' and Fair Use." *Harvard Law Review* 115.4 (2002): 1193–1216. Print.

Gordon, Lewis. "A Questioning Body of Laughter and Tears: Reading *Black Skin, White Masks* through the Cat and Mouse of Reason and a Misguided Theodicy." *Parallax* 8.2 (2002): 10–29. Print.

Gossett, Thomas F. *Race: The History of an Idea in America.* New ed. New York: Oxford UP, 1997. Print.

Grant, Madison. *The Passing of the Great Race.* 1916. New York: Charles Scribner's and Sons, 1921. Print.

Gray, Herman. *Watching Race: Television and the Struggle for "Blackness."* Minneapolis: U of Minnesota P, 1995. Print.

Gray, Jonathan, Jeffrey P. Jones, and Ethan Thompson. *Satire TV: Politics and Comedy in the Post-Network Era.* New York: New York UP, 2009. Print.

Greenberg, Lynn Cheryl. *Troubling the Waters: Black-Jewish Relations in the American Century.* Princeton: Princeton UP, 2006. Print.

Gregson, Ian. *Postmodern Literature.* London: Arnold, 2004. Print.

Griffin, John Howard. *Black Like Me.* 1961. Boston: Houghton Mifflin, 1971. Print.

———. *Black Like Me.* 1961. New York: Signet, 1996. Print.

Griffiths, Frederick T. "Copy Wright: What Is an (Invisible) Author?" *New Literary History* 33 (2002): 315–41. Print.

Gubar, Susan. *Racechanges: White Skin, Black Face in American Culture.* New York: Oxford UP, 1997. Print.

Guerrero, Ed. *Framing Blackness: The African-American Image in Film.* Philadelphia: Temple UP, 1993. Print.

———. "The Black Man on Our Screens and the Empty Space in Representation." *Black Male: Representations of Masculinity in Contemporary American Art.* Ed. Thelma Golden. New York: Whitney Museum of American Art, 1994. 181–90. Print.

Guy-Sheftall, Beverly. "The Body Politic: Black Female Sexuality and the Nineteenth-Century Euro-American Imagination." *Skin Deep, Spirit Strong: The Black Female Body in American Culture.* Ed. Kimberly Wallace-Sanders. Ann Arbor: U of Michigan P, 2002. 13–35. Print.

Haddox, Thomas. "Alice Randall's *The Wind Done Gone* and the Ludic in African American Historical Fiction." *Modern Fiction Studies* 53.1 (2007): 120–39. Print.

Haizlip, Shirlee Taylor. *The Sweeter the Juice: A Family Memoir in Black and White.* New York: Simon and Schuster, 1994. Print.

Hale, Grace Elizabeth. *Making Whiteness: The Culture of Segregation in the South, 1890–1940.* New York: Vintage, 1998. Print.

Hall, Gwendolyn Midlo. *Africans in Colonial Louisiana: The Development of Afro-Creole Culture in the 18th Century.* Baton Rouge: Louisiana State UP, 1995. Print.

Hall, Stuart. "Cultural Identity and Diaspora." *Theorizing Diaspora: A Reader.* Ed. Jana Evans Braziel and Anita Mannur. Oxford: Blackwell, 2003. 233–46. Print.

———. "New Ethnicities." *Black British Cultural Studies: A Reader.* Ed. Houston A. Baker Jr., Manthia Diawara, and Ruth H. Lindeborg. Chicago: U of Chicago P, 1996. 163–72. Print.

Halsell, Grace. *Soul Sister.* 30th Anniversary ed. Washington, DC: Crossroads International, 1999. Print.

Haraway, Donna. "A Cyborg Manifesto: Science, Technology, and Socialist Feminism in the Late Twentieth Century." *Simians, Cyborgs, and Women: The Reinvention of Nature.* New York: Routledge, 1991. 149–81. Print.

Hardt, Michael, and Antonio Negri. *Empire.* Cambridge and London: Harvard UP, 2000. Print.

Harper, Frances E. W. *Iola Leroy.* 1892. Boston: Beacon, 1999. Print.

Harper, Phillip Brian. "Passing for What? Racial Masquerade and the Demands of Upward Mobility." *Callaloo* 2.2 (1998): 381–97. Print.

Harris, Cheryl I. "Whiteness as Property." *Harvard Law Review.* 106.8 (June 1993): 1710–91. Print.

Harris, Keith M. "'That Nigger's Crazy': *Richard Pryor,* Racial Performativity, Cultural Critique." *Richard Pryor: The Life and Legacy of a "Crazy" Black Man.* Ed. Audrey Thomas McCluskey. Bloomington: Indiana UP, 2008. 23–38. Print.

Harris, Wendell B. Telephone Interview. 10 March 1996.

———. E-mail Interview. 4 Dec. 2011.

Harrison-Kahan, Lori. *The White Negress: Literature, Minstrelsy, and the Black-Jewish Imaginary.* New Brunswick: Rutgers UP, 2011. Print.

Heard, Danielle Christine. "Buggy Jiving Comic Strategies of the Black Avant-Garde." Diss. Cornell University, 2010.

Henry, Neil. *Pearl's Secret: A Black Man's Search for his White Family.* Berkeley: U of California P, 2001. Print.

Ho, Jennifer. "Ambiguous Movements: Paisley Rekdal's Passing Identity in *The Night My Mother Met Bruce Lee: Observations on Not Fitting In.*" *Women & Performance: A Journal of Feminist Theory* 15.1 (2005): 141–65. Print.

Hobson, Laura Z. *Gentleman's Agreement.* New York: Simon and Schuster, 1946. Print.

Holder, Eric. "Remarks as Prepared for Delivery by Attorney General Eric Holder at the Department of Justice African American History Month Program." 18 Feb. 2009. Web. 10 June 2009.

Hollinger, David A. "Amalgamation and Hypodescent: The Question of Ethnoracial Mixture in the History of the United States." *American Historical Review* 108.5 (Dec. 2003): 1363–90. Print.

———. "Obama, the Instability of Color Lines, and the Promise of a Postethnic Future." *Callaloo* 31.4 (2008): 1033–37. Print.

———. *Postethnic America: Beyond Multiculturalism.* New York: Basic Books, 2000. Print.

Hollinger, Karen. "Film Noir, Voice Over, and the Femme Fatale." *Film Noir Reader*. Ed. Alain Silver and James Ursini. New York: Limelight Editions, 1996: 243–59. Print.

Hollywood Shuffle. Dir. Robert Townsend. The Samuel Goldwyn Co., 1987.

Holmlund, Chris. *Impossible Bodies: Femininity and Masculinity at the Movies*. New York: Routledge, 2002. Print.

Honigman-Smith, Charlotte. "Portrayed, or Betrayed?" *Lilith* 26.2 (Summer 2001): 16–17. Print.

hooks, bell. *Black Looks: Race and Representation*. Boston: South End Press, 1992. Print.

Howells, Richard. " 'Is It Because I Is Black?' Race, Humour, and the Polysemiology of Ali G." *Historical Journal of Film, Radio and Television* 26.2 (2006): 155–77. Print.

Howells, William Dean. *An Imperative Duty*. 1892. Ed. Edwin Cady. New York: Twayne, 1962. Print.

Huggins, Nathan. "Passing is Passe." *Revelations: American History, American Myths*. Ed. Brenda Smith Huggins. New York: Oxford UP, 1995. 245–47. Print.

Hughes, Langston. "Limitations of Life." *Black Theatre U.S.A.* Ed. James Hatch and Ted Shine. New York: Free Press, 1974. 655–57. Print.

———. "The Negro Artist and the Racial Mountain." In Gates and McKay 1311–14. Print.

Huh, Jinny. "Whispers of Norbury: Sir Arthur Conan Doyle and the Modernist Crisis of Racial (Un)Detection." *Modern Fiction Studies* 49.3 (2003): 550–80. Print.

The Human Stain. Dir. Robert Benton. Miramax Films, 2003.

Hunter, Tera. " 'It's a Man's Man's Man's World': Specters of the Old Re-Newed in Afro-American Culture and Criticism." *Callaloo* 38 (1989): 247–49. Print.

Huq, Rupa. "Global Youth Cultures in Localized Spaces: The Case of the UK New Asian Dance Music and French Rap." *The Post-Subcultures Reader*. Ed. David Muggleton and Rupert Weinzierl. New York: Berg, 2003. 195–208. Print.

Hurst, Fannie. *Imitation of Life*. Ed. Daniel Itzkovitz. Durham: Duke UP, 2004. Print.

Hutcheon, Linda. *A Poetics of Postmodernism: History, Theory, Fiction*. New York: Routledge, 1988. Print.

———. *A Theory of Parody: The Teachings of Twentieth-Century Art Forms*. New York: Methuen, 1985. Print.

"I Refuse to Pass." Janice Kingslow. *Negro Digest* (May 1950): 22–31. Print.

Ibrahim, Habiba. *Troubling the Family: The Promise of Personhood and the Rise of Multiracialism*. Minneapolis: U of Minnesota P, 2012. Print.

Ignatiev, Noel. *How the Irish Became White*. New York: Routledge, 1995. Print.

———, and John Garvey, eds. *Race Traitor*. New York: Routledge, 1996. Print.

Imitation of Life. Dir. Douglas Sirk. Universal International Pictures, 1959.

———. Dir. John M. Stahl. Universal Pictures, 1934.

"Information About Suntrust Bank v. Houghton Mifflin Company." 17 April 2001. Web. 22 Dec. 2008.

iona rozeal brown a3 . . . black on both sides. 2004. Spellman College Museum of Fine Art. Web. 3 March 2008.

"Is Passing for White a Dying Fad?" L. Masco Young. *Color* (April 1957): 46–49. Print.

Itzkovitz, Daniel. "Introduction." *Imitation of Life*. By Fannie Hurst. Durham: Duke UP, 2004. Print.

———. "Passing Like Me: Jewish Chameleonism and the Politics of Race." *Passing: Identity and Interpretation in Sexuality, Race, and Religion*. In Sánchez and Schlossberg 38–63. Print.

Jacobs, Harriet. *Incidents in the Life of a Slave Girl*. 1861. Ed. Jean Fagin Yellin. Cambridge: Harvard UP, 1987. Print.

Jacobs, Joanne. "Mixing of Races Makes Categories Obsolete." *Tampa Tribune*. 16 July 1997, final ed., Nation/World 7. *Lexis-Nexis*. 2 Dec. 2004.

Jacobson, Matthew Frye. *Whiteness of a Different Color*. Cambridge: Harvard UP, 1998. Print.

Jacobson, Robin Dale. *The New Nativism: Proposition 187 and the Debate over Immigration*. Minneapolis: U of Minnesota P, 2008. Print.

Jackson, Lawrence. "Ralph Ellison, Sharpies, Rinehart, and Politics in *Invisible Man*." *The Massachusetts Review* 40.1 (1990): 71–95. Print.

Jameson, Fredric. *Postmodernism or, The Cultural Logic of Late Capitalism*. Durham: Duke UP, 1991. Print.

Johnson, Charles. *The Oxherding Tale*. 1982. New York: Plume, 1995. Print.

———. "A Phenomenology of the Black Body." *Michigan Quarterly Review* 32.4 (1993): 595–614. Print.

Johnson, James Weldon. *The Autobiography of an Ex-Colored Man*. 1912. Ed. William L. Andrews. New York: Penguin, 1990. Print.

———. *The Autobiography of an Ex-Coloured Man*. 1912. New York: Hill and Wang, 1960. Print.

———. *The Autobiography of an Ex-Colored Man*. 1927. *Three Negro Classics*. Intro. John Hope Franklin. New York: Avon Books, 1965. 393–511. Print.

———. "The Autobiography of an Ex-Colored Man." *The Norton Anthology of African American Literature*. Ed. Henry Louis Gates Jr. and Nellie Y. McKay. New York: Norton, 1977. 777–861. Print.

Jones, Nicholas A., and Amy Symens Smith. *The Two or More Races Population: 2000*. U.S. Census Bureau. Washington, DC: GPO, 2001. Web.

Kane, Gregory P. "Push for 'Multiracial' Label Gives Rise to Suspicions Among Blacks." *Tampa Tribune*. 18 July 1997, final ed., Nation/World: 13. *Lexis-Nexis*. Web. 2 Dec. 2004.

Kane, Pat. "Ali G: Da New White and Black Minstrel." *Sunday Herald*. 10 March 2002. Web. 3 March 2008.

Kaplan, Erin Aubry. "Sort of Black Like Me." Rev. of *One Drop: My Father's Hidden Life—A Story of Race and Family Secrets* by Bliss Broyard. *Los Angeles Times.* 30 Sept. 2007: R10. Print.

Kawash, Samira. "*The Autobiography of an Ex-Coloured Man*: (Passing for) Black Passing for White." In Ginsberg 59–74. Print.

Kennedy, Randall. "Racial Passing." *Mixed Race America and the Law: A Reader.* Ed. Kevin Johnson. New York: New York UP, 2003. 157–68. Print.

———. *Selling Out: The Politics of Racial Betrayal.* New York: Random House, 2008. Print.

Kercher, Stephen E. *Revel with a Cause: Liberal Satire in Postwar America.* Chicago: U of Chicago P, 2006. Print.

Kim, Claire Jean. "The Racial Triangulation of Asian Americans." *Politics and Society* 27.1 (1999): 105–38. Print.

Kim, Jinah. "Immigrants, Racial Citizens, and the (Multi)Cultural Politics of Neoliberal Los Angeles." *Social Justice* 35.3 (2008): 36–56. Print.

Klein, Naomi. *No Logo: No Space, No Choice, No Jobs.* New York: Picador, 2002. Print.

Klein, Sybil. *Creole: The History and Legacy of Louisiana's Free People of Color.* Baton Rouge: Louisiana State UP, 2000. Print.

Kramer, Paul A. *The Blood of Government: Race, Empire, the United States, and the Philippines.* Chapel Hill: U of North Carolina P, 2006. Print.

Kraszewski, Jon. "Country Hicks and Urban Cliques: Mediating Race, Reality, and Liberalism on MTV's *The Real World*." *Reality TV: Remaking Television Culture.* Ed. Susan Murray and Laurie Ouellette. New York: New York UP, 2004. 179–96. Print.

Kroeger, Brooke. *Passing: When People Can't Be Who They Are.* New York: Public Affairs, 2004. Print.

Kun, Josh. *Audiotopia: Music, Race, and America.* Berkeley and Los Angeles: U of California P, 2005. Print.

Kydd, Elspeth. " 'The Ineffaceable Curse of Cain': Racial Marking and Embodiment in *Pinky*." *Camera Obscura* 43.15 (2000): 95–121. Print.

LaMarre, Heather L., Kristen D. Landreville, and Michael A. Beam. "The Irony of Satire: Political Ideology and the Motivation to See What You Want to See in The Colbert Report." *The International Journal of Press/Politics* 14.2 (2009): 212–32. Print.

Larsen, Nella. *Quicksand and Passing.* New Brunswick: Rutgers UP, 1986. Print.

"Law & Order." *IMDb.* IMDb.com, Inc. n.d. Web. 10 Aug. 2011.

Lazarre, Jane. *Beyond the Whiteness of Whiteness: Memoir of a White Mother of Black Sons.* Durham: Duke UP, 1997. Print.

Leab, D. J. *From Sambo to Superspade: The Black Experience in Motion Pictures.* Boston: Houghton Mifflin, 1975. Print.

League of Gentlemen, The. BBC, UK. 11 Jan. 1999-31 Oct. 2002.

Lee, Felicia R. "Confronting America's Racial Divide, in Blackface and White." *The New York Times.* 16 Feb. 2006: E1, E7. Print.

Lemire, Elise. *"Miscegenation": Making Race in America.* Philadelphia: U of Pennsylvania P, 2002. Print.

Lemon, Alaina. "Without a 'Concept'? Race as Discursive Practice." *Slavic Review* 61.1 (2002): 54–61. Print.

Lerner, Michael, and Cornel West. *Jews and Blacks: A Dialogue on Race, Religion, and Culture in America.* New York: Penguin, 1995. Print.

Lessig, Lawrence. *Free Culture: The Nature and Future of Creativity.* New York: Penguin, 2005. Print.

Lipsitz, George. "The Possessive Investment in Whiteness: Racialized Social Democracy and the White Problem in American Studies." *American Quarterly* 47 (Sept. 1995): 369–87. Print.

———. *The Possessive Investment in Whiteness: How White People Profit from Identity Politics.* Rev. ed. Philadelphia: Temple UP, 2006. Print.

"Libertyville." *Cold Case.* CBS. WJZ. Baltimore. 29 March 2009.

Little Britain. BBC, UK. 16 Sept. 2003-31 Dec. 2006.

Locke, Alain. "The New Negro." In Gates and McKay 984–92. Print.

López, Ian F. Haney. "Chance, Context, and Choice in the Social Construction of Race." *The Latino/a Condition.* Ed. Richard Delgado and Jean Stefancic. New York: New York UP, 1998. 9–16. Print.

Lost Boundaries. Dir. Alfred L. Werker. Film Classics, 1949.

Lott, Eric. *Love and Theft: Blackface Minstrelsy and the American Working Class.* New York: Oxford UP, 1995. Print.

———. "Response to Trey Ellis's 'The New Black Aesthetic.'" *Callaloo* 12.1 (1989): 244–46. Print.

Lovely, Erica. "Obama's Roots Have Irish Smiling Eyes." *Politico* Web. 11 March 2009.

Lowe, Lisa. *Immigrant Acts: On Asian American Cultural Politics.* Durham: Duke UP, 1996. Print.

Lucia, Cynthia. "Race, Media and Money: A Critical Symposium on Spike Lee's *Bamboozled*." *Cineaste* 26.2 (2001): 10–17. Print.

Mackey, Nathaniel. *Discrepant Engagement: Dissonance, Cross-Culturality, and Experimental Writing.* Cambridge: Cambridge UP, 1993. Print.

Major, Clarence. *Come By Here: My Mother's Life.* New York: John Wiley and Sons, 2002. Print.

Malcolm X. Dir. Spike Lee. Forty Acres and a Mule Filmworks, 1992.

Malik, Sarita. *Representing Black Britain: Black and Asian Images on Television.* London: Sage, 2002. Print.

———. "The Black and White Minstrel Show." *The Museum of Broadcast Communications.* Web. 3 March 2008.

Malkani, Gautam. *Londonstani.* London: Fourth Estate, 2006. Print.

Massood, Paula. *Black City Cinema: African American Urban Experiences in Film.* Philadelphia: Temple UP, 2003. Print.

Matthews, David. *Ace of Spades: A Memoir.* New York: Henry Holt, 2007. Print.

McBride, James. *The Color of Water: A Black Man's Tribute to His White Mother.* New York: Riverhead, 1996. Print.

McCaig, Donald. *Rhett Butler's People.* New York: St. Martin's, 2007. Print.

McHale, Brian. *Postmodernist Fiction.* New York: Methuen, 1987. Print.

Meagher, Timothy J. "Racial and Ethnic Relations in America, 1965–2000." *Race and Ethnicity in America: A Concise History.* Ed. Ronald H. Bayor. New York: Columbia UP, 2003. 193–240. Print.

Melamed, Jodi. *Represent and Destroy: Rationalizing Violence in the New Racial Capitalism.* Minneapolis: U of Minnesota P, 2011. Print.

Melnick, Jeffrey. "Rattling the Cage of Black-Jewish Relations." *"Jewishness" and the World of "Difference" in the United States.* Ed. Marc Lee Raphael. Williamsburg, VA: College of William and Mary, 2001. 50–64. Print.

Meyer, Julie. *Age: 2000.* U.S. Census Bureau. Washington, DC: GPO, 2001. Web.

Miller, Karen E. Quinones. *Passin': A Novel.* New York: Grand Central Publishing, 2008. Print.

Miller, Monica L. *Slaves to Fashion: Black Dandyism and the Styling of Black Diasporic Identity.* Durham: Duke UP, 2009. Print.

Millner, Denene. "In Creating a Word to Describe his Racial Makeup, Golfer Tiger Woods has also Stirred up a Round of Controversy Among Blacks." *(New York) Daily News.* 8 June 1997, Sunday Extra: 2. *Lexis-Nexis.* Web. 2 Dec. 2004.

Mills, Charles W. "Non-Cartesian Sums: Philosophy and the African-American Experience." *Blackness Visible: Essays On Philosophy and Race.* Ithaca: Cornell UP, 1998. 1–20. Print.

"Minstrelsy, Passing, and the Location of an American Racial Identity." Special Issue. Guest Ed. Joshua J. Masters. *LIT: Literature, Interpretation, Theory* 18.2 (2007). Print.

Mitchell, Margaret. *Gone With the Wind.* 1936. New York: Scribner's, 2007. Print.

Moon, Spencer. *Reel Black Talk: A Sourcebook of 50 American Filmmakers.* Westport, CT.: Greenwood, 1997. Print.

Moran, Rachel F. "Demography and Distrust: The Latino Challenge to Civil Rights and Immigration Policy in the 1990s and Beyond." *La Raza Law Journal* 8:1 (Spring 1995): 1–24. Print.

Morrison, Toni. "Comment." *The New Yorker.* 5 Oct. 1998: 1–2. Web.

———. *a mercy.* New York: Knopf, 2008. Print.

———. "On the Backs of Blacks." *Time.* 2 Dec. 1993. 57. Print.

Mosley, Walter. *Devil in a Blue Dress.* New York: Washington Square Press, 1990. Print.

"Most Children Younger Than Age 1 Are Minorities, Census Bureau Reports." *United States Census Bureau.* Department of Commerce. 17 May 2012. Web. 12 June 2012.

Moynihan, Sinéad. *Passing Into the Present: Contemporary American Fiction of Racial and Gender Passing.* Manchester: Manchester UP, 2011. Print.

Mullen, Harryette. "Optic White: Blackness and the Production of Whiteness." *Diacritics* 24.2/3 (1994): 71–89. Print.

Murray, Susan. "'I Think We Need a New Name for It': The Meeting of Documentary and Reality Television." *Reality TV: Remaking Television Culture.* Ed. Susan Murray and Laurie Ouellette. New York: New York UP, 2004. 40–56. Print.

Nakashima, Cynthia L. "An Invisible Monster: The Creation and Denial of Mixed-Race People in America." *Racially Mixed People in America.* Ed. Maria P. P. Root. Newbury Park: Sage, 1992. 162–80. Print.

Nerad, Julie Cary. "Slippery Language and False Dilemmas in Passing Novels by Child, Howells, and Harper." *American Literature* 75.4 (2003): 813–41. Print.

"The New Face of America: How Immigrants Are Shaping the World's First Multicultural Society." *Time* Special Issue. 18 Nov. 1993. 2. Print.

"The New Face of Race." *Newsweek* Special Report. 18 Sept. 2000. 38–41. Web.

Ngai, Mae. *Impossible Subjects: Illegal Aliens and the Making of Modern America.* Princeton: Princeton UP, 2004. Print.

Nina Simone: Live At Montreux. Dir. Raymond Jaussi. 1976. Eagle Rock Entertainment, 2006.

Obama, Barack. "Press Conference of the President." The White House, Washington, DC. Web. 24 March 2009.

Obeidallah, Dean. "Sacha Cohen's Movie a Minstrel Show." *CNN* Web. 11 May 2012.

Okihiro, Gary Y. "Colonial Vision, Racial Visibility: Racializations in Puerto Rico and the Philippines during the Initial Period of U.S. Colonization." *Racial Transformations: Latinos and Asians Remaking the United States.* Ed. Nicholas De Genova. Durham: Duke UP, 2006. 23–39. Print.

"Older and More Diverse Nation by Midcentury." *United States Census Bureau.* Department of Commerce. Web. 14 Aug. 2008.

Oliver, Kelly, and Benigno Trigo. *Noir Anxiety.* Minneapolis: U of Minnesota P, 2003. Print.

Omi, Michael, and Howard Winant. *Racial Formation in the United States: From the 1960s to the 1990s.* 2nd ed. New York: Routledge, 1994. Print.

Ono, Kent A., and John M. Sloop. *Shifting Borders: Rhetoric, Immigration, and California's Proposition 187.* Philadelphia: Temple UP, 2002. Print.

Out of Sight. Dir. Steven Soderbergh. Universal Pictures, 1998.

Palumbo-Liu, David. *Asian/American: Historical Crossings of a Racial Frontier.* Stanford: Stanford UP, 1999. Print.

Pascoe, Peggy. *What Comes Naturally: Miscegenation Law and the Making of Race in America.* New York: Oxford UP, 2009. Print.

"pass·ing." *Women & Performance: a journal of feminist theory* 15.29 (2005). Print.

"Passing." *Transition: An International Review* 58 (1992). Print.

Paumgarten, Nick. "Central Casting: The Race Card." *The New Yorker.* 10 Nov. 2003. CondéNet. Web. 2 March 2007.

Pépé le Moko. Dir. Julien Duvivier. 1937. DVD. The Criterion Collection, 2004.

Perlmann, Joel. "Reflecting the Changing Face of America: Multiracials, Racial Classification, and American Intermarriage." In Sollors, *Interracialism* 506–33. Print.

Pfeiffer, Kathleen. *Race Passing and American Individualism*. Amherst: U of Massachusetts P, 2003. Print.

Phillips, William M. Jr. *An Unillustrious Alliance: The African American and Jewish American Communities*. New York: Greenwood, 1991. Print.

Pilgrim, David. "The Tragic Mulatto Myth." *Jim Crow Museum of Racist Memorabilia at Ferris State University*. Web. Nov. 2000.

Pinky. Dir. Elia Kazan. Twentieth Century Fox, 1949.

Pitts, Leonard. "It Comes Down to This: Black Matters." *Buffalo News*. 28 Apr. 1997, city ed.: Viewpoints 3B. *Lexis-Nexis*. Web. 2 Dec. 2004.

Pool, Hannah. "Return to the Dark Ages." *The Guardian*. 22 Sept. 2006. Web. 3 March 2008.

Potok, Mark, ed. "Resurgence on the Right." *Intelligence Report*. Southern Poverty Law Center. Summer 2009. Web. 28 June 2009.

Pouzoulet, Catherine. "The Cinema of Spike Lee: Images of a Mosaic City." *Spike Lee's* Do the Right Thing. Ed. Mark A. Reid. New York: Cambridge UP, 1997. 31–49. Print.

Powell, A. D. *"Passing" for Who You Really Are: Essays in Support of Multiracial Whiteness*. Palm Coast, FL: Backintyme, 2005. Print.

Prell, Riv-Ellen. *Fighting to Become Americans: Assimilation and the Trouble Between Jewish Women and Jewish Men*. Boston: Beacon, 1999. Print.

Pulido, Laura. *Black, Brown, Yellow, and Left: Radical Activism in Los Angeles*. Berkeley: U of California P, 2006. Print.

Pynchon, Thomas. *The Crying of Lot 49*. 1965. New York: Harper Perennial, 2006. Print.

Qian, Zhenchao and Daniel T. Lichter. "Changing Patterns of Interracial Marriage in a Multiracial Society." *The Journal of Marriage and Family* 73.5 (Oct. 2011): 1065–84. Print.

Raimon, Eve Allegra. *The "Tragic Mulatta" Revisited: Race and Nationalism in Nineteenth-Century Antislavery Fiction*. New Brunswick: Rutgers UP, 2004. Print.

Randall, Alice. *The Wind Done Gone*. New York: Houghton Mifflin, 2001. Print.

Rehling, Nicola. "White Heterosexual Masculinity in Contemporary Popular Cinema." Unpublished PhD thesis, Aristotle U of Thessaloniki, 2005. Print.

Retman, Sonnet. "*Black No More*: George Schuyler and Racial Capitalism." *PMLA* 123 (2008): 1448–64. Print.

Rich, Frank. "Guess Who's Coming to Dinner." *The New York Times*. 2 Nov. 2008. Late ed sec. WK: 10. Print.

Road Trip. Dir. Todd Phillips. Dream Works, 2000.

Robinson, Amy. "Forms of Appearance of Value: Homer Plessy and the Politics of Privacy." *Performance and Cultural Politics*. Ed. Elin Diamond. New York: Routledge, 1996. 237–60. Print.

———. "It Takes One to Know One: 'Passing' and Communities of Common Interest." *Critical Inquiry* 20.4 (1994): 715–36. Print.

Robertson, Gil. "The Chameleon." *Savoy*. Sept. 2002. 56–59. Print.

Rodriguez, Richard. *Brown: The Last Discovery of America*. New York: Penguin, 2002. Print.

Roediger, David. "Race Will Survive the Obama Election." *The Chronicle of Higher Education: Chronicle Review* (2008): B6. Print.

Rogin, Michael. *Blackface, White Noise: Jewish Immigrants in the Hollywood Melting Pot*. Berkeley: U of California P, 1996. Print.

Roley, Brian Ascalon. *American Son*. New York: Norton, 2001. Print.

———. "*American Son* Epilogue." *Growing Up Filipino: Stories for Young Adults*. Ed. Cecilia Manguerra Brainard. Santa Monica: Palh, 2003. Print.

Root, Maria P. P. "Five Mixed Race Identities: From Relic to Revolution." In Winters and DeBose 3–20. Print.

———. *The Multiracial Experience: Racial Borders as the New Frontier.* Newbury Park: Sage, 1996. Print.

Rosaldo, Renato. *Culture and the Remaking of Social Analysis*. Boston: Beacon, 1989. Print.

Rostand, Edmund. *Cyrano de Bergerac*. 1897. Trans. Anthony Burgess. New York: Applause Books, 1998. Print.

Roth, Philip. *The Human Stain*. Boston and New York: Houghton Mifflin, 2000. Print.

Rottenberg, Catherine. *Performing Americanness: Race, Class, and Gender in Modern African-American and Jewish-American Literature*. Hanover, NH: UP of New England, 2008. Print.

Rouse, Roger. "Thinking through Transnationalism: Notes on the Cultural Politics of Class Relations in the Contemporary United States." *Public Culture* 7 (1995): 353–402. Print.

Rushdie, Salman. "The New Empire Within Britain." 1982. *Imaginary Homelands: Essays and Criticism 1981–1991*. London: Granta, 1991. 129–38. Print.

Russet, Margaret. "Race Under *Erasure*." *Callaloo* 28.2 (2005): 358–68. Print.

Saint-Amour, Paul K. *The Copywrights: Intellectual Property and the Literary Imagination*. Ithaca: Cornell UP, 2003. Print.

Saks, Eva. "Representing Miscegenation Law." In Sollors, *Interracialism* 61–80. Print.

Salzman, Jack, and Cornel West, eds. *Struggles in the Promised Land: Toward a History of Black-Jewish Relations in the United States*. New York: Oxford UP, 1997. Print.

Sánchez, Maria Carla, and Linda Schlossberg, eds. *Passing: Identity and Interpretation in Sexuality, Race, and Religion.* New York: New York UP, 2001. Print.

Sandweiss, Martha A. *Passing Strange: A Gilded Age Tale of Love and Deception Across the Color Line.* New York: Penguin, 2009. Print.

Sartre, Jean-Paul. "Portrait of the Inauthentic Jew." *Commentary* 5.5 (May 1948): 389–97. Print.

Saunders, Robert S. *The Many Faces of Sacha Baron Cohen: Politics, Parody, and the Battle over Borat.* Lanham, MD: Lexington Books, 2009. Print.

Scales-Trent, Judy. *Notes of a White Black Woman: Race Color Community.* 1995. University Park: Pennsylvania State UP, 2001. Print.

Scary Movie. Dir. Keenen Ivory Wayans. Miramax Films, 2000.

Schlossberg, Linda. "Introduction: Rites of Passing." In Sánchez and Schlossberg 1–12. Print.

Schuyler, George. *Black No More.* New York: Macaulay, 1931. Print.

———. "Negro Art-Hokum." In Gates and McKay 1221–23. Print.

Seeman, Melvin. "Status and Identity: The Problem of Inauthenticity." *The Pacific Sociological Review* 9.2 (1966): 67–73. Print.

Senna, Danzy. *Caucasia.* New York: Riverhead Books, 1998. Print.

Sharfstein, Daniel J. *The Invisible Line: Three American Families and the Secret Journey from Black to White.* New York: Penguin, 2011. Print.

Shohat, Ella, and Robert Stam. *Unthinking Eurocentrism: Multiculturalism and the Media.* New York: Routledge, 1994. Print.

Slow Burn. Dir. Wayne Beach. Lionsgate Productions, 1995.

Smith, Cherise. *Enacting Others: Politics of Identity in Eleanor Antin, Nikki S. Lee, Adrian Piper, and Anna Deavere Smith.* Durham: Duke UP, 2011. Print.

Smith, John David. *Anti-Black Thought: 1863–1925.* New York: Garland, 1993. Print.

Smith, Shawn Michelle. *American Archives: Gender, Race, and Class in Visual Culture.* Princeton: Princeton UP, 1999. Print.

Smith, Sidonie. "Performativity, Autobiographical Practice, Resistance." *Women, Autobiography, Theory: A Reader.* Ed. Sidonie Smith and Julia Watson. Madison: U of Wisconsin P, 1998. 108–15. Print.

———, and Julia Watson. *Reading Autobiography: A Guide for Interpreting Life Narratives.* 2nd ed. Minneapolis: U of Minnesota P, 2010. Print.

Smith, Valerie. "Reading the Intersection of Race and Gender in Narratives of Passing." *Diacritics* 24.2–3 (1994): 43–57. Print.

Smith-Pryor, Elizabeth M. *Property Rites: The Rhinelander Trial, Passing, and the Protection of Whiteness.* Chapel Hill: U of North Carolina P, 2009. Print.

Sollors, Werner. *Neither Black Nor White Yet Both: Thematic Explorations of Interracial Literature.* New York: Oxford UP, 1997. Print.

———, ed. *Interracialism: Black-White Intermarriage in American History, Literature, and Law.* New York: Oxford UP, 2000. Print.

Song, Min-Hyoung. *Strange Future: Pessimism and the 1992 Los Angeles Riots.* Durham: Duke UP, 2005. Print.

Soul Man. Dir. Steve Miner. New World Pictures, 1986.

Spencer, Rainier. *Reproducing Race: The Paradox of Generation Mix.* Boulder: Lynne Rienner, 2010. Print.

Spickard, Paul. "The Subject is Mixed Race: the Boom in Biracial Biography." *Rethinking "Mixed Race."* Ed. David Parker and Miri Song. London, VA: Pluto Press, 2001. 76–98. Print.

Spivak, Gayatri Chakravorty. "Can the Subaltern Speak?" *Marxism and the Interpretation of Culture.* Ed. Cary Nelson and Lawrence Grossberg. London: Macmillan, 1988. 271–313. Print.

Squires, Catherine R. *Dispatches from the Color Line: The Press and Multiracial America.* Albany: State U of New York P, 2007. Print.

Steele, Shelby. "Obama Seduced Whites with a Vision of Their Racial Innocence Precisely to Coerce Them into Acting out of a Racial Motivation." *Los Angeles Times.* 5 Nov. 2008: A31. Print.

Stern, Julia. "Spanish Masquerade and the Drama of Racial Identity in *Uncle Tom's Cabin.*" In Ginsberg 103–30. Print.

Stewart, Mart A. "Teaching *Gone With the Wind* in the Socialist Republic of Vietnam." *Southern Cultures* 11.3 (2005): 9–34. Print.

Stoddard, Lothrop. *The Rising Tide of Color Against White World Supremacy.* Intro. Madison Grant. New York: Scribner, 1920. Print.

Stowe, Harriet Beecher. *Uncle Tom's Cabin.* 1851–52. Ed. and Intro. Christopher G. Diller. Ontario: Broadview, 2009. Print.

Streeter, Caroline. "The Hazards of Visibility: 'Biracial' Women, Media Images, and Narratives of Identity." In Winters and DeBose. 301–22. Print.

Sullivan, Andrew. "Good Bye to All That: Why Obama Matters." *The Atlantic Online.* Web. Dec. 2007.

Swift, Jonathan. *The Battle of the Books.* Lenox, MA: Hard Press, 2006. Print.

Talty, Stephan. *Mulatto America: At the Crossroads of Black and White Culture.* New York: Harper, 2003. Print.

Tate, Greg. "Nigs R Us, or How Blackfolk Became Fetish Objects." *Everything But The Burden: What White People Are Taking From Black Culture.* Ed. Greg Tate. New York: Broadway Books, 2003. 1–14. Print.

Taylor, Clyde. "Two Way Street." *Black Film Review* 1.6 (1990): 8–9. Print.

Taylor, Helen. *Circling Dixie: Contemporary Southern Culture Through a Transatlantic Lens.* New Brunswick: Rutgers UP, 2001. Print.

———. "Women and Dixie: The Feminization of Southern Women's History and Culture." *American Literary History* 18.4 (2006): 847–60. Print.

Thomas, Piri. *Down These Mean Streets.* 1967. New York: Vintage, 1997. Print.

Thompson, Debby. " 'Is Race a Trope?': Anna Deavere Smith and the Question of Racial Performativity." *African American Review* 37.1 (2003): 127–38. Print.

"TI Timeline." *CBP.gov*. Web. 10 Nov. 2011.

"Tiger Woods Profile." *CNN.com*. 2001. Cable News Network. n.d. Web. 20 June 2008.

Time (Fall 1993) 142:21. Special Issue. Web.

Top of the Heap. Dir. Christopher St. John. The Fanfare Corp, 1972.

Torres, Sasha. *Black, White and In Color: Television and Black Civil Rights*. Princeton: Princeton UP, 2003. Print.

Tropic Thunder. Dir. Ben Stiller. Dreamworks, 2008.

True Identity. Dir. Charles Lane. Sandollar Productions, 1991.

Ty, Eleanor. "Abjection, Masculinity, and Violence in Brian Roley's *American Son* and Han Ong's *Fixer Chao*." *MELUS* 29.1 (2004): 119–36. Print.

Tyler, Carole-Anne. "Passing: Narcissism, Identity, and Difference." *differences: A Journal of Feminist Cultural Studies* 6.2+3 (1994): 212–48. Print.

Udovitch, Mim. "Vin Diesel Shows His True Colors." *Details*. June/July 2004. 158–62. Print.

Wacks, Jamie L. "Reading Race, Rhetoric, and the Female Body in the *Rhinelander* Case." In Sollors, *Interracialism* 162–77. Print.

Wald, Gayle. *Crossing the Line: Racial Passing in Twentieth-Century U.S. Literature and Culture*. Durham: Duke UP, 2000. Print.

Walker, Lisa. *Looking Like What You Are: Sexual Style, Race, and Lesbian Identity*. New York: New York UP, 2001. Print.

Walker, Rebecca. *Black, White, and Jewish: Autobiography of a Shifting Self*. New York: Riverhead, 2001. Print.

Weaver, Simon. "Comprehending Ambivalence: Ali G and Conceptualisations of the 'Other.'" *Connections* 4 (n/d): 1–16. Web. 3 March 2008.

Webb, Frank J. *The Garies and Their Friends*. 1857. Intro. Robert Reid-Pharr. Baltimore: Johns Hopkins UP, 1997. Print.

Weber, Donald. "From Limen to Border: A Meditation on the Legacy of Victor Turner for American Cultural Studies." *American Quarterly* 47.3 (Sept. 1995): 525–36. Print.

Weinbaum, Alys Eve. *Wayward Reproductions: Genealogies of Race and Nation in Trans-Atlantic Modern Thought*. Durham: Duke UP, 2004. Print.

Weiner, Rex. "One Way Street." *Variety*. 22 Jan. 1996: 13. Print.

Weisenburger, Steven. *Fables of Subversion: Satire and the American Novel, 1930–1980*. Athens: U of Georgia P, 1995. Print.

"Wentworth Miller." *Wikipedia*. Wikipedia: The Free Encyclopedia. 20 June 2008. Web. 23 June 2008.

West, Cornel. "Foreword." *Fires in the Mirror*. By Anna Deavere Smith. New York: Anchor Books, 1993. xvii–xxii. Print.

White, Armond. "Apostasy: Anti-hype in Four Steps." *The Resistance*. Woodstock, NY: Overlook, 1995. 278–82. Print.

White Chicks. Dir. Keenen Ivory Wayans. Columbia Pictures, 2004.

White, Mimi. *Tele-Advising: Therapeutic Discourse in American Television*. Chapel Hill: U of North Carolina P, 1992. Print.

White, W. L. *Lost Boundaries*. New York: Harcourt, Brace, & Co., 1947. Print.

White, Walter. *Flight*. 1926. Baton Rouge: Louisiana State UP, 1998. Print.

———. *A Man Called White: The Autobiography of Walter White*. 1948. Foreword Andrew Young. Athens: U of Georgia P, 1995. Print.

Whitehead, Colson. *The Intuitionist*. New York: Anchor Books, 1999. Print.

"Why 'Passing' Is Passing Out." *Jet*. 17 July 1952. 12–16. Print.

Williams, Bettye J. "Glimpsing Parody, Language, and Post-Reconstruction Themes in Alice Randall's *The Wind Done Gone*." *CLA Journal* 47.3 (2004): 310–25. Print.

Williams, Gregory Howard. *Life on the Color Line: The True Story of a White Boy Who Discovered He Was Black*. New York: Penguin, 1995. Print.

Williams, Kim M. "From Civil Rights to the Multiracial Movement." In Winters and DeBose 85–98. Print.

———. *Mark One or More: Civil Rights in Multiracial America*. Ann Arbor: U Michigan P, 2008. Print.

Williams, Linda. *Playing the Race Card: Melodramas of Black and White from Uncle Tom to O. J. Simpson*. Princeton: Princeton UP, 2001. Print.

Williamson, Joel. *New People: Miscegenation and Mulattoes in the United States*. Baton Rouge: Louisiana State UP, 1980. Print.

Willis, Ellen. "The Myth of the Powerful Jew." *Strangers and Neighbors: Relations Between Blacks and Jews in the United States*. Ed. Maurianne Adams and John Bracey. Amherst: U of Massachusetts P, 1999. 720–28. Print.

Winters, Loretta I., and Herman L. DeBose, eds. *New Faces in a Changing America: Multiracial Identity in the 21st Century*. New York: Sage, 2002. Print.

Wright, Richard. "Blueprint for Negro Writing." In Gates and McKay 1380–88. Print.

———. *Native Son*. 1940. New York: Perennial, 1987. Print.

———. *Native Son*. 1940. New York: Library of America, 1991. Print.

———. *White Man Listen!* 1957. New York: Anchor Books, 1964. Print.

Wright, Susan Prothro. "In the Wake of D. W. Griffith's *The Birth of a Nation* Chesnutt's *Paul Marchand, F.M.C.* as Command Performance." In Wright and Glass 67–83. Print.

———, and Ernestine Pickens Glass, eds. *Passing in the Works of Charles W. Chesnutt*. Jackson: U of Mississippi P, 2010. Print.

Yaeger, Patricia. "Cicum-Atlantic Superabundance: Milk as World-Making in Alice Randall and Kara Walker." *American Literature: A Journal of Literary History, Criticism, and Bibliography* 78.4 (2006): 769–98. Print.

Young, Robert. *White Mythologies: Writing History and the West*. London: Routledge, 1996. Print.

Zack, Naomi. *Race and Mixed Race*. Philadelphia: Temple UP, 1993. Print.

Zanger, Jules. "The 'Tragic Octoroon' in Pre–Civil War Fiction." In Sollors, *Interracialism* 284–90.

Zayd, Daniel Ibn. "Sacha Cohen and Arab Minstrelsy." *Dissident Voice: A Radical Newsletter in the Struggle for Peace and Social Justice.* Web. 19 May 2012.

Zhou, Min, and Yang Sao Xiong. "The Multifaceted American Experiences of the Children of Asian Immigrants: Lessons for Segmented Assimilation." *Ethnic and Racial Studies* 28.6 (2005): 1119–52. Print.

Zinsser, William, ed. *Inventing the Truth: The Art and Craft of Memoir.* New York: Mariner Books, 1998. Print.

Contributor Biographies

Michael B. Gillespie is an assistant professor of film in the School of Interdisciplinary Arts, School of Film, and Department of African American Studies at Ohio University. His teaching and research focus on film theory, black visual and expressive culture, historiography, global cinema, film adaptation, and genre theory. His recent publications include "Reckless Eyeballing: *Coonskin,* Film Blackness, and the Racial Grotesque," in *Contemporary Black American Cinema: Race, Gender and Sexuality at the Movies* (Routledge, 2012) and "Dirty Pretty Things: The Racial Grotesque, Historiography, and Contemporary Art," in *Post-Soul Satire: An Interdisciplinary Critical Overview* (UP of Mississippi, forthcoming). He is completing a book entitled *Film Blackness: American Cinema and the Idea of Black Film* and co-editing two volumes, *Black Cinema Aesthetics Revisited* with Akil Houston and *New Chester Himes Criticism* with Gary Holcomb.

Lori Harrison-Kahan is the author of *The White Negress: Literature, Minstrelsy, and the Black-Jewish Imaginary* (Rutgers University Press, 2011). She has published essays in *Cinema Journal, MELUS, Legacy, Modern Language Studies, Modern Fiction Studies,* and *Tulsa Studies in Women's Literature.* After receiving her PhD in English and Comparative Literature from Columbia University, she held a postdoctoral fellowship at the University of Pennsylvania and has taught American literature and culture at Connecticut College and Harvard University. She currently teaches in the English department at Boston College.

Meredith McCarroll earned her PhD at University of Tennessee, where she wrote a dissertation entitled "Seeing Whiteness: Twentieth Century Literary and Cinematic Images," which calls for a remapping of race that complicates both the readings of race in traditional African American texts and of nonwhite bodies in twenty-first century popular culture by arguing for a non-dichotomous reading of race. McCarroll has recently published in *Pluck! Journal of Affrilachian Literature and Culture,* and is at work on a longer project with the Affrilachian Poets. Her book *Unwhite: Appalachia, Race, and Film* is forthcoming from University of Georgia Press. She is the writing fellows coordinator and teaches at Clemson University.

Ana Cristina Mendes is a researcher at ULICES (University of Lisbon Centre for English Studies) in Portugal. Her interests span postcolonial cultural production and its intersection with the culture industries. Her publications include *O Passado em Exibição* (Cosmos, 2011) and the co-edited book *Re-Orientalism and South Asian Identity Politics: The Oriental Other Within* (Routledge, 2011), as well as articles on Indian and British Asian film, and on Indian Writing in English published in *Third Text* and *Journal of Commonwealth Literature.* Her edited collection *Salman Rushdie and Visual Culture: Celebrating Impurity, Disrupting Borders* was published in 2011 by Routledge and her monograph *Salman Rushdie and Cultural Brokerism in the Twenty-First Century* is forthcoming from Ashgate.

Irina Negrea is an assistant professor at Shaw University in Raleigh, N.C. She completed her doctoral degree at Lehigh University. Her teaching interests include African American literature, twentieth-century American literature, film, and popular culture. Her current monograph (in progress) establishes a working typology of passing, along with a discussion of race, the racial status quo, and their subversion through passing in fiction and memoirs written by African American writers throughout the past century.

Julie Cary Nerad is an associate professor of American literature and a member of the Women's and Gender Studies program at Morgan State University in Baltimore, Maryland. Her essays have appeared in *American Literature, African American Review, ESQ: A Journal of the American Renaissance,* and *LIT: Literature, Interpretation, Theory.* She was the contributing editor for a special issue of *SLI: Studies in the Literary Imagination* entitled "Leaping into the Fire: Representations of Women in U.S. Race Riots" and is revising a monograph on racial passing in the nineteenth and early twentieth centuries.

Eden Osucha is assistant professor of English at Bates College where she is also affiliated with the Program in American Cultural Studies and teaches courses in American literature, cultural theory, and creative writing. She is currently completing a book project, *The Post-Racial Past: Race, Pri-*

vacy and Identity Before the Obama Era, which examines historical productions of "post-racial" discourse in U.S. law, literature, and media. Recent and forthcoming publications include articles on the linked articulations of "privacy" and "whiteness" in nineteenth-century visual culture and law, Toni Morrison's *Paradise* and the racialized regulations of intimacy in "The Moynihan Report" and *Griswold v. Connecticut,* and depictions of historical memory in the fiction of Colson Whitehead and Octavia Butler.

Amanda Page is an assistant professor at Juniata College. She has published articles on the passing narrative in *Southern Quarterly* and *MELUS.* Her manuscript in progress, "Passing Affinities," focuses on depictions of people outside the racial binary of black and white as a rhetorical strategy of disruption in U.S. passing narratives of the late nineteenth and early twentieth centuries. She is also currently at work on a book about novelist Chang-rae Lee for the University of South Carolina Press.

Jené Schoenfeld is an assistant professor at Kenyon College, where she teaches courses in African American literature. Her research explores representations of the mulatto in American fiction and culture, particularly the way that the mulatto figure serves as a central site for negotiations concerning post-Reconstruction conceptions of race and racial identity. She is currently working on a book on how, under segregation, the incorporation of the mulatto into the category "black" occasioned a reconsideration of the meaning of blackness itself in the fiction of Frances E. W. Harper, Charles Chesnutt, Nella Larsen, Jean Toomer, and others.

Gayle Wald is professor of English and American Studies at George Washington University. She is author of *Crossing the Line: Racial Passing in 20th-Century U.S. Literature and Culture* (Duke UP, 2000) and *Shout, Sister, Shout! The Untold Story of Rock-and-Roll Trailblazer Sister Rosetta Tharpe* (Beacon Press, 2007). She is currently completing "It's Been Beautiful," a study of the pioneering PBS TV show *SOUL!,* for Duke University Press.

Lynn Washington holds a postdoctoral position at James Madison University. As a Fulbright Scholar, she conducted research on the reggae aesthetic in literature at the University of the West Indies in Mona, Jamaica. She has served as an editor for the revised second edition of *Black Fire: An Anthology of Afro American Writing.* Her other research and teaching interests are passing narratives from 1850–1950, twentieth-century African American women writers, African American and Caribbean literature, and musico-literary aesthetics.

Index

Abbott, Stacey, 118
Ace of Spades: A Memoir (Matthews), 62, 89
Adorno, Theodor, 291
Affirmative Action, 16, 72, 111
African American family, 42–48, 124–26, 131–32, 168; and the color line, 17, 43, 53–56, 60, 69–70; and passing, 41–48, 52–53, 64, 71–72, 74–88, 90, 96, 98, 111–12, 233; and slavery, 46
Agnew v. State, 118
Ali G, 19–20, 29, 205–26
Ali G Indahouse: The Movie, 208
Ali G in da USAiii, 207
Ali G, Innit, 210, 220
Allen, Sarah A., 62
Allen, Theodore W., 24
Althusser, Louis, 283, 288
American Son (Roley), 19, 178–200
Angel, 13, 18, 28, 95, 99–105, 107, 113–14, 115, 117, 118
anthropoemic, 218–19
anthropophagic, 218–19
anti-immigration, 22, 179. *See also* immigrants
anti-Semitism, 238, 240, 245, 250. *See also* Jews/Jewish/Jewishness
Antler, Joyce, 249
Anzaldúa, Gloria, 53, 63, 182–83, 185, 190, 243, 245, 284, 300, 301; *Borderlands/La Frontera*, 182, 301. *See also* mestiza
Appadurai, Arjun, 284, 300, 301
Appiah, Anthony, 24
appropriative rejoinders, 157
Asian, 7, 8, 20, 23, 42, 179–200, 204, 206, 211, 213, 220, 224, 242, 248
Asian American, 179–200; stereotypes of, 194–95
atavism, 16, 92, 106, 118, 119. *See also* black baby trope/fable
Authenticity: cultural, 18, 22; historical, 154; identity, vii, 10, 16, 135, 174, 206, 244, 288; racial, 16, 73, 84–86, 109, 119, 126–27 131–33, 135, 143, 184–85, 189–91, 199, 204, 208, 215, 243, 258, 285–87, 288, 290–91, 295, 298, 301, 302; televisual, 154
Autobiography of An Ex-Colored Man (Johnson), 55, 91, 196, 198, 265, 275

Babb, Valerie, 45
Bagdikian, Ben H., 151, 153
Bahktin, Michael, 158
Baker, Houston, viii
Balshaw, Maria, 87
Bamboozled, 22, 210, 276, 286–302
Band of Angels, 29
Bangladeshis, 224

Banks, William M., 299
Baraka, Amiri, 302
Barrington, Judith, 62
Barthes, Roland, 288, 293, 302; *S/Z*, 288, 293, 302
Bartholomew, Anne, 155
Baschirotto, Corinna, 154, 161, 166–67, 170
Bauman, Zygmunt, 218–19
Beam, Michael A., 174
Beatty, Paul, 301; *White Boy Shuffle*, 301
Beauty and The Beast, 270
Beck, Evelyn Torton, 152, 172
Beck, Joseph M., 173
Beck, Warren, 173
Bell, Kevin, 278
Bellafante, Gina, 128, 129, 145
Belluscio, Steven J., 27
Benetton, 204
Bennett, Juda, 12, 13, 27
Benston, Kimberly, 274
Berger, Maurice, 249; *White Lies: Race and the Myths of Whiteness*, 249
Berzon, Judith R., 99, 116, 117, 118. *See also* black baby trope/fable
Beyond Passing (Galindo), 62
Beyond the Whiteness of Whiteness: Memoir of a White Mother of Black Sons (Lazarre), 249
Bhabha, Homi, 205, 215–16, 232, 250, 264, 286, 300, 301
Biale, David, 242
biology, relation to race, 16, 21, 24, 72, 188
biracial, ix, 17, 20, 25, 41, 43, 49, 50, 60, 62, 63, 71, 73, 8, 97, 116, 160, 184, 229, 231, 238; biography, 43, 63; memoir, 39–68, 69–94, 231–49
Birth of a Nation, The, 154, 294, 303
Black and White Minstrel Show, The, 208–209, 211
black baby trope/fable, 18, 92, 106–107, 109, 111, 165. *See also* Berzon and atavism
blackface, 15, 20, 23, 28, 126, 129–34, 139, 141–43, 204–205, 208–209, 210, 212, 224, 292, 296–97, 300, 302. *See also* minstrelsy
Black Girl, 265
black-Jewish relations. *See* Jews/Jewish/Jewishness
Black Like Me (Griffin), 26, 27, 42, 136, 137, 146
blackness, 2, 5, 8, 17, 18, 24, 45, 48, 50, 55–79 passim, 82–88, 89, 96, 99, 106–107, 111–16 passim, 124–26, 129–34, 139–45 passim, 161–62, 166–68, 175, 176, 199, 206, 209, 212, 220, 223, 230, 232–49, 258–59, 262–63, 265–68 passim, 274, 284, 295, 297, 300–303 passim; and authenticity, 18, 109, 129, 133; cultural, 132, 139, 143, 287, 297; displaced, 45, 58; film, 258–59, 274, 276; metaphoric, 24; of mulattos, 88, 99; and parody, 287, 294–97; as property, 17, 82, 84; as scapegoat, 45; and spectacle, 129, 131, 140; valuation of, 17, 70, 72, 82–83, 87–88, 92
Black No More (Schuyler), 29, 146
black pride, 142, 230
Black.White., 13, 18, 123–47
Black, White and Jewish (Walker), 20, 231–51
black-white binary, vii, ix, 15, 20, 43, 49, 58, 60, 61, 70, 95, 99, 102, 104, 105, 111, 139, 167, 175, 180, 181, 183–84, 196–97, 214, 219, 223, 231, 234, 242, 246, 270, 284, 286, 289, 290, 301
Bland, Sterling L., 45
blood, 7–8, 14, 17, 21, 57, 71–72, 79, 88, 99, 101–102, 103, 107–15

passim, 150, 165–68, 176, 188, 199, 242, 251, 265; black, 71, 79, 96, 102, 105, 115, 119, 150, 166–68, 251; as carrier of racial traits, 7, 17, 72, 99, 102, 107, 119; white, 57. *See also* one-drop rule
Bogle, Donald, 292
Bondswoman's Narrative, The (Crafts), 13
Booth, Wayne, 13
borderlands, 50, 60, 61, 284; cultural, 19. *See also* racial borders
Borderlands/LaFrontera (Anzaldúa), 182, 301
Bowman, Elizabeth Atkins, 13; *Dark Secret*, 13
Boyle, James, 159, 173, 174
Branigan, Edward, 275
Britain/British, 2, 20, 26, 29, 145, 173, 203, 206–19, 222, 224, 275, 277
Brodie, John, 119
Brodkin, Karen, 224, 238, 239, 250
Browder, Laura, 63, 66
Brown, Cecil, 302
brown, iona roseal, 212–13
Brown, John Gregory, 13; *Decorations in a Ruined Cemetery*, 213
Brown, Nancy G., 116
Brown, Wesley, 13; *Darktown Strutters*, 13
Brown, William Wells, 11; *Clotel, or the President's Daughter*, 11
browning, racial, 22, 25
Broyard, Anatole, 13, 69–92, 269
Broyard, Bliss, 13, 17, 62, 69–92, 250; *One Drop: My Father's Hidden Life*, 17, 62, 69–92, 250
Bunn, Austin, 245
Bush Mama, 276
Butler, Judith, 231, 236, 259, 290. *See also* performativity, gender
Cablinasian, 8, 97
Cain, Herman, 176
Call of the South, The (Durham), 118
capitalism(ist), 15, 16, 20, 22, 24, 144, 210, 286, 295
Caribbean, 26, 91, 213, 224
cartesian sum, 261–62
Catonese, Brandi Wilkins, 145
Caucasia (Senna), ix, 12, 20, 27, 229–51
Caughie, Pamela L., 27, 269
Chameleon Street, 21, 255–78
Chappelle, Dave, 209, 225
Chesnutt, Charles W., 12, 13, 113–14, 199, 284; *House Behind the Cedars, The*, 199; *Mandy Oxendine*, 13; *Paul Marchand, F. M. C.*, 13; *Quarry, The*, 13
Cheung, King-Kok, 180
Chicana/o, 19, 182–200, 245–46
Chin, Daryl, 277
Christian, Barbara, viii, 251
citizenship, 30, 46, 52, 56, 182, 292
Civil Rights Act of 1964, 24, 179
Civil Rights Act of 1990, 6, 24
Civil Rights Act of 1991, 6, 24
Civil Rights Era/Movement, 12, 16, 29, 42–43, 63, 75, 134, 155, 175, 179–80, 188, 198, 229–30, 232, 234, 237, 241, 249, 250, 295. *See also* post-Civil Rights era
Civil War, The, 117, 153–55, 173, 174
Clansman, The (Dixon), 173, 303
Clinton, William Jefferson, 6, 24–25, 144
Clotel, or the President's Daughter (Brown), 11
Clowers, Myles, 173
Cocteau, Jean, 270
Cohen, Sacha Baron, 20, 29, 205–25
Colbert Report, The, 158, 174, 207. *See also* Colbert, Steven

Colbert, Steven, 144, 158, 174, 207, 224. See also *The Colbert Report*
Cold Case, 13, 28
Colonization: internal, 170; cultural, 204; of the Philippines, 182, 186, 191, 199
color blind(ness), 3–5, 14, 15, 18, 23, 24, 105, 114, 116, 129, 144, 155, 170–71, 172
color conscious(ness), 24, 199
color line, 11, 17, 19, 22, 40–45, 47–49, 52–55, 57, 60–61, 63, 65, 70, 72, 74–75, 82, 96, 106, 113, 119, 130, 137, 139, 161, 166–67, 172, 206, 223, 230–31, 233, 284, 286, 291; crossing of, 11, 40, 44–45, 47–48, 53, 57, 61, 63, 72, 74–75, 113, 119, 130, 137, 206, 230, 233, 284, 286
colored, 47, 55–60, 101, 221, 234, 261, 265
Color of Water: A Black Man's Tribute to His White Mother, The (McBride), 249
Condé, Mary, 173
Conservatism: cultural, 18; political, 4, 174, 225; racial, 15
Cooper, J. California, 13; *Family*, 13
Cooper, James Fenimore, 11; *Last of the Mohicans, The,* 11
copyright law, 151–59, 171–74, 208
Couch, Greg, 112
Crafts, Hannah, 13; *Bondswoman's Narrative, The*, 13
Crenshaw, Kimberlé, 25
Creole, 77, 79, 84, 87, 91, 198
Cripps, Thomas, 302
Crowdus, Gary, 293, 294
Crying of Lot 49, The (Pynchon), 156
Culler, Jonathan, 288
cultural borrowing, 14–15, 20
cultural mulatto. *See* mulatto
cultural tourism, 134, 136
Cutler, R. J., 127, 145
Cutter, Martha J., 189, 284
Cyrano de Bergerac (Rostand), 269

Da Ali G Show, 29, 207, 222
DaCosta, Kimberly McClain, 6, 9, 25, 43
Daily Show, The, 158, 207. *See also* Stewart, Jon
Dalmage, Heather, 25
Daniel, G. Reginald, 25, 29
Darder, Antonia, 184
Dark Secret (Bowman), 13
Darktown Strutters (Brown), 13
Dash, Julie, 275
Davis, F. James, 61, 62, 64, 96, 115–16
Davis, Rebecca Harding, 62; *Waiting for the Verdict*, 62
Dawkins, Laura, 106
Dawkins, Marcia Alesan, 27
DeBose, Herman L., 25
Decorations in a Ruined Cemetery (Brown), 13
Deleuze, Gilles, 278
Deloria, Philip, 300
Dennis, Felix, 222
Derrida, Jacques, viii
Descartes, René, 261–62
Devil in a Blue Dress, film, 13
Devil in a Blue Dress, novel (Mosley), 13
Dickerson, Debra, 116
Diesel, Vin, 114, 119
Dinerstein, Joel, 276
discrimination, racial, 3, 4, 24, 26, 29, 40, 56, 58, 72–73, 82, 84, 87, 179–80, 200, 208
Dixon, Thomas, 173, 303; *Clansman, The*, 173, 303
documentary, 62, 127–29, 135, 137, 143, 146
Dominguez, Virginia, 91
Donaldson, Susan V., 149, 153, 172, 173

double consciousness, 136, 143, 237, 277, 289. *See also* Du Bois, W. E. B.
Douglas, Ramona E., 116
Dovey, Jon, 145
Down these Mean Streets (Thomas), 199
Dreisinger, Baz, 5, 13, 14, 26, 27, 198, 225
Du Bois, W.E.B., 55, 56, 63, 136, 143, 237, 261, 289; *Souls of Black Folk, The*, 56, 63
Durham, Robert Lee, 118; *Call of the South, The*, 118
During, Simon, 303
Duvall, J. Michael, 119
Duvivier, Julien, 270
Dyer, Richard, 28, 132

Edge, 271, 277
Edmonds, Patricia, 274
Elam, Michelle, 9, 11, 13, 14, 27, 29
Ellis, Trey, 22, 283–84, 286, 296, 298–99, 300–301, 303
Ellison, Ralph, 12, 13, 45, 262, 263–64, 272, 274, 276, 283; *Invisible Man*, 45, 64, 262, 272, 274, 289; *Juneteenth*, 12, 13; *Shadow and Act*, 283
Erasure (Everett), 22, 286–303
ethnicity, x, 7, 19, 20, 25–26, 29, 30, 114, 180, 187, 192, 223, 231
Everett, Percival, 22, 286–303; *Erasure*, 22, 286–303

F for Fake, 268
Fabi, M. Giulia, 27
Family (Cooper), 13
Fanon, Franz, 175, 270
Faulkner, William, 118; *Light in August*, 118
Fauset, Jessie Redmon, 90, 233, 251, 275, 301; *Plum Bun*, 90, 233, 251, 275, 301
Favor, J. Martin, 299, 303
Filipina/o, 180–200
Film Blackness, 259, 274, 276
First Amendment, The, 151–52, 170, 173
Fish, Stanley, 288
Fishbone, 300
Flight (White), 198
fluidity: racial, 215, 273, 300; sexual, 245–47
Foote, Shelby, 151
Frank, Anne, 235–37, 240
Freedman, Jonathan, 249

Galindo, Elaine, 13, 62; *Beyond Passing*, 62
Gallego, Mar, 27
ganguro, 20, 212–13
Garies and their Friends, The (Webb), 11, 73, 89, 160
Garvey, John, 62
Gates, Jr., Henry Louis, viii, 13, 69, 80, 151, 172, 269
gay, 8, 10, 25, 145, 150, 160, 225, 245, 247. *See also* homosexual
generation mix, 5, 24
genes, in relation to race, 48, 107, 118
genetic difference, in relation to race, 5, 144, 283, 284
Gennocchio, Benjamin, 212
Gentleman's Agreement (Hobson), 250
Georgakas, Dan, 293, 294
Gerima, Haile, 276
Gillespie, Michael B., 255–81
Gilroy, Paul, 203, 206–208, 216–20, 225, 263, 278, 284, 300, 301
Ginsberg, Elaine K., 10, 12, 27, 28, 39, 61, 181, 225, 249, 257
Glaser, Jennifer, 249
Glass, Ernestine Pickens, 12, 225
Glazer, Nathan, 232
Goldberg, David Theo, 24
Goldstein, David S., 24
Goldstein, Eric, 250

Gone With the Wind, film, 149–76
Gone With the Wind, novel (Mitchell), 18, 149–76
Gordon, Lewis, 276
Gossett, Thomas F., 24
Grant, Madison, 7
Gray, Herman, 131, 139, 147
Gray, Jonathan, 158, 224–25, 302
Greenberg, Lynn Cheryl, 250
Gregson, Ian, 175
Griffin, John Howard, 26, 27, 42, 63, 137, 146; *Black Like Me*, 26, 27, 42, 136, 137, 146
Griffith, D. W., 154, 173, 303; *Birth of a Nation, The*, 154, 294, 303
Griffiths, Frederick, 262
Gubar, Susan, 28, 276
Guerrero, Ed, 264, 267, 277
Gutman, Amy, 24
Guy-Sheftall, Beverly, 163

Haddox, Thomas, 154, 172, 176
Haizlip, Shirlee Taylor, 13, 16, 17, 41–49, 50, 53–54, 56, 60, 64, 66, 250; *Sweeter the Juice: A Family Memoir in Black and White, The*, 16, 41–50, 250
Hale, Grace Elizabeth, 173, 299
Hall, Gwendolyn Midlo, 91
Hall, Stuart, 184, 214, 215, 225
Halsell, Grace, 26; *Soul Sister*, 26
Haraway, Donna, 284, 300, 301
Hardt, Michael, 223
Harlem Renaissance, 4, 27, 106–107, 230, 298
Harper, Frances E. W., 63, 70, 73, 83–84, 160; *Iola Leroy*, 65, 70, 73, 83, 88, 92, 160
Harper, Phillip Brian, 74, 78
Harris, Cheryl I., viii, 61, 118, 199
Harris, Keith M., 267
Harris, Wendell B., 21, 255–59, 274–77
Harrison-Kahan, Lori, 229–53
Heard, Danielle, 302
Hegelian dialectic, 160
Henry, Neil, 13
heterosexuality, 141–42, 147, 246, 247
Hilfiger, Tommy, 210, 223
hip hop, 128, 210–13, 277, 301
Hispanic, 7, 30, 31, 47, 119, 198, 242–44
historical fiction, 158, 170, 176
Ho, Jennifer, 183–84, 185
Hobson, Laura, 250
Holder, Eric, 171, 276
Hollinger, David A., 63, 242
Hollinger, Karen, 276
Hollywood Shuffle, 276
Holmlund, Chris, 147
Holocaust, the 237–38
homophobia, 10, 145, 210, 225. *See also* homosexuality
homosexuality, 27, 246. *See also* gay
Honigman-Smith, Charlotte, 244
hooks, bell, 248
Hopkins, Pauline E. W., 62; "Test of Manhood, A Christmas Story, The," 62
Horkheimer, Max, 291
Houghton Mifflin, 151–53, 172
House Behind the Cedars, The (Chesnutt), 199
Howells, Richard, 211, 213, 220, 221, 222
Howells, William Dean, 198; *Imperative Duty, An,* 198
Hudlin brothers, 300
Huggins, Nathan, 28
Hughes, Langston, 29, 89, 303; *Limitations of Life*, 29
Huh, Jinny, 266
Human Stain, The, film, 13, 29
Human Stain, The, novel (Roth), 12, 13, 27, 29, 114, 231, 285
Hunter, Tara, 299, 303

Huq, Rupa, 211
Hurst, Fannie, 73, 89, 230, 234, 249, 250, 275; *Imitation of Life*, film: 1934 version, 29, 73; 1959 version, 29, 73, 225, 234; *Imitation of Life*, novel, 230, 234, 275
Hutcheon, Linda, 151, 158, 172
hybrid, 8, 49, 63, 64, 102, 185, 198, 213, 215, 284, 285, 286, 296, 298
hybridity, ix, 16, 19–20, 22, 43, 53, 56, 60, 161, 166–67, 170, 182, 215, 219, 286; cultural, 215, 216; thriving, 284, 299
hypodescent, 3, 41, 69, 70, 183, 184–85, 198, 245

Ibrahim, Habiba, 29
Ice Cube, 13, 128
Ignatiev, Noel, 23, 62, 175
Illusions, 275
imaginary, 161, 167; white cultural, 139, 193
Imitation of Life, film: 1934 version, 29, 73; 1959 version, 29, 73, 225, 234
Imitation of Life, novel (Hurst), 230, 234, 275
Immigration Act of 1924, 7, 25
Immigration Act of 1965, 192
Immigrants, 7–8, 22, 23, 26, 30, 31, 44, 52, 138, 165, 179, 181–82, 188–89, 191, 193–94, 197, 236, 240; Asian, 179, 188; Chicana/o, 188; European, 23, 138; Filipina/o, 194; Irish, 44; Jewish, 236; Korean, 180; Latina/o, 31, 179, 188, 197; Mexican, 188, 193, 197; Polish, 26
Imperative Duty, An (Howells), 198–99
Incidents in the Life of a Slave Girl (Jacobs), 11
Indian: East Asian, 26, 50, 192, 224; Native American, 8, 197, 300
intellectual property, 157, 159, 171, 174
interracial(ism), 1, 5, 16, 23, 25, 26, 41, 54, 71, 82, 84, 89, 96, 116, 118, 125, 145, 159, 164, 180–83, 191, 197–99, 230, 234, 247; adoptions, 71; coalitions, 180–87, 191, 197, 198, 230; family, 25, 41, 46, 71, 82, 84, 89, 98; marriage, 23, 89, 96, 116, 118, 247; solidarity, 25, 181, 191, 198
Intersectionality, 25
Intuitionist, The (Whitehead), 13, 27, 156
I Passed for White (Lee), 42, 62–63
invisibility: and passing, 10, 43, 100, 241; racial, 43, 45–46, 54, 56, 58, 60–61, 63; of whiteness, 132
Invisible Man (Ellison), 45, 64, 262, 272, 274, 289
Iola Leroy (Harper), 65, 70, 73, 83, 88, 92, 160
Irish, 1–3, 7, 23, 44, 175
Itzkovitz, Daniel, 241, 249, 250

Jackson, Lawrence, 274
Jackson, Michael, 6–7, 224
Jacobs, Harriet, 11; *Incidents in the Life of a Slave Girl*, 11
Jacobs, Joanne, 116
Jacobson, Matthew Frye, 23, 25, 250
Jacobson, Robin Dale, 188, 199
Jameson, Fredric, 175
Japan/Japanese, 26, 185, 193, 212–13. *See also* ganguro
Jewish American Princess, 237
Jew/Jewish/Jewishness, ix, 7, 8, 20, 26, 29, 48, 85, 88, 114, 119, 205, 206, 208, 214, 220, 224, 230–49; and assimilation, 231–32, 235, 237, 240–42; passing for, 20, 23–38, 242, 250; passing for black, 249, 250; passing for Muslim, 214; passing for white, 20, 27, 29, 230–31, 233, 249, 250; relationships with African

Jew/Jewish/Jewishness *(continued)* Americans, 232–34, 240, 250; and whiteness, 224, 229–42, 248–50
Jim Crow Era, 2, 11, 19, 42, 51, 54, 61, 72, 78, 95–96, 98, 118, 137, 143, 153, 155, 188, 285, 291. *See also* segregation
Johnson, Charles, 12, 151, 275; *Oxherding Tale*, 12
Johnson, James Weldon, 55, 91, 196, 198, 265, 275; *Autobiography of An Ex-Colored Man*, 55, 91, 196, 198, 265, 275
Johnson-Reid Act, 25 *See also* Immigration Act of 1924
Jolson, Al, 208, 222
Jones, Jeffrey P., 158, 302
Jones, Nicholas A., 116
Jones v. Commonweath, 107
Juneteenth (Ellison), 12, 13

Kalman, Tibor, 204, 224
Kane, Gregory P., 116
Kane, Pat, 222
Kaplan, Erin A., 87
Kawash, Samira, 9, 183, 198
Kennedy, Randall, 26, 61
Kercher, Stephen E., 302
Kim, Claire Jean, 199
Kim, Jinah, 179
King, Martin Luther, Jr., 48–49, 294
Klein, Naomi, 210
Klein, Sybil, 91
Kramer, Paul A., 198
Kraszewski, Jon, 145
Kreyling, Michael, 151
Kroeger, Brooke, 28
Ku Klux Klan, 57, 160, 173
Kun, Josh, 276
Kydd, Elspeth, 117

Lacan, Jacques, 160–61, 175, 198
LaMarre, Heather L., 174
Landreville, Kristen D., 174
Lane, Charles, 28, 275
language, as marker of racial identity, 8–9, 16–17, 19, 21, 43, 85, 166, 170, 185, 191–92, 199, 207, 225, 236, 241
Larsen, Nella, 160, 233, 251, 301; *Passing*, 160, 233, 251, 301
Last of the Mohicans, The (Cooper), 11
Latina/o, 5, 23, 26, 31, 100, 117, 179–99, 243, 244
Law & Order, 13, 18, 28, 95, 105–15, 117, 118
Lazarre, Jane, 249; *Beyond the Whiteness of Whiteness: Memoir of a White Mother of Black Sons*, 249
Leab, D. J., 302
League of Gentlemen, The, 209
Lee, Felicia R., 127, 128
Lee, Harper, 151
Lee, Reba, 42, 62–63; *I Passed for White*, 42, 62–63
Lee, Spike, 22, 204, 210, 276, 277, 286–95, 299–300, 302
Lemire, Elise, 24, 301
Lemon, Alaina, 71
Lerner, Michael, 250–51
lesbian(ism), 26, 245–47
Lessig, Lawrence, 174
Leventhal, Mel, 231, 239
liberalism, 4, 15, 17, 97, 105, 111, 114, 129, 134, 138, 141, 144, 174, 209, 216, 222, 248, 249, 299. *See also* neo-liberalism
Lichter, Daniel T., 31
Life on the Color Line: The True Story of a White Boy Who Discovered He Was Black (Williams), 16, 41, 53–61, 250
Light in August (Faulkner), 118
liminality, 19, 49, 53, 56, 60, 99, 181, 183, 185, 188, 197, 224, 269, 286, 296, 298

Limitations of Life (Hughes), 29
Lipsitz, George, 61, 92, 118, 286
literary echo, 174
Little Britain, 209
Live at Montreux, 263
Living Colour, 300
Locke, Alain, 303
Londonstani (Malkani), 211
López, Ian F. Haney, 186
Los Angeles: entertainment industry, 126; gang culture, 183; immigration, 179, 180, 187; riot, 6, 25, 180; South Central, 127, 133
Lost Boundaries, film, 27, 29, 62
Lost Boundaries, novel (White), 42, 62
Lott, Eric, 139, 140, 141, 224, 298–99, 302
Lovely, Erica, 1
Loving v. Virginia, 96, 116
Lowe, Lisa, 182–83, 185
Lucia, Cynthia, 286, 290
Ludacris, 209
Lumière brothers, 208
lynching, 65, 103, 110

Mackey, Nathaniel, 263
Major, Clarence, 13
Malcolm X, 276
Malik, Sarita, 207, 209, 211, 220, 222
Malkani, Gautam, 211; *Londonstani*, 211
Man Called White, A (White), 42
Mandy Oxendine (Chesnutt), 13
masquerade: and blackface, 132, 138, 208; and impersonation, 255, 257–58, 264, 268, 300; as passing, 40, 128, 205, 208; racial, 15, 20, 28, 74, 127, 129–32, 134, 142, 190, 204, 213, 223, 258; Spanish, 11, 27; white, 249
Massood, Paula, 276
Matthews, David, 13, 62, 72, 89; *Ace of Spades: A Memoir*, 62, 89
McBride, James, 249–50; *Color of Water: A Black Man's Tribute to His White Mother, The*, 249–50
McCarroll, Meredith, 283–306
McCaig, Donald, 154–55; *Rhett Butler's People*, 154–55
McGoy, David, 302
McHale, Brian, 172
Meagher, Timothy J., 25
Melamed, Jodi, 5, 23, 24, 25, 28, 30
Melnick, Jeffrey, 232, 233
memoir, 9, 12, 13, 16–17, 21, 39–66, 69–92, 231–51
Mendes, Ana Cristina, 203–27
mercy, a (Morrison), 175
mestiza/o, 19, 63, 182–85; consciousness, 53, 243; identity, 19, 182–84, 190, 196; passing, 191, 199
Mexican, 23, 27, 185–97, 248
Meyer, Julie, 116
Middle East/Middle Eastern, 7, 20, 206, 213
Miller, Karen E. Quinones, 13; *Passin': a novel*, 13
Miller, Monica L., 268
Miller, Wentworth, 114
Millner, Denene, 97
Mills, Charles W., 45, 64, 262
mimicry, 159, 205, 235, 259, 264, 267, 270, 276, 302
minstrelsy: Arab-faced, 225; blackface, 15, 129–30, 139, 205, 208–10, 224; global, 225; as performance, 87, 143, 211, 223; shows, 22, 208–10, 211, 212, 225, 287, 292, 297, 302. *See also* blackface
miscegenation, 96, 104, 107, 115–16, 118, 284
Mitchell, Elvis, 277
Mitchell, Margaret, 18, 149–59, 169, 172, 173; *Gone With the Wind*, film, 149–76; *Gone With the Wind*, novel, 18, 149–76

mixed-race: identity, 12, 249; people, 6, 8–9, 49, 54, 63, 70, 81, 99, 117. *See also* biracial, interracial, and multiracial
model minority myth: Asian, 187–89, 194, 199, 200; Jews, 242
Moon, Spencer, 255–56, 274, 277
Moran, Rachel F., 179, 180
morphing: facial, 6; racial, 20, 204–205, 224; identity, 213, 236, 296
Morrison, Toni, 12, 24, 151, 175, 251; *mercy, a*, 175
Mos Def and Talib Kweli are Black Star, 278
Mosley, Walter, 13
Moss, Kate, 20, 203–205, 223
Moynihan, Sinéad, 27, 225
Mr. Arkadin/Confidential Report, 278
mulatta/o, 7, 9, 16, 43, 55, 97, 99, 100, 107, 113–17 passim, 151, 183, 184, 191, 198, 199, 243, 283–84, 301; cultural, 22, 283–86, 289, 292, 296–99, 301, 303; degenerate, 57, 98, 99, 101, 102, 118, 119; as hybrid, 63; stereotype of, 18, 98, 102, 247; tragic, 17, 18, 70, 73–74, 84, 88, 101, 117, 183, 187, 234, 247, 284; trope, 98, 102–105, 234
Mullen, Harryette, 264
multicultural(ism), 5, 6, 7, 14, 16, 23, 24, 25, 28, 30, 83, 114, 139, 179, 215–17, 225, 229, 232
multiracial(s), 1, 6, 14–18, 20, 25, 30, 41, 43–44, 49, 53, 60–63 passim, 83, 96–98, 102, 105, 113–19 passim, 125, 144, 184–85, 190, 204, 231, 232, 242, 248, 250, 283; on reality television, 125; on U. S. Census, 6–7, 22, 25, 96–97, 114, 115, 116
multiracial movement, 6, 17, 43, 61, 63, 70–71, 283, 298
multiracialism, 9, 14, 16, 43, 230, 285
Murphy, Eddie, 136–37, 146–47
Murray, Susan, 127–28
Muslim, 2–3, 8, 213–14, 225–26

N.A.A.C.P., 62, 91
Nakashima, Cynthia L., 98, 117–18
Native American, 8, 197, 300
Native Son (Wright), 196, 287, 292, 302
nativism, 181, 193
Negrea, Irina, 39–67
Negri, Antonio, 223
neo-borderlands, 19, 22
neo-colonialism, 224
neo-liberalism, 5, 23, 24, 28, 30, 87, 144
neo-slave narrative, 150, 170, 172
Nerad, Julie Cary, 1–31, 54, 65, 69–93, 119, 149–78
New Black Aesthetic, 283, 298–300, 301. *See also* Post-Soul Aesthetic
Ngai, Mae, 179, 197
Nietzsche, Friedrich, 278
"Nigger Minstrel." *See* minstrelsy
Notes of a White Black Woman (Scales-Trent), 16, 39, 41, 49–53

Obama, Barack, ix, 1–4, 7–9, 23, 25, 116, 123–25, 143–44, 170, 176
Obeidallah, Dean, 225
Okihiro, Gary Y., 186
Oliver, Kelly, 276
Omi, Michael, 124, 129, 144, 197, 198
One Drop: My Father's Hidden Life (Broyard), 17, 62, 69–92, 250
one-drop rule, 14, 17, 69, 79, 80, 83, 115, 166. *See also* hypodescent
Ono, Kent A., 188
Orton, Harlow S., 64
Osucha, Eden, 123–48
Out of Sight, 277
Oxherding Tale, The (Johnson), 12

Page, Amanda, 179–201
Pakistan(i), 2–3, 224, 242
Palumbo-Liu, David, 187

parody, 18–19, 20, 22, 29, 134, 150–59, 170–74 passim, 212, 223, 265, 287–98, 301, 302
Pascoe, Peggy, 96, 98, 116
Passin': a novel (Miller), 13
Passing (Larsen), 160, 233, 251, 301
passing: as betrayal, 10, 11, 53, 72, 78, 258, 265, 285; for Chicano, 186, 189–91; as con, 58, 266; definition of, 10–13, 39–41, 72–75, 181, 257, 284–85; for economic benefit, 12, 40, 46, 53, 73–77, 90, 189–91; as fraud, 83, 99, 100, 102; and invisibility, 10, 43, 100, 241; as a joke on whites, 58–59, 151, 285; for Jewish, 20, 23–38, 235, 242, 250; for Muslim, 214; numbers of, 13, 26, 40, 61; postmodern, 19, 20, 21, 205, 223, 285–86; as self-hate, 17, 74–75, 77, 90; situational, 12, 40, 77; as straight, 174; as transgression, 9, 73, 181, 285; unintentional, 12, 54, 61, 65, 90, 160, 165, 174; white fear of, 50–51; white to black, 26 (*see also* Halsell and Griffin)
Paul Marchand, F. M. C. (Chesnutt), 13
Paumgarten, Nick, 114
Pépé le Moko, 270
performativity: autobiographical, 231; gender, 235, 290; identity, 264, 268; racial, 14, 21, 72, 130, 160, 235, 259–60, 274, 290, 292
Perlmann, Joel, 26
Pfeiffer, Kathleen, 27
phenotype, 21, 23, 42, 73, 109, 119, 258, 289–91
Philippines, 182, 186, 198, 199. *See also* Filipino
Phillips, Todd, 277
Phillips, William M., Jr., 251
Pilgrim, David, 73
Pinky, 27, 29, 117
Piper, Adrian, viii, 28
Pitts, Leonard, 97
Platitudes, 303
Plessy vs. Ferguson, 58
Plum Bun (Fauset), 90, 233, 251, 275, 301
Pool, Hannah, 203, 204
"Portrait of the Inauthentic Jew" (Sartre), 85
"Portrait of the Inauthentic Negro" (Broyard), 85
post-Civil Rights era, vi, 14, 22, 42, 61, 70, 77, 170, 181, 184, 229, 285. *See also* Civil Rights Era/ Segregation
postcolonial(ism), 149, 160, 175, 216–17, 265, 298
post-ethnic, 242, 245
postmodern, 1, 8 86, 149, 160, 170, 184, 205–206, 209–14, 223, 224, 225, 300; passer/passing, 19, 20, 21, 205, 223, 285–86; text, 18, 20, 149–50, 155–56, 160, 170, 172, 175, 176, 288
post-racial(ism), vii, ix, 2, 14, 16, 18, 23, 24, 70, 116, 123–25, 127, 129, 131, 138–39, 143–44, 146, 170–72
Post-Soul Aesthetic, ix, 16, 285, 286
Potok, Mark, 31
Pouzoulet, Catherine, 302
Powell, A. D., 28
Prell, Riv-Ellen, 250
Presidential election, 2008, 1–2, 5, 123
Proposition 187, 193
proteophobia, 218
Puerto Rican, 23, 199, 242, 244
Pulido, Laura, 188
Pynchon, Thomas, 156; *Crying of Lot 49, The*, 156

Qian, Zhenchao, 31
Quarry, The (Chesnutt), 13
queerness, 141, 145, 234, 245–47

race: and consumerism, 16, 20, 132, 133, 142, 196, 210, 213, 237, 244, 286–88, 291–97, 299; and criminality, 91, 98, 99, 101, 103, 195; and masculinity, 132, 196, 199, 210, 235; as property, 17, 21, 30, 39, 57, 61, 82, 118, 195, 199, 296, 298, 301 (*see also* whiteness); as social construction, viii, ix, 20, 70–71, 170, 215, 231, 235; and social space, 64, 16–27, 218–19, 223; and youth culture, 133, 207, 210–13

racial: authenticity, 16, 73, 84–86, 109, 119, 126–27, 131–33, 135, 143, 184–85, 189–91, 199, 204, 208, 215, 243, 258, 285–87, 288, 290–91, 295, 298, 301, 302; betrayal, 10, 11, 53, 72, 78, 258, 265, 285; binary, vii, ix, 15, 20, 43, 49, 58, 60, 61, 70, 95, 99, 102, 104, 105, 111, 139, 167, 175, 180, 181, 183–84, 196–97, 181, 183–84, 196–97, 214, 219, 223, 231, 234, 242, 246, 270, 284, 286, 289, 290, 301; border, 49–50, 53, 56, 64, 113, 147, 182, 284–85, 298, 300 (*see also* borderlands); caricature, 18 223, 286, 290, 292, 295, 297, 300; choice, 17, 20, 40, 43, 46, 53, 66, 70, 71, 73, 78, 89, 114, 123, 184, 186, 190, 242; classification, 6, 10–12, 16, 17, 21, 45, 50, 53, 58, 60–61, 63, 66, 71, 79, 88, 96–99, 146, 165, 170, 181, 184, 214, 219; dichotomy, 19, 22, 43, 181, 186, 198, 284, 289, 298; difference, viii, 5, 6, 15, 16, 24, 50, 72, 76, 81, 86, 89, 90, 97, 101–102, 106, 117, 125, 128, 130–31, 133, 136, 139, 143, 145, 146, 160–61, 166, 176, 181, 184, 204, 214–18, 219, 232, 238, 243–44, 299; discrimination, 3, 4, 24, 26, 29, 40, 56, 58, 72–73, 82, 84, 87, 179–80, 200, 208; epistemology, 4, 8, 18, 23, 139, 185; essence, 11, 71, 92, 102, 166, 176, 185, 196, 205, 215; fetishism, 134, 141, 143, 210, 213–14; fluidity, vii, 19, 20, 146, 204, 245–46, 272; formation, ix, 19, 20, 146, 204, 245–46, 272; fraud, 83, 99, 100, 102; heritage, 1, 3, 8, 10, 14, 19, 23, 42, 48, 50, 54, 60, 70–71, 79, 80, 83, 89, 96, 114, 164–65, 175, 186, 190–91, 229–30, 289; hierarchy, 15, 41, 56, 84, 102, 105, 113, 138, 146, 173, 179, 183, 187, 196, 198, 199, 216, 221, 232, 286, 288, 291, 298; imitation, 276, 290, 298; indeterminacy, 9, 19, 147, 205, 208, 214, 223; invisibility, 43, 45–46, 54, 56, 58, 60–61, 63; liminality, 49, 53, 60, 183, 185, 269, 286; masquerade, 15, 20, 28, 74, 127, 129–32, 134, 142, 190, 204, 213, 223, 258 (*see also* masquerade); morphing, 20, 204–205, 224 (*see also* morphing); performance, vii–viii, 9–11, 15, 18–22, 58, 72, 85, 86, 109, 126, 129, 130–31, 133, 135, 139–42, 183, 185–86, 190–91, 193, 199, 204–205, 235–36, 239, 242, 244–45, 284, 303; performativity, 14, 21, 72, 130, 160, 235, 259–60, 274, 290, 292 (*see also* performativity); pride, 25, 74–75, 142, 198, 230; property, (*see* race, as property); purity, 50, 52, 63, 64, 72, 102, 172, 216, 219, 286; realism, 139 (*see also* racial authenticity); self-hate, 12, 17, 75, 77, 90, 97, 186; solidarity, 25, 41, 181, 191, 198, 234; spectacle, 18, 125, 129–32, 143; stereotypes, 16, 18, 20, 22, 58, 70, 81, 84, 85–88, 98, 102, 134, 139, 142–43, 154–59 passim, 163, 169, 180, 186, 187, 190, 194–95, 205, 211, 214, 225, 237, 244, 247,

287, 291, 292, 294–97, 303 (*see also* stereotypes); transgression, 9, 73, 84, 113, 181, 234, 289; uplift, 41, 72, 83, 198; visibility, viii, 8–9, 26, 45, 56, 60, 107–109, 184, 214, 250
racism, ix, 2–3, 11, 12, 16, 19, 22, 24, 26, 40, 42, 44, 47, 51, 80, 81, 95, 98, 101–13, 125, 135, 137–38, 143–45, 150, 153, 158–59, 170–72, 181, 184, 186–97, 204, 209, 216–17, 223, 225, 232, 234, 271, 294; internalized, 8, 12, 90, 175, 196; structural or systemic, 4, 12, 21–22, 25, 103, 111–12, 171
Raimon, Eve Allegra, 154, 164, 175
Randall, Alice, xii, 13, 18, 19, 149–76; *Wind Done Gone, The*, 13, 18, 149–76
Rawls, J., 277
realness, discourse of, 129, 132, 133
Reconstruction, 155, 173, 303
Rehling, Nicola, 206, 210, 213, 222
Retman, Sonnet, 129–30
Rhett Butler's People (McCaig), 154–55
Rhinelander, Leonard and Alice, 118
Ripley, Alexandra, 173; *Scarlett*, 173
Road Trip, 277
Robertson, Gil, 119
Robinson, Amy, 73, 119, 136, 258
Rock, Chris, 300
Rodriguez, Richard, 208
Roediger, David, 123–24
Rogin, Michael, 224, 232
Roley, Brian Ascalon, 19, 179–200; *American Son*, 19, 178–200
Root, Maria P. P., 12, 116
Rosaldo, Renato, 49, 50, 64
Rostand, Edmund, 269
Roth, Philip, 12, 13, 27, 29, 114, 231, 249, 285; *Human Stain, The*, film, 13, 29; *Human Stain, The*, novel, 12, 13, 27, 29, 114, 231, 285
Rottenberg, Catherine, 29
Rouse, Roger, 276
Rushdie, Salman, 216
Russet, Margaret, 289

Saks, Eva, 107, 118
Saint-Amour, Paul K., 157, 174
Salzman, Jack, 250
Sánchez, Maria Carla, 12, 27, 61, 225
Sandweiss, Martha A., 26, 29
Sartre, Jean Paul, 85; "Portrait of the Inauthentic Jew," 85
satire, 16, 19, 20, 29, 174, 220, 224, 291–98, 300, 302
Saunders, Robert A., 225
Scales-Trent, Judy, 16–17, 39–43, 49–53, 56, 60, 64; *Notes of a White Black Woman*, 16, 39, 41, 49–53
Scarlett (Ripley), 173
Schlossberg, Linda, 10, 12, 27, 61, 63, 225
Schuyler, George, 19, 146, 303; *Black No More*, 29, 146
Schwartz, Russell, 271
Seeman, Melvin, 76, 85
segregation, 2, 11, 17, 42, 54, 96–100, 109–10, 153, 155, 285–86. *See also* Jim Crow Era
Selznick, David O., 153, 173
Sembene, Iusmane, 265
Senna, Danzy, ix, 12, 20, 27, 229–41, 248–49, 250; *Caucasia*, ix, 12, 20, 27, 229–51; *Where Did You Sleep Last Night? A Personal History*, 250
sexuality, vii, 9, 25, 233, 245–47
Shadow and Act (Ellison), 283
Sharfstein, Daniel J., 11, 26, 29, 40, 47, 71, 115
Shohat, Ella, 270
Simone, Nina, 263
skin color, vii, 2, 4, 11, 19–20, 21, 24, 26, 28, 29, 39, 42–47 passim, 50, 51, 54–58, 60–66 passim, 71–73, 75–76, 78–79, 82–83, 87, 89, 90,

skin color *(continued)*
97, 98, 100, 106, 113, 117, 118, 119, 130, 132, 161, 164–65, 184, 199, 203, 212, 225, 229–30, 235–36, 239, 246–48, 249–50, 276, 285, 289; dark-skinned, 11, 21, 26, 40, 47, 57, 62, 75, 76, 83, 87, 89, 90, 92, 100, 106, 108, 109, 117, 118, 130, 164–65, 194, 199, 212, 229, 230, 246–47, 248, 249, 289; light-skinned, 2, 11, 19, 20, 21, 29, 39, 42–44, 51, 54, 56, 58, 62, 64, 66, 71, 74, 75–76, 78–79, 90, 98, 107, 130, 132, 161, 225, 250, 285
slavery, 2, 11, 46, 52, 115, 149–50, 153, 168–69, 172, 173, 273
Sloop, John M., 188, 193
Slow Burn, 13
Smith, Anna Deavere, 259
Smith, Amy Symens, 116
Smith, Cherise, 258
Smith, John David, 64
Smith-Pryor, Elizabeth M., 29
Smith, Shawn Michelle, 7, 25, 28
Smith, Sidonie, 62, 88, 231
Smith, Valerie, viii, 250, 258, 275
Soderbergh, Steven, 277
Sollors, Werner, viii, 9, 13, 24, 26, 27, 39, 54, 63, 64, 99, 116, 117, 284, 301
Song, Min-Hyoung, 197
Souls of Black Folk, The (Du Bois), 56, 63
Soul Man, 28
Soul Sister (Halsell), 26
South Asian, 211, 224, 242. *See also* Pakistan(i)
South Central Los Angeles. *See* Los Angeles
spectatorship, 18, 128–32, 139–43, 258
Spencer, Rainier, 24
Spickard, Paul, 43, 49, 63, 65
Spivak, Gayatri Chakravorty, 298. *See also* subaltern
Squires, Catherine R., 63
Stam, Robert, 270
Stereotypes: of African Americans/Blacks/blackness, 16–22 passim, 58, 70, 81, 84–89, 98, 139, 142–43, 156, 163, 211, 287, 291, 292, 294–97, 303; of Asians, 186, 195; of Asian Americans, 194–95; of Chicanos, 190; of gays, 225; of Jews, 237, 244; of Mexicans, 187; of mulattos, 18, 98, 102, 247; of teens, 146; of whiteness/whites, 84, 134, 156, 290
St. John, Christopher, 276
Stern, Julia, 27
Stewart, Jon, 158, 207, 224
Stewart, Mart A., 153, 172
Stiller, Ben, 28, 31
Stoddard, Lothrop, 7
Stowe, Harriet Beecher, 11; *Uncle Tom's Cabin*, 11
Streeter, Caroline, 28
Street, William Douglas, Jr., 21, 255–78
subaltern, 157, 160, 169, 298. *See also* Spivak, Gayatri
Sullivan, Andrew, 2–3, 7
Sweeter the Juice: A Family Memoir in Black and White, The (Haizlip), 16, 41–50, 250
Swift, Jonathan, 293
S/Z (Barthes), 288, 293, 302

Talty, Stephan, 301
Tate, Greg, 267, 297–98
Taylor, Clyde, 268
Taylor, Helen, 172, 173, 174
television, reality, 18, 124–29, 132, 135, 140, 145–46
"Test of Manhood, A Christmas Story, The" (Hopkins), 62
Thacker, Audrey B., 24
third race, 284, 286, 297, 299, 300
Thomas, Piri, 199

Thompson, Debby, 259
Thompson, Ethan, 158, 302
Top of the Heap, 276
Torres, Sasha, 129
Townsend, Robert, 276
tragic mulatta/o, 17, 18, 70, 73–74, 84, 88, 101, 117, 183, 187, 234, 247, 284. *See also* mulatta/o
traitor, racial, 41, 46, 53, 62
transformation: identity, 129, 240–41, 247; global, 216; physical, 137, 145; racial, 48, 230, 232, 239, 241, 250; sexual, 147; structural, 123
Trigo, Benigno, 276
Tropic Thunder, 28, 31
True Identity, 28, 275
25th Hour, 302
Ty, Eleanor, 195, 199
Tyler, Carole-Anne, 251

U. S. Census Bureau, 29–30, 97, 114, 115, 198
U. S. Census, 2000, 6, 7, 22, 25, 96–97, 116
U. S. Census, 2010, 25
Udovich, Mim, 114, 119
Uncle Tom's Cabin (Stowe), 11, 169, 296

visibility, 26, 43, 46, 58, 63, 100; and passing, 10, 15, 28; racial, viii, 8–9, 26, 45, 56, 60, 107–109, 184, 214, 250; social, 45, 183

Wacks, Jamie L., 118
Waiting for the Verdict (Davis), 62
Wald, Gayle, vii–x, 4, 12, 27, 28, 39, 61, 62–63, 89, 146, 181, 225
Walker, Alice, 173, 231
Walker, Kara, 176
Walker, Lisa, 26
Walker, Rebecca, 13, 20, 229–51
Washington, Lynn, 69–93
Watson, Julia, 62, 88
Wayans brothers, 28, 205–206
Wayans, Damon, 289
Weaver, Simon, 207, 217, 219, 225
Webb, Frank J., 11, 73, 89, 160; *Garies and Their Friends, The*, 11, 73, 89, 160
Weber, Donald, 49
Weinbaum, Alys Eve, 144
Weiner, Rex, 274
Weisenburger, Steven, 302
Welles, Orson, 268, 278
West, Cornel, 233, 250
Where Did You Sleep Last Night? A Personal History (Senna), 250
White, Armond, 271
White Boy Shuffle (Beatty), 301
White Chicks, 28, 205
whiteface, 28, 30, 32–33, 142, 205
white fear, 22, 31, 61, 48, 50–51, 57, 106, 108, 111, 118
Whitehead, Colson, 13, 27, 156; *Intuitionist, The*, 13, 27, 156
White Lies: Race and the Myths of Whiteness (Berger), 249
"White Like Me," 136, 146
White Man Listen! (Wright), 278
White, Mimi, 145
whiteness, 5, 7, 14, 21, 23, 44–45, 46–48, 50, 55, 62, 73, 77–78, 83, 98, 109, 115, 119, 131–33, 136, 137, 139–40, 142–43, 147, 161–62, 167, 168, 184, 192–93, 195, 206, 224, 229–35, 240–42, 248–49, 258, 264–65, 267, 284, 291, 295, 297, 300, 301, 303; as absence of race, 45, 63–64, 132, 248; hegemonic power of, 19, 22, 40, 43, 45, 50–51, 102, 132, 196, 206, 240; and Jewishness, 224, 229–42, 248–50; as masquerade, 300; phenotypic, 40, 76; as property, 21, 30, 39, 56–57, 61, 83, 92, 99, 102, 118, 195, 199,

whiteness *(continued)*
286, 298; stereotypes of, 84, 134, 156, 290
white privilege, 29, 30, 45–46, 51, 55, 62, 87, 98, 102, 110, 112, 118, 119, 135, 136–37, 143, 161, 163, 166, 167, 199, 204, 206, 229, 250, 258, 288, 299
white supremacy, 7, 22, 23, 39, 153, 159, 160, 182, 186, 191–92, 194, 196, 199, 286
White, Walter, 42, 61, 62, 65, 198; *Flight,* 198; *Man Called White, A,* 42
White, W. L., 42, 62; *Lost Boundaries,* film, 27, 29, 62; *Lost Boundaries,* novel, 42, 62
white womanhood, 160, 171
wigger, 211
Williams, Bettye J., 151, 173
Williams, Gregory Howard, 13, 16, 17, 41–43, 53–60, 65–66, 250; *Life on the Color Line: The True Story of a White Boy Who Discovered He Was Black*, 16, 41, 53–61, 250
Williams, Kim M., 25, 63
Williams, Linda, 29
Williamson, Joel, 61, 96, 115
Willis, Ellen, 251
Wilson, Woodrow, 154, 294, 303
Winant, Howard, 124, 129, 144, 197, 198
Wind Done Gone, The (Randall), 13, 18, 149–76
Winters, Loretta I., 25
Without a Trace, 13, 28
Woods, Tiger, 8, 9, 97, 98, 112, 114, 119
Wright, Richard, 196, 278, 287, 292, 293, 302; *Native Son*, 196, 287, 292, 302; *White Man Listen!*, 278
Wright, Susan Prothro, 12, 225, 306

Xiong, Yang Sao, 189, 200

Yaeger, Patricia, 162, 170, 176
Young, Robert, 219

Zack, Naomi, 96, 98, 99, 115, 117
Zanger, Jules, 98
Zayd, Daniel Ibn, 225
Zhou, Min, 189, 200
Zinsser, William, 62